MW00583740

7/25/13
#32.99

The Political Question Doctrine and the Supreme Court of the United States

The Political Question Doctrine and the Supreme Court of the United States

Edited by
Nada Mourtada-Sabbah
and
Bruce E. Cain

Published in cooperation with the Berkeley Public Policy Press of
the Institute of Governmental Studies at the University of
California, Berkeley

LEXINGTON BOOKS

A division of
ROWMAN & LITTLEFIELD PUBLISHERS, INC.
Lanham • Boulder • New York • Toronto • Plymouth, UK

CHABOT COLLEGE LIBRARY

LEXINGTON BOOKS

A division of Rowman & Littlefield Publishers, Inc.
A wholly owned subsidiary of The Rowman & Littlefield Publishing Group, Inc.
4501 Forbes Boulevard, Suite 200
Lanham, MD 20706

Estover Road
Plymouth PL6 7PY
United Kingdom

British Library Cataloguing in Publication Information Available

Library of Congress Cataloging-in-Publication Data

The political question doctrine and the Supreme Court of the United States / edited by
Nada Mourtada-Sabbah and Bruce E. Cain.
    p. cm.
Includes bibliographical references and index.
ISBN-13: 978-0-7391-1283-0 (cloth : alk. paper)
ISBN-13: 978-0-7391-1284-7 (pbk. : alk. paper)
ISBN-10: 0-7391-1283-X (cloth : alk. paper)
ISBN-10: 0-7391-1284-8 (pbk. : alk. paper)
1. Political questions and judicial power—United States—Cases. 2. Constitutional
law—United States—Cases. 3. United States. Supreme Court. I. Mourtada-Sabbah,
Nada. II. Cain, Bruce E.
KF8748.P565 2007
347.73'26—dc22   2006030122

Printed in the United States of America

♾™ The paper used in this publication meets the minimum requirements of American
National Standard for Information Sciences—Permanence of Paper for Printed Library
Materials, ANSI/NISO Z39.48–1992.

To my father, who spurred a deep interest in the meanings of the law and its due process.

—Nada Mourtada

Contents

Introduction

Jesse H. Choper[1]

With roots tracing to *Marbury v. Madison*,[2] the political question doctrine—that courts should abstain from resolving constitutional issues that are better left to other departments of government, mainly the national political branches—has rarely served as a meaningful restraint on the Supreme Court's authority. Now, catalyzed by the Court's decision in *Bush v. Gore*,[3] in which the justices voted five to four to resolve a presidential election dispute without so much as mentioning the doctrine, scholars have concluded that political questions are in serious decline, if not fully expired, being clearly at odds with the notion of judicial supremacy adopted by the Court in recent years. Moreover, within the past dozen years, the Court has also raised the possibility that the Guarantee Clause may again become part of the judiciary's repertoire.[4] But other decisions over the past three decades suggest that reports of the political question's demise are premature. Two rulings, each authored by the Court's then-chief justice, specifically invoked the doctrine in refusing to subject to judicial review either control

---

[1] Earl Warren Professor of Public Law, University of California, Berkeley (Boalt Hall). I wish to express appreciation to Katherine Florey, Boalt '04, for her very able assistance in preparing this Introduction.
[2] 5 U.S. 137, 165-66 (1803).
[3] 531 U.S. 98 (2000).
[4] *New York v. United States*, 505 U.S. 144 (1992).

of the national guard[5] or the congressional impeachment process.[6] Indeed, as recently as 2004, four members of the Court urged its application to partisan political gerrymandering, one deferred consideration of the matter, and none of the remaining justices even suggested that nonjusticiability was no longer a viable approach.[7] Thus, it appears to be an appropriate occasion to ask both what remains of the political question doctrine and what role it should play in the future.

The scholars contributing to this volume accept this challenge by considering the political question doctrine from a wide range of historical and theoretical perspectives. Rachel E. Barkow reviews its doctrinal evolution. Mark Tushnet describes the decline of its prudential elements. Two articles—Richard L. Hasen on the Guarantee Clause and Nada Mourtada and John Fox on presidential war making—take primarily historical perspectives. Other authors consider contemporary as well as historical topics: Nancy Kassop surveys current war on terrorism cases, while Pierre Avril discusses recent controversies within the distinctive French system of judicial review. Erwin Chemerinsky makes the case for dispensing with the political question doctrine entirely. Louis Fisher and Nathaniel Persily examine various consequences of judicial involvement in politics. Jonathan R. Siegel highlights the weaknesses of the political process as an alternative to judicial action.

In this introduction, I briefly review each author's arguments, and then indicate some of my own views on the subject,[8] which center primarily on questions of comparative institutional competence and the distinction between structural constitutional issues and individual rights. While many of my thoughts are longstanding and closely tied to my conception of the role of judicial review in American representative democracy, they have been informed and illuminated by the works collected in this book.

Rachel E. Barkow's comprehensive historical account of the political question provides a good starting point for consideration of its present viability. Tracing what she views as the early "rise"[9] and the twentieth-century "fall"[10] of the doctrine, she argues that it is on the verge of becoming "completely defunct"[11] because its premise that the political branches have a role in determining the meaning of the Constitution is impossible to reconcile with the vision of judicial supremacy embraced by recent Supreme Courts. Barkow urges that the justices' theory of "judicial superiority"[12] and their path toward a wholly "Court-centric

---

[5] *Gilligan v. Morgan*, 413 U.S. 1 (1973).
[6] *Nixon v. United States*, 506 U.S. 224 (1993).
[7] *Vieth v. Jubelirer*, 541 U.S. 267 (2004).
[8] See generally Jesse H. Choper, *The Political Question Doctrine: Suggested Criteria*, 54 Duke L. J. 1457 (2005).
[9] Barkow.
[10] Barkow.
[11] Barkow.
[12] Barkow.

view of the Constitution"[13] are at odds with the Constitution's history and structure.

In particular, Barkow would revive the "classical strain"[14] of the political question doctrine. In contrast to the "prudential strain," advocated by Alexander Bickel as a technique of judicial abstention,[15] the classical version asks only whether there is "some textual reason for concluding that the question lies within the interpretive powers of a political branch."[16] Because this approach is rooted in constitutional text and structure, Barkow contends, it is capable of serving as an independent limit on "a judge's ability to use her or his own policy preferences to avoid deciding a case."[17] By contrast, the prudential strand contains nothing to "keep[ ] a judge's use of the [political question] doctrine in check" and may well simply be a device to avoid an issue that is "too complicated or . . . too politically charged."[18]

However, as Mark Tushnet's chapter demonstrates, Barkow overstates the constraining power of the "classical" approach because "textual commitment" often provides an unreliable boundary for judicial policy preferences. Tushnet's appraisal of the political question doctrine's decline conflicts somewhat with Barkow's. He argues that the Court hastened its end by the rationale in *Baker v. Carr* and subsequent cases that the political question issue was simply an "ordinary question of constitutional interpretation."[19] This conflicts with Bickel's justification for a prudential avoidance technique which was defined by "precisely the characteristic . . . that it cannot be captured in rules."[20]

In the second part of his essay, Tushnet contends that a similar process of "doctrinalization"[21] has occurred with regard to the prudential elements of standing law, that standing has largely become a question of "congressional interference with the executive's discretion to choose how to enforce the law," rather than a way of "allowing the courts to express a generalized concern about their role."[22] The waning of both avoidance theories in favor of an approach that always results in a judicially authoritative "ordinary constitutional interpretation"[23] illustrates a phenomenon highlighted most recently by *Bush v. Gore*: an "acceptance in our political and legal culture of a strong form of judicial supremacy that was only uncertainly accepted when *Baker v. Carr* was decided."[24]

---

[13] Barkow.
[14] Barkow.
[15] Barkow.
[16] Barkow.
[17] Barkow.
[18] Barkow.
[19] Tushnet.
[20] Tushnet.
[21] Tushnet.
[22] Tushnet.
[23] Tushnet.
[24] Tushnet.

As I will discuss shortly, I agree with much of Tushnet's analysis. In my view, however, he underplays a major qualification of his conclusion in regard to political questions. As his own examples suggest (and as he himself recognizes),[25] there is no reason why the Court's weighing of prudential factors cannot greatly influence, if not resolve, whether the Court will find a textual commitment to another branch, a judgment that may well be significantly affected by all of the *Baker v. Carr* criteria.

Believing that only in regard to Guarantee Clause (and foreign affairs) issues does the "political question doctrine continue[ ] to have any viability,"[26] Richard L. Hasen's chapter comprehensively reviews the Court's treatment of the Guarantee Clause. Although he persuasively contends that neither the "textual commitment" nor the "manageable standards" criteria of *Baker v. Carr* are very convincing for all Guarantee Clause claims,[27] he nevertheless argues that Guarantee Clause issues should continue to be treated as political questions. This is necessary because such claims are likely to arise in charged political contexts, such as the state initiative process at issue in *Pacific States Telephone & Telegraph Co. v. Oregon* or proposals to impose cumulative voting by judicial decree.[28] Hasen is sympathetic to such challenges "[a]s a matter of politics," feeling, for example, that the initiative process tends to "trample upon the rights of minorities" and "create budgetary chaos."[29] Nonetheless, such "serious questions about political structure," whether favored by liberals or conservatives, should not be removed from everyday politics and left "in the hands of judges to ossify."[30]

The difficulty with Hasen's position is that it requires a broader definition of "political question" than he proposes. As he concedes, constitutional provisions other than the Guarantee Clause can be readily used to afford judicial review of voting and election claims, thus preventing courts from escaping questions about state initiative and election processes entirely. This drains his thesis regarding the Guarantee Clause of much of its import.

Providing a different perspective on judicial interference with political processes, Louis Fisher questions widespread academic condemnation of *Bush v. Gore*, whose merits the Court might have readily avoided by invoking a fairly straightforward version of the political question doctrine. While Fisher does not fully endorse the Court's reasoning, he does contend that criticism of the decision by scholars in both law and political science have "relied too much on hyperbole rather than close analysis."[31] Although he believes that *Congress* is a "competent forum for resolving disputes about close elections,"[32] he argues that the Court was

---

[25] See Tushnet's discussion of the decisions in the *Nixon*, *Powell*, and *Goldwater* cases.

[26] Hasen.

[27] Hasen.

[28] Hasen.

[29] Hasen.

[30] Hasen.

[31] Fisher.

[32] Fisher.

"compelled to intervene because of serious issues created by the Florida Supreme Court,"[33] whose opinion had already taken over from the state legislature, a political body far more capable than an unelected judiciary of accurately expressing the people's will.

Fisher's general preference for leaving questions of partisan electoral politics to a political forum is sound, but he does not persuasively explain why it should not have prevailed in this instance. Whether or not the Florida court had exceeded its proper role, the Constitution provided a perfectly adequate mechanism for resolution of the issue in Congress.[34] The Supreme Court's intervention thus had the effect of *stopping* the opportunity that would otherwise have existed for a legislative body to resolve the controversy.

Although Nathaniel Persily takes a sharply different view of *Bush v. Gore* than Fisher, he is similarly skeptical about judges' incursions into the electoral process. He suggests that many "judicial involvement[s] in politics"[35] should be considered to present political questions. Over the last quarter-century, in his view, the Court's attempts to address the merits of such issues have resulted in its invalidating genuine innovations in the workings of the political system (such as majority-minority legislative districts and cross-voting in primaries). Since he believes that these reform efforts may be justified as "protecting minorities or providing greater political access,"[36] he concludes that the *Carolene Products* rationale for judicial review as a guarantee of minority political rights has been "co-opt[ed]"[37] by mainstream political actors. Consequently, he argues that what was once a "judicial revolution" has unfortunately "matured into opportunities for partisan manipulation and judicial reinforcement of traditional power structures."[38]

Persily recommends as a criterion for determining a political question in the arena of electoral politics whether the Court's intervention responds to the *Carolene Products* preference for protecting "discrete and insular minorities." He suggests that the Court might avoid claims by "established political parties," because they have sufficient resources to defend their interests without judicial review. Political gerrymandering (as in *Davis v. Bandemer* and *Vieth v. Pennsylvania*) falls into this category, as does *Bush v. Gore*.

While Persily may well provide a perceptive and valuable insight, it may go more to the merits of some rulings rather than to their justiciability. In any event, it is not immediately obvious whether many claims relating to electoral politics will aid or hurt political minorities. For example, Persily criticizes the Court's invalidation of congressional term limits in *U.S. Term Limits v. Thornton*, arguing that this represents another instance in which the Court defended traditional voting proce-

---

[33] Fisher.

[34] See Jesse H. Choper, *Why the Supreme Court Should Not Have Decided the Presidential Election of 2000*, 18 Const. Comm. 335 (2001).

[35] Persily.

[36] Persily.

[37] Persily.

[38] Persily.

dures at the cost of stifling electoral innovation.[39] Yet while the imposition of term limits, to be sure, stops majorities from prevailing, it does not necessarily follow that it also advances minority rights. At the very least, then, Persily's proposal needs to be more specific in explaining the circumstances under which courts should avoid "politics," as he defines the term.

Nada Mourtada and John Fox examine the political question issue from a yet different perspective, taking the view that the political question doctrine has evolved over the years to reflect cultural and generational changes (such as the late twentieth-century shift to greater executive authority in corporate and religious life, which may have produced greater public receptivity to Executive war-making power). The authors survey in detail courts' treatment of issues of war and peace over a two-century span. They commence with cases between 1794 and 1800 raising the question whether France was an "enemy," in which the courts accepted the premise that all war powers rested in Congress. Mourtada and Fox then describe how the federal courts continued to support congressional supremacy through the 1850s, but during the Civil War generally upheld executive decisions that trumped individual liberties and states' rights. They go on to reason that the "presidentially ordered wars" in Korea and Vietnam led the way to executive preeminence, concluding with the argument that present-day political questions reflect a context of "globalism and American unilateralism" in which "the Executive is obligated to protect investments abroad and to insure the secure flow of labor and goods."

Nancy Kassop discusses a similar and much-contested area of the political question doctrine: judicial handling of individual rights claims in matters of foreign affairs and national security. Kassop examines several current war on terrorism cases in order to consider what role judicial avoidance doctrines might ultimately play. Taking a historical look at the Court's rulings during the World War II era, she points out that the justices usually decided such cases on the merits. *Baker v. Carr*, however, changed that model by "hand[ing] the president a virtual road map of claims he could use to make the case for nonjusticiability in foreign affairs."[40] As a result, she argues, from the Vietnam period onward, the Court has largely declined to interfere in controversies of this kind, thus leaving presidents "with a fair degree of confidence that they have broad discretion to make policy in this area with minimal fear of judicial intervention."[41] From her examination of briefs and other documents filed in the lower federal courts in the *Hamdi* and *Padilla* cases, Kassop concludes, however, that the courts' and government's embrace of a "judicial avoidance posture"[42] may be changing. The thrust of the government's argument in the current cases, she argues, is to urge judicial resolution on the merits rather than abstention, and district and circuit courts have generally adopted this position.

---

[39] Persily.
[40] Kassop.
[41] Kassop.
[42] Kassop.

Pierre Avril's article describes the operation of the political question doctrine in France, tracing the modern development of that country's independent judiciary and a judicial review process quite different from the Anglo-American system. He outlines how "the well established principle according to which the political authorities should respect the law has evolved, moving from the idea of . . . judicial review of the actions of these [political authorities] to ensure their conformity to the law, to the generalized intervention of the judge to protect individual rights."[43] He points to two principal examples of the ways in which judicial entities have dealt with sensitive political issues: first, how a decision on immigration and asylum by the Constitutional Court, subsequently overturned by political amendment, "ventured beyond what [was] politically acceptable at a time when the legitimacy of the political leaders was affirmed by the electorate," [44] and second, the complexities involved in adjudicating prosecutions of political officials for "incompetent administration."[45]

Erwin Chemerinsky most straightforwardly argues that there is no reason for the political question doctrine to exist at all. In Chemerinsky's view, the judiciary should *always* be the "ultimate interpreter of the Constitution."[46] He explores possible responses to this position—that "no branch of government is authoritative"[47] and that different branches of government should have final responsibility for construing different parts of the Constitution.[48] Ultimately, though, he contends that "the federal courts, and especially the Supreme Court, are best suited to engage in constitutional interpretation,"[49] and that it is "the institution most able to protect the Constitution's structure and values from majoritarian pressures."[50] Moreover, he argues that the judiciary's "decision-making method is preferable for constitutional interpretation and evolution"[51] because, in contrast to the political branches, the judiciary is "compelled to hear the complaints of a single person"[52] and to "decide each matter . . . on its own merits" rather than through "logrolling and voting trade-offs."[53] Although Chemerinsky acknowledges the desirability of judicial caution and deference to the political branches in certain cases, he rejects any doctrine that would mandate "total noninvolvement no matter what the circumstances."[54]

Subscribing to much of Chemerinsky's reasoning, but not explicitly endorsing his conclusion, Jonathan R. Siegel argues that the structure of judicial review gives

---

[43] Avril.
[44] Avril.
[45] Avril.
[46] Chemerinsky.
[47] Chemerinsky.
[48] Chemerinsky.
[49] Chemerinsky.
[50] Chemerinsky.
[51] Chemerinsky.
[52] Chemerinsky.
[53] Chemerinsky.
[54] Chemerinsky.

courts a unique and irreplaceable role in resolving constitutional claims. Siegel's main purpose is to expose the weaknesses in one central defense of the political question doctrine: the "electoral process provides an appropriate substitute" for judicial review in enforcing constitutional barriers.[55] He effectively contends that the political system is inadequate, largely because it lacks those "characteristics of the judicial process that are essential to the task of enforcing such constraints."[56] Courts have multiple "practical and theoretical"[57] advantages, which include "the mandatory nature of the judicial process, its focus on precisely stated issues, its articulation of reasons for decisions, and its use of precedent."[58] Invocation of the political question doctrine, he urges, may deny litigants the benefit of the orderly, reasoned resolution that judges alone provide.

In his discussion, Siegel focuses on a critical element for any workable approach to the political question doctrine: the precise definition of what a "political question" is. He contends that many issues courts treat as nonjusticiable are "bogus" political questions.[59] As an example at the extreme: A lawsuit alleging that income tax rates are "just too high" "would of course deserve immediate dismissal," since the Constitution contains "no constraint that would prevent Congress from imposing the current set of income tax rates."[60] The claim is "obviously frivolous,"[61] and has nothing to do with the political question doctrine. Siegel thus helpfully distinguishes between rulings that constitutional provisions provide no "legal constraints" (these are true decisions on the ultimate merits) and those that commit determinations as to whether "legal constraints" are violated to another branch (these are true political questions and plainly not decisions on the merits).[62] While this distinction may, of course, make little difference to the litigants challenging the official action in the case before the Court, it is highly important from a theoretical standpoint in defining the role and responsibility of the various branches of government, and (as I will suggest further below) it may well prove significant in guiding the future conduct of the political departments.

I would define "political question" from a similar perspective: a substantive ruling by the justices that a constitutional issue regarding the scope of a particular provision (or some aspects of it) should be authoritatively resolved not by the Supreme Court but usually by one (or both) of the national political branches or by an organ of state government. A further refinement, however, is needed. Thus, Tushnet describes the political question "issue" in two separate ways: (1) "Who gets to decide what the right answer to a substantive constitutional question is?"[63] and (2) "Does the Constitution give a political branch the final power to interpret

---

[55] Siegel.
[56] Siegel.
[57] Siegel.
[58] Siegel.
[59] Siegel.
[60] Siegel.
[61] Siegel.
[62] Siegel.
[63] Tushnet.

the Constitution?"[64] The first comports with my formulation. The second differs significantly, invoking what the Court in *Baker v. Carr* labelled a "textually demonstrable constitutional commitment,"[65] resting essentially on conventional constitutional interpretation.

While I readily accept the "textual commitment" principle (as I discuss shortly), my approach, drawing heavily on an earlier analysis,[66] is an essentially functional one rather than being grounded in constitutional text or original understanding. I basically subscribe to Chemerinsky's description of the current system: "that for each part of the Constitution one branch of government . . . [should be] assigned the role of final arbiter of disputes, but it is not the same branch for all parts of the Constitution." And I generally join his belief that the Court should have the ultimate say as to "which branch decides."[67] In most respects, I see the justices' analysis on the political question doctrine as involving the same justifications that govern the institutional role of judicial review in our democracy, especially in regard to whether the political branches at both the national and local levels may trustworthily determine the meaning and scope of a particular constitutional provision.

I believe that the Court should consider four criteria in determining whether to relegate questions of constitutional interpretation to the political branches. First: courts should refrain from deciding questions where there is a "textual commitment" to a coordinate political department—that is, when the Constitution itself is interpreted as clearly referring the resolution of a question to an elected branch. Second: pursuant to a functional rather than a textual approach, when judicial review is thought to be unnecessary for the effective preservation of our constitutional scheme, the Court should decline to exercise its interpretive authority. Third: the Court should not decide issues for which it cannot formulate principled, coherent tests as a result of "a lack of judicially discoverable and manageable standards."[68] Finally: I would tentatively suggest that constitutional injuries that

---

[64] Tushnet.

[65] 369 U.S. at 217.

[66] Jesse Choper, *Judicial Review and the National Political Process* (University of Chicago Press, 1980). It may be worth noting that, because of the ongoing controversy over the doctrine of "political questions," I never used the phrase in the book, instead describing the inquiry as involving the "justiciability" of various constitutional issues.

[67] One cannot unqualifiedly accept Chemerinsky's formulation without rejecting the venerable positions of Jefferson, Jackson, and Lincoln that no branch of government is authorized to act as final arbiter and that each may determine constitutionality when exercising its constitutionally assigned powers. My functionally grounded instincts coincide with our developed thinking that the Court should possess the ultimate decision-making authority *and* that the other departments should feel bound thereby. See *Cooper v. Aaron*, 358 U.S. 1 (1958). Still, there are situations where I lean in the opposite direction, particularly when this produces greater security for individual rights, e.g., after the Court upholds the constitutionality of a federal statute, a president who disagrees with the Court's judgment declines to enforce it, or he pardons those convicted under it, or he vetoes similar legislation.

[68] 369 U.S. at 217.

are general and widely shared are also candidates for being treated as political questions. These four criteria have a common thread: They identify questions either that the judiciary is ill-equipped to decide or where committing the issue to some political branch promises a reliable, perhaps even a superior, resolution.

The first criterion, "textual commitment" to a coordinate national branch, is perhaps the most straightforward. It is difficult to disagree with the proposition that if the text of the Constitution or the original understanding of its meaning, as reflected in its "structure and underlying political theory,"[69] persuasively leads to the conclusion that the elected branches rather than the Court should be the final arbiter of its meaning, then the justices should withdraw. Although, in my view, this will very rarely be true, it merits emphasizing that the Court's finding a political question under any of my four suggested criteria does *not* instruct either Congress or the president or state legislators or executive officials that they have an *unbounded discretion* to settle the matter, but rather that their task is to make as *informed and sensitive a constitutional judgment* as possible.

The consequences of removing the prophylaxis of judicial oversight by vesting full authority in the political branches are, of course, incalculable. Still, it must be remembered that political action by multimember bodies often depends on the votes of just a few. Thus, the possibility that the product of the decision-making process of the political branches, when they consciously exercise final constitutional authority, will be undertaken with a greater adherence to principle than when they engage in ordinary lawmaking is greatly increased by the fact that only a small number of legislators (or executive officers) are usually needed to determine the outcomes. Only *their* sense of duty must be affected. Consequently, there is at least some reasonable chance (as could arise by the Court's possible ruling that certain claims of individual rights in the area of military and foreign affairs are committed for resolution by the political branches) that acceptance of this responsibility by the president and legislature may result in greater protection for personal liberties than would the Court's ruling on the merits while giving great deference to the political decision makers (as shown in Kassop's discussion of the government's briefs and some of the lower court decisions in the war on terrorism cases).

The operation of the firm rule in place between 1935 and 1990 respecting the scope of Congress's power under the Commerce Clause, which upheld exercises of authority over state and local matters as long as "Congress had a rational basis for finding that . . . [the regulated activity] affected commerce,"[70] illustrates how judicial review may tend to enhance rather than deter national hegemony. The rationale is simple enough: If those members of Congress who ignore constitutional questions of states' rights prevail in the legislative process, and if the Court then upholds the statute in deference to a congressional judgment as to constitu-

---

[69] Robert J. Pushaw, Jr., *Judicial Review and the Political Question Doctrine: Reviving the Federalist "Rebuttable Presumption" Analysis*, 80 N.C. L. Rev. 1165, 1177 (2002).

[70] *Heart of Atlanta Motel, Inc. v. United States*, 379 U.S. 241, 258 (1964).

tionality that has never really been made, then judicial review is self-defeating. It will encourage those lawmakers who believe that constitutionality is the equivalent of what the Supreme Court will uphold; and it will embolden them to take further national steps into what were previously thought to be state preserves. Indeed, even those senators and representatives who are most sensitive to the limits of national power, and who treat the constitutional question very seriously, cannot help but be affected by judicial validation of earlier federal regulations.

Even prior to his historic pronouncements in *Marbury*, John Marshall expressed his view that although some "interpretation[s] of rules of law . . . demanded the exercise of the type of discretionary judgment that characterizes political action," this "did not thereby cease to be a matter of applying legal norms" and "principles,"[71] and he "believed in the ability of the political branches conscientiously to interpret and obey the Constitution . . . especially in those cases beyond the power of the judiciary to resolve."[72] Thus, even if the Court had adopted a "color blind" or "strict neutrality" standard for its review of all race- and sex-based state action under the Fourteenth Amendment, in contemporary America, were the justices to subsequently rule that the criteria for the selection of high ranking cabinet officials are exclusively within the province of the executive, a constitutionally sensitive president might well conclude that, regardless of the validity of other kinds of race- or sex-based state action, it is important (or "compelling" in equal protection terms) that appointed government leaders reflect the racial, ethnic, and gender makeup of the general population.

The second criterion, like the first, concerns the division of authority among the Congress, President, and the Court, but, like the third and fourth focuses on the functional role of judicial review rather than on constitutional text and original understanding. This second gauge distinguishes between matters of constitutional structure—questions relating to federalism and separation of powers between the political branches[73]—and those involving individual rights. The basic rationale is that by abstaining when the political branches may be trusted to produce a sound constitutional decision, the justices reduce the discord between judicial review and majoritarian democracy (and enhance their ability to render enforceable decisions when their participation is vitally needed). Although I share *much* of Chemerinsky's (as well as Siegel's) thesis, I do not agree that it should be universally employed or used in contexts where it does not realistically apply. Moreover, since Congress and the executive are well-equipped to handle constitutional structure issues because the competing interests are forcefully represented in the national

---

[71] Walter Dellinger & H. Jefferson Powell, 2 Green Bag 367, 373 (Summer 1999).

[72] *Id.* at 377.

[73] With respect to constitutional conflicts between the political branches, on the one hand, and the Supreme Court, on the other, I urge that since the federal judiciary is not well represented in the national political process, the Court should continue to use its power of judicial review to reject laws that improperly restrict or expand the Court's authority.

political process, the justification for judicial review, the most antimajoritarian exercise of national government power, is at a low ebb in those matters.[74] Again, I wish to emphasize the *functional* rather than *textual* basis for this view because the clauses of the Constitution that allocate power between the national government and the states (such as the commerce, taxing, and spending powers) and that divide authority between Congress and the president (such as the appointments and treaty provisions) no more plainly reveal, either by text or intent, which institution of government should determine the constitutionally proper balance than does Article IV's proviso that "the United States shall guarantee to every State in this Union a Republican Form of Government" or Article V's procedures for amending the Constitution. While the Court has ruled that both the Guarantee Clause and Article V raise political questions, they no more satisfy the "textual commitment" criterion than most other clauses of the Constitution whose language plainly vests power in the political branches but still have been traditionally subject to judicial interpretation. And, as above, I wish also to underline that although these matters of constitutional structure are nonjusticiable under my approach, they are still outside the realm of everyday politics in the sense that they should not be resolved by *conventional political criteria* for majoritarian decision making, but rather by a *deliberative constitutional judgment*. To whatever extent this occurs, however, in my view, such questions are still best decided by a branch that, unlike the judiciary, is capable of being politically accountable and dealing with matters of practicality.

This second criterion, in particular, also takes account of John Marshall's understanding: As indicated above, "Marshall thought that the Constitution expects of political officials no less than of judicial ones the ability and willingness to interpret and apply legal norms. But he did not think that in doing so the politicians could or would renounce politics. Indeed, on some issues only the political capacity to make judgments of prudence and policy can fulfill the Constitution's requirements."[75] Barkow discusses at some length Marshall's view that the constitutional division of authority is founded largely on questions of institutional compe-

---

[74] Of course, it is important to make clear that individual rights claims, subject to normal judicial review, may arise in such cases, independently of constitutional structure issues. For example, in *United States v. Darby*, 312 U.S. 100 (1941), it was contended that the Fair Labor Standards Act of 1936 (which regulated wages and hours in factories that produced goods for interstate commerce) exceeded Congress's commerce power, *and*, even if it were within that power because the matter substantially affected interstate commerce, nonetheless such regulation of personal economic freedom was a deprivation of property without due process of law. Similarly, in *United States v. Belmont*, 301 U.S. 324 (1937) and *United States v. Pink*, 315 U.S. 203 (1942), it was charged both that President Franklin D. Roosevelt's executive agreement with the Soviet Union respecting Russian assets within the states was an invasion of states' rights *and* that it violated the Fifth Amendment by depriving individual creditors of property without due process of law and by taking private property without just compensation.

[75] Dellinger & Powell, *supra* at 376.

tence.[76] For example, Marshall believed that the constitutionally established power to extradite under a treaty is properly committed to the executive department because only that branch can have a complete view of how this judgment will affect the nation's foreign relations. Similarly, he upheld a statute granting the president the unreviewable decision respecting an emergency that justified activating the militia to repel an attack.[77] Moreover, the Court has subsequently invoked the political question doctrine when venturing into areas where it believed that the executive had special responsibilities. Thus, in *Gilligan v. Morgan*, the Court declined to exercise close supervision over training of the Ohio National Guard, explaining that the executive was better equipped for this task.[78]

Adjudication of individual rights claims should similarly depend on the special qualifications of each of the branches. The necessity of vindicating constitutionally secured personal liberties is the principal justification for the awesome (and antimajoritarian) power that judicial review confers upon the federal judiciary. As Barkow recounts, in *Marbury v. Madison*, Chief Justice Marshall adverted to this precept when first raising the notion of a political question, concluding that no judicial involvement is warranted when a claim's "subjects are political," one that "respect[s] the nation, not individual rights. . . ."[79] This distinction exists because, where personal rights are at stake, it cannot always (or even often) be assumed that the majoritarian political process can produce a trustworthy result – particularly because of the defects of the electoral and political systems that Siegel identifies.

Consequently, although the Court may find some issues arising under a constitutional provision to be nonjusticiable, it should be exceedingly reluctant to foreclose consideration of an individual rights claim, even though it may concern "politics," the political process or the internal workings of the political branches.[80] Of course, this in no way guarantees that the personal liberty appeal will succeed. Apart from an ordinary rejection on the merits, there may also be controversies implicating personal liberties which the Court concludes are governed by the political question doctrine. Thus, as we have seen, if the Constitution is read to commit authoritative interpretation of a constitutional provision to the political branches, the Court must decline to rule for the claimant. Nonetheless, in my judgment, the text or original understanding would have to be exceptionally clear to persuade the Court to reach this result in order to defeat what it otherwise be-

---

[76] Barkow.

[77] *Martin v. Mott*, 25 U.S. 19 (1827).

[78] See discussion at Barkow. In *Gilligan*, the Court relied mainly on the "textual commitment" criterion, 413 U.S. 1, 6 (1973). To the extent that the conclusions in all three cases just discussed are ultimately influenced by the judiciary's inability to gather and assess the relevant data, the matter falls within the "manageable standards" criterion (to be discussed shortly), although such factors may surely influence the Court's judgment on original understanding.

[79] Barkow.

[80] See generally John H. Ely, *Democracy and Distrust* (Harvard University Press, 1980).

lieves may be a violation of a constitutionally protected individual right; few (if any) constitutional provisions unambiguously require such a determination.

The situation arises in cases when, on the one hand, a constitutional provision is judged to allocate broad discretion to a political branch and, on the other, there is an individual rights claim grounded in some other clause, such as Due Process, Equal Protection, or the freedoms of speech, press and religion. For example, suppose Congress removed a federal judge who claimed that the impeachment was motivated solely by race. The judge would have a powerful equal protection claim, presumptively calling for the normal operation of nondeferential judicial review respecting alleged violations of constitutionally secured personal liberties. It is possible, however, that the Court would rule that the Impeachment Power grants Congress *unreviewable authority to determine* its scope (a true political question). This may be based on a "textual commitment" which "makes clear that the Senate sits as judge and jury, and its rulings of fact and law therefore stand as res judicata in all other tribunals"[81] (although I probably would not interpret this as going beyond the Senate's determining the adjudicative facts alleged for impeachment[82] and not to the constitutionality of procedural protections that are, at least in most instances, distinct from trial of the substantive charges, or to factors—such as racial prejudice—that are wholly external to the litigation proceedings).[83] Or it may be grounded on the Court's judgment that it lacks "judicially discoverable and manageable standards," whose complexities will be discussed below, but include the difficulties of ferreting out the needed adjudicative facts, or of determining the motivation of the relevant government actors—535 members of Congress are different from a handful of senators on the Judiciary Committee for this purpose.[84] (The president's nomination and appointments powers present similar scenarios.[85]) But it bears repeating that in my view, this course may well

---

[81] Paul Brest, Sanford Levinson, J. M. Balkin and Akhil Reed Amar, *Processes of Constitutional Decisionmaking,* 4th ed. (Gaithersburg: Aspen Law & Business, 2000), 735. See generally Akhil Reed Amar, *On Impeaching Presidents,* 28 Hofstra L. Rev. 291 (1999).

[82] Accord, *Powell v. McCormack,* 395 U.S. 486, 548 (1969).

[83] For the view that neither the text nor intention of the "sole Power to try all Impeachments" language supports the conclusion that the judiciary has no role whatever, see Rebecca L. Brown, *When Political Questions Affect Individual Rights: The Other Nixon v. United States,* 1993 Sup.Ct.Rev. 125, 127–34.

[84] For a strongly presented description of the formidable problems connected with ascertaining the motives of even a single legislator, see Justice Scalia's dissenting opinion in *Edwards v. Aguillard,* 482 U.S. 578, 636–39 (1987).

[85] Siegel gives examples of other constitutional provisions that have been said to fall into this category. He cites Robert Pushaw's position that the president's decision whether to veto a bill is unreviewable by the courts because "the President's discretion with regard to the veto power is absolute." See Siegel (summarizing Pushaw, n. 69 *supra*). Although Siegel finds it "pointless" to invoke the political question doctrine in a case so easily resolved on the merits, he agrees with Pushaw's view that the Constitution does not limit the veto power. Siegel also discusses then-Judge Scalia's opinion in *Morgan v. United States,* 801 F.2d 445 (D.C. Cir. 1986), where a candidate in a closely con-

provide better protection for individual rights than would a judicial ruling on the merits that affords substantial deference to the political decisionmakers.[86] While the judge in *United States v. Nixon* did not specifically allege an individual rights violation, his argument—that the full Senate did not participate in the evidentiary hearing on the charges brought against him and thus abused the Senate's authority to "try" all impeachments—could readily have been framed as a due process infraction.[87] While the *Nixon* Court was right to rule against the judge, it would have been preferable, in my view, to have decided the merits of the due process claim (if properly presented)—finding that the Senate's action, while not posing a political question, was not unconstitutional. This is the position taken by Justice White's concurrence; indeed, it is strongly suggested in Chief Justice Rehnquist's opinion for the Court, which undertook an historical inquiry into the meaning of the word "try" before pronouncing the matter a political question.

My third criterion, the absence of "judicially discoverable and manageable standards," is drawn from *Baker v. Carr*. It is concerned not only with issues arising at the national level, it (and my fourth criterion as well) also includes acts of state or local governments and addresses mainly issues of individual rights.[88] The "manageable standards" test reflects the judgment that, under some circumstances, a decidedly practical restraint on justiciability may be necessary. There may be constitutional provisions for which the Court simply lacks the capacity to develop clear and coherent principles to govern litigants' conduct. This is true even though the justices can always produce *some* standard. Tushnet argues, for example, that the "one person, one vote" precept developed by the Court in *Reynolds v. Sims* exceeds the extent to which the Court may properly go to fashion creative standards while using what it claims are simply "ordinary methods of [constitutional] interpretation." For me, however, the real question is whether a particular standard

---

tested congressional election challenged the decision by the House of Representatives to seat his rival. Dismissing the case for lack of jurisdiction, the opinion held that the text and history of the Elections Clause were "entirely consistent with . . . [the] plain exclusion of judicial jurisdiction" because it provides that the House is not merely a judge but "the Judge" of its members' qualifications. Siegel (citing 801 F.2d at 447). Neither Scalia (nor Siegel) argue that Congress's power under the Elections Clause is unlimited, only that it is unreviewable by the Court. In practice, however, the result may be the same as in the veto case—that is, the Court may be required to dismiss a claim that the coordinate branch has exercised its power in a way that violates individual rights.

[86] For forceful criticism of anything greater than a "certain degree" of judicial deference so as to avoid "grave potential dangers to individual liberty," see Martin H. Redish, *Judicial Review and the "Political Question,"* 79 Nw. U. L. Rev. 1031, 1061 (1984).

[87] See *Hastings v. United States,* 802 F.Supp. 490 (D.D.C. 1992), vacated, 988 F.2d 1280 (D.C. Cir. 1993), 837 F.Supp. 3 (D.D.C. 1993).

[88] For the view that this is consistent with the pre-*Baker* use of the political question doctrine, see Fritz Scharpf, *Judicial Review and the Political Question: A Functional Analysis,* 75 Yale.L. J. 517, 538–39 (1966). See also Alexander M. Bickel, *The Least Dangerous Branch* (Indianapolis: Bobbs-Merrill, 1962), 184 (one element of the political question doctrine is "the Court's sense of lack of capacity . . . [because of] the strangeness of the issue and its intractability to principled resolutiona").

is constitutionally warranted ("judicially discoverable"), desirable, and sufficiently principled to guide the lower courts and constrain all jurists from inserting their own ideological beliefs in ad hoc, unreasoned ways. Although my thinking as to this is still tentative, examples of the constitutional problems that may resist judicial efforts to resolve in accordance with the criteria just set out include whether a partisan gerrymander violates the Equal Protection Clause, limiting punitive damages under the Due Process Clause, and (probably most controversially) the definition of a regulatory "taking" under the Just Compensation and Takings Clause.

To briefly explore just one of these difficulties: Partisan political gerrymandering unquestionably implicates the individual right to vote on an equal basis, and—as was the case in *Baker v. Carr* and its progeny dealing with malapportionment—entrenched politicians have an obvious disincentive to address the issue. The Court could adopt a standard similar to that it has chosen for racial gerrymandering. But the prevailing sentiment (both judicial and scholarly) strongly questions whether it would be constitutionally warranted or desirable to interpret the Equal Protection Clause so as to invalidate all apportionments that made political factors dominant and controlling, subordinating usual districting criteria. Yet it would seem that other informed solutions regarding whether gerrymandering had occurred and how to remedy it would require judges to make complex and imponderable factual determinations involving such factors as the extent of party loyalty among voters, qualities such as personal appeal or political skill that might have contributed to the success of particular candidates, and the degree of influence the minority party retained through lobbying or political patronage. None of these matters is easily measured or readily within the realm of judicial expertise.

Moreover, this may be one of those contexts in which the Court cannot develop effective safeguards of individual rights, but where the political process may afford some meaningful protection, however flawed. A political party in power, for example, may restrain itself from the worst excesses of gerrymandering because of fear of retaliation should the electorate reverse its advantage, or of the possibility that its avarice will be presently emulated in other states where its opponents are in control.

A final observation respecting the "manageable standards" criterion: In *Nixon*, the Court reasoned that its absence "may strengthen the conclusion that there is a textually demonstrable commitment to a coordinate branch."[89] Similarly, as Barkow points out, *Luther v. Borden* suggested that the definitional difficulties that the Court would face in deciding whether a challenged state government was "republican" influenced its conclusion that the Guarantee Clause was intended to be ultimately interpreted by Congress.[90] Nonetheless, I am doubtful that the text or original understanding of either the Impeachment or Guarantee Clauses is sufficiently clear to negate all judicial review, especially because of the legitimate individual rights claims that may be made in the impeachment context (as I have already discussed), as well as those that might be presented in the *Luther* situation

---

[89] 506 U.S. 224, 228–29 (1993). See n. 78 *supra*.
[90] See Barkow.

(as will be discussed shortly). Therefore, if the Court were to determine that a constitutional issue presents a political question because of the "manageable standards" criterion—as was suggested by the plurality opinion in *Coleman v. Miller* on the question of a reasonable time for the pendency of a constitutional amendment—its conclusion should not be based on the "textual commitment" theory but rather on the functional approach of judicial review not being feasible. Once again, however, I want to be clear that this criterion is grounded in judicial incapacity to fashion a governing rule, and not in the Court's judgment that the political branches ought to have "discretion free of principled rules."[91] To the contrary, the ideal is that Congress and the executive will develop their own principles, albeit norms informed by political needs and experience.

A fourth criterion for nonjusticiability, about which I am yet more uncertain than the third, borrows from standing doctrine the concept of a "generalized grievance": a harm by which people are injured or affected in a similar way. Generalized grievance cases may encompass individual constitutional rights insofar as all (or almost all) persons may truly be said to have suffered comparable injury in respect to their personal liberties. This may fairly lead to the conclusion that a decision by a government body that is accountable to an electoral majority trustworthily represents all affected. Although I believe there are very few examples of this phenomenon, cases such as *United States v. Richardson*,[92] involving the contention that the Statement and Account Clause mandated that the CIA publish its budget even though a federal statute allowed the CIA to keep it secret, and *Schlesinger v. Reservists*,[93] presenting the argument that a senator's or representative's membership in the Armed Forces Reserves violates the Incompatibility Clause, are potential candidates.

It is clear that neither clause involves national power versus states rights. Nor does either appear to cover clashes between Congress and the president. It is debatable, though, as to whether they pose individual rights issues. It may be that they fall into yet a different category that I have described as "housekeeping" matters, dealing with administrative details of the federal departments (for example, the minimum age for elected national officials) or with relations among the states (for example, the Extradition Clause).

But assuming (though very doubtfully on my part) that *Richardson* and *Reservists* embrace constitutionally secured personal freedoms, they are clearly distinguishable, in regard to whether the injury is really uniformly distributed, from the more usual situations concerning constitutional provisions that are plainly understood to affect individual rights such as the freedoms of speech and religion or the protections of the accused. Thus, for example, a statute that required everyone to attend religious services on Sunday may be read as treating all the same, but its enormously disparate impact is obvious. So, too, for a law that compelled all citizens to pay an annual $100 fee in order to vote.

---

[91] Bickel, n. 88 *supra*, at 186.
[92] 418 U.S. 166 (1974).
[93] 418 U.S. 208 (1974).

It might be argued that the *Richardson* plaintiff's injury, for example, is in fact of the same variety, since the denial of information about the CIA's budget also affects people to varying degrees. Some will think the withholding of information a desirable precaution, most will be indifferent, and a few, like the *Richardson* plaintiff, will protest. Nevertheless, it appears unlikely that the minority objecting to the CIA measure is a stable or identifiable one, and as a result there is little reason to believe that the ordinary political process is not a fair and trustworthy method for resolving its concerns.[94] This conclusion stems largely from the nature of the constitutional provision at issue. Even if the Statement and Account Clause might be said to establish a kind of personal liberty, it does not appear to be one that falls within the class of "fundamental" rights that serve to protect an identifiable racial, religious, or political minority that might be subject to majority abuse, consequently requiring that the constitutionally secured right be withdrawn from authoritative interpretation by the ordinary political process. Instead, the Statement and Account Clause may be seen as creating a right that belongs to the majority (rather than an endangered, constitutionally guarded minority), which it may at its own option choose to forego as was done in respect to maintaining secrecy for the CIA budget. If a future majority wishes to reclaim the right, it is a simple matter for it to repeal the legislation so as to require normal publication of the information.

Similarly, should the generalized grievance criterion apply to a situation in which a majority of voters attempts to restrict its own exercise of democratic powers, such as by agreeing to an unevenly apportioned legislature or by imposing term limits for elected officials? Does the right at issue belongs to the "public at large"—as might be argued about the right to receive information about the CIA's budget—or is it, rather, an individual right that is not subject to majority infringement? In the 1964 *Reapportionment Cases*, the Court ruled that a malapportioned legislature violates equal protection even if approved "by a vote of the majority of the state's electorate,"[95] reasoning that because the constitutional principle safeguards the right of each citizen "to cast an equally weighted vote," it extends even to the situation in which the majority creating the malapportionment includes a majority of those who would be underrepresented by it.[96] This ruling seems to be contrary to the generalized grievance test. It may be helpful to contrast the one

---

[94] See the discussion of which minorities merit judicial protection in *Judicial Review and the National Political Process* 76–77.

[95] *Lucas v. Colorado Gen. Assembly*, 377 U.S. 713, 736 (1964).

[96] *Id.* at 736. It is conceivable that a majority might agree to such a scheme even though it would appear to be voting against its own interest. At the time the *Reapportionment Cases* were decided, I noted that white urban voters might support a malapportioned legislature in the belief that rural voters would take a firmer stand against integration. See Jesse H. Choper, *On the Warren Court and Judicial Review*, 27 Cath. U. L. Rev. 31 (1967). Though less likely, it is even possible to imagine a similar scenario occurring today. For example, voters in a state whose cities were experiencing a wave of pro-tax newcomers might be persuaded to rest a greater share of voting power in the reliably anti-tax countryside.

person, one vote guarantee with the constitutional right at stake in a case involving laws allegedly respecting an establishment of religion. For example, the fact that a majority of non-Methodists had authorized a state appropriation to construct a Methodist church should not bar a court from granting an injunction against the use of state funds for this purpose. Disregarding majority preferences here would be necessary to vindicate the rights of a specially protected minority: non-Methodists who did not want to support the Methodist Church.

Term limits and popularly enacted malapportionments, however, present a different problem. In *U.S. Term Limits v. Thornton*, the Court invalidated term limits as applied to members of Congress, finding that the requirements for congressional service imposed by the Qualifications Clause were meant to be exclusive. The Court also emphasized the principle, drawn from the *Powell* decision, that "sovereignty confers on the people the right to choose freely their representatives to the National Government."[97] Although the Court did not treat the issue of term limits as a political question (even the dissent did not advocate this position[98]), it deserves consideration under the "generalized grievance" criterion. In the absence of proof to the contrary, neither the imposition of term limits nor an informed referendum establishing unequally sized legislative districts would appear to have either the motive or effect of preventing a minority group from attaining power. Moreover, in contrast to malapportionments that are the exclusive creation of a legislature, and which current legislators have a stake in perpetuating, there is no structural barrier to the electorate's repealing term limits if they no longer command the majority's support. Therefore, although term limits and *all* malapportionments unquestionably restrict the individual's right to vote, it is not clear to me that this is the sort of a personal liberty that courts must intervene to protect. Rather, the ordinary political process appears to provide a viable alternative. Still, even on the fair assumption that there is no reason to think that the political branches cannot be trusted to fairly resolve at least several of the constitutional claims discussed above, there are major hurdles to be overcome before they may be labeled as nonjusticiable. For one thing, as Siegel points out,[99] the fact that a grievance is widely shared neither guarantees nor even makes it likely that the political branches will correct it. While the traditional electoral process or other forms of direct political activity are available in theory, it may well be that various impediments will make them unlikely to respond very often. Perhaps, though, because of the fact (as I argued elsewhere[100]) that when the issue is significant enough, the political process will (and has) answered, and because failure on the part of the legislative or executive branches to act in situations of this kind (where the burden is very widely shared) does not necessarily make the outcome unfair, the criterion (if administrable) may still be viable.

---

[97] 514 U.S. 779, 794 (1995).

[98] Justice Thomas in dissent did suggest, however, that any individual rights issues posed by the denial of ballot access to particular candidates were best analyzed under the First or Fourteenth Amendments rather than the Qualifications Clause. See *id.* at 925.

[99] See Siegel et seq.

[100] *Judicial Review and the National Political Process* 312–13.

Although the criteria I have discussed, especially the second one, may alter the way the Court approaches alleged political questions, adherence to them would not depart substantially from what has actually been done. For example, justiciability of questions under the Guarantee Clause, whose political question status has been frequently debated, would turn largely on the extent to which the issue involved individual rights. Thus, as I have already suggested, *Luther v. Borden* might plausibly be argued under a theory similar to that of the reapportionment cases that resulted in their removal from the Guarantee Clause category: denial of the fundamental right to vote because the government in power was not legitimately elected (in the same way that an executive order making the incumbent governor-for-life would deny voting rights to the population at large).[101] Under like reasoning, at least some claims related to the Art. V constitutional amendment process might clear the political question hurdle, e.g., an argument that a state ratifying convention had been inequitably apportioned. Indeed, *Powell v. McCormack* may be seen from this perspective in that the House of Representatives' refusal to seat the congressman may credibly be characterized as a denial of his constituents' right to vote. Some of these claims, however, even if valid from an individual rights perspective, could founder under the "manageable standards" criterion.

Finally, a most prominent proposal for identifying political questions merits further consideration: the expedient technique of avoiding especially contentious disputes that the justices may feel disinclined to decide according to adequately principled rules because of a fear of weakening their already vulnerable branch of government. This path of prudence, most famously developed by Alexander Bickel (for political questions[102] as well as other tools of judicial abstinence), suggested (albeit inexplicitly) in the *Baker v. Carr* formulation, and historically identified by scholars as an element of the political question doctrine,[103] is plainly most questionable when applied to the Court's refusal to decide matters that are brought before it under its congressionally imposed mandatory jurisdiction.[104] The Court has never determined—when faced with a controversy that is sufficiently concrete, developed, and adverse to fulfill the explicit requirements of Article III—whether the political question doctrine is rooted in the Constitution or is simply a judicial construct that exists at the sufferance of the political branches. Of course, under the "textual commitment" criterion, all the Court need do is to hold as a matter of constitutional interpretation that resolution is committed to the political branches and that, as a consequence, no ordinary act of Congress may supersede the command of the fundamental charter. But this does not work for my other three crite-

---

[101] This was suggested in *Luther*, 48 U.S. at 45 ("unquestionably a military government, established as the permanent government of the State, would not be a republican government"), as well as in *Minor v. Happersett*, 88 U.S. 162 (1874), raising the question of whether a republican government could deny the vote to women.

[102] Bickel, n. 88 *supra*, at 125–26, 183–84.

[103] See, e.g., Maurice Finkelstein, Judicial Self-Limitation, 37 Harv. L. Rev. 338 (1924).

[104] See Gerald Gunther, *The Subtle Vices of the "Passive Virtues"—A Comment on Principles and Expediency in Judicial Review*, 64 Colum. L. Rev. 1 (1964).

ria. I have argued elsewhere, however, that if the Court concludes that the resolution of certain constitutional questions would be inconsistent with proper performance of its essential role in our system of government, then it should invalidate efforts by the political branches to require it to do so.[105] Bickel's prudential approach may well be more appropriately used, however, pursuant to the Court's discretionary system of certiorari, now covering almost all of its docket, but this is totally different from a holding of political question which does not merely put off a final decision to another day but prevents all federal courts from adjudicating the merits of a constitutional issue.

Although I concur in Justice Robert H. Jackson's famous bon mot, offered to inform the Court's task of interpreting our fundamental charter, that the justices should not "convert the constitutional Bill of Rights into a suicide pact,"[106] and I am not unsympathetic to the pragmatic notions about discretion sometimes being the better part of valor and living to fight another day, still, I would be much troubled in concluding that the Court's concern for individual rights should be affected by its judgment of whether a particular result will bring criticism, hostility, or disobedience. Such speculation must be based on social-scientific predictions that judges are poorly equipped to make. More importantly, for the Court to make this an element of how it finally interprets the Constitution is inconsistent with the politically neutral and principled role supporting its antimajoritarian existence in a democratic government. And to do so in any but the most extraordinary and compelling circumstances would be to shirk its vital function as that government agency of last resort for guarding the constitutional rights of those without political influence.

The considerations underlying the political question doctrine are fundamental to the judicial role, important both as limits to and justifications for the power of judicial review. The contributions to this book should play a significant part in the ongoing discussion.

---

[105] *Judicial Review and the National Political Process* 404–15.
[106] *Terminiello v. City of Chicago*, 337 U.S. 1, 37 (1949) (dissenting opinion).

The Rise and Fall of the Political Question Doctrine[1]

Rachel E. Barkow[2]

At least in areas outside foreign affairs, the political question doctrine appears to be on the verge of dying, if it is not already dead. My aim in this chapter is to offer an account of the doctrine's decline and to explain why this development should concern, not comfort, us.

Part I begins this task by tracing the constitutional roots of the political question doctrine and its relationship to a theory of interpretive deference. Part II continues by documenting the beginning of the doctrine's demise and the correlation of that demise with the ascendancy of a theory of judicial review that is one of judicial hegemony. Part III then argues that the diminishment of the doctrine—and, in particular, its classical strain—is troublesome precisely because it fosters this vision of judicial supremacy.

[1] A longer version of this chapter initially appeared as an article entitled *More Supreme than Court? The Fall of the Political Question Doctrine and the Rise of Judicial Supremacy*, 102 Colum. L. Rev. 237 (2002). It is reprinted here with the permission of the Columbia Law Review.

[2] Associate Professor of Law, New York University School of Law.

I. The Origins and the Rise

As Robert Pushaw has explained,[3] Alexander Hamilton "foreshadowed" the political question doctrine's development when he stated in the Federalist Papers:

> If it be said that the legislative body are themselves the constitutional judges of their own powers and that the construction they put upon them is conclusive upon the other departments it may be answered that this cannot be the natural presumption *where it is not to be collected from any particular provisions in the Constitution.*[4]

In other words, although judicial review is the norm, there are exceptions, which are expressed in "particular provisions in the Constitution." Hamilton therefore recognized a constitutionally based political question doctrine, or what can be termed the "classical" formulation of the doctrine: The Constitution carves out certain categories of issues that will be resolved as a matter of total legislative or executive discretion. Under this view of the doctrine, judicial abstinence is not merely prudential or expedient but constitutionally required. Application of the classical political question doctrine does not depend on the particular parties in the case or on the particular remedy being sought. It is a doctrine that is rooted in the text and structure of the Constitution itself.

Alexander Hamilton was not alone in acknowledging that the resolution of certain constitutional questions belongs with the politically accountable branches. Chief Justice Marshall, another great defender of the judiciary, was also a vigorous advocate of what came to be known as the political question doctrine. Indeed, he acknowledged the political question doctrine in *Marbury v. Madison.* Marshall argued for judicial modesty by making clear that the Supreme Court's remedial power did not extend to all legal questions. "Questions, in their nature political, or which are, by the constitution and laws, submitted to the executive, can never be made in this court."[5] In particular, because some questions are committed by the Constitution to the absolute discretion of Congress or the president, there is no place for judicial oversight.

Chief Justice Marshall did make clear, however, that it was for the Court to determine whether an issue presented a political question, committed to the discretion of the political branches, or a judicial question, which the Court could answer.[6] Although the allocation would "always depend on the nature of [the]

---

[3] Robert J. Pushaw, Jr., *Justiciability and Separation of Powers: A Neo-Federalist Approach,* 81 Cornell L. Rev. 393, 424 (1996).

[4] *The Federalist* No. 78 (Alexander Hamilton) 467 (Clinton Rossiter ed., 1961) (emphasis added).

[5] *Marbury v. Madison,* 5 U.S. (1 Cranch) 137, 170 (1803).

[6] *Id.* at 167, 170–71.

act,"[7] Marshall provided key guiding factors for identifying a political question: "The subjects are political. They respect the nation, not individual rights. . . ."[8] They involve areas in which the Constitution vests the political branches with discretion. "The province of the court is, solely, to decide on the rights of individuals, not to enquire how the executive, or executive officers, perform duties in which they have discretion."[9]

Marshall's stance in *Marbury* was hardly surprising. Three years earlier, when he was in the House of Representatives, Marshall explained to his fellow congressmen that some issues under the Constitution presented questions of political law that must be answered by the political branches. Marshall noted that this was a jurisdictional limit, based on the Constitution's enumeration of judicial powers to extend only to "cases." "By extending the judicial power to all *cases in law and equity*, the constitution had never been understood to confer on that department any political power whatever."[10] On the contrary, "[i]f the judicial power extended to every question under the constitution, it would involve almost every subject proper for legislative discussion and decision." That, according to Marshall, would destroy the separation of powers: "The division of power . . . could exist no longer, and the other departments would be swallowed up by the judiciary."[11]

Marshall explained that there were reasons of institutional competence underlying this constitutional division of power. For instance, he argued that the executive should make the determination to extradite under a treaty because it is the "department whose duty it is to understand precisely the state of the political intercourse and connection between the United States and foreign nations, to understand the manner in which the particular stipulation is explained and performed by foreign nations, and to understand completely the state of the Union."[12] Walter Dellinger and Jefferson Powell summarized Marshall's position, noting that, from the examples he gave, it is clear that political questions include "a judgment about where the nation's interests lay, including its interests in justice to itself and others and in the preservation of national security," as opposed to questions involving individual rights.[13] Marshall made clear that, although he believed the judiciary had the power to "say what the law is," he also believed that the judiciary was not the *only* branch with that power.[14] Indeed, as Dellinger and Powell note, "on some issues only the political capacity to make judgments

---

[7] *Id.*
[8] *Id.* at 166.
[9] *Id.* at 170.
[10] Speech of the Honorable John Marshall (March 7, 1800), in 18 U.S. (5 Wheat.) app. note I, at 16–17 (1820).
[11] *Id.*
[12] *Id.* at 28.
[13] Walter Dellinger and H. Jefferson Powell, *Marshall's Questions*, 2 Green Bag 2d 367, 372–74 (1999).
[14] *Id.* at 375.

of prudence and policy can fulfill the Constitution's requirements."[15] Thus, although its critics believe the doctrine has no place in a country where judicial review is a fundamental part of the constitutional structure, the classical version of the political question doctrine can trace its pedigree to the Constitution itself and its original understanding.

At the time Marshall was writing, judicial review and the political question doctrine did not present the courts with the strictly binary choice that appears today, with the latter seen as so fundamentally opposed to the former. Judicial review involved a spectrum of broad deference to the political branches, with the political question doctrine occupying one end. Also along the spectrum were issues on which the political branches enjoyed considerable, but not absolute, deference. Finally, at the other end were the questions that are so much more familiar to us today: those questions on which the Court alone provides interpretation without giving any deference to the other branches. As Larry Kramer has recently explained, it was this end of the spectrum that was more controversial at the founding. "[E]ven a limited power of judicial review remained controversial in the 1780s. At the time, the most that could be said . . . was that courts might exercise review where the legislature unambiguously violated an established principle of fundamental law."[16] Hamilton, for instance, believed that a court should declare a statute unconstitutional only if there were an "irreconcilable variance" between the Constitution and the statute.[17] In 1796, Justice Chase stated that he would declare an Act of Congress void only "in a very clear case."[18] Similarly, Justice Paterson stated in 1800 that the Court should strike only "a clear and unequivocal breach of the Constitution, not a doubtful and argumentative application."[19] Courts at the founding recognized and respected the fact that "it is the duty of legislators as well as judges to consult [the Constitution] and conform their acts to it, so it should be presumed that all their acts do conform to it unless the contrary is manifest."[20] This idea of clear mistake "is not founded on the idea that only manifestly abusive legislative enactments are unconstitutional, but rather on the idea that only such manifest error entitles a court to displace the prior constitutional ruling of the enacting legislature."[21]

Thus, when Hamilton and Marshall recognized that there were political questions outside judicial review, they were simply acknowledging one end of a

---

[15] *Id.* at 376.

[16] Larry D. Kramer, *Putting the Politics Back into the Political Safeguards of Federalism*, 100 Colum. L. Rev. 215, 238–40 (2000).

[17] *Federalist* No. 78 at 467.

[18] *Hylton v. United States*, 3 U.S. (3 Dall.) 171, 175 (1796).

[19] *Cooper v. Telfair*, 4 U.S. (4 Dall.) 14 (1800).

[20] James B. Thayer, *The Origin and Scope of the American Doctrine of Constitutional Law*, 7 Harv. L. Rev. 129, 142 (1893), quoting Chancellor Waties of South Carolina (internal quotation marks and citation omitted).

[21] Lawrence Gene Sager, *Fair Measure: The Legal Status of Underenforced Constitutional Norms*, 91 Harv. L. Rev. 1212, 1223 (1978).

spectrum of congressional and executive discretion to interpret and enforce the Constitution. The constitutional judgments of the political branches were highly respected and the courts gave them great deference. It was appropriate at that time for courts to engage in a threshold inquiry to determine how much interpretive room a constitutional delegation of power gave the branch receiving that power.[22] While the courts remained responsible for declaring the boundaries, it was recognized that the Constitution contemplated room for the political actors to give substantive meaning within those boundaries.

Perhaps no other case illustrates this concept of interpretive deference better than *M'Culloch v. Maryland* and its treatment of the Necessary and Proper Clause. Chief Justice Marshall's opinion for the Court recognized that, although "the powers of the government are limited," the sound interpretation of the Constitution "must allow the national legislature that discretion, with respect to the means by which the powers it confers are to be carried into execution, which will enable that body to perform the high duties assigned to it, in the manner most beneficial to the people."[23] The Court described its role as policing the boundaries of legislative power, not dictating legislative conclusions within those bounds. If the Court were to inquire into whether an action was "necessary," it would "pass the line which circumscribes the judicial department, and . . . tread on legislative ground."[24] In other words, the substantive content of "necessary" would be supplied by Congress, not the Court.

To a generation that recognized such different degrees of deference to the political branches in their interpretation of constitutional questions, the notion of some questions sitting entirely outside judicial review was far from shocking.

Identifying these questions, however, is not a straightforward task. Given that the Constitution does not contain an express textual commitment of judicial review in the Supreme Court, it is not surprising that provisions of the Constitution do not explicitly strip the Court of power and vest interpretive authority with Congress or the executive. Instead, the interpretive deference given to the political branches must be inferred from a textual grant of power to a political branch and from structural clues that the grant of power cannot be shared with the judicial branch. In addition, some insight on whether the question is for the political branches alone can be gleaned from the historical background of the provision.[25]

Because this is obviously a difficult interpretive enterprise, the structural considerations in particular leave room for prudential or functional considerations to enter the analysis. Chief Justice Marshall in *Marbury* gave one structural

---

[22] Thayer, *Origin and Scope,* 144.

[23] *M'Culloch v. Maryland,* 17 U.S. (4 Wheat.) 316, 421 (1819).

[24] *Id.* at 423.

[25] See Steven G. Calabresi, *The Political Question of Presidential Succession,* 48 Stan. L. Rev. 155, 157 (1995); Marcella David, *Passport to Justice: Internationalizing the Political Question Doctrine for Application in the World Court,* 40 Harv. Int'l L. J. 81, 129 (1999). Pushaw, *Justiciability and Separation of Powers,* 501.

characteristic for courts to use in deciding whether a constitutional question presents a political question: Does it involve an individual right, or does it involve a more general question of political judgment and discretion?[26] Another interpretive guidepost is provided by the type of information that will be needed to resolve the underlying constitutional determination. Will it require factfinding that is particularly suited to the resources and expertise of the political branches? Will it implicate sensitive questions of foreign relations or other national interests? A third interpretive clue is whether there are established legal standards to apply in resolving the constitutional question, the presence of which makes it more likely that the matter is suited for the courts.[27]

Originally, these questions were answered as part of a larger inquiry into how a particular grant of authority to a political branch in the Constitution should be interpreted.[28] For instance, in *Luther v. Borden*, the Court relied on a grant of authority to Congress in the Guarantee Clause, as well as the practical difficulties of deciding whether a particular state government was "republican," to conclude that the interpretation of the Guarantee Clause rests with Congress.[29] There was, then, a textual anchor to the prudential analysis. The Guarantee Clause states that the "*United States* shall guarantee to every State in this Union a Republican Form of Government,"[30] and the Court interpreted "United States" to mean "Congress."[31]

To this textual anchor, the Court added the structural inference that the Court could not share interpretive responsibility with Congress because of the difficulties of judicial involvement. The case grew out of the extraordinary events of the Rhode Island Dorr Rebellion in 1841 and 1842, which resulted in two different state governments claiming legitimacy.

Chief Justice Taney, writing for a majority of the Court, began his analysis by noting the practical effects of deciding which sovereign was legitimate.[32] He argued that a decision that the charter government was illegitimate would entail consequences such as invalidating its laws and taxes and nullifying its courts' judgments.[33] These practical concerns colored the Court's perception and interpretation of the Constitution. As the Court argued, "[w]hen the decision of this court might lead to such results, it becomes its duty to examine very carefully its own powers before it undertakes to exercise jurisdiction."[34]

---

[26] *Marbury*, 5 U.S. at 166.
[27] Oliver P. Field, *The Doctrine of Political Questions in the Federal Courts*, 8 Minn. L. Rev. 485, 512 (1924).
[28] See Thomas M. Franck, *Political Questions/Judicial Answers* 45 (1992).
[29] *Luther v. Borden*, 48 U.S. (7 How.) 1, 47 (1849).
[30] U.S. Const. art. IV, sec. 4 (emphasis added).
[31] *Luther*, 48 U.S. at 42
[32] *Id.* at 39–40.
[33] *Id.*
[34] *Id.* at 39.

The Court then focused on the text of the Guarantee Clause itself. Insofar as the Constitution "has provided for an emergency of this kind, and authorized the general government to interfere in the domestic concerns of a State," it "has treated the subject as political in its nature, and placed the power in the hands of that department."[35] The Court concluded that, under Article IV of the Constitution, "it rests with Congress to decide what government is the established one in a State. For as the United States guarantee to each State a republican government, Congress must necessarily decide what government is established in the State before it can determine whether it is republican or not."[36] When Congress accepts the state's representatives, it recognizes the authority of the government under which they were appointed and its republican nature. Congress's "decision is binding on every other department of the government, and could not be questioned in a judicial tribunal."[37] In conclusion, Chief Justice Taney restated the classical theory of the political question doctrine and dismissed the notion that anything other than the Constitution itself could override the Court's responsibility to decide constitutional questions:

This tribunal, therefore, should be the last to overstep the boundaries which limit its own jurisdiction. And while it should always be ready to meet any question confided to it by the Constitution, it is equally its duty not to pass beyond its appropriate sphere of action, and to take care not to involve itself in discussions which properly belong to other forums. No one, we believe, has ever doubted [this] proposition. . . .[38]

The Court's analysis in *Luther* thus shows how prudential factors colored the Court's application of the classical political question doctrine, but the opinion makes clear that the Court's holding was anchored in the text and structure of the Constitution itself. It also establishes the importance of having the Court make the threshold inquiry as to what the Court's "appropriate sphere of action" in the case is (i.e., who decides who decides). There was no assumption that the Court's sphere of action in all cases is complete interpretive power.

The Court engaged in a similar analysis in *Pacific States Telephone & Telegraph Co. v. Oregon*, but it relied on prudential factors to a much greater extent.[39] In *Pacific States*, the Court was faced with a challenge to an Oregon tax law on the ground that Oregon lacked a republican form of government. Specifically, the petitioners argued that the Oregon constitution improperly permitted the people to legislate by initiative and referendum.[40]

The Court could have simply cited *Luther*'s interpretation of the Guarantee Clause. Instead, it began by listing the parade of horribles that would ensue if the Court were to conclude that Oregon lacked a republican form of govern-

---

[35] *Id.* at 42.
[36] *Id.*
[37] *Id.*
[38] *Id.* at 46.
[39] 223 U.S. 118 (1912).
[40] *Id.* at 137.

ment. First, the Court concluded that it would open the door for every citizen to
challenge taxes or other government duties by "assail[ing] in a court of justice
the rightful existence of the State."[41] Second, such a holding would "practically
award a decree absolving from all obligation to contribute to the support of or
obey the laws of such established state government."[42] Finally, just in case the
disincentives were not already great enough, the Court added that "as a consequence of the existence of such judicial authority a power in the judiciary must
be implied, unless it be that anarchy is to ensue, to build by judicial action upon
the ruins of the previously established government a new one."[43]

Faced with what it viewed as the prospect of having to establish a state government from scratch, it is not surprising that the Court concluded it had no authority to decide the question. What is interesting about *Pacific States*, however,
is that the Court appeared to reach its result, to a much greater degree than even
the *Luther* Court, by reasoning backward from these consequences without regard for the language or structure of the Constitution itself. The Court listed the
implications of ruling that Oregon lacked a republican form of government and
then asked whether Article IV demands "these strange, far-reaching and injuri-
ous results."[44] In answering its own seemingly rhetorical question, the Court
relied on the prudential aspects of *Luther*, noting in particular that *Luther* detailed at the outset "the far-reaching effect and gravity of the consequences
which would be produced" by a finding that a state lacked a republican form of
government.[45] Thus, the Court made the prudential concerns even more prominent than it had in *Luther*.

The Court's analysis in both *Luther* and *Pacific States* demonstrates that the
consequences of judicial involvement are legitimate considerations in determining how to interpret a constitutional provision. But the use of prudential factors
as part of an interpretation of the Constitution eventually set the stage for those
factors to take on independent significance—regardless of the text, structure, or
history of the particular constitutional provision at issue.

Thus, cases like *Luther* and *Pacific States* established the groundwork for
the Court's subsequent expansion of the political question doctrine into a more
general tool of avoidance. This became an especially attractive option for a New
Deal Court seeking to reclaim its legitimacy. After its judicially activist substantive Due Process and Commerce Clause decisions sparked President Roosevelt's
Court-packing plan, the Supreme Court began a marked shift toward judicial
restraint. Judicial review of congressional acts was at its most deferential.

---

[41] *Id.* at 141–42.
[42] *Id.* at 142.
[43] *Id.*
[44] *Id.*
[45] *Id.* at 144.

As part of that pattern of deference, the Court stretched the contours of the political question doctrine and, in particular, the prudential strain.[46] One such instance is *Coleman v. Miller*. In 1924, Congress proposed an amendment, known as the Child Labor Amendment, to the Constitution in response to the Court's rejection of legislation to the same effect. In 1925, the Kansas Legislature rejected the amendment. In 1937, however, the amendment was still pending, and the Kansas Legislature sitting at that time voted to ratify.[47] A group of Kansas state legislators opposed to the amendment challenged the ratification, arguing that it violated Article V because the state legislature failed to ratify within a reasonable time.[48]

The Court was therefore faced with a question involving a constitutional amendment to overturn one of its decisions. Unsurprisingly, given the political pressure it was under, the Court did not take the bait. Seven of the justices concluded that the validity of the legislature's ratification was a "political question" for Congress to judge.

Three of the seven concluded that whether a proposed amendment "lost its vitality through lapse of time" is for Congress to decide.[49] In writing the opinion for himself and the two other justices who held that view, Chief Justice Hughes distinguished the Court's decision in *Dillon v. Gloss*, a case decided eighteen years earlier. In *Dillon*, the Court had reviewed whether Congress could properly place a seven-year ratification limit on the Eighteenth Amendment and had upheld the limit as a "reasonable time."[50] Chief Justice Hughes explained that Dillon had not reached the question as to whether the Court should determine what constitutes a reasonable time when Congress has not exercised its power to fix one. Rather, that case established only that Congress has the power to fix the time limit. The Court itself could not establish a time when Congress has not acted, Chief Justice Hughes explained, because there are no criteria for a judicial determination, and such a decision would involve "an appraisal of a great variety of relevant conditions, political, social, and economic."[51]

Justice Black, in an opinion joined by three other justices, would have gone even further to hold that the constitutional amendment process is "'political' in its entirety, from submission until an amendment becomes part of the Constitution, and is not subject to judicial guidance, control, or interference at any point."[52] Therefore, they would not have reviewed the issue presented in Dillon.

---

[46] See Louis Henkin, *Is There a "Political Question" Doctrine?* 85 Yale L. J. 597, 625 (1976); Robert A. Schapiro, *Judicial Deference and Interpretive Coordinacy in State and Federal Constitutional Law*, 85 Cornell L. Rev. 656, 685 (2000).

[47] *Coleman v. Miller* 307 U.S. 433, 435–36 (1939).

[48] *Id.* at 436.

[49] *Id.* at 451, 456.

[50] *Id.* at 452, citing *Dillon v. Gloss*, 256 U.S. 368 (1921).

[51] *Id.* at 453–54.

[52] *Id.* at 459 (Black, J., concurring).

What is interesting about Coleman is the extent to which the justices relied on prudential factors alone to reach their conclusion. The seven justices who thought the case raised a political question did not make the text, history, or structure of Article V central to—or even part of—their analysis. Instead, "the lack of satisfactory criteria for a judicial determination" drove the Hughes opinion,[53] and the four concurring justices offered almost no analysis to support their view. Yet, there is a strong textual and structural argument to be made that the Article V question rests with Congress.[54]

The Supreme Court made similar use of prudential factors in *Colegrove v. Green*. Justice Frankfurter, in an opinion joined by Justices Reed and Burton, concluded that a suit brought by Illinois voters alleging unconstitutional vote dilution in the establishment of congressional election districts was "beyond [the Court's] competence."[55] Justice Frankfurter observed that the history of apportionment reveals its "embroilment in politics" and concluded that "[c]ourts ought not to enter this political thicket."[56] Justice Frankfurter's opinion did not even bother to address whether the determination of each constitutional claim raised by petitioners had been delegated to Congress. To be sure, he stated that Congress's power under Article I, Section 4 to make or alter regulations regarding the time, place, or manner of House elections vests exclusive control of those elections with Congress.[57] But he did not address separately the petitioners' Fourteenth Amendment claim. Instead, he stated generally that "no court can affirmatively remap the Illinois districts so as to bring them more in conformity with the standards of fairness for a representative system. At best we could only declare the existing electoral system invalid."[58] This would "bring courts into immediate and active relations with party contests."[59] Instead, he argued, the remedy for unfair districting lies with state legislatures or with Congress.

Justice Rutledge's concurrence argued that the concerns raised by Justice Frankfurter were better addressed as a matter of equitable remedies.[60] Justice Rutledge believed that the Court's precedent made clear that the issue did not present a political question, but he would have nevertheless dismissed the complaint for want of equity, given that the cause was "of so delicate a character."[61]

---

[53] *Id.* at 454–55

[54] See, e.g., Rachel E. Barkow, *More Supreme than Court? The Fall of the Political Question Doctrine and the Rise of Judicial Supremacy*, 102 Colum. L. Rev. 237, 280 (2002).

[55] *Colegrove v. Green,* 328 U.S. 549, 552 (1946).

[56] *Id.* at 554–56.

[57] *Id.* at 554.

[58] *Id.* at 553.

[59] *Id.*

[60] *Id.* at 565 (Rutledge, J., concurring).

[61] *Id.*

He therefore disagreed that a prudential political question doctrine was necessary to decide the case.

To understand this development of a wholly prudential political question doctrine, it is helpful to turn to Alexander Bickel, who gave what is perhaps its finest defense.[62] Bickel was writing in the aftermath of *Brown v. Board of Education*[63] and the Court's desegregation orders, and it was imperative in his view that the Court maintain its legitimacy at that critical juncture in its history.[64] Bickel believed that the Court's treatment of cases had to be principled, but he also believed that the Court's actions upholding legislation would be perceived as legitimating the policies underlying the law.[65] Bickel believed the Court could avoid legitimating "bad" laws and still stay true to principle by refusing to reach the merits in controversial cases.[66]

The Court thus needed means to avoid deciding such difficult matters, and the prudential political question doctrine was one such tool. Bickel observed that "judicial review is at least potentially a deviant institution in a democratic society," and the political question doctrine would enable courts to avoid "rampant activism" by staying out of certain matters.[67] The "passive virtues" of the prudential political question doctrine coincided with the judicial restraint and extreme deference of the New Deal Court. The Court's vision of its own powers—and, more importantly, its own limitations—admitted a strong political question doctrine.

The problem with the prudential theory, however, is that once the political question doctrine is unleashed entirely from the Constitution itself, what keeps a judge's use of the doctrine in check? What prevents a court from avoiding a case simply because it believes the issue is too complicated or is too politically charged? And what stops a judge from deciding questions constitutionally committed to another branch, as long as the judge believes it would be more expedient for the court to decide the issue instead?

II. The Fall

The strong version of the political question doctrine that developed did not sit comfortably alongside the aggressive judicial review of the Warren Court. In 1962, four years after the Warren Court announced that federal courts are "supreme in the exposition of the law of the Constitution,"[68] the Court began to cut

---

[62] Alexander M. Bickel, *The Least Dangerous Branch* 69 (2d ed. 1986).

[63] 347 U.S. 483 (1954).

[64] Bickel, *The Least Dangerous Branch*, 251–54.

[65] *Id.* at 29–31.

[66] *Id.* at 169–70.

[67] Alexander M. Bickel, *The Supreme Court, 1960 Term—Foreword: The Passive Virtues*, 75 Harv. L. Rev. 40, 47 (1961).

[68] *Cooper v. Aaron*, 358 U.S. 1, 18 (1958).

back on the political question doctrine. In *Baker v. Carr*, Justice Brennan set out to reverse the course laid out by Justice Frankfurter in *Colegrove*. The Court in *Baker* held that a complaint alleging that a state apportionment statute violated the Equal Protection Clause presented a justiciable cause of action.

In so doing, the Court engaged in its most detailed discussion of the political question doctrine to date. Justice Brennan's opinion catalogued a host of political question doctrine cases, involving issues ranging from foreign relations to the validity of constitutional amendments to the status of Indian tribes. This summary was necessary, according to the Court, "to expose the attributes of the doctrine—attributes which, in various settings, diverge, combine, appear, and disappear in seeming disorderliness."[69] The Court found two areas of common ground among the disarray. First, *Baker* held that the political question doctrine was inapplicable to cases involving the federal judiciary's relationship to the states. Rather, the doctrine applied only to the relationships among the three branches of the federal government. Thus, although the Court's prior Guarantee Clause cases had suggested that some questions were left to the state political process,[70] *Baker* made clear that the doctrine would not go so far. This view of the doctrine therefore coincided with *Cooper*'s view of the federal-state relationship.

Second, and relatedly, the Court stated that the doctrine is "primarily a function of the separation of powers."[71] The Court noted that "several formulations which vary slightly according to the settings in which the questions arise may describe a political question, although each has one or more elements which identify it as essentially a function of the separation of powers."[72] The Court then synthesized its prior cases to create a list of six factors that should be evaluated on a "case-by-case" basis:

> Prominent on the surface of any case held to involve a political question is found a textually demonstrable constitutional commitment of the issue to a coordinate political department; or a lack of judicially discoverable and manageable standards for resolving it; or the impossibility of deciding without an initial policy determination of a kind clearly for nonjudicial discretion; or the impossibility of a court's undertaking independent resolution without expressing lack of the respect due coordinate branches of government; or an unusual need for unquestioning adherence to a political decision already made; or the potentiality of embarrassment from multifarious pronouncements by various departments on one question.[73]

The Court in *Baker* therefore recognized not only the classical theory of the political question doctrine (the first factor and perhaps the second, depending on

---

[69] *Baker v. Carr*, 369 U.S. 186, 210 (1962).
[70] E.g., *Luther*, 48 U.S. at 47, 51.
[71] *Baker*, 369 U.S. at 210.
[72] *Id.* at 217.
[73] *Id.*

whether it is used to inform the first), but the prudential strand as well (the remaining four factors and perhaps the second). To dismiss on political question grounds, at least one of these factors must be applicable. The Court concluded that none of the factors was applicable in *Baker* and that the petitioners' equal protection challenge could go forward.

Justice Frankfurter, joined by Justice Harlan, dissented. Although his opinion largely amplified the arguments he made in *Colegrove*, those arguments now seemed out of step with the Warren Court's more aggressive judicial review. Nevertheless, echoing Alexander Bickel, he cautioned that the Court's authority "ultimately rests on sustained public confidence in its moral sanction" and that "feeling must be nourished by the Court's complete detachment, in fact and in appearance, from political entanglements and by abstention from injecting itself into the clash of political forces in political settlements."[74]

As he retraced the Court's Guarantee Clause cases, Justice Frankfurter noted only their prudential roots, not the classical constitutional basis for holding such cases to be "political questions." He highlighted the Court's reluctance to interfere without clear standards for judicial enforcement and its unwillingness to become an arbiter of "broad issues of political organization historically committed to other institutions and for whose adjustment the judicial process is ill-adapted."[75] Just as in *Colegrove*, Justice Frankfurter seemed to recognize that he could not make a classical argument for the political question doctrine to apply under the Fourteenth Amendment as the Court had done in *Luther v. Borden* for the Guarantee Clause. His solution was to engage in a somewhat revisionist version of judicial history. He claimed that "Art. IV, sec. 4, is not committed by express constitutional terms to Congress."[76] "It is the nature of the controversies arising under it," he proclaimed, "nothing else, which has made it judicially unenforceable."[77] Thus, he attempted to turn the entire political question doctrine into a prudential one.

Although Justice Frankfurter's arguments had held sway in 1946, those same arguments could not be reconciled with the theory of judicial review that prevailed in the 1960s. The judiciary had brought an end to segregation and was seen as the political savior for the disenfranchised, without seeming to pay much of a price in terms of its legitimacy.[78] The prevailing sentiment was in favor of an active judiciary—and that sentiment continues in large measure today, although the activism tends to run in a different direction. In this climate, "abstaining" from questions not because the Constitution demands it but because the Court prefers it would be unthinkable. Indeed, for this reason, the political question doctrine—especially its prudential aspects—has drawn scathing re-

---

[74] *Id.* at 267 (Frankfurter, J., dissenting).

[75] *Id.* at 289.

[76] *Id.* at 297.

[77] *Id.*

[78] See David, *Passport to Justice,* 131 n. 212; Samuel Issacharoff, *The Structures of Democratic Politics*, 100 Colum. L. Rev. 593, 595 (2000).

bukes from scholars, with some calling for complete abandonment of the doctrine.[79]

As it turned out, critics of the prudential political question doctrine had little to fear. Although *Baker* gave us a new test for political questions that seemed quite flexible, the case actually signaled the beginning of the end of the prudential political question doctrine, at least in cases not involving foreign affairs. In fact, in the almost forty years since *Baker v. Carr* was decided, a majority of the Court has found only two issues to present political questions, and both involved strong textual anchors for finding that the constitutional decision rested with the political branches. At the same time, the Court has sent signals that the prudential doctrine was disfavored.

For example, seven years after *Baker*, the Court considered on the merits Representative Adam Clayton Powell, Jr.'s claim that the House of Representatives improperly excluded him from the Ninetieth Congress, even though many scholars thought the case presented a political question. The House had concluded that Powell satisfied the standing qualifications of Article I, Section 2, but voted to exclude him based on a finding that he had wrongfully diverted House funds for the use of others and himself.[80] Respondent members of the House argued to the Supreme Court that "a careful examination of the pre-[Constitutional] Convention practices of the English Parliament and American colonial assemblies demonstrates that by 1787," the legislature's power to assess the qualifications of its members included the power to exclude or expel a member "on the ground that an individual's character or past conduct rendered him unfit to serve."[81] Despite the broad grant of authority given the House to judge the qualifications of its members in Article I, Section 5, the Court held that it could decide the matter on the merits.[82] It therefore rejected the applicability of the political question doctrine in an area that some believed presented a strong case for it.[83]

---

[79] See, e.g., Charles L. Black, *Inequities in Districting for Congress:* Baker v. Carr *and* Colegrove v. Green, 72 Yale L. J. 13, 13–14 (1962); Wayne McCormack, *The Political Question Doctrine—Jurisprudentially*, 70 U. Det. Mercy L. Rev. 793, 822 (1993); Michael Stokes Paulsen, *Nixon Now: The Courts and the Presidency After Twenty-Five Years*, 83 Minn. L. Rev. 1337, 1378 (1999); Martin H. Redish, *Judicial Review and the "Political Question,"* 79 Nw. U. L. Rev. 1031, 1045–46 (1985); Michael E. Tigar, *Judicial Power, The "Political Question Doctrine," and Foreign Relations*, 17 UCLA L. Rev. 1135, 1163 (1970); Erwin Chemerinsky, *Interpreting the Constitution* 95–105 (1987); John H. Ely, *War and Responsibility: Constitutional Lessons of Vietnam and Its Aftermath* 55–57 (1993); Franck, *Political Questions*, 4–5; Harold H. Koh, *The National Security Constitution: Sharing Power After the Iran-Contra Affair* 221–24 (1990).]

[80] *Powell v. McCormack*, 395 U.S. 486, 492–93 (1969).

[81] *Id.* at 521–22.

[82] *Id.* at 550.

[83] See, e.g., Herbert Wechsler, *Toward Neutral Principles of Constitutional Law*, 73 Harv. L. Rev. 1, 7–8 (1959).

In reaching this conclusion, the Court followed the "classical" model. The Court conducted an extensive analysis of the historical background of Article I, Section 5, and, based on that evaluation, concluded that the House is "without authority to *exclude* any person, duly elected by his constituents, who meets all the requirements for membership expressly prescribed in the Constitution."[84] "Art. I, § 5, is at most a 'textually demonstrable commitment' to Congress to judge only the qualifications expressly set forth in the Constitution."[85] Prudential factors seemed to have no bearing on the Court's decision.

Three years later, however, the Court sent a brief signal that the prudential strand of the doctrine was not yet dead. In *O'Brien v. Brown*, the Supreme Court granted a stay of a D.C. Circuit judgment that held justiciable a dispute about which groups of delegates should be seated from Illinois and California at the Democratic Convention in 1972.[86] Although the Court's decision to grant the stay was not a determination of whether a political question was presented, the Court strongly suggested that the matter would be deemed a political question. That is, although the Court was "unwilling to undertake final resolution of the important constitutional questions presented without full briefing and argument," it did note that the case "involve[d] claims of the power of the federal judiciary to review actions heretofore thought to lie in the control of political parties."[87] There was little classical analysis in the Court's opinion, suggesting that prudential concerns could still support abstention.

That signal proved to be a false one, however, as the classical analysis prevailed in the two post-*Baker* cases in which the Court found a political question. The first such case was *Gilligan v. Morgan*, in which the Court dismissed a suit brought by Kent State students alleging that student protestors were killed due to the government's negligent training of the National Guard. The students asked the Court to "assume continuing regulatory jurisdiction over the activities of the Ohio National Guard."[88] This would include "establish[ing] standards for the training, kind of weapons and scope and kind of orders to control the actions of the National Guard."[89] The Court rejected the request, stating that Article I, Section 8, Clause 16 vests in Congress the "responsibility for organizing, arming, and disciplining the Militia (now the National Guard)."[90] Chief Justice Burger's opinion noted that "[t]he complex, subtle, and professional decisions as to the composition, training, equipping, and control of a military force are essentially professional military judgments, subject *always* to civilian control of the Legislative and Executive Branches."[91]

---

[84] *Powell*, 395 U.S. at 522.
[85] *Id.* at 548.
[86] *O'Brien v. Brown*, 409 U.S. 1, 4–5 (1972).
[87] *Id.*
[88] *Gilligan v. Morgan*, 413 U.S. 1, 5 (1973).
[89] *Id.* at 6.
[90] *Id.*
[91] *Id.* at 10.

It took another twenty years for a majority of the Court to conclude that another issue presented a political question. In the meantime, the Court sent other signals that the doctrine was disfavored.[92] For instance, in *New York v. United States*, Justice O'Connor's opinion for the Court noted that both case law and scholarship had called into question the nonjusticiability of Guarantee Clause claims and suggested that the Court might no longer adhere to the view that questions under the Guarantee Clause present political questions.[93] This was hardly mere dicta, as the Court went on to decide that the Guarantee Clause claim failed on the merits.[94] In *Webster v. Doe*, the Court's conclusion that the CIA director's decision to fire an employee was judicially reviewable led Justice Scalia to observe that "[t]he assumption that there are any executive decisions that cannot be hauled into the courts may no longer be valid."[95] In *Japan Whaling Ass'n v. American Cetacean Society*, the Court suggested that statutory issues could not present political questions.[96] The Court's failure to apply the doctrine led many commentators to pronounce the entire doctrine, not just its prudential strand, dead.[97] Most commentators hardly mourned its departure, as they viewed the doctrine as a harmful relic from the past that could not coexist with an active federal bench.

Their predictions were just a bit premature, however. The Court concluded in *Nixon v. United States* that whether the Senate could impeach a federal judge pursuant to Article I, Section 3, Clause 6 based on the report of a factfinding committee presented a nonjusticiable political question. Chief Justice Rehnquist's opinion for the Court was based predominantly on the classical political question doctrine. In fact, he made an effort to cut back the prudential aspect of the doctrine. The opinion listed only the first two *Baker* factors—a textually demonstrable commitment to a coordinate political branch and the lack of judicially manageable standards—as relevant to the inquiry.[98] In addition, the opinion used the second factor only to inform the first—as the Court had done previously, before the New Deal Court expanded the doctrine: "[T]he lack of judicially manageable standards may strengthen the conclusion that there is a

---

[92] For cases rejecting arguments that they presented political questions, see *Davis v. Bandemer*, 478 U.S.109, 118–27 (1986) (political gerrymandering); *County of Oneida v. Oneida Indian Nation*, 470 U.S. 226, 248–50 (1985), (Indian affairs); *INS v. Chadha*, 462 U.S. 919, 940–43 (1983) (one-House veto); *Elrod v. Burns*, 427 U.S. 347, 351–53 (1976) (political patronage).

[93] *New York v. United States*, 505 U.S. 144, 184–86 (1992).

[94] *Id.* at 185.

[95] *Webster v. Doe*, 486 U.S. 592, 621 (1988) (Scalia, J., dissenting).

[96] *Japan Whaling Ass'n v. American Cetacean Society*, 478 U.S. 221, 230 (1986).

[97] See, e.g., Ely, *War and Responsibility*, 55; Franck, *Political Questions*, 61; Nat Stern, *The Political Question Doctrine in State Courts*, 35 S.C. L. Rev. 405, 406 (1984); *Ramirez de Arellano v. Weinberger*, 745 F.2d 1500, 1514 (D.C. Cir. 1984); *Tel-Oren v. Libyan Arab Republic*, 726 F.2d 774, 796 (D.C. Cir. 1984) (Edwards, J., concurring).

[98] *Nixon v. United States*, 506 U.S. 224 (1993).

textually demonstrable commitment to a coordinate branch."[99] The Court in *Nixon* did add, however, that "[i]n addition to the textual commitment argument, we are persuaded that the lack of finality and the difficulty of fashioning relief counsel against justiciability."[100] Thus, although the Court minimized the independent significance of the prudential factors, it does not appear that it meant to foreclose their use entirely, even apart from their relationship to the textual commitment prong.

In *Nixon*, the textual, structural, and historical evidence all pointed to an interpretation of Article I, Section 3, Clause 6 that vests the Senate with the interpretive authority to determine what the Constitution means by the "tr[ial]" of impeachments. The text of the provision itself gives "sole" power to the Senate, and the history of the impeachment provision demonstrates that the framers thought this judicial power belonged exclusively to the Senate and not to the courts.[101] Moreover, as the Court's opinion in *Nixon* points out, impeachment is a political check on the judicial branch, providing a structural reason for not vesting coordinate interpretive powers with the judicial branch itself.[102] For these reasons, commentators frequently cited impeachment as the prototypical example of a political question, if one is to be found at all.[103] As Judge Williams pointed out in his opinion for the D.C. Circuit in *Nixon*, "[i]f the political question doctrine has no force where the Constitution has explicitly committed a power to a coordinate branch and where the need for finality is extreme, then it is surely dead."[104]

Nixon, then, presented perhaps the most powerful case for applying the classical strand of the political question doctrine. Yet, even in that case, three justices concluded that the judiciary had a role to play in determining what kind of "trial" the Constitution contemplated. After *Nixon*, it was unclear whether *Nixon* would be an outlier—the last exception to the rule of judicial supremacy—or whether the classical political question doctrine would undergo a renaissance. As the history of the doctrine establishes, the answer to that question would depend on the Court's view of its interpretive role as a more general matter. Would the Court continue its move toward constitutional hegemony over the other branches, or would it return to the classical roots of the political question

---

[99] *Id.* at 228–29.

[100] *Id.* at 236.

[101] For discussions of this history, see Michael J. Gerhardt, *Rediscovering Nonjusticiability: Judicial Review of Impeachments After* Nixon, 44 Duke L. J. 231, 252–58 (1994); Pushaw, *Justiciability and Separation of Powers,* 429 n.166.

[102] *Nixon,* 506 U.S. at 235.

[103] See, e.g., Erwin Chemerinsky, *Cases under the Guarantee Clause Should Be Justiciable,* 65 U. Colo. L. Rev. 849, 855 (1994); Gerhardt, *Rediscovering Nonjusticiability,* 233-34; Pushaw, *Justiciability and Separation of Powers,* 505; but see Raoul Berger, *Impeachment: The Constitutional Problems* 103–21 (1973).

[104] *Nixon v. United States,* 938 F.2d 239, 246 (D.C. Cir. 1991).

doctrine and consider as a threshold matter in all cases how much interpretive power the Constitution vests with the political branches?

There is perhaps no starker illustration of the answer to that question than the 2000 presidential election cases. The argument for applying the political question doctrine to the Article II question in both *Bush v. Palm Beach County Canvassing Board* (Bush 1)[105] and *Bush v. Gore* (Bush II)[106] is a powerful one.[107] Indeed, one could make a powerful argument under either the classical or prudential strand of the doctrine. Yet, a unanimous Court in Bush I and the concurrence in Bush II addressed the Article II question without even mentioning the doctrine, let alone applying it. Instead, the justices took for granted that they had the "responsibility to resolve the federal and constitutional issues the judicial system has been forced to confront."[108] If the political question doctrine did not merit even discussion in those cases, it is quite apparent that the doctrine is in serious decline—if not completely defunct.

III. Why We Should Resuscitate the Classical Political Question Doctrine

The political question doctrine requires the Court to acknowledge that the other branches "may make constitutional law—i.e., make judgments about the scope and meaning of its constitutionally authorized . . . functions—subject to change only if [the branch] later changes its mind or by a constitutional amendment."[109] It is therefore not surprising that the doctrine has declined as the Supreme Court has become of the view that it alone among the three branches has been allocated the power to provide the full substantive meaning of all constitutional provisions. The current Court appears to believe that it alone provides the final answer to almost all constitutional questions, while the interpretations of the other branches are to be accepted at the Court's discretion. If "[a] strong view of judicial supremacy implies an absence of judicial deference,"[110] a fortiori it demands the demise of the political question doctrine. If the Court does not trust the political branches enough to give their decisions deference in cases over which the Court has jurisdiction, it would be anomalous for the Court to conclude that the political branches possess institutional advantages that justify giving them complete control over some constitutional questions.

---

[105] 531 U.S. 70 (2000).

[106] 531 U.S. 98 (2000).

[107] See Barkow, *More Supreme than Court*, 273–300. *Bush v. Gore*, 531 U.S. 98 (2000).

[108] *Bush v. Gore*, 531 U.S. at 111.

[109] Gerhardt, *Rediscovering Nonjusticiability*, 233

[110] Schapiro, *Judicial Deference*, 665.

Or, to state the matter conversely, the existence of the political question doctrine is a powerful weapon for those who advocate coordinate review.[111] Indeed, it is no coincidence that judges and scholars have relied on the existence of the political question doctrine to support their theories that other branches are charged with the responsibility of interpreting the Constitution. Justice Scalia has cited the political question doctrine to support the argument that not all constitutional violations must be remediable in the courts.[112] Paul Brest, arguing against a theory of judicial exclusivity in interpretation, notes that such a theory "takes no account of so-called 'political questions.'"[113] Lawrence Sager has observed that "[t]he very existence of the political question doctrine in our constitutional jurisprudence thus reflects a partial recognition" of his thesis of judicially underenforced constitutional norms.[114] Erwin Chemerinsky has similarly relied on the political question doctrine to support his claim "that for each part of the Constitution one branch of government is assigned the role of final arbiter of disputes."[115] Archibald Cox has asserted that "[t]he underlying considerations . . . are hardly different" between the deference accorded "political determinations under the commerce, due process or equal protection clauses," and the determination "whether a question is political."[116] Michael McConnell has used political question doctrine cases to support his view that Congress has the power to interpret the Fourteenth Amendment to enforce Section 5 of that amendment.[117]

The most expedient way to remove the intellectual tension between the Court's theory of judicial superiority and the political question doctrine is to eliminate one or the other. And so the Court has ushered out the doctrine—allowing its supremacy theory to flower and its confidence in its own constitutional abilities to grow. The decline of the political question doctrine—at least in its classical form—is therefore extremely troublesome, for it paves the way for this Court-centric view of the Constitution. This trend can be seen in a variety of substantive areas, from the Court's cases under Section 5 of the Fourteenth Amendment to its Commerce Clause cases to its increasing use of substantive canons of interpretation.[118]

---

[111] See Scott E. Gant, *Judicial Supremacy and Nonjudicial Interpretation of the Constitution*, 24 Hastings Const. L. Q. 359, 371 (1997); Learned Hand, *The Bill of Rights*, 15–18 (1958).

[112] *Webster v. Doe*, 486 U.S. 612–13 (Scalia, J., dissenting).

[113] Paul Brest, *Congress as Constitutional Decisionmaker and Its Power to Counter Judicial Doctrine*, 21 Ga. L. Rev. 57, 63 (1986).

[114] Sager, *Fair Measure,* 1225.

[115] Chemerinsky, *Interpreting the Constitution,* 84.

[116] Archibald Cox, *The Role of Congress in Constitutional Determinations*, 40 U. Cin. L. Rev. 199, 206 (1971).

[117] Michael W. McConnell, Comment, *Institutions and Interpretation: A Critique of City of Boerne v. Flores*, 111 Harv. L. Rev. 153, 171 and n. 123 (1997).

[118] See Barkow, *More Supreme than Court*, 303–17.

This vision of judicial supremacy is troublesome for many reasons. It is at odds with the historical understanding of the judiciary's role, as Larry Kramer has persuasively explained.[119] It is in tension with the Constitution's structure.[120] And it is normatively worrisome because the different branches bring different strengths and weaknesses to the interpretive enterprise. The purpose of this chapter is to not to recount those arguments in detail. But it is important to note that a judicial monopoly on interpretation risks losing the advantages of political branch interpretation and exacerbating the disadvantages of judicial interpretation. In particular, a more balanced approach could allow greater input by the people themselves and all the benefits that brings.[121] Deferring to the political branches in some cases also requires the Court to acknowledge the views of the political branches, which may cause the Court to question its own interpretation. A spectrum of deference, therefore, helps to promote a dialogue between the Court and the political branches.

The same institutional and structural concerns that support giving some deference to Congress's interpretative decisions also justify giving absolute deference to the political branches in certain circumstances. As Walter Dellinger and Jefferson Powell have noted, questions are left to the political branches "not only because of the judiciary's limitations, but also because of the political branches' virtues."[122] Thus, a recent trend in the academic literature is to identify issues that are better left to the political branches instead of the courts.[123]

But while there is great value in acknowledging that a question rests with the political branches, there is also a great danger that this power could be

---

[119] See Larry D. Kramer, *The Supreme Court, 2000 Term—Foreword: We the Court*, 115 Harv. L. Rev. 4 (2001).

[120] Barkow, *More Supreme than Court*, 320–23.

[121] See Kramer, *We the Court, passim*; Barkow, *More Supreme than Court*, 323–30.

[122] Dellinger and Powell, *Marshall's Questions*, 376.

[123] See, e.g., Barkow, *More Supreme than Court*, 273–300 (Article II. Section 1, Clause 2); Calabresi, *Presidential Succession*, 175 (presidential succession statutes); Chemerinsky, *Cases under the Guarantee Clause*, 859 (impeachment of judges, foreign policy decisions); Viet D. Dinh, *Executive Privilege: The Dilemma of Secrecy and Democratic Accountability*, 13 Const. Comment 346, 352–55 (1996) (executive privilege claims in response to congressional requests for information); Rex D. Khan, *Why Refugee Status Should Be Beyond Judicial Review*, 35 U.S.F. L. Rev. 57, 74–77 (2000) (refugee status); Pushaw, *Justiciability and Separation of Powers*, 505–07 (presidential veto, impeachment, appointments, declarations of war, making of treaties); John C. Yoo, *The Continuation of Politics by Other Means: The Original Understanding of War Powers*, 84 Cal. L. Rev. 167, 288–90, 300 (1996) (interbranch war powers disputes); John C. Yoo, *Treaties and Public Lawmaking: A Textual and Structural Defense of Non–Self-Execution*, 99 Colum. L. Rev. 2218, 2248 (1999) (foreign affairs); see also Mark Tushnet, *Taking the Constitution Away from the Courts* 95–123 (1999); Neal Kumar Katyal, *Legislative Constitutional Interpretation*, 50 Duke L. J. 1335, 1341, 1363 (2001); Abner J. Mikva, *Justice Brennan and the Political Process: Assessing the Legacy of Baker v. Carr*, U. Ill. L. Rev. 683, 698 (1995).

abused if there is no principled basis for determining when a decision should rest with another branch. It is for this reason that the classical political question doctrine must be distinguished from the prudential strand that has developed. The classical political question doctrine reflects the constitutional structure of deference, for it is rooted in the language, structure, and history of the Constitution itself. Just as the Court could conclude from the language and purpose of the Necessary and Proper Clause that Congress was entitled to great deference, the text and structure of the Constitution provides clues about whether Congress is entitled to absolute deference. The premise of the classical political question doctrine is that there must be some textual reason for concluding that the question lies within the interpretive powers of a political branch. As part of that textual analysis, of course, a court could look to the structural design of the Constitution and consider the consequences of judicial involvement and whether judicially manageable standards exist. Those factors would be used only to shed light on the interpretation of the Constitution itself and would not be decisive on their own. Thus, they would be anchored to the Constitution and would therefore limit a judge's ability to use her or his own policy preferences to avoid deciding a case or to lay claim to a case that properly rests with the political branches.

To be sure, tying the political question doctrine to constitutional interpretation will cure the problem of unprincipled application only insofar as the method of constitutional interpretation itself is principled. Thus, my endorsement of the classical political question doctrine must be tempered by this reality. Even without debating which method of constitutional interpretation is optimal—a debate that will undoubtedly rage indefinitely among legal scholars—one can assume that grounding a decision in the Constitution itself will constrain a judge more than allowing him or her to use any prudential factors he or she deems important, regardless of what the Constitution has to say about the matter. At the very least, the classical political question doctrine makes it more difficult for judges to decide or not to decide cases when doing so is flatly at odds with the text, history, or structure of the Constitution. Perhaps even more importantly, it requires the Court—as a threshold matter—to focus on the language of the Constitution itself and whether that language suggests that some interpretive deference (or even complete deference) is appropriate.

It is on this basis that the classical doctrine diverges from the prudential doctrine. Unfortunately, because the two strands of the political question doctrine have been blurred over the years—and because *Baker v. Carr* seemed to weld them together in its six-part test—most commentators have failed to bifurcate the doctrine. Indeed, some of the foremost legal scholars have come to believe that the prudential strain is the *only* aspect of the doctrine, forgetting its classical, constitutionally based roots.[124] And, because of the weaknesses of the

---

[124] Chemerinsky, *Cases under the Guarantee Clause,* 852–53; Michael J. Glennon, *Foreign Affairs and the Political Question Doctrine,* 83 Am. J. Int'l L. 814, 815–16 (1989); Richard A. Posner, *Path-Dependency, Pragmatism, and Critique of History in Adjudication and Legal Scholarship,* 67 U. Chi. L. Rev. 573, 601 (2000).

prudential strand of the doctrine, many have advocated the abandonment of the doctrine in its entirety.

These calls for abandonment should apply only to the prudential strand of the doctrine. As these commentators rightly point out, there is no principled basis for distinguishing the cases that are avoided on prudential grounds from those that are decided.[125] It would be difficult to determine, *ex ante*, when the prudential factors listed in *Baker* would dictate abstention and when they would permit review. After all, many legal questions involve vague standards and require an "initial policy determination." It is difficult to explain substantive due process or Eighth Amendment cases on any other basis. All cases reversing a political judgment of constitutionality express a similar "lack of the respect due coordinate branches of government." It would be hard to predict when there is an "unusual need for unquestioning adherence to a political decision already made" or when "the potentiality of embarrassment from multifarious pronouncements" demands abstention. Ironically, then, the *Baker* prudential factors themselves appear to be judicially unmanageable.

Moreover, the prudential strain aims to address problems that might be handled more directly by other doctrines, including standing[126] and the courts' general powers of equitable discretion.[127] What the prudential aspect of the doctrine adds, if anything, is an even more flexible escape hatch for a court that wishes to avoid deciding a tough case.

Because the prudential doctrine allows the Court to avoid deciding a case without an anchor in constitutional interpretation, it is this aspect of the political question doctrine that seems most troublesome. It would be unwise, however, to reject the entire political question doctrine because of the failings of the prudential doctrine. Indeed, the classical political question doctrine is critically important in the constitutional order, and its demise is cause for concern. In particular, the disappearance of the classical political question doctrine has a negative effect on two fronts.

First, it has a direct negative impact in that it prevents the political branches from exercising constitutional judgment in those cases in which a classical political question is presented. Admittedly, this is a small category of cases that are not likely to arise very often. Electoral count disputes, judicial impeachments, and constitutional amendment ratification questions do not occur with much frequency. These questions are of fundamental importance, however, and judicial interference in these circumstances could have a negative effect on our government that transcends the scope of the particular case. Nothing provides a

---

[125] See, e.g. Redish, *Judicial Review*, 1045-46; Fritz W. Scharpf, *Judicial Review and the Political Question: A Functional Analysis*, 75 Yale L. J. 517, 552–53 (1966).

[126] See Rebecca L. Brown, *When Political Questions Affect Individual Rights: The Other* Nixon v. United States, 1993 Sup. Ct. Rev. 125, 143–48; Linda Sandstrom Simard, *Standing Alone: Do We Still Need the Political Question Doctrine?* 100 Dick. L. Rev. 303, 306 (1996).

[127] Henkin, *Is There a "Political Question" Doctrine?*, 617–22.

more poignant illustration than the Article II issue in the 2000 election cases. The doctrine strikes at the heart of the separation of powers and the need for each branch to stay within its sphere to maintain the constitutional order.

Second, the end of the classical political question doctrine has a much broader secondary effect. The Supreme Court is effectively left alone to police the boundaries of its power. This is, perhaps, the most difficult of all the Court's tasks, for it requires the most extreme form of willpower. It also dramatically displays the tension that exists beneath the surface of all the Court's decisions. That is, when the Court is protecting individual rights against congressional action, deciding whether authority resides with the states or with Congress, or resolving controversies between the executive and Congress, its own interest is not at the fore in the decision. Ostensibly, the Court is protecting one entity from another. When the Court decides whether the political question doctrine applies, however, what is merely implicit in those other decisions becomes explicit: the Court's institutional interests and strengths *vis-à-vis* the other branches.

Thus, when the Court conducts the threshold inquiry of whether a matter rests exclusively with another branch, it must inevitably weigh the advantages and disadvantages of judicial review versus pure political analysis. This process therefore highlights for the Court its own strengths and weaknesses, as well as the upsides and downsides of giving the question to Congress or the executive. This is a healthy analysis for the Court to undertake, for it highlights the functional concerns behind the separation of powers and forces the Court to take a more modest view of its own powers and abilities. Therefore, eliminating this jurisdictional question from the Court's tasks helps pave the way for a much broader vision of judicial supremacy and a much more limited view of deference to the political branches. The end of the classical political question doctrine thus threatens to disrupt our constitutional order and turn the framers' vision of a constitutional conversation among three coordinate branches into a monologue by the Supreme Court.

Law and Prudence in the Law of Justiciability: The Transformation and Disappearance of the Political Question Doctrine

Mark Tushnet[1]

I. Introduction

Alexander Bickel and Fritz Scharpf treated the political question doctrine as one of the devices the Supreme Court could use in structuring the way it interacted with the overall political system.[2] Bickel in particular conceded that the Court had to justify the decisions it made on the merits of constitutional questions by invoking principle.[3] The problem with principle, as Bickel and Scharpf saw it,

---

[1] Carmack Waterhouse Professor of Constitutional Law, Georgetown University Law Center. I would like to thank Rachel Barkow, Susan Low Bloch, Steve Goldberg, Heather Gerken, Vicki Jackson, and Louis Michael Seidman for their comments on drafts of this essay.

[2] Alexander M. Bickel, *The Least Dangerous Branch: The Supreme Court at the Bar of Politics* (Indianapolis, Ind.: Bobbs Merrill, 1962), 183–97; Fritz Scharpf, *Judicial Review and the Political Question: A Functional Analysis*, 75 Yale L. J. 517 (1966).

[3] I use the term *principle* in the sense made familiar by Herbert Wechsler [Herbert Wechsler, *Toward Neutral Principles of Constitutional Law*, 73 Harv. L. Rev. 1 (1959)]. Wechsler argued that our legal system accommodated the power of judicial review with democratic theory by insisting that judges exercise that power in a principled manner, by

was that invoking a rule might be imprudent, entangling the courts with the other institutions of the political system in ways that would not benefit the nation.[4] The political question doctrine, along with other justiciability doctrines, provided the Court with techniques for refraining from deciding cases on the merits when doing so would be imprudent.

The difficulty with this analysis is that the political question doctrine is itself a rule, in the minimal sense that the Court has to provide reasons for invoking it.[5] In providing reasons for invoking the doctrine, the Court creates a doctrine that inevitably undermines the possibility of deploying the political question doctrine in the service of prudent judgment, for it is precisely the characteristic of prudential judgment that it *cannot* be captured in rules. Bickel thought that the political question doctrine "resists being domesticated."[6] By that he meant that applying the doctrine inevitably required the courts to respond to prudential concerns that could not be reduced to rules, criteria, or even standards. He was wrong.

That, in short, is the story of *Baker v. Carr.*[7] The Court treated the political question doctrine as a principle, as it had to within the framework, accepted by the justices, that constitutional decisions had to be principled.[8] It thereby made the political question doctrine effectively unavailable as a technique for coordinating the Court with the nation's other political institutions. But, as Scharpf noted, the political question doctrine did serve important functions for the Court and the na-

---

which he meant that judges had to deploy rules that were neutral in the sense that they did not systematically prefer one class of litigants to another except to the extent that the rules the judges invoked made the characteristics of the favored class relevant to the outcome. For present purposes, I use a more modest and defensible definition: *principle* means that the Court has to decide by invoking a rule-like formulation that specifies the conditions under which one result rather than another follows.

[4] As Louis Michael Seidman has pointed out to me, for Bickel prudence might sometimes require the courts to refrain from acting because acting would require that they pursue principle when a principled decision—one compelled by law—would not benefit the nation.

[5] Gerald Gunther's powerful criticism of Bickel's argument rested precisely on this insight, although Gunther phrased the point differently. Gerald Gunther, *The Subtle Vices of the "Passive Virtues": A Comment on Principle and Expediency in Judicial Review,* 64 Colum. L. Rev. 1 (1964).

[6] Bickel, *supra* n. 2, at 125.

[7] 369 U.S. 186 (1962).

[8] Bickel's most effective arguments about prudence derived from his consideration not of justiciability doctrine but of the Court's discretionary power to deny review. See, e.g., Bickel, *supra* n. 2, at 133–42. Translating those arguments to the context of doctrine proved impossible. And, even in the context of discretionary denials of review, dissents from refusals to review cases routinely describe rule- or standard-like considerations that the dissenters assert ought to govern the decision to review or not. Finally, it may be worth mentioning that the very fact that the Court granted review in the two 2000 election cases suggests that the Court sees a reduced role for prudential considerations even at the stage of granting review.

tion.[9] Not surprisingly, then, the concerns that made the political question doctrine attractive before *Baker v. Carr* remained important. Prudence simply migrated from the political question doctrine to the law of standing. But, once again, standing is a legal doctrine, and doctrinalization occurred again.

By the late 1990s, justiciability doctrine had been thoroughly domesticated. *Baker v. Carr*[10] gave us a list of criteria for deciding when to invoke the political question doctrine; standing cases had developed the litany of "injury, causation, and redressability" to structure a purely doctrinal analysis.[11] By the turn of the century, a complete transformation had occurred, as shown by the fact that only old-fashioned scholars noted what prior generations would have thought serious political question and standing problems in *Bush v. Gore*.[12] This is a transformation of constitutional consciousness that can best be understood by historicizing the justiciability doctrines, that is, by trying to identify the historical circumstances under which those doctrines seemed appropriate vehicles for prudential judgments and the circumstances that led later constitutional thinkers to conclude that they were not such vehicles.

This essay develops the foregoing argument by examining, in Section II, the transformation of the political question doctrine from *Baker v. Carr* through *Walter Nixon v. United States*.[13] Section III charts a similar, perhaps even more dramatic transformation of the law of standing. Section IV then examines *Bush v. Gore*, explaining how older doctrines of standing and political questions might have been thought relevant there. It argues as well that the very fact that those doctrines went unmentioned by the Court shows why we must take a historically grounded view of justiciability doctrines. Section V sketches the historical settings in which the political question doctrine as a counsel of prudence arose and disappeared. The conclusion suggests that, in the current historical period, it may be impossible to retrieve the possibility of a practice of judicial review constrained by prudence.

---

[9] Scharpf, *supra* n. 2, at 566–82 identifies functional reasons such as differential access to information and, important in the present context, the responsibilities of the political branches as among the bases for the political question doctrine.

[10] 369 U.S. 186 (1962).

[11] See, e.g., *Allen v. Wright*, 468 U.S. 737 (1984) (denying standing to litigants who did not allege facts showing that they had suffered an injury that a judicial order would redress); *Schlesinger v. Reservists Committee to Stop the War*, 418 U.S. 208 (1974) (denying standing to litigants who asserted only a generalized grievance).

[12] 531 U.S. 98 (2000).

[13] 506 U.S. 224 (1993).

II. *Baker v. Carr* and the Doctrinalization of the
Political Question Doctrine

I begin, boringly, by quoting the familiar catalog of criteria *Baker v. Carr* discerned in the Court's political question cases:

> a textually demonstrable constitutional commitment of the issue to a coordinate political department; or a lack of judicially discoverable and manageable standards for resolving it; or the impossibility of deciding without an initial policy determination of a kind clearly for nonjudicial discretion; or the impossibility of a court's undertaking independent resolution without expressing lack of the respect due coordinate branches of government; or an unusual need for unquestioning adherence to a political decision already made; or the potentiality of embarrassment from multifarious pronouncements by various departments on one question.[14]

Louis Henkin provided the definitive guide to understanding this catalog in his challenge to the very existence of a political question doctrine.[15] According to Henkin, most of the political question cases involved decisions by the Court (1) that the Constitution gave the political branches discretion to decide what to do and the political branches had not abused their discretion, or (2) that the Constitution placed no limits on the discretion of the political branches to decide what to do. Henkin's important point was that the Court's decisions are *on the merits*. That is, the Court in these cases interprets the Constitution to say one thing rather than another. Here Henkin drew on a thought in *Baker v. Carr* itself, arguing that no political question arises when all the Court must do is engage in ordinary constitutional interpretation.[16]

Henkin also identified an important residual category, which in my judgment provides the best explanation for whatever true political question doctrine there is: "there might be constitutional provisions which can properly be interpreted as wholly or in part 'self-monitoring' and not the subject of judicial review."[17] Understanding this suggestion requires that we resolve an ambiguity in *Baker v. Carr*'s reference to a "constitutional commitment *of the issue* to a coordinate political branch." One possibility is that the "issue" is the question presented on the merits, where we want to know what the right answer to a substantive constitutional question is. The issue on the merits in *Baker v. Carr* was whether the Constitution requires some degree of equality in apportionments. *Marbury v. Madison*, saying that "it is emphatically the province and duty of the

---

[14] 369 U.S. at 217.

[15] Louis Henkin, *Is There a Political Question Doctrine?* 85 Yale L. J. 597 (1976).

[16] For completeness, I would add that there is a cluster of cases involving foreign affairs where the pull of some sort of political question doctrine seems strong.

[17] *Id.* at 622–23.

courts to say what the law is,"[18] strongly suggests that ordinary constitutional interpretation, done by the courts, tells us the answers to substantive constitutional questions.

For the political question doctrine to raise interesting questions about the *Marbury* tradition, the "issue" to which the Court refers must be different. For the political question doctrine, the "issue," in the Court's sense, is who gets to decide what the right answer to a substantive constitutional question is. Again, in *Baker v. Carr*, the issue in this sense is who gets to decide whether the Constitution requires some degree of equality in apportionments. That is, the Court asks, Does the Constitution give a political branch the final power to interpret the Constitution?[19]

Self-monitoring provisions are those to which the answer is, yes, this provision gives Congress or the president the final power to specify the meaning of the Constitution that the litigants have raised. I have argued elsewhere that self-monitoring constitutional provisions are those as to which we have some confidence that the political branches will do at least as good a job as the courts in interpreting the Constitution.[20]

We are now in a position to understand why the political question doctrine came under pressure once *Baker v. Carr* gave it the form of law. *Baker v. Carr* made it natural to reject political question arguments by noting that all that was at stake was an ordinary question of constitutional interpretation of the sort courts routinely answer. Notions of judicial supremacy make doubtful any assertion that a constitutional provision should be self-monitoring in Henkin's sense, while skepticism about the ability of the political branches to behave in a constitutionally responsible manner undermines the claim that any constitutional provision should be self-monitoring in the sense I have urged.

With this as background, I now review the Court's major political question cases from *Baker* to *Walter Nixon*. *Baker* itself, of course, asserted that the equal protection challenge it allowed to go forward presented an ordinary question of constitutional interpretation: "Judicial standards under the Equal Protection Clause are well developed and familiar."[21] The post-*Baker* reapportionment decisions illuminate what ordinary questions of constitutional interpretation are, even though the reapportionment decisions are not themselves political question

---

[18] *Marbury v. Madison*, 5 U.S. (1 Cranch) 137, 177 (1803).

[19] In *Baker*, the question is, Does the Constitution give a political branch the final power to determine whether the Constitution requires some degree of equality in apportionments? In *United States v. Munoz-Flores,* 495 U.S. 385 (1990), the question was, Does the Constitution give Congress the ultimate authority to determine that a particular bill is indeed one "for raising revenue" that must originate in the House of Representatives?

[20] Mark Tushnet, *Taking the Constitution Away from the Courts* 107–08 (Princeton, N.J.: Princeton University Press, 1999).

[21] 369 U.S. at 226.

decisions.[22] The post-*Baker* judicial standards demonstrate judicial creativity in constitutional interpretation: If ordinary constitutional interpretation produces a quite rigid "one person, one vote" rule, what if anything lies outside the domain of ordinary constitutional interpretation?

The Court's answer is, "not much," when it rejects political question arguments. *Powell v. McCormack* is the paradigm.[23] The House of Representatives refused to seat Adam Clayton Powell because he had been the subject of public scandals. Powell sought judicial relief. The House officers he sued said that the Constitution gave the House the exclusive power "to Judge . . . the . . . Qualifications of its own Members."[24] Powell said that this was a textual commitment only of the power to determine whether members satisfied the "qualifications" listed elsewhere in the Constitution. The Court agreed, holding that the House lacked power to refuse to seat a member who it conceded satisfied the enumerated qualifications.[25] The analytic point is that the Court applies ordinary processes of interpretation to the clauses said to commit the question to the political branches in deciding whether a question *is* a political question. *Powell* and the reapportionment cases following *Baker v. Carr* show how easy it is to interpret the clauses at issue *not* to commit the question to the political branches.[26]

United States v. Munoz-Flores has the same structure.[27] The Victims of Crime Act contained a provision added in the Senate requiring people convicted of federal crimes to pay a special assessment to a Crime Victims Fund. Munoz-Flores said that the assessment violated the Constitution's requirement that "all Bills for raising Revenue shall originate in the House of Representatives."[28] The Court replied that Munoz-Flores could prevail only if the special assessment provision was a "Bill for raising Revenues." Determining what the Constitution

---

[22] See, e.g., *Avery v. Midland County*, 390 U.S. 474 (1968) (applying the one-person, one-vote rule to a county commission); *Kirkpatrick v. Preisler*, 394 U.S. 526 (1969) (developing standards for determining when a deviation from one-person, one-vote is excessive); *Mahan v. Howell*, 410 U.S. 315 (1973) (same).

[23] 395 U.S. 486 (1969). See also *Japan Whaling Ass'n v. American Cetacean Society*, 478 U.S. 221, 230 (1986) (asserting that "under the Constitution, one of the judiciary's characteristic roles is to interpret statutes, and we cannot shirk this responsibility merely because our decision may have significant political overtones.").

[24] U.S. Const., art. I, sec. 5.

[25] The Court's confidence in its role is suggested by the fact that it reserved the question of whether it could review a decision by the House that a member did not satisfy one of the enumerated requirements. 395 U.S. at 521 n. 42 ("federal courts might still be barred by the political question doctrine from reviewing the House's factual determination that a member did not meet one of the standing qualifications. This is an issue not presented in this case and we express no view as to its resolution.").

[26] See also *United States Department of Commerce v. Montana*, 503 U.S. 442 (1992) (rejecting a political question argument and finding justiciable a claim challenging Congress's choice of methods of apportioning seats among the states).

[27] 495 U.S. 385 (1990).

[28] U.S. Const., art. I, sec. 7, cl. 1.

meant when it referred to such bills was an ordinary question of constitutional interpretation. The Court then held that Origination Clause did not refer to provisions aimed at funding particular programs but only at bills that support general government programs.

The Court's only recent decision purporting to invoke the political question doctrine shows how hard it is to resist the pull of the argument that the Court can come up with a constitutional interpretation that answers what is said to be a political question, that is, one as to which the answer must come from the political branches. *Walter Nixon v. United States* involved Judge Nixon's challenge to the processes used in the Senate's impeachment trial that resulted in his conviction.[29] Having found that conducting trials of impeachments before the entire Senate was, in the Senate's view, unduly burdensome, the Senate adopted a rule that allowed testimony to be presented before a committee, which would send to the entire Senate the transcript and a report summarizing the testimony. Under this procedure, not every senator actually heard live witness testimony; the Senate's vote on whether to convict was based on the transcript and report. The relevant constitutional language is that the Senate has "the sole Power to try all Impeachments."[30] The term *sole* in this provision might seem to stand in Judge Nixon's way, but he relied on the proposition that the courts have the power to engage in ordinary constitutional interpretation. What the Constitution meant, Judge Nixon said, was that only the Senate—and no one else—could try him for the offenses with which he was charged. But, he argued, the Senate had to give him a *trial*, not some truncated proceeding: True, the Senate has the sole power to try him, but it has to *try* him.

The Court seemed to hold that Judge Nixon's claim presented a political question, concluding that "the word 'try' in the Impeachment Clause does not provide an identifiable textual limit on the authority which is committed to the Senate."[31] Justice White's concurring opinion pointed out difficulties with that conclusion. His example was this: No one would contend that the Senate had given a judge a trial in any sense whatever if it followed a "practice of automatically entering a judgment of conviction whenever articles of impeachment were delivered from the House."[32] As Justice White put it, in terms that recall the aftermath of *Baker v. Carr*, "'try' presents no greater, and perhaps fewer, interpretive difficulties than some other constitutional standards that have been found amenable to *familiar techniques of judicial construction.* . . ."[33] He conceded that his example involved an improbable hypothetical case, but emphasized that, as long as the courts were able to say that *something* was *not* a trial, the word "try" had a meaning the courts could discern.

---

[29] 506 U.S. 224 (1993).

[30] U.S. Const., art. I, sec. 3.

[31] 506 U.S. at 238.

[32] *Id.* at 246-47 (White, J., concurring in the judgment).

[33] *Id.* at 247 (White, J. concurring in the judgment) (emphasis added).

And, as it happens, elements of the Court's opinion seem to agree with Justice White. It noted that "[t]he word 'try,' both in 1787 and later, has considerably broader meanings than those to which [Judge Nixon] would limit it."[34] That comes close to rejecting on the merits Judge Nixon's claim that he had not received a trial within the meaning of the Impeachment Clause. As Henkin noted, some cases described as posing political questions actually involve only the question of whether the political branches abused a discretion given them by the Constitution. Justice White would have interpreted the Constitution to give the Senate substantial discretion to specify trial procedures, that is, to pin down in detail what the word *try* meant. But, Justice White said, and the Court's discussion of the broad meanings of the word seems to agree, that even though the Senate was given wide latitude in specifying trial procedures, the courts are not precluded from deciding that the Senate had abused the discretion the Constitution gave it to define terms.[35]

The Court engages in the interpretive enterprise all the time. Though nominally holding that the case presented a political question, *Walter Nixon* shows how difficult it is for the justices to assert unqualifiedly that a particular constitutional provision really has no meaning it can identify. And, in a world where the Court is comfortable with interpreting the Constitution and uncomfortable with allowing anyone else to do so, once it is conceded that a provision means something, the "textually demonstrable commitment" element simply falls away.

Goldwater v. Carter, the only other recent case in which the political question doctrine figured prominently, illustrates the problem as well.[36] The United States and the Republic of China, located in Taiwan, had a mutual defense treaty, which the Senate had ratified. The People's Republic of China insisted that the United States abrogate the treaty if the United States and the People's Republic were to have diplomatic relations. Acting without the participation of the Senate, President Jimmy Carter announced that the mutual defense treaty was abrogated and no longer bound the United States. Senator Barry Goldwater challenged the abrogation, arguing that the Constitution, in giving the Senate a role in creating treaties, also gave it a role in abrogating them. The Constitution expressly said that Senate agreement was necessary to *enter into* a treaty relation, and, Senator Goldwater asserted, the Constitution should be interpreted to require Senate agreement to *get out of* a treaty relation.

---

[34] *Id.* at 229.

[35] See also *id.* at 254–55 (Souter, J., concurring in the judgment) (asserting that the courts would have a role if "the Senate's action [was] . . . so far beyond the scope of its constitutional authority . . . as to merit a judicial response. ").

[36] 444 U.S. 996 (1979). The case also indicates the pull of the foreign affairs context on the political question doctrine. But see *Japan Whaling Ass'n v. American Cetacean Society*, 478 U.S. 221 (1986) (rejecting the argument that the foreign affairs context of a statutory interpretation case should limit the Court's role).

The Supreme Court ultimately rejected Senator Goldwater's claim, with the justices expressing a variety of views on why he should not prevail. For present purposes the position of then–Justice Rehnquist and the responses of Justice Brennan and Powell are the most important. Justice Rehnquist and three others found that Senator Goldwater's claim raised a political question.[37] In part that was because of the foreign affairs setting. But, in addition, Justice Rehnquist said that the Constitution committed the question of who must participate in a treaty abrogation to the political branches.[38] His argument was that the Constitution expressly said that the Senate had to participate in creating a treaty relation, and that, in saying nothing about whether it had to participate in abrogating such a relation, the Constitution implicitly left that question to the political branches to resolve: "[W]hile the Constitution is express as to the manner in which the Senate shall participate in the ratification of a treaty, it is silent as to that body's participation in the abrogation of a treaty."[39] Silence meant that the question was left to the political branches.

Justice Powell did not reach the merits, believing that Senator Goldwater's claim was not ripe, but disagreed with Justice Rehnquist's analysis. Justice Powell posed the following problem: "Assume that the President signed a mutual defense treaty with a foreign country and announced that it would go into effect despite its rejection by the Senate. Under Mr. Justice Rehnquist's analysis that situation would present a political question even though Art. II, sec. 2, clearly would resolve the dispute."[40] But, Justice Powell said, the "legal issue" presented by a unilateral presidential commitment to a treaty relation was no different from the legal issue presented by a unilateral presidential decision to end such a relation: "In both cases, the Court would interpret the Constitution to decide whether congressional approval is necessary to give a Presidential decision on the validity of a treaty the force of law."[41] The only difference, to Justice Powell, was that his hypothesized case presented "textual" analysis while Senator Goldwater's real one required "interstitial analysis," that is, interpretation based on inferences from what the Constitution said and what it did not say. That, to Justice Powell, was an exercise in ordinary constitutional interpretation.

In reviewing this history, we see that the overall effect of *Baker v. Carr* was what I have referred to as the doctrinalization of the political question doctrine. The Court converted into a set of legal rules an approach that had some flexibility and that therefore might be invoked whenever a majority thought that the prudent course was to avoid involvement in a constitutional dispute. *Baker v. Carr* specified six elements of the doctrine and came to be understood as insisting that at least one be present when the Court finds a case to raise a political

---

[37] 444 U.S. at 1002–06 (Rehnquist, J., concurring).

[38] *Id.* at 1002 (Rehnquist J., concurring).

[39] *Id.* at 1003 (Rehnquist, J., concurring).

[40] *Id.* at 999–1000 (Powell, J., concurring).

[41] *Id.*

question.[42] Even more, the Court has not invoked the more obviously flexible criteria articulated in *Baker v. Carr*—the last four of the six on its list—in any recent case, to the point where it seems fair to say that the only real components of the doctrine are the first two: a textually demonstrable commitment to the political branches and the lack of judicially manageable standards.[43]

As Bickel understood, however, prudent judgment cannot be captured in rules. If, as Scharpf emphasized, techniques of avoiding decision for prudential reasons were functional for the Court, *Baker v. Carr*'s elimination of one such technique might impel the Court to find another. For a while, the Court settled on the doctrine of standing, but it too lost its functional value as an avoidance device as it became doctrinalized. By the time that happened, the functional need for avoidance doctrines disappeared.

III. Standing as a Prudential Approach and Its Doctrinalization

Although sounding some prudential themes, *Flast v. Cohen* initiated the doctrinalization of standing law.[44] The standing doctrine's potential to replace the political question doctrine was apparent in the Court's assertion that the Constitution's "case or controversy" language "define[s] the role assigned to the judiciary in a tripartite allocation of power to assure that the federal courts will not intrude into areas committed to the other branches of government."[45] Justice Powell's observation in a case about standing that justiciability doctrines were "founded in concern about the proper—and properly limited—role of the courts in a democratic society" is to the same effect.[46]

A series of cases involving what the Court called generalized grievances blurred the lines between standing law and the political question doctrine. *United States v. Richardson* denied standing to taxpayers who challenged Congress's failure to disclose the budgets of several national security agencies as a violation of the Constitution's requirement that "a regular Statement and Account of the Receipts and Expenditures of all public Money shall be published

---

[42] See Erwin Chemerinsky, *Constitutional Law: Principles and Policies* 119 (New York: Aspen Law & Business, 1997) ("Virtually every case considering the political question doctrine quotes" the list of six factors.).

[43] The Court has not explicitly reduced the doctrine to these two components, and presumably the other four remain available in the event that the Court chooses to revive a more discretionary doctrine than the one it has recently invoked. Still, it seems worth noting that it would not have been difficult to say that deciding the merits of the question presented in *Powell v. McCormack* would express a lack of respect for the House of Representatives, and yet the Court did not do so.

[44] 392 U.S. 83 (1968).

[45] 392 U.S. at 95.

[46] *Warth v. Seldin*, 422 U.S. 490, 498 (1975).

from time to time."[47] After saying that the plaintiffs lacked standing because they presented only a generalized grievance shared by every taxpayer, the Court concluded:

> It can be argued that if respondent is not permitted to litigate this issue, no one can do so. In a very real sense, the absence of any particular individual or class to litigate these claims gives support to the argument that the subject matter is Committed to the surveillance of Congress, and ultimately to the political process.[48]

This comes very close to asserting that the question presented was a political one.

As a *law* of standing developed, the possibility of deploying it in the service of prudent judgment disappeared, to be replaced by a doctrinalized concern about congressional interference with the executive's discretion to choose how to enforce the law. Standing doctrine, that is, was transformed from something allowing the courts to express a generalized concern about their role into a doctrine about the division of power between Congress and the presidency.

Flast v. Cohen might have been developed in a way that would have eliminated the standing doctrine entirely. It quoted *Baker v. Carr* for its central proposition that standing required only that the litigant have "such a personal stake in the outcome of the controversy as to assure that concrete adverseness which sharpens the presentation of issues upon which the court so largely depends for illumination of difficult constitutional questions."[49] As scholars noted, no one seriously pursues expensive litigation without doing the best to present the strongest arguments to illuminate the questions presented.[50] Were "concrete adverseness" the governing standard, only quirky cases presented by *pro se* litigants would be dismissed on standing grounds.

Perhaps because the Warren Court did not get a chance to push its standing doctrine through to maturity, the Court tried to define tests for identifying when concrete adverseness existed. A shorthand summary of the modern test is that standing law requires that a litigant have suffered a harm of a type the courts are willing to acknowledge to be a harm, caused by unconstitutional actions taken by the government defendants and likely to be eliminated or at least alleviated by some remedy the courts are in a position to award.[51]

---

[47] 418 U.S. 166 (1974).

[48] *Id.* at 179.

[49] 392 U.S. at 99, quoting *Baker v. Carr,* 369 U.S. 186, 204 (1962).

[50] See, e.g., Robert Scott, *Standing in the Supreme Court: A Functional Analysis,* 86 Harv. L. Rev. 645 (1973).

[51] In what follows, I focus on the problem of determining what are cognizable harms; the contours of developments regarding causation and redressability are essentially the same as the ones I describe with respect to harm.

The law of cognizable harm developed along two tracks. In terms of timing, the Court, influenced by the economic regulatory programs associated with the New Deal, initially thought that identifying cognizable harms was an essentially judicial task, albeit sometimes with guidance from Congress.[52] The Court rethought its position as the Great Society Congresses enacted environmental and consumer-oriented programs. The Court concluded that Congress had a large role in specifying constitutionally cognizable harm.[53] Ultimately, the only constraint the Court recognized on Congress's power to specify harms that give rise to standing was based on Article II, not Article III.[54] Once *that* occurred, the cases involving judicial identification of cognizable harm could be seen in a new light. They became cases in which standing would exist had Congress conferred it. But, in the absence of congressional action, the courts would say, in effect, "The injury you say you have suffered simply does not count *with us*, even though it might be an injury in some sense." And, in saying that, the courts necessarily decided that *the Constitution* provided no remedy for that kind of injury. The decisions were on the merits of the constitutional claims presented.

To the extent that the courts had a doctrine of standing before the New Deal, that doctrine required plaintiffs to allege that they were injured in a way closely analogous to the injuries remedied in traditional common law actions.[55] The government had to do something that the courts saw as resembling a trespass onto the plaintiff's land, for example. The rise of the administrative state placed this notion of harm under such pressure that it simply disappeared. *FCC v. Sanders Bros. Radio Station* is usually cited as the case where the Court abandoned the requirement of common-law-like injury.[56] The radio station sought judicial review of an FCC decision awarding a broadcast license to a competitor. The radio station had no right to be free from competition, but the Court held it could assert the general public interest in radio station licensing. *Sanders Bros.* highlighted the legal realist point that *harm* was not a category that existed in the natural world. It was, rather, a category *created by* law. Congress might identify special harms that the courts would not, but the conceptual underpinnings of *Sanders Bros.* showed that decisions, whether by Congress or by the courts, treating some things as harms and others as not-harms were exercises of lawmaking power.

---

[52] See, e.g., *FCC v. Sanders Bros. Radio Station,* 309 U.S. 470 (1940) (allowing a competitor to challenge a grant of a radio license on the ground that the license did not serve the public interest).

[53] See, e.g., *Sierra Club v. Morton,* 405 U.S. 727 (1972) (denying standing in the particular case, but acknowledging that esthetic, conservation, or recreational harm could support standing).

[54] See text accompanying notes 62–63 *infra*.

[55] See Geoffrey R. Stone et al., *Constitutional Law* 101 (4th ed., Gaithersburg: Aspen Law & Business, 2001) ("In the early days of standing doctrine—the first decades of the twentieth century—a common law interest was often treated as a necessary basis for standing.").

[56] 309 U.S. 470 (1940).

The critical development came when the Court recognized that Congress could actually *create* interests, the infringement of which would cause constitutionally cognizable harm.[57] Classical environmental law protected people against nuisances, which were readily assimilated to common law trespass; modern environmental law protected people against injuries to their aesthetic interests, which had no obvious common law analogues. The Freedom of Information Act gave everyone an interest in access to government information, an interest for which there was no obvious common law analogue. Racial discrimination was similar to classical harms; refusing to show available apartments to racial "testers" who had no interest in renting was not.[58] The Court conceptualized the testers' interest as one in acquiring information. It knew, of course, that such an interest arose not from anything analogous to practices causing common law harms but simply from the fact that Congress wanted information about apartments distributed without regard to race.

The Court's decisions *restricting* standing in the modern era are to some extent misleading. With respect to harm, all they were really about was whether the particular plaintiff had in fact suffered harm to an interest created by Congress. The most dramatic example of this phenomenon is *Lujan v. Defenders of Wildlife*.[59] The case involved a challenge to a rule interpreting the Endangered Species Act to be applicable only to projects within the United States or on the high seas. The plaintiffs were environmentalists whose affidavits alleged that they had traveled abroad, and intended to continue to travel abroad in the future, to view endangered species whose habitats were threatened by projects receiving support from the U.S. government. A majority of the Court found that they had not alleged that they would be harmed by the failure to apply the Act to those projects.[60] But, it turned out, the problem was that the plaintiffs said only that they *hoped* to travel abroad in the future. A majority of the justices indicated that the plaintiffs would have had standing if they had had concrete plans to engage in that travel. As many have observed, a law of standing that can be satisfied by buying a ticket to fly to Egypt is not doing much serious work.

The plaintiffs in *Lujan* also sought standing under a citizen-suit provision allowing "any person" to bring suit. They argued that the provision gave standing because it created an interest in seeing that the law was obeyed.[61] More important for present purposes, they argued that the cases acknowledging congres-

---

[57] See *Linda R.S. v. Richard D.*, 410 U.S. 614, 617 n. 3 (1973) ("Congress may enact statutes creating legal rights, the invasion of which creates standing, even though no injury would exist without the statute.").

[58] *Havens Realty Corp. v. Coleman*, 455 U.S. 363 (1982) (finding standing for an African-American "tester" who had no interest in renting but who had received discriminatory misrepresentations, where Congress had acted to assure that representations about apartment availability would be made in a nondiscriminatory way).

[59] 504 U.S. 555 (1992).

[60] *Id.* at 562–64.

[61] *Id.* at 576–77.

sional power to create interests that, if infringed, gave rise to standing, allowed Congress to create precisely the interest in seeing the law obeyed. The Court invoked the principle barring the courts from hearing cases that present only generalized grievances to dismiss this claim. It acknowledged that the prior cases had not involved claims based on statutory provisions giving anyone a right to sue, but denied that that distinction mattered. It continued, "Vindicating the public interest . . . is the function of Congress and the Chief Executive. . . . To permit Congress to convert the undifferentiated public interest in executive officers' compliance with the law into an 'individual right' vindicable in the courts is to permit Congress to transfer from the President to the courts the Chief Executive's most important constitutional duty, to 'take Care that the Laws be faithfully executed.'"[62] With this, standing shifted from Article III to Article II, at least when a litigant relied on a congressional statute purporting to confer standing.[63]

Federal Elections Commission v. Akins seems to transform the generalized grievance rule.[64] The Federal Election Campaign Act had a provision broadly allowing "any person" who thought the commission erred in dismissing a complaint to seek judicial review. The plaintiffs thought the commission had committed legal error in failing to require a political action committee to disclose information that the statute required to be disclosed. The Court agreed that the plaintiffs had standing. It said that the commission's "strongest argument is its contention that this lawsuit involves only a 'generalized grievance.'"[65] The Court said that its prior cases invoking the generalized grievance rule involved what the Court called "abstract and indefinite" harms that were *also* widely shared.[66] "The abstract nature of the harm . . . deprives the case of the concrete specificity" that Article III required.[67] It contrasted such harms with widely shared harms that are "concrete." Informational injury, that is, the deprivation of access to information that Congress wanted available, was a widely—indeed, I would think, universally—shared concrete harm, whereas the "interest in seeing

---

[62] *Id.* at 576.

[63] But see *Raines v. Byrd,* 521 U.S. 811 (1997). There the Court denied standing to a member of Congress challenging the Line Item Veto Act because Congress members did not have a sufficient personal stake in the dispute and did not allege a sufficiently concrete injury. The statute authorized suit by "[a]ny Member of Congress or any individual adversely affected" by the Act, 2 U.S. C. sec. 692 (a)(1). The Court appears to have read this provision as requiring that the members of Congress authorized to sue must be adversely affected as the Court had traditionally interpreted that phrase. This is not the most natural reading of the provision, because it makes the reference to members of Congress redundant (a member of Congress adversely affected is necessarily an individual adversely affected).

[64] 524 U.S. 11 (1998).

[65] *Id.* at 22.

[66] *Id.* at 23.

[67] *Id.* at 24.

that the law is obeyed" was a widely, indeed perhaps universally, shared abstract harm.

The distinction between widely shared abstract harms and widely shared concrete ones remains undeveloped and unclear. Still, take the rule that there is standing when a plaintiff alleges a widely shared concrete harm to an interest Congress wanted to protect, join it with the rule that plaintiffs can show individualized harm to such interests by careful pleading, and we have a law of standing that comes close to requiring the minimal concrete adverseness that *Flast v. Cohen* identified as the constitutional requirement.

Some qualifications are necessary. First, the concrete adverseness requirement probably still does screen out the frivolous *pro se* litigant. Second, standing law now has an Article II basis[68]—but only when the litigant challenges actions by federal executive officials, a much smaller class of cases than the one to which earlier standing doctrine applied. Third, as the Court in *Akins* said, the fact that an injury is widely shared might "counsel[] against . . . interpreting a statute as conferring standing."[69] So, to the extent that standing law is not Article II law, it is now a law about rules of statutory interpretation.

After the Court acknowledged broad congressional power to identify constitutionally cognizable harms, limited only by Article II, judicial decisions about which harms gave rise to standing and which did not became transparently decisions on the merits, rather than decisions about some question prior to the merits. *Northeastern Florida Contracts v. Jacksonville,*[70] read against the background of *Allen v. Wright,*[71] demonstrates the inseparability of the merits from the supposedly antecedent question of harm. The Internal Revenue Code allows private schools to obtain tax-exempt status but only if they do not discriminate on the basis of race.[72] *Allen v. Wright* rejected a challenge to the methods the Internal Revenue Service (constrained by congressional dictates) used to determine whether private schools receiving such exemptions were in fact operating without racial discrimination. The parents of African-American school children, who alleged that the assertedly feeble IRS enforcement program violated their constitutional rights, brought the challenge. The Court held that the plaintiffs did not have standing.

Allen v. Wright contained several themes. One touched on Article II concerns: The Court noted the principle "'that the Government has traditionally been granted the widest latitude in the 'dispatch of its own affairs.'"[73] It cited Article II in support of its observation that the principle, "[w]hen transported

---

[68] See *Lujan,* 504 U.S. at 577.

[69] *Akins,* 524 U.S. at 24.

[70] 508 U.S. 656 (1993).

[71] 468 U.S. 737 (1984).

[72] See *Bob Jones University v. United States,* 461 U.S. 574 (1983) (holding that a racially discriminatory private school was not entitled to tax-exempt status as a charitable institution).

[73] *Allen,* 468 U.S. at 761, quoting *Rizzo v. Goode,* 423 U.S. 362, 378–79 (1976).

into the Art. III context, . . . counsels against recognizing standing in a case
brought . . . to seek a restructuring of the apparatus established by the Executive
Branch to fulfill its legal obligations."[74] My present concern is with the way in
which the Court dealt with one of the harms the plaintiffs alleged they suffered,
characterized by the Court as a claim of stigmatic injury. That is, the plaintiffs
said that the IRS's feeble enforcement effort communicated a message to them
and others that the interests of African Americans in reducing discrimination
were not worth serious consideration. The Court said that this did not "constitute
judicially cognizable injury."[75] The Court in *Allen v. Wright* tried to explain why
it should not recognize stigmatic injury as a constitutionally cognizable harm:
"A black person in Hawaii could challenge the grant of a tax exemption to a
racially discriminatory school in Maine."[76] Stigmatic injury was deemed a generalized grievance, and the law of standing precluded courts from hearing cases
resting on generalized grievances.

In *Northeastern Florida Contractors*, the plaintiffs were a group of contractors who challenged a local affirmative action program that set aside a portion of
city contracts for minority contractors.[77] The court of appeals denied standing
because none of the plaintiffs alleged that it would have been awarded a contract
had there been no set aside program. The Supreme Court reversed, saying that
the contractors' injury was the denial of opportunity to compete on an equal
footing, not denial of the contracts themselves.[78]

Denial of an opportunity, even if having the opportunity would not eventu-
ate in any material benefit to the plaintiff, is a judicially cognizable injury, while
suffering from communications by the government that devalue one's race-
based concerns is not. Put that way, it would seem that the courts recognize injuries pretty much by fiat: This one counts, that one does not. Or, more precisely,
as a matter of substantive constitutional interpretation, the Constitution does not
protect African Americans against stigmatic injury, while it does protect against
denials of opportunity to compete on an equal basis. One can defend both of
those conclusions in substantive constitutional terms, but the defense would operate on the level of substance, not on the level of standing to sue. Further, if the
problem in *Allen* was that the case presented only a generalized grievance, it is
hardly obvious that one can consistently assert both that stigmatic injury suffered, on the *Allen* litigants' theory, only by African Americans, is a generalized

---

[74] *Id.*

[75] *Id.* at 753.

[76] 468 U.S. at 756.

[77] 508 U.S. at 659 (describing the plaintiffs).

[78] 508 U.S. at 666 ("When the government erects a barrier that makes it more difficult for members of one group to obtain a benefit than it is for members of another group,
a member of the former group seeking to challenge the barrier need not allege that he
would have obtained the benefit but for the barrier in order to establish standing. The
'injury in fact' in an equal protection case of this variety is the denial of equal treatment
resulting from the imposition of the barrier, not the ultimate inability to obtain the benefit.").

grievance and that denial of the opportunity to compete on an equal basis suffered in *Northeastern Florida Contractors* by all nonminority contractors is not.[79]

Even if one can distinguish between *Allen* and *Northeastern Florida Contractors* in some way that does not ultimately define *injury* with reference to the merits of the constitutional claim, other difficulties remain. The Court's recognition of congressional power to create standing in large classes of citizens—in effect, to *make* generalized grievances justiciable—is in tension with the notion that the Constitution relegates the resolution of generalized grievances to Congress. Because Congress has the power to confer standing, the only real question in any standing case should be whether Congress has done so—that is, how the courts should interpret the statutes under which they act.

The rule that results from the Court's cases is then that the Constitution requires something other than an assertion of a generalized grievance so that Congress can resolve the problem, unless Congress wants the courts to resolve it, in which case the Constitution requires the courts to do Congress's bidding, unless doing so would interfere with the president's duty to execute the laws. The law of standing, once fully doctrinalized, becomes a combination of a narrow Article II–based rule and some presumptions about how to interpret statutes. As with the political question doctrine, the law of standing can no longer be the vehicle for the expression of prudential judgments about when the courts might properly participate in resolving questions about the overall operation of our system of government.

IV. The Silences of *Bush v. Gore*

Judicial conservatives of a prior generation would at least have worried about the justiciability of the challenges raised in *Bush v. Gore*. They would have noticed standing and political question problems in the case. What accounts for the striking silences about those problems in the Court's opinion finding an equal protection violation and in the opinion for the three justices finding a violation of Article II?

The facts of *Bush v. Gore* need no restating.[80] A majority of the Supreme Court held that the system devised by the Florida Supreme Court violated principles of equal protection.[81] The standing problem is this.[82] We can identify two

---

[79] Perhaps the distinction introduced in *Akins* between abstract and concrete generalized grievances might be developed in a way that shows why a stigmatic injury is abstract while the denial of the opportunity to compete on an equal basis is concrete. What that account might be, however, is unclear to me; stigmatic injury seems to me fairly described as concrete.

[80] 531 U.S. 98 (2000).

[81] *Id.* at 106 ("The want of those rules here has led to unequal evaluation of ballots in various respects.").

equal protection problems that might arise from the recounting system. First, the system might have been skewed, intentionally or otherwise, to favor Vice President Al Gore by making it more likely that new votes for him would turn up than would new votes for Governor George Bush. On this theory the equal protection problem is a straightforward one of partisan vote dilution. Either George Bush or a Florida voter who voted for George Bush would clearly have standing.

Unfortunately, that is not the theory the Court adopted. Instead, the Court said that the constitutional violation occurred because the recount system did not guarantee that ballots cast by voters in different precincts that either were identical in physical appearance or otherwise equally reflected a clear voter intent would be given identical treatment (whether counted or cast aside). Why should George Bush have standing to raise this claim? One thing should be obvious: Bush cannot assert standing on the ground that the constitutional flaw in the recount system adversely affected him. The flaw identified by the Supreme Court majority has no systematic relationship to votes for either candidate: On the Court's analysis, a recount conducted under the Florida court's system might have produced more votes for George Bush, not Al Gore.[83]

A more plausible argument about standing is also more complex. On the Supreme Court's analysis we know that there is a group of voters whose votes might not be counted when physically identical ballots were counted. It would be a miracle if no Bush voters were among that group. But no individual Bush voter can confidently assert that his/her ballot would not be counted. Governor Bush might then have third-party standing to assert the interests of the Bush voters among the group disadvantaged by the recount system. Equally, of course, Vice President Gore would have standing to assert the interests of the Gore voters in that group. This leads one to wonder whether, with respect to the constitutional violation the Court actually found, the case should have been seen as nonadversarial.[84]

An even more plausible argument for standing exists. Richard Pildes has identified a distinct form of injury associated with certain voting systems, which

---

[82] For a more complete analysis, see Pamela Karlan, *The Newest Equal Protection: Regressive Doctrine on a Changeable Court*, in *The Vote: Bush, Gore, and the Supreme Court* (Cass R. Sunstein and Richard A. Epstein eds., University of Chicago Press, 2001), 77; Pamela Karlan, *Nothing Personal: The Evolution of the Newest Equal Protection from* Shaw v. Reno *to* Bush v. Gore, 79 N.C. L. Rev. 1345 (2001).

[83] Perhaps we might defend the Court's rule as a prophylactic one guarding against partisan vote dilution that is difficult to detect. If so, a person claiming to have been the victim of partisan vote dilution would have standing to raise the equal protection claim the Court recognized.

[84] Perhaps we might develop an idea of "pendent" standing, which would operate like this: A litigant clearly has standing to raise legal argument X, but the court rejects that argument while accepting argument Y, which the litigant would not otherwise have standing to raise. Pendent standing allows the court to enter a judgment predicated on argument Y even though it would not have been able to do so had the litigant raised only argument Y in the complaint.

he says work *expressive* harm.[85] Pildes developed the concept to deal with the problems of finding standing under traditional notions of injury in cases involving race-conscious districting.[86] Pamela Karlan has suggested that *Bush v. Gore* also involves this sort of harm, worked by a flaw in the election process of a sort that does not generate identifiable individuals who have suffered from having their votes diluted or otherwise devalued.[87]

Pildes and Karlan point out that *anyone* within a jurisdiction operating a voting system that implicates expressive discrimination has standing to raise the objection.[88] That, however, raises another problem. As we have seen, the Court has said that the very fact that anyone can raise a particular constitutional claim is a reason for denying standing to all.[89] Standing so broadly available demonstrates that the plaintiff has a generalized grievance better addressed through the political process than through constitutional adjudication.[90]

The answer to this objection, if there is one, comes from *Baker v. Carr* itself. It is that equal protection claims of any sort, including claims of expressive harm, are justiciable. To quote the key passage from *Baker v. Carr* again, "Judicial standards under the Equal Protection Clause are well developed and familiar."[91] The *Bush v. Gore* Court's reluctance to commit itself to any equal protection doctrine casts some shadows on an approach that would allow standing in anyone to raise any equal protection claim,[92] but *Baker v. Carr* supplemented by

---

[85] Richard H. Pildes and Richard G. Niemi, *Expressive Harms, "Bizarre Districts," and Voting Rights: Evaluating Election-District Appearances After* Shaw v. Reno, 92 Mich. L. Rev. 483 (1993).

[86] *Id.*

[87] Karlan, *supra* n. 82.

[88] Once again, this suggests that the litigation on the legal issue the Court accepted in *Bush v. Gore* was nonadversarial.

[89] See text accompanying notes 47–48 *supra.*

[90] I have been discussing who might have standing, at the outset, to raise the equal protection claim the Court recognized. Perhaps, however, the only relevant question is whether Bush had standing at the Supreme Court level. (State courts need not restrict standing to litigants who satisfy the federal Article III standards.) There, he could claim that the Florida Supreme Court's action deprived him of a victory; that is, his claim would not be against anything associated with the recount, but would be against the Florida Supreme Court's decision. Cf. *ASARCO, Inc. v. Kadish,* 490 U.S. 605 (1989) (finding that litigants who might not have had Article III standing nonetheless had standing to raise, in the Supreme Court, the claim that the state court decision appealed from itself injured them; Chief Justice Rehnquist and Justice Scalia dissented on this issue, and Justice O'Connor did not participate in the decision).

[91] *Baker,* 369 U.S. at 226. Erwin Chemerinsky, Bush v. Gore *Was Not Justiciable,* 76 Notre Dame L. Rev. 1093 (2001), argues that *Baker v. Carr* found justiciability not for all equal protection claims associated with elections but only for cases claiming malapportionment.

[92] *Bush v. Gore,* 112 S. Ct. 525, 532 (2000) ("Our consideration is limited to the present circumstances, for the problem of equal protection in election processes generally presents many complexities.").

later voting discrimination cases at least provides some basis for finding standing in *Bush v. Gore*.

No one would today contend that the equal protection claim in *Bush v. Gore* raised a political question. The argument accepted by three justices in their concurring opinion that the Florida Supreme Court's action violated Article II is another matter.[93] The argument they accepted was that the Florida Supreme Court's interpretation of the Florida statutes regulating elections and recounts was so eccentric as to amount to a judicial displacement of the power committed by the Constitution to the state legislature to direct how presidential electors are to be appointed. But, critics suggest, the Constitution committed the decision about whether there had been such a displacement to Congress.[94]

There appears to be an emerging consensus that the Article II issue in *Bush v. Gore* was indeed a political question.[95] The relevant clauses are in the Twelfth Amendment. Much in the argument for the proposition that the Article II issue presented a political question turns on what I call the atmospherics of the Twelfth Amendment. Reading the Amendment, one certainly gets the general impression that Congress was supposed to play a large, and perhaps the only, role in resolving contested presidential elections. Certainly nothing in the amendment refers directly to a judicial role in resolving such elections. Still, the political question doctrine, considered as a doctrine, requires not atmospherics but an analysis of constitutional text.

Atmospherics may influence the way one looks at constitutional text, however. In *Walter Nixon*, the Supreme Court framed its discussion of the meaning of the word *try* by first discussing the meaning and role of the word *sole* in the phrase, "sole Power to try all Impeachments."[96] Formally speaking, that analysis was not responsive to Judge Nixon's claim, but the atmospherics of the impeachment clause seem to have induced the Court to find that there were no judicially manageable standards for determining the meaning of *try*.

The precise question to ask is, Is there a demonstrable textual commitment of the Article II question to Congress? Here it is important to describe the Article II question carefully. The Article II question is not a general or abstract one, such as, Does the Constitution give the courts a role in resolving disputed presidential elections? Rather, it is this: Did the Florida Supreme Court exceed the

---

[93] For a more complete analysis of the political question issue, see Samuel Issacharoff, *Political Judgments,* in *The Vote, supra* n. 82, at 55.

[94] See Steven Calabresi, *A Political Question,* in *Bush v. Gore: The Question of Legitimacy* (Bruce Ackerman ed., Yale University Press, 2002). Cf. Chemerinsky, *supra* n. 42, at 866–67 (suggesting that the equal protection claim also presented a political question).

[95] In addition to Calabresi, *supra* n. 94, see also Rachel E. Barkow, *More Supreme than Court? The Fall of the Political Question Doctrine and the Rise of Judicial Supremacy,* 102 Colum. L. Rev. 237 (2002); Jesse H. Choper, "Why the Supreme Court Should Not Have Decided the Presidential Election of 2000," UC Berkeley Public Law and Legal Theory Working Paper Series, Working Paper No. 65, 2001.

[96] 506 U.S. 224, 229 (1993).

discretion granted it by the Florida legislature in interpreting Florida election law as applied in a presidential election? The political question issue, then, is whether there is a textually demonstrable commitment to the political branches of the power to answer *that* question. The answer might be influenced by the atmospherics of the Twelfth Amendment, but it cannot be determined by language in that amendment dealing with problems other than the one presented in *Bush v. Gore.*

The political question argument gets its force from the provision on counting the ballots cast by the electors: "The President of the Senate shall, in the presence of the Senate and House of Representatives, open all the certificates and the votes shall then be counted."[97] The Constitution says that the Senate and the House shall be present, and says nothing about judges having any role. Further, if no candidate has a majority of the electoral votes cast and counted (by whatever means), the choice of who is to become president devolves upon the House of Representatives.[98] So far, then, the Twelfth Amendment does not seem to contemplate a role for the courts.

There is more to say, however. Start with the passive voice: "shall be counted." Does the constitutional text commit to anyone in particular resolution of disputes over which votes should be counted? Here the problem is analogous to that in *Goldwater v. Carter.*[99] There the Constitution said something about entering treaties but nothing about getting out of them; here the Constitution says something about counting electoral votes but nothing about what to do when someone says, "This isn't a valid vote." In *Goldwater,* then–Justice Rehnquist treated constitutional silence as supporting the conclusion that the political question doctrine made nonjusticiable the claim that the Senate had to participate in treaty abrogation.[100] Perhaps, however, the foreign affairs context made *Goldwater* special for Justice Rehnquist.[101] The domestic context of *Bush v. Gore* may have allowed him and Justices Scalia and Thomas to treat the constitutional silence over resolving disputes over electoral votes as permitting courts to exercise their traditional role of interpreting the Constitution, as Justice Powell said in *Goldwater.*

With this view of the Twelfth Amendment in hand, we can examine a simpler defense of the proposition that the Constitution did not commit the Article II claim to Congress. The first words of the Twelfth Amendment are, "The Electors shall meet in their respective states."[102] The dispute in *Bush v. Gore* can be put as one over identifying exactly who the electors were, and nothing in the Twelfth Amendment suggests that resolving disputes over identity is committed

---

[97] U.S. Const., Amend. XII.
[98] *Id.*
[99] 444 U.S. 996 (1979).
[100] *Id.* at 1003 (Rehnquist, J., concurring).
[101] *Id.* (noting that the case "involves foreign relations").
[102] U.S. Const., Amend. XII.

to Congress.[103] The electors referred to in the Twelfth Amendment are the Bush electors, if that amendment restricts a state legislature's ability to delegate interpretive authority to state courts, or if the Florida Supreme Court exceeded the bounds of what the legislature had delegated to it. The questions of whether the amendment does restrict state legislatures and whether the Florida Supreme Court acted impermissibly are classically *legal* questions ordinarily committed to the courts for resolution.

It is at the least not obvious that the Constitution contains a demonstrable textual commitment of the Article II question to Congress. The availability of judicial standards to determine whether the Florida Supreme Court so deviated from ordinary statutory interpretation as to displace the legislature as the body defining the manner of selecting electors is clear, no matter how controversial the application of those standards might be. It involves no "initial policy determination," and of course there was no "political decision already made" that counseled in favor of "unquestioning adherence."[104]

The only component of the *Baker v. Carr* standards that might support the conclusion that the Article II claim presented a political question, other than the "textual commitment" standard, is that "undertaking independent resolution" might "express[] lack of the respect due coordinate branches of government."[105] After all, nothing in the Constitution says that Congress *cannot* resolve disputes over who the electors are or over which votes should be counted.[106] Further, the most cogent retrospective defenses of *Bush v. Gore* are that the Court acted properly to avert a constitutional crisis.[107] Yet, that crisis would have consisted of actions by one of the political branches, and perhaps both.[108] Suggesting that

---

[103] Perhaps one can read the Twelfth Amendment to remit to Congress the choice of which electors to count in the event that it receives two slates from a single state. A federal *statute* establishes an elaborate procedure for Congress to use in making that choice, which commentators have taken as indicating Congress's belief that it had at least the first word in determining which votes to count. But, of course, that is true of all constitutional questions. It is not clear to me that the enactment of a statute governing how to count disputed electoral slates demonstrates that the Constitution gives Congress both the first and last words on which slate should be counted.

[104] See *Baker*, 369 U.S. at 186.

[105] *Id.*

[106] And, of course, in the nation's only prior experience with a similar election problem, the 1876 election, Congress did resolve these questions by appointing a commission whose report it adopted.

[107] See, e.g., Richard Posner, *Breaking the Deadlock: The 2000 Election, The Constitution, and the Courts* (Cambridge: Harvard University Press, 2001).

[108] The characterization of action by the political branches as a crisis depends in addition on the delay occasioned by the necessity for the political branches to act. The idea appears to be that there was a crisis because the nation might not know who its next president would be until January. There are, however, many things a nation's people would benefit from knowing earlier rather than later, and in the circumstances of late 2000 uncertainty about who the president would be does not seem much different from many of those other things.

the courts must act because the political branches would, if left alone, provoke a constitutional crisis seems rather close to expressing a lack of the respect due those branches.

What is most notable about *Bush v. Gore* in the present context is that no one said anything at all about justiciability questions. I do not claim that the case should actually have been dismissed for lack of standing or because it raised a political question. I do claim that the justiciability questions are obvious to someone schooled in the Bickel tradition, and that to such a person the silence in *Bush v. Gore* about justiciability is quite remarkable. But, of course, a person attuned to the justiciability questions is a person whose legal consciousness was shaped in a period that has now passed.

V. Bickel's World, and Ours[109]

Bickel gave a catalog of "the foundation[s]" of the political question doctrine that sounds quite different from the doctrinalized criteria in *Baker v. Carr*:

> (a) the strangeness of the issue and its intractability to principled resolution; (b) the sheer momentousness of it, which tends to unbalance judicial judgment; (c) the anxiety, not so much that the judicial judgment will be ignored, as that perhaps it should but will not be; (d) finally ("in a mature democracy"), the inner vulnerability, the self-doubt of an institution which is electorally irresponsible and has no earth to draw strength from.[110]

Bickel's catalog not only sounds quite different from *Baker v. Carr*'s, it invokes prudential concerns quite remote from the legal ones Justice Brennan articulated. *Bush v. Gore* shows how foreign Bickel's intellectual universe is from ours. In particular, Bickel's catalog includes items arguably not present in *Bush v. Gore*: anxiety and self-doubt.

The equal protection question was strange, as the Court's reluctance to develop any doctrine indicates, but as the aftermath of *Baker v. Carr* showed, initial strangeness does not foreclose the possibility of developing principles (in the Wechslerian sense) to resolve it and its cousins. The issue in *Bush v. Gore* was unquestionably momentous, and virtually everyone thinks that *someone's* judgment was distorted: Bush's supporters think that the justices of the Florida Supreme Court were out of control,[111] and Gore's supporters think that the U.S. Supreme Court's majority acted in an entirely partisan manner.[112]

---

[109] The title intentionally echoes Robert A. Burt, *Alex Bickel's Law School and Ours*, 104 Yale L. J. 1853 (1995), and the argument is at least kin to Burt's.

[110] Bickel, *supra* n. 2, at 184.

[111] See, e.g., Richard Epstein, *In Such Manner as the Legislature Thereof May Direct: The Outcome in* Bush v. Gore *Defended*, in *The Vote, supra* n. 82. Criticism of the Court's dissenters on this ground is less common, but I have run across it, mostly in the

More interesting, I think, is that Bickel's remaining items make no appearance in *Bush v. Gore*. Anxiety never attended the Supreme Court's decision, and particularly not anxiety over the possibility that the nation would comply with a mistaken decision. A certain kind of positivism seems to have settled in along with the nation's acceptance of a theory of strong judicial supremacy.[113] That is, our only worry is that the nation will not comply with the Court's decisions. Compliance is unproblematic because we no longer have available to us the sense that a Court decision might be mistaken. Nor, finally, did anyone on the Court demonstrate self-doubt or a sense of inner vulnerability.

The proximate reason for the foreignness of Bickel's formulation to today's constitutional sensibility, I think, is the acceptance in our political and legal culture of a strong form of judicial supremacy that was only uncertainly accepted when *Baker v. Carr* was decided. The ultimate reason, though, lies in the political setting in which today's Court operates.[114] I have already emphasized the effect doctrinalization has on prudential analysis. The second element we must examine is the historical setting in which the Court Bickel and Scharpf operated and the setting of today's Court.

Bickel and Scharpf were right to see that the task of combining prudence and law was particularly important for the time at which they wrote. They were dealing with a Supreme Court that had only recently emerged from the crisis precipitated by the Court's obstruction of the New Deal and that was simultaneously attempting to redefine the scope of government power by developing civil rights and civil liberties restrictions on government power.[115] Bickel's mentor Felix Frankfurter was centrally concerned with the legacy of the pre-New Deal Court but clearly believed that judicial power should be used to achieve racial justice.[116] For Frankfurter and Bickel, success required that the Court carefully calculate when it could succeed in disciplining local and national majorities that acted against the vision of civil rights and civil liberties to which Frankfurter and Bickel were committed.

---

form of the observation that only someone whose judgment was distorted could fail to recognize how out of control the Florida Supreme Court was.

[112] See, e.g., Alan Dershowitz, *Supreme Injustice: How the High Court Hijacked Election 2000* (New York: Oxford University Press, 2001); Bruce Ackerman, *The Court Packs Itself,* The American Prospect, Feb. 12, 2001, 48.

[113] See sources cited in n. 124 *infra* for indications of a commitment among legal scholars to a theory of strong judicial supremacy.

[114] See text accompanying nn. 132–33 *infra*.

[115] For essays on the New Deal crisis and the Court's response, see William E. Leuchtenberg, *The Supreme Court Reborn: The Constitutional Revolution in the Age of Roosevelt* (New York: Oxford University Press, 1995).

[116] For a discussion of Frankfurter's complex position in the school desegregation cases of 1954–1955, see Mark Tushnet, *Making Civil Rights Law: Thurgood Marshall and the Supreme Court, 1936–1961* (New York: Oxford University Press, 1994), 192–93, 203–04.

Sympathetic with the main thrust of the Warren Court's decisions through the early 1960s, Bickel was concerned that the Court would not be able to sustain its initiatives unless the Court acted with prudence. The setting in which he wrote provides the key to his interest in justiciability doctrines and to their disappearance. Southern members of Congress had attacked the Court in 1956 over *Brown v. Board of Education.*[117] In 1959 the Conference of State Chief Justices challenged the Court over some of the Court's preemption and criminal procedure decisions.[118] The Court had weathered a substantial effort to restrict its jurisdiction in 1958–1959, which Chief Justice Warren later said "came dangerously close to passing."[119] *Baker v. Carr* came in 1962, only four years after the Court had articulated the strongest theory of judicial supremacy it could, in response to defiance of its desegregation decisions by the governor of Arkansas.[120] The Court's reapportionment and school prayer decisions provoked a substantial adverse reaction in Congress.[121]

All this led Bickel to conclude that success in the Court's reformist enterprise, with which he generally agreed when he wrote *The Least Dangerous Branch*, required that the Court act with prudence. Bickel sometimes saw prudence embodied in the Court's actions, as in its adoption of the "all deliberate speed" formula for desegregation.[122] But, prudence also sometimes meant that the Court should not act. Judicial action had to be principled, and sometimes principle—faithfully adhering to legal principle—would actually lead the nation astray. Justiciability doctrines would give the Court additional tools to avoid harm to itself or to the nation.

As it happened, the Court had a different view of what prudence required than Bickel. He thought that prudence required caution; the Warren Court thought, probably correctly, that boldness was at least as prudent a course. Even so, the Warren Court, composed mainly of seasoned politicians,[123] agreed with Bickel that the Court was a political institution.

The Court weathered the assaults on it during the early 1960s. Since then political liberals, recalling the triumphs of the Warren Court, and political conservatives, savoring the prospect of getting the Supreme Court on their side, have gone along with judicial supremacy.[124] Of course, the Court itself has been

---

[117] See Bickel, *supra* n. 2, at 256–58 (quoting the Southern Manifesto).

[118] See Lucas S. Powe, *The Warren Court and American Politics* (Cambridge: Harvard University Press, 2000), 139 (discussing the Conference criticism).

[119] Warren quoted in *id.* at 133.

[120] *Cooper v. Aaron,* 358 U.S. 1 (1958).

[121] See Powe, *supra* n. 118, at 203–04 (describing the reaction to the Court's decisions).

[122] Bickel, *supra* n. 2, at 247–54.

[123] See Mark Tushnet, *Constitutional Interpretation, Character, and Experience,* 72 BU L. Rev. 747, 757 (1992).

[124] The examples I use, somewhat self-defensively, are the reviews of my book, *Taking the Constitution Away from the Courts, supra* n. 20, which challenged judicial

quite comfortable in asserting its own supremacy.[125] Nor do any current justices appear to believe that law, faithfully invoked, might sometimes be bad for the country.

Today's version of judicial supremacy, however, has a different foundation from the one on which the Warren Court rested. As I have suggested, the Warren Court asserted judicial supremacy because it believed that judicial supremacy was a politically astute method of achieving its political goals. In contrast, today's justices see the Court as an institution devoted to law alone. The doctrinalization of justiciability law is untroubling to today's Court, because it sees no need for approaches—they cannot be called doctrines—that would allow them to temper law with prudence. Professor Cass Sunstein, Bickel's jurisprudential heir, has argued that the Court should incorporate prudence into its decision making, but for Sunstein prudence operates as a component of judgments on the merits. Sometimes, according to Sunstein, the Court should act boldly—render what Sunstein calls maximalist decisions—but frequently it should act cautiously, issuing decisions that address the constitutional merits but do so in what Sunstein calls a minimalist way.[126] The reasons that make minimalism sometimes appropriate, in Sunstein's view, are not identical to the ones that, for Bickel, should lead to a prudential abstention from decision on the merits, but they are at least cousins of Bickel's reasons.

A parallel development has occurred on the Court as well. Frankfurter's heirs on the Court are today's balancers, who articulate doctrines that allow them to decide cases on the merits while preserving the possibility of a different decision should circumstances change.[127] For the balancers, prudence is a component of judgment but not an element of legal doctrine.

In the 1950s and 1960s, balancing decisions were thought to be conservative relative to the positions taken by the Warren Court majority and, more important for present purposes, they were thought to be inconsistent with the demands imposed on judicial decision making by the rule of law.[128] The political valence of balancing has changed: Relative to the most prominent advocates of

---

supremacy. For liberal reactions defending judicial supremacy, see James E. Fleming, *The Constitution Outside the Courts* (Book Review), 86 Corn. L. Rev. 215 (2000), and Erwin Chemerinsky, *Losing Faith: America without Judicial Review?* (Book Review), 98 Mich. L. Rev. 1416 (2000); for conservative reactions doing so, see Saikrishna Prakash, *America's Aristocracy* (Book Review), 109 Yale L. J. 541 (1999); Joan Larsen, *Constitutionalism without Courts?*, 94 Nw. U. L. Rev. 983 (2000).

[125] The best example, because the assertion of judicial supremacy elicited no disagreement from within the Court, is *City of Boerne v. Flores*, 521 U.S. 507 (1997).

[126] Cass Sunstein, *One Case at a Time: Judicial Minimalism on the Supreme Court* (Cambridge: Harvard University Press, 1999).

[127] Among the Court's recent cases, *Eastern Enterprises v. Apfel*, 524 U.S. 498 (1998) best illustrates the balancing phenomenon.

[128] See, e.g., Laurent B. Frantz, *Is the First Amendment Law?—A Reply to Professor Mendelson*, 51 Calif. L. Rev. 729 (1963).

the rule of law as a law of rules,[129] balancing is a liberal technique.[130] It is now reasonably common to describe today's Court as a conservative version of the Warren Court.[131] It is that, but only in a sense. Like the Warren Court, today's Court has no general constitutional theory that cautions against invalidating statutes. But the Warren Court, believing that constitutional law was an exercise in political decision making, acted boldly when and because it thought it could accomplish its political goals by doing so. Today's Court acts boldly because it believes the law requires it to do so.

Today's Court is in a position to act in that way precisely because it is *not* under imminent threat of retaliation. For the Warren Court, it was a close question whether legislative majorities could be assembled to challenge the Court's decisions. Today we have a divided government, which means that Court decisions can be overturned or successfully challenged only if a substantial majority of the people disagrees with the Court.[132] But, on that question, the facts surrounding *Bush v. Gore* can be taken as emblematic. The members of today's Court know that whatever they do, close to half of the nation's people will think they did the right thing. After *Bush v. Gore*, neither the Court nor its defenders thought it disrespectful to assume that leaving resolution of the election dispute to Congress would either provoke or itself *be* a constitutional crisis. In contemporary circumstances, a constitutional jurisprudence of boldness predicated on refusing to temper legal with political judgment is a politically sound jurisprudence.[133]

VI. Conclusion

The story of *Baker v. Carr* combines two elements. First, doctrinalization substantially reduced the possibility of the Court's deploying the political question and standing doctrines in the service of prudential judgments about what would be the best structures of governance in a democratic society. Second, the Warren Court's legacy was a theory of judicial supremacy accepted along every point of

---

[129] The reference here is obviously Antonin Scalia, *The Rule of Law as a Law of Rules*, 56 U. Chi. L. Rev. 1175 (1989).

[130] Again, Gerald Gunther saw this first. Gerald Gunther, *In Search of Judicial Quality on a Changing Court: The Case of Justice Powell*, 24 Stan. L. Rev. 1001 (1972). I suspect that Gunther would have a different account of the origins of his perception.

[131] See, e.g., John C. Jeffries, Jr., and Daryl Levinson, *The Non-Retrogression Principle in Constitutional Law*, 86 Calif. L. Rev. 1211, 1212 (1998); Donald H. Zeigler, *The New Activist Court*, 45 Am. U. L. Rev. 1367 *passim* (1996).

[132] For an introduction to the argument, see Mark Tushnet, *Foreword: The New Constitutional Order and the Chastening of Constitutional Ambition*, 113 Harv. L. Rev. 29 (1999).

[133] Why today's justices believe—if they do—that faithful adherence to law can never damage the nation is another question, and one to which I have no answer.

the political spectrum. No one likes every Supreme Court decision, but everyone hopes—in my view, against hope—that the Court will eventually decide every case in accordance with his or her own views. No one, therefore, is willing to say that judicial supremacy is in principle a bad thing. When Bickel wrote a generation or two ago, that possibility was available in the legal and political culture. I think we should retrieve it, but I do not think we will.

Leaving the Empty Vessel of "Republicanism" Unfilled:
An Argument for the Continued Nonjusticiability of Guarantee Clause Cases

Richard L. Hasen[1]

Introduction

Many commentators trace the beginning of the end of the political question doctrine to the Supreme Court's 1962 *Baker v. Carr* decision. In *Baker*, as Mark Tushnet has explained, the Court domesticated the doctrine by reducing it from an amorphous prudential doctrine to a set of six legal rules.[2] Tushnet is one of many commentators to note the much more recent failure of Supreme Court justices in the *Bush v. Gore* majority and concurrence even to *consider* applicability of the political question doctrine to the issues raised in the case. These commentators question whether the dispute over Florida presidential electors

---

[1] Professor and William M. Rains Fellow, Loyola Law School. Thanks to Rachel Barkow, Pam Karlan, Hans Linde, Rick Pildes, Roy Schotland, and Mark Tushnet for useful comments and suggestions and to Amber Star Healy for excellent research assistance.

[2] Mark Tushnet, *Law and Prudence in the Law of Justiciability: The Transformation and Disappearance of the Political Question* Doctrine, 80 N.C. L. Rev. 1203–35 (2002).

was for Congress (or the Florida Legislature) to resolve rather than for Court resolution, and, more broadly, whether there is anything left of the doctrine at all.[3]

If the political question doctrine continues to have any vitality, it is in the area of foreign affairs[4] and in cases raising "Guarantee Clause" claims. I will ignore the foreign affairs area in this chapter and focus on the Guarantee Clause, contained in Article IV, section 4 of the United States Constitution. The clause provides that "[t]he United States shall guarantee to every State in this Union, a Republican Form of Government. . . ."

The Supreme Court held a Guarantee Clause claim to be a nonjusticiable political question in 1849, when it refused to enter a dispute over which of two rival governments was the legitimate government of Rhode Island.[5] Although the Court adjudicated some disputes raising Guarantee Clause claims after 1849, by 1912 the Court viewed the clause as essentially a dead letter.[6] It had been unclear whether the Court in *Baker* meant to bury or revive Guarantee Clause claims. Now, cases raising even Guarantee Clause claims stand on the cusp of justiciability. In 1992, the Court strongly suggested some Guarantee Clause claims would be justiciable and the rationales supporting nonjusticiability appear no longer to be persuasive.

In Part I of this chapter, I argue that there is good reason to believe that the Court will soon consider claims arising under the Guarantee Clause. First, as a textual matter, the argument for nonjusticiability is weak. Second, the prudential rationale offered by the Court in *Baker v. Carr* for not deciding Guarantee Clause claims—that the Guarantee Clause is "not a repository of judicially manageable standards"—has failed to hold up in the face of the Court development of manageable standards in other areas of the law. Thus, all that stands in the way of justiciability is weakly reasoned (though longstanding) precedent.

In Part II of this chapter, I argue that the Court should nonetheless continue to treat cases raising Guarantee Clause claims as nonjusticiable. The most likely claims advanced under the clause would challenge the initiative process (or particular initiatives) and provide additional arguments for Court intervention in election law (particularly voting rights) disputes. The success of such claims would further entrench courts in political regulation with little benefit and at a great potential cost. It also may have unintended consequences for those who see the clause as the next means of advancing a liberal activist agenda on the Court; it may just as well promote a conservative activist agenda. Thus, the history of the

---

[3] Rachel E. Barkow, *More Supreme than Court? The Fall of the Political Question Doctrine and the Rise of Judicial Supremacy*, 102 Colum. L. Rev. 237–336 (2002); Erwin Chemerinsky, Bush v. Gore *Was Not Justiciable*, 76 Notre Dame L. Rev. 1093–1112 (2001); Samuel Issacharoff, *Political Judgments*, in *The Vote: Bush, Gore and the Supreme Court* 55–76 (Cass R. Sunstein and Richard A. Epstein, eds., University of Chicago Press, 2001).

[4] Tushnet 2002, 1206 n. 19.

[5] *Luther v. Borden*, 48 U.S. (7 How.) 1 (1849).

[6] *Pacific States Telephone & Telegraph Co. v. Oregon*, 223 U.S. 118 (1912).

Guarantee Clause could well parallel the history of the Equal Protection Clause from its liberal use in post-*Baker* cases to more conservative uses in cases like *Bush v. Gore.* I conclude that both liberal and conservative Court justices concerned about the overinvolvement of the courts in political regulation would do well to keep the political question doctrine on life support, if only to insure that Guarantee Clause claims remain nonjusticiable.

The Fall (and Potential Resurrection) of Guarantee Clause Claims in the Supreme Court

A. A Brief History of Guarantee Clause Justiciability

Others have provided detailed histories of the origins of the Guarantee Clause in the Constitution and its fate in the Supreme Court.[7] What follows here is a brief and updated survey of key cases in the area.

Luther v. Borden stands as the poster child for the nonjusticiability of political question cases to come before the Court. The case arose out of a civil war in Rhode Island in the 1840s pitting those who wanted to expand the franchise against supporters of the existing government who wished to continue use of Rhode Island's narrow suffrage requirements. The factions formed rival governments. The president of the United States ultimately sided with the existing government and the rebellion was quashed.

Years after the insurrection ended, the case of *Luther v. Boren* made it to the Supreme Court. *Luther* was a trespass case in which police from the existing government broke into plaintiff's home looking for evidence that he was participating in the rival electoral process. The plaintiff claimed trespass on grounds that the police officers had no authority to enter his home because the government for which they worked was not a "republican" government under the Guarantee Clause.

The Court refused to consider whether the existing Rhode Island government was "republican" under the Guarantee Clause, declaring in the 1849 case that "[u]nder this article of the Constitution it rests with Congress to decide what government is the established one in a State."[8]

In the years following *Luther*, the Supreme Court occasionally decided Guarantee Clause cases. For example, in the 1874 case of *Minor v. Happersett*, the Court held that a state's denial of the right to vote to women did not make that government nonrepublican for purposes of the Guarantee Clause. But the trend ceased in 1912, when the Court decided *Pacific States Telephone & Telegraph Co. v. Oregon.* Oregon had adopted the initiative and referendum process in 1902, and

---

[7] Arthur E. Bonfield, *The Guarantee Clause of Article IV, Section 4: A Study in Constitutional Desuetude*, 46 Minn. L. Rev. 513–72 (1962); William M. Wiecek, *The Guarantee Clause of the U.S. Constitution* (Cornell Univeristy Press, 1972).

[8] *Luther v. Borden*, 48 U.S. at 42.

in 1906 voters passed an initiative establishing a tax on telephone and telegraph companies. The companies contested the tax on grounds "that the creation by a State of a power to legislate by the initiative and referendum causes the prior lawful state government to be bereft of its lawful character" as not a republican form of government.[9]

Relying on *Luther*, the Court held the telephone company's claim to be nonjusticiable. It held that the question whether a state was republican was a "subject committed" to the judgment of Congress.[10] The Court also listed a "parade of horribles"[11] should the Court rule otherwise, including a suggestion that holding the Oregon government not republican in this case would invalidate every other statute passed and every court decision rendered in Oregon since the state adopted the initiative process.[12] Following *Pacific States*, the Court consistently held Guarantee Clause challenges to be nonjusticiable.[13]

Among the post–*Pacific States* cases was the 1946 case of *Colegrove v. Green*, in which a plurality of the Court, led by Justice Frankfurter, held challenges to the malapportionment of state legislative districts to be a nonjusticiable question under the Guarantee Clause.[14] *Colegrove* is the case in which Justice Frankfurter warned courts to stay out of the "political thicket."

By 1962, however, a shifting Court majority now believed malapportionment cases to be justiciable. In *Baker v. Carr*, the Court held that courts could consider such cases under the Equal Protection Clause of the Fourteenth Amendment even if such cases were deemed nonjusticiable under the Guarantee Clause. Justice Brennan's opinion for the Court set forth six criteria for determining whether a case presented a nonjusticiable political question. One criterion asked the courts to consider whether there were "judicially discoverable and manageable standards for resolving" the case.[15] Justice Brennan then contrasted the Guarantee Clause as "not a repository of judicially manageable standards" with the supposedly "well developed and familiar" standards of the Equal Protection Clause.[16]

Scholars[17] and the Court itself in subsequent cases have disputed whether the Court in *Baker* intended to close or open the door to future Guarantee Clause claims. Two years after *Baker*, the Court characterized the case as standing for the limited proposition that "some questions raised under the Guaranty Clause are nonjusticiable, where 'political' in nature and where there is a clear absence of

---

[9] *Pacific States*, 223 U.S. at 137.

[10] *Id.* at 142.

[11] See Barkow 2002 at 257.

[12] *Pacific States*, 223 U.S. at 141–42.

[13] Erwin Chemerinsky, *Cases Under the Guarantee Clause Should Be Justiciable*, 65 U. Colo. L. Rev. 863–64 (1994).

[14] *Colegrove v. Green*, 328 U.S. 549 (1946).

[15] *Baker v. Carr*, 369 U.S. 186 (1962) at 217.

[16] *Id.* at 223, 226.

[17] Compare Arthur E. Bonfield, Baker v. Carr: *New Light on the Constitutional Guarantee of Republican Government*, 50 Cal. L. Rev. 245–63 (1962) with Wiecek.

judicially manageable standards."[18] Yet in 1980 the Court refused to consider whether certain provisions of the Voting Rights Act violated the Guarantee Clause, citing *Baker* flatly for the proposition that the "issue is not justiciable."[19] Finally, in 1992, the Court in *New York v. United States* announced that "not all claims under the Guarantee Clause present nonjusticiable political questions," citing *Reynolds*' earlier weak statement on justiciability, and emphasizing *Reynolds*' statement that only "*some* questions" under the clause cannot be considered. The Court further noted that "[c]ontemporary commentators have likewise suggested that courts should address the merits of such claims, at least in some circumstances."[20] Though purporting not to resolve what it termed the "difficult question" of justiciability, the court "assumed" justiciability and proceeded to decide the merits of the dispute, finding no Guarantee Clause violation in the particular case. It is here where the matter now sits doctrinally.

B. Why the Supreme Court May Soon Consider Guarantee Clause Cases on the Merits

New York v. United States came awfully close to adjudicating (indeed some say it actually adjudicated) a Guarantee Clause case on the merits. Scholars have been predicting the Court would do so for some time. Writing in 1972, Wiecek thought the "future of the clause seems bright."[21] Ely remarked in 1980 that "it seems likely that this unfortunate doctrine—that all Republican Form cases are necessarily cases involving political questions—will wholly pass from the scene one of these days."[22] In 1994, following the *New York* case, Chemerinksy remarked that "the time is clearly approaching in which the Court may be quite willing to reject the view that cases under the Guarantee Clause should always be dismissed on political question grounds."[23]

These scholars have good reason for optimism that the new trend will continue. Besides the strong signal on justiciability sent by the Court in *New York v. United States*, neither the textual argument nor the prudential argument against justiciability seems particularly strong under current constitutional jurisprudence.

The textual argument, advanced in both *Luther v. Borden* and *Pacific States*, is that the Guarantee Clause commits enforcement of the guarantee to Congress, not the states. The argument is weak. "The clause does not say 'Congress shall

---

[18] *Reynolds v. Sims*, 377 U.S. 533 (1964) at 582.

[19] *City of Rome v. United States*, 446 U.S. 156 (1980) at 182 n. 17.

[20] *New York v. United States*, 505 U.S. 144 (1992) at 185.

[21] Wiecek at 271.

[22] John Hart Ely, *Democracy and Distrust: A Theory of Judicial Review* 118 (Harvard University Press, 1980).

[23] Chemerinksy 1994 at 851.

guarantee;' it unambiguously says 'the United States' and includes all branches of the federal government."[24]

This textual argument is buttressed by a structural argument put forward by Deborah Merritt: the Guarantee Clause appears in Article IV of the Constitution; if the framers intended to limit the enforcement power of the clause solely to Congress, the clause should have appeared in Article I, which sets forth other congressional powers.[25] This structural argument is somewhat weakened by the fact that Article IV, Section 3 explicitly grants Congress other powers, specifically the power to admit new states into the Union and the power to dispose of and make rules and regulations concerning the territory or other property belonging to the United States. In any case, the drafting history of the clause, as set forth in Wiecek's book, does not show that the framers intended to insulate Guarantee Clause claims from judicial review.

Perhaps a more formidable nonjusticiability argument (at least formidable at one time in the Court's history) is that the term "republican form of government" is incapable of any set meaning to be construed by the courts. Over time, commentators have put forward varied meanings of the term "republican," from arguing that any form of state government sanctioned at the time the states ratified the Constitution was "republican," to stating that the clause simply banned monarchical and hereditary forms of government, to advancing the more ambitious argument that the meaning of "republicanism" is subject to change over time to reflect current views on what republican government now requires.

Such indeterminacy—which coincides with what the *Baker* Court meant in talking about some political questions involving a "lack of judicially discoverable and manageable standards"—may once have been a problem for the Supreme Court, but it hardly seems a problem now. Chemerinksy termed "fatuous" the manageability distinction drawn by the Supreme Court in *Baker* between a Guarantee Clause Claim and an Equal Protection Claim regarding legislative apportionment.[26]

The Equal Protection Clause provides that no state may deny any person "equal protection of the laws." From this vague language, the Court has constructed a one person, one vote rule applicable not only in state elections but in local ones as well.[27] The Court also has used the clause to: ban poll taxes;[28] strike down a law limiting voting in school board elections to parents and taxpayers;[29] strike down a one-year but uphold a fifty-day durational residency requirement for

---

[24] Chemerinsky 1994 at 871; see also Barkow 2002 at 255, 257 (calling the Supreme Court's equation of "United States" with "Congress" a "textual anchor" used by the court to address prudential concerns).

[25] Deborah Jones Merritt, *The Guarantee Clause and State Autonomy: Federalism for a Third Century*, 88 Colum. L. Rev. 75–76 (1988).

[26] Chemerinksy 1994 at 871.

[27] *Reynolds v. Sims*; *Avery v. Midland County*, 390 U.S. 474 (1968).

[28] *Harper v. Virginia Board of Elections*, 383 U.S. 663 (1966).

[29] *Kramer v. Union Free School District No. 15*, 395 U.S. 621 (1969).

voting;[30] limit the extent to which race may be taken into account in the redistricting process;[31] and overrule the recount procedures mandated by the Florida Supreme Court in the 2000 election controversy.[32] All that from the words "equal protection of the laws."

Writing before *Harper*, Bonfield considered it unthinkable that the Court would use the Equal Protection Clause to strike down poll taxes (especially given earlier contrary precedent upholding poll taxes against equal protection challenge), suggesting instead that the Court use the Guarantee Clause to strike down such taxes.[33] But that route turned out to be unnecessary; the Court has been able to do a great deal of political regulation by reading meaning into the words of the Equal Protection Clause.

Thus, neither the textual claim nor the prudential claim about unmanageable standards likely would carry much weight these days. Of course, the Court might balk at deciding a case as extreme as *Luther v. Borden*; it is hard to imagine the Court being forced again to choose between two rival state governments, especially after the president had recognized the existing state government and the insurrection was quashed in the interim. But in the absence of such an extreme case (which seems unlikely as I write now at the beginning of the 21st century in the United States), all that stands in the way of justiciability is overruling some old precedent. *New York v. United States* shows that even old precedent may not pose much of a barrier to a Court that has a use for a Guarantee Clause claim.

Finally, in discussing the justiciability of the Guarantee Clause, it is worth mentioning the "parade of horribles" featured in the *Pacific States* case. This argument is surely makeweight. Nothing in the Constitution requires the Supreme Court, in holding that an aspect of state law is nonrepublican, to find all actions of that state to be nonrepublican as well. The Court could have simply declared the particular feature of state law—in *Pacific States*, the initiative power—to be nonrepublican, leaving the rest of state law intact. As early as 1886, the Court had recognized a similar concept in what later became known as the "de facto officer doctrine,"[34] which "confers validity upon acts performed by a person acting under the color of official title even though it is later discovered that the legality of that person's appointment or election to office is deficient."[35]

---

[30] *Dunn v. Blumstein*, 405 U.S. 330 (1972); *Martson v. Lewis*, 410 U.S. 679 (1973).

[31] *Shaw v. Reno*, 509 U.S. 630 (1993).

[32] *Bush v. Gore*, 531 U.S. 98 (2000).

[33] Bonfield, *Guarantee Clause*, at 514, 564.

[34] *Norton v. Shelby County*, 118 U.S. 425 (1886) at 442.

[35] *Ryder v. United States*, 515 U.S. 177 (1995) at 180.

Do Not Wake the "Sleeping Giant:"
The Argument for Continued Nonjusticiability

A. The Guarantee Clause and Individual Rights

John Adams and Charles Sumner made the two most memorable comments about the Guarantee Clause. Adams, writing in 1807, remarked that he never understood the clause's meaning and believed "no man ever did or ever will."[36] Sumner, speaking on the floor of the Senate in 1867 in favor of a bill to expand African-American suffrage throughout the United States under the power he claimed the Guarantee Clause granted Congress, called the clause a "sleeping giant."[37] Together, the comments allude to both the clause's potential manipulability and its potential power as a judicial doctrine (though Sumner of course was speaking of the power the clause conferred on *Congress*, not the courts).

Since the 1960s, scholars have called upon the Court to use the Guarantee Clause to handle a wide variety of potential individual rights claims. "Republicanism" is an empty vessel to be filled by whatever individual right the particular writer desires the courts to enforce. Indeed, back in 1964, Mitchell Franklin believed the clause "should be understood as a guarantee of equal, integrated education, without distinction between private and public schools," subject only to the First Amendment freedoms of communication for teacher and student.[38] More common were arguments like those of Bonfield. Writing before the Supreme Court decided to use the Equal Protection Clause to engage in general political regulation, Bonfield saw the Guarantee Clause as the natural repository for political rights.[39]

Contemporary scholars have continued to claim that the Supreme Court erred in not grounding its malapportionment jurisprudence in the Guarantee Clause.[40] Michael McConnell recently wrote the Court's choice in *Baker* to use the Equal Protection Clause rather than the Guarantee Clause to regulate apportionment pushed the Court to choose particularly manageable standards like the one person, one vote rule in *Reynolds v. Sims,* leading to later problems of partisan and racial gerrymandering. McConnell argued that the Equal Protection Clause language committed the Court to a focus on equal populations while a Guarantee Clause

---

[36] See Wiecek at 72.

[37] *Id.* at 214.

[38] Mitchell Franklin, *Influence of the Abbé de Mably and of Le Mercier de la Rivière on American Constitutional Ideas Concerning the Republic and Judicial Review,* in *Perspectives of Law: Essays for Austin Wakeman Scott* 99 (Roscoe Pound et al., eds., Little, Brown, 1964).

[39] Bonfield, *Guarantee Clause* and *Baker v. Carr.*

[40] See, e.g., Jesse H. Choper, *Observations on the Guarantee Clause—As Thoughtfully Addressed by Justice Linde and Professor Eule,* 65 U. Colo. L. Rev. 741–44 (1994).

claim could have allowed the Court to focus on preserving the right of a state not to be trampled by a permanent political minority.[41]

McConnell probably overstated the role that the choice of constitutional provision would have made to subsequent developments. In other equal protection election cases the Court has not imposed any exacting requirement of strict equality such as in *Reynolds*. For example, in cases such as *Davis v. Bandemer*, regulating partisan gerrymandering, the Equal Protection Clause has proven quite malleable.[42] And, as a matter of Court politics, the Guarantee Clause route was impossible at the time of *Baker*, given that Justice Stewart simply refused to overrule any existing precedent.[43]

Although the courts since *Baker* have used the Equal Protection Clause to engage in a great deal of political regulation securing particular individual rights, the Guarantee Clause still could be used in the future to regulate those aspects of politics currently out of the bounds of the Equal Protection Clause. Two provocative areas commentators have proposed for Guarantee Clause regulation are the initiative process and voting rights claims not covered by the Equal Protection Clause.

Hans Linde has been the champion of the argument that the Guarantee Clause should be used to police the initiative process.[44] Linde, a former Oregon Supreme Court justice, would like to see *Pacific States* overruled, or at least have *state courts* adjudicate Guarantee Clause challenges. According to Linde, an initiative violates the Guarantee Clause when it places in the state constitution beyond the reach of the legislature laws that "govern private relationships or conduct or impose burdens or penalties on private persons." Thus, initiatives that put tax laws or sentencing laws beyond legislative change (such as California's infamous Proposition 13) are nonrepublican and should be struck down because they defeat the ability of representative government to function.[45] In an earlier work, Linde also explained his belief that antigay initiatives imposing constitutional amendments fall

---

[41] Michael W. McConnell, *The Redistricting Cases: Original Mistakes and Current Consequences*, 24 Harv. J. L. & Pub. Pol'y 106–09 (2000).

[42] *Davis v. Bandemer*, 478 U.S. 109 (1986).

[43] Roy A. Schotland, *The Limits of Being "Present at the Creation,"* 80 N.C. L. Rev. 1508-09 (2002). Issacharoff, Pildes, and Karlan call *Colegrove* "absolutely square precedent refusing to entertain malapportionment claims under the Fourteenth Amendment." They question why, "[i]f the Court had to overrule some precedent to review apportionment and the refusal to reapportion," it overruled the Fourteenth Amendment holding and not the Guarantee Clause holding [Samuel Issacharoff, Pamela S. Karlan, and Richard H. Pildes, *The Law of Democracy: Legal Structure of the Political Process* 159 (2d. rev. ed., Foundation Press, 2002)]. From my understanding of the drafting history of *Baker*, the answer is that at least some of the justices did not view *Colegrove*'s plurality decision as binding precedent.

[44] Hans A. Linde, *When Initiative Lawmaking is Not "Republican Government": The Campaign Against Homosexuality*, 72 Or. L. Rev. 19–45 (1993); *Who is Responsible for Republican Government?* 65 U. Colo. L. Rev. 709–31 (1994); State *Courts and Republican Government*, 41 Santa Clara L. Rev. 951–71 (2001).

[45] Linde 2001 at 963.

into a category of nonrepublican initiatives that "by their terms [are] directed against identifiable racial, ethnic, linguistic, religious, or other social groups."[46]

Kathryn Abrams has a less well-developed but equally provocative view of the Guarantee Clause in the area of voting rights. In the 1982 case of *City of Mobile v. Bolden*, the Supreme Court had rejected a claim by African-American plaintiffs to roughly proportional representation on a city council.[47] Abrams would resurrect such a claim (though she does not say so directly) using the Guarantee Clause. According to Abrams, one of the "important questions that could be asked under the rubric of the Guarantee Clause [is] how the state structures its internal political processes in a strongly differentiated and frequently polarized political world."[48] She suggests that "the place to begin" understanding the meaning of republicanism in the Guarantee Clause is to ask whether schemes of cumulative voting as proposed by Lani Guinier are necessary to prevent "bare numerical majorities" from exercising "sustained political power under circumstances where their interests are in persistent tension with those of a minority."[49]

B. Courts and Contested Republican Government Claims

As a matter of politics, I have a great deal of sympathy with the arguments of both Linde and Abrams. To the extent that the initiative process makes it easy to trample upon the rights of minorities[50] or create budgetary chaos through tax policies, perhaps the initiative process (or large portions of it) should be curtailed. And given the long history of political discrimination, particularly against African Americans, voting schemes such as cumulative voting may make a great deal of sense.

Linde and Abrams should direct their concerns toward political change. If the people of California abolished the initiative process tomorrow, that would be fine. And Congress, in my view correctly, created more proportional (though not strictly proportional) representation for minority groups in passing the amended section 2 of the Voting Rights Act in 1982.[51] The problem with the arguments of

---

[46] Linde 1993 at 41.

[47] *City of Mobile v. Bolden*, 446 U.S. 55 (1980).

[48] Kathryn Abrams, *No "There" There: State Autonomy and Voting Rights Regulation*, 65 U. Colo. L. Rev. 841 (1994).

[49] *Id.* at 842.

[50] See Julian N. Eule, *Judicial Review of Direct Democracy*, 99 Yale L. J. 1503–86 (1990).

[51] Congress has justified such legislation under its enforcement powers contained in the Fourteenth and Fifteenth Amendments; it may be possible, as the Supreme Court narrows those enforcement powers [see Richard L. Hasen, *The Supreme Court and Election Law: Judging Equality from* Baker v. Carr *to* Bush v. Gore ch. 4 (New York Univeristy Press, 2003)] that Congress will seek to justify such legislation under the Guarantee Clause. For more on expansive congressional power under the clause, see Ethan J. Leib,

Linde and Abrams is that they would take these very serious questions about political structure out of the political process and leave them in the hands of judges to ossify in constitutional decisions binding on the entire nation.

Their calls to further judicialize political regulation should be read in light of the history of the Supreme Court's regulation of politics through other clauses of the Constitution, particularly the Equal Protection Clause. As I argue in great detail elsewhere,[52] the Court wrongly has gone well beyond the protection of core equality rights in its jurisprudence toward adopting and enshrining in constitutional doctrine essentially contested views of political equality.

The Court was right in a case like *Harper* to strike down the poll tax because a near social consensus had developed that the use of wealth taxes for voting was inegalitarian under contemporary standards of democracy. And, if we were writing on a blank slate, I would care very little about whether the Court reached that result, as it did, under the Equal Protection Clause or, as Bonfield proposed, through the Guarantee Clause.

But both liberal and conservative Supreme Court majorities have gone well beyond social consensus to entrench in constitutional law their view of the best political arrangements. Conservatives can point to liberal decisions going well beyond social consensus: *Avery v. Midland County*, for example, extended the one person, one vote rule to all local government, thereby dooming any federal-like arrangements for regional government.[53] Liberals similarly can point to conservative decisions going well beyond social consensus: *Bush v. Gore*, for example, ended the 2000 election on equal protection grounds, and *Shaw v. Reno*, which limited the extent to which legislatures may take race into account in constructing legislative districts, even for the purpose of bolstering minority representation in the legislature.

I have little doubt that the Court could follow the same path in determining what "republican government" requires in the 21st century. The Court likely would go beyond what I believe would be a social consensus that "republican government" means that a state may not establish a monarchy. Would it strike down as nonrepublican an initiative preventing gay marriage or an initiative preventing property taxes from rising more than a certain amount per year? Would it require a city like Mobile, Alabama, to restructure the procedures by which it chooses members of its city council so as to assure more proportional representation of racial groups in the city? If these examples seem fanciful, they should not, for they go no further in interpreting the Guarantee Clause than the Supreme Court has gone in the last forty years of interpreting the Equal Protection Clause.

Redeeming the Welshed Guarantee: A Scheme for Achieving Justiciability, 24 Whittier L. Rev. 143–218 (2002).

[52] Hasen 2003.

[53] Bruce E. Cain, *Election Law as a Field: A Political Scientist's Perspective*, 32 Loy. L.A. L. Rev. 1105–19 (1999).

C. Liberal and Conservative Agendas

By now, I have probably convinced readers with conservative leanings that reviving the sleeping giant is not a good idea; "republican" government may turn out to be whatever a liberal group of judges says it is. I now turn to convince the liberals, who may think that judicial activism in the service of greater individual rights is justified.[54] In the course of convincing the liberals, however, I run the risks of reviving the interests of conservatives in the clause's justiciability.

What liberals should fear is that the Guarantee Clause could well become another tool used in the federalism litigation pitting "states rights" against the power of the federal government. In the last decade, we have witnessed a federalism revolution in the Supreme Court.[55] Among other things, the Court has limited congressional power under the Commerce Clause (previously thought to be virtually limitless)[56] and, through its Eleventh Amendment jurisprudence, it has increased the scope of the immunity of states from suits for damages or other retrospective relief for violation of federal law.[57]

Thus far, the Guarantee Clause has played little role in this federalism revolution; but that could well change. As Laurence Tribe has pointed out, "the Supreme Court has never held that the Guarantee Clause . . . confers judicially cognizable rights upon *individuals*. . . . [I]t need not follow from the unavailability of the Guarantee Clause as a textual source of protection for *individuals* that the clause confers no judicially enforceable rights upon *states as states*. It is, after all, '*to every State*' that the promise of the Guarantee Clause is addressed."[58]

Deborah Merritt has advanced in detail the argument that the *states* could use the Guarantee Clause against the power of the federal government.[59] The concern, as put by Merritt, is that "states cannot enjoy republican governments unless they retain sufficient autonomy to establish and maintain their own forms of government. The Guarantee Clause, therefore, implies a modest restraint on federal power to interfere with state autonomy."[60]

Merritt directs much of her argument at preserving a realm of state autonomy from federal government intrusion—such as the federal rules thrust on the states

---

[54] See Chemerinsky 1994 at 869 and n. 83.

[55] See Mark Tushnet, *The New Constitutional Order* (Princeton Univeristy Press, 2003).

[56] See *United States v. Lopez*, 514 U.S. 549 (1995); *United States v. Morrison*, 529 U.S. 598 (2000).

[57] *Seminole Tribe v. Florida*, 517 U.S. 44 (1996); *Alden v. Maine*, 527 U.S. 706 (1999).

[58] Laurence H. Tribe, *American Constitutional Law* 910–11 (3d ed., Foundation Press, 2000).

[59] Merritt 1988; see also Deborah Jones Merritt, *Republican Governments and Autonomous States: A New Role for the Guarantee Clause*, 65 U. Colo. L. Rev. 815–33 (1994).

[60] Merritt 1988 at 2.

regarding disposal of low-level nuclear waste at issue in the *New York v. United States* case. Merritt also believes that the clause may limit the ability of Congress to bar states from enacting voter qualification requirements like literacy tests or to require states to lowering the voting age to eighteen.[61] She recognizes, however, that there is tension between her argument that the Guarantee Clause limits power in this area and the Supreme Court's interpretation of the Equal Protection Clause to allow Congress to regulate the franchise to assure equal representation.

Lest anyone dismiss Merritt's attempt to turn the Guarantee Clause into a sword to be used by states against the federal government, the argument has been taken very seriously in Tribe's influential constitutional law treatise.[62] More importantly, Justice O'Connor cited Merritt's article in her majority opinion in *New York v. United States.*[63] *New York* featured a Guarantee Clause argument *advanced by a state* against the *federal government.* The claim was that federal laws on nuclear waste disposal infringed too much on New York's sovereign prerogative to make its own laws. The *New York* majority indicated its willingness to reconsider the justiciability question, though it found no Guarantee Clause problem in the particular case. Indeed, it is much easier to imagine the current conservative Court using the Guarantee Clause to advance the cause of federalism than to expand the scope of individual political rights.

This is not to say that Merritt's argument *should* be accepted by the Court; it should not. On its face, Merritt's claim is as plausible an interpretation as Linde's or Abrams' about how a court might interpret the Guarantee Clause. All of these authors bolster their arguments by citing selected tidbits from the Federalist Papers and other sources ostensibly showing the founders' intent in drafting the Guarantee Clause. Such attempts have led to serious questioning as to whether the authors have accurately described original intent of the clause's framers.[64]

But the argument against Merritt goes beyond originalism. As Abrams points out, subsequent amendments to the Constitution, including the Civil War Amendments, changed the nature of the federal-state relationship to give greater power to the federal government.[65] More importantly, there is far from social consensus that a state loses its "republican" character when the federal government imposes mandates upon it in its otherwise lawful exercise of powers. To accept Merritt's argument is to ossify and entrench the meaning of the Guarantee Clause as much as it would be to accept Linde's or Abrams' arguments; the clause should not be put

---

[61] See *Oregon v. Mitchell,* 400 U.S. 112 (1970).

[62] Tribe at 908–12.

[63] At 185.

[64] See, e.g., Robert G. Natelson, *A Republic, Not a Democracy? Initiative, Referendum and the Constitution's Guarantee Clause,* 80 Texas L. Rev. 807–57 (2002) [disputing Linde's historical claims]; Akhil Reed Amar, *The Central Meaning of Republican Government: Popular Sovereignty, Majority Rule, and the Denominator Problem,* 65 U. Colo. L. Rev. 749–86 (1994) [same]; Robert F. Nagel, *Terminator 2,* 65 U. Colo. L. Rev. 843–47 (1994) [disputing Merritt's historical claims].)

[65] Abrams at 836–38.

into the hands of the judiciary as another tool to regulate politics on a national scale.

Conclusion

Back in 1789, there was good reason to include the Guarantee Clause in the Constitution: to provide the federal government with power to send an army to prevent states from becoming monarchies or lapsing into civil war. Whether the clause's drafters intended the clause to give the federal government the power to regulate state politics further (or, as Merritt has argued, to limit federal government intervention in state governance) and whether the drafters intended the federal courts to play a role in enforcing the clause remain important questions of historical debate.

Writing at the beginning of the 21st century, there seems little social benefit in making the Guarantee Clause justiciable. We already have a wide and deep equal protection jurisprudence to protect minorities from laws that trample on their rights. *Romer v. Evans* provides a good example. In *Evans*, voters passed an initiative purporting to deny homosexuals any "special rights." Plaintiffs challenged the law on equal protection grounds. The Supreme Court held the law violated equal protection as wholly irrational: "A law declaring that in general it shall be more difficult for one group of citizens than for all others to seek aid from the government is itself a denial of equal protection of the laws in the most literal sense."[66] The Guarantee Clause is simply unnecessary to protect minority rights.[67]

Nor is there any pressing need to craft federalism arguments out of the Guarantee Clause in a further effort to protect the states from the federal government. The Supreme Court has created ample doctrine in the last decade to rework the federal-state relationship. Part of the reason a Guarantee Clause claim was unnecessary in *New York v. United States* was that the Supreme Court struck down one of the federal laws as a Tenth Amendment violation. It is not clear what important state rights might be protected by the Guarantee Clause that are not already protected by the Court's existing interpretation of the Constitution.

To be sure, there might be a case where the Guarantee Clause would come in handy to a Court intent on reaching a particular result. But the Court should resist the urge to expand judicial power yet again with the empty vessel of "republican government." The history of the Equal Protection Clause shows how much awesome power a judicially activist Supreme Court—liberal or conservative—can find in vague phrase.

---

[66] *Romer v. Evans*, 517 U.S. 620 (1996), 633.
[67] Cf. Linde 1994 at 727 (arguing that a Guarantee Clause challenge should have preceded the equal protection challenge in *Evans* on grounds that "logically" issues of process should precede issues of substance.).

Two Centuries of Changing Political Questions in Cultural Context[1]

Nada Mourtada-Sabbah and John W. Fox[2]

This chapter explores how government mirrors contemporaneous cultural values and sentiment in applying the political question doctrine. Changes in the national culture are reflected in new meanings, interpretations, and applications of the political question doctrine. After establishing the initial cultural setting and meaning of the doctrine at the onset of the Republic, the chapter examines new interpretations at roughly generational intervals (thirty years), down to the present day.

This chapter thus presents a longitudinal analysis of contentious social contexts when the political question doctrine was upheld and when it exceeded the intended limited authority. Then, legal rulings were the "weather vanes" of society as basic economic, political, and ideological relations crosscutting the Republic changed. Throughout the span of U.S. history, the scope of the political question doctrine broadened to deal with new factors: the growth of the Republic across the

---

[1] This chapter draws in part on a CRS Report to Congress authored by Louis Fisher and Nada Mourtada-Sabbah, "Is War Power a Political Question?" September 2000.

[2] Nada Mourtada-Sabbah is Associate Professor of Political Science and Chair, Department of International Studies, American University of Sharjah (AUS), and Visiting Professor of Public Law at the University of Paris II. John W. Fox is Professor of Political Anthropology at AUS.

vast North American continent during the first century and the extension of U.S. economic and political interests abroad during the second century.

When the states formed a confederation, powers were apportioned in the Constitution to unite the thirteen states into a union while preserving some of their sovereign powers. The three branches of the federal government were designed as both separate and equal, with checks and balances to ensure an inherent equality. In analyzing the two centuries of the political question doctrine being applied and contested, it should be borne in mind that the executive could not consistently impose his will over Congress or vice versa. Institutions with their legal interpretations change to remain adaptive; and the Constitution, with its built-in ambiguities, has proven surprisingly resilient and flexible in serving a society that has radically transformed from agrarian to industrial to postindustrial/global.

At the onset of the Republic, objectives of concern for the collectivity of states were placed under federal authority. The states encoded in the Constitution a union in which the federal government was only empowered to carry out policies of mutual concern in arenas beyond the individual state boundaries, such as protecting economic ventures abroad or threats at home by foreign forces. Thus, the thirteen once autonomous states, confederated to achieve mutually agreeable benefits, especially to defend possible encroachments by the British, French, and Spanish forces ensconced in colonies surrounding the newly independent and militarily vulnerable Republic.

Throughout much of the early Republic, the egalitarian American folk mores of largely independent farmers resonated with the constitutionally balanced though separate powers of the executive, legislature, and judiciary. With a healthy suspicion of powers being held by one person, such as the president, the federal courts ruled against war-making ventures even with the implicit compliance of Congress. During these two centuries the courts sometimes curtailed the excesses of war-making activities by the political branches when they impinged upon civil liberties of individual citizens. Many of these cases involved persons engaged in entrepreneurial activities related to the war efforts in which the courts ruled in favor of the rights of the individuals. Thus, the rights of individuals were deemed to supersede particular executive actions. As stated in the Preamble to the Constitution and in the Declaration of Independence, the nation existed for the pursuit of happiness by its citizenry, which was interpreted to involve the quest for wealth in general, and thus commercial interests beyond the shores of the nation.

The inherent balance between the branches reflects symmetry in process in their concurring on the legality of federal actions. Political questions were actions by the executive that the courts decided not to settle, leaving them as prerogatives of the elected branches to define. In 1803, Chief Justice Marshall recognized in *Marbury v. Madison* that some discretionary actions by the elected branches lie outside the scope of judicial review. Marshall argued that the Constitution invested the president "with certain important political powers, in the exercise of which he is to use his own discretion, and is accountable only to his country in his political character, and to his own conscience."[3] Political subjects "respect the nation, not individual rights, and being entrusted to the executive, the decision of the executive is conclusive."[4] Political questions submitted to the president "can never be made in this court."[5] In this line of reasoning, war-making was a collective concern requiring the endorsement of the states through Acts of War passed by their representatives in Congress. The decision to take the country from a state of peace to a state of war rested first with the legislative branch and is to be carried out by the executive branch. Courts ideally protected the legislative prerogative against encroachment by the executive.[6] Nevertheless, as a practical concern, the executive as commander in chief came to be allowed flexibility to pursue small-scale foreign military forays (e.g., the "defensive" foray against the Barbary Pirates). These actions became legal precedents for later political prerogatives.

It remained constitutionally undefined whether one limited foreign policy initiative is discretionary of the executive or of the legislature. In any event, the judiciary defers in these instances to the judgment of the elected or political branches of government. The doctrine came to function well with its intended ambiguity in limited actions. However, as conflicts progressed from small operations under presidential directive to full-blown wars, the constitutionality of the action came to be challenged. We argue that it was during times of rapid social change, when cultural norms were redefined, that the legality in applying the doctrine was most often adjudicated. Yet, many political episodes were sufficiently ambiguous to require judicial review within the cultural meanings of the times. The federal courts evaluated if the action was constitutional and how much latitude the agents of government or the law enforcement bodies could assume in carrying out their duties.

American Society Industrializes and Political Questions Change

The law is an artifact of society. As society changed, so did its legal meanings. In order to understand how the law was interpreted, we need to understand the specific society it served. We may conceptualize the United States as manifesting several thresholds of social change, which correlate with episodes of judicial reinterpretation: (1) when American society metamorphosed from agrarianism to industrialism (ca. 1860s), and (2) when society changed from industrialism to globalism (ca. 1973–1980s).

Early contestations of the political question doctrine arose from armed conflicts as the nation expanded west during its first century (1790–1890s). However,

---

[3] *Marbury v. Madison*, 5 U.S. (1 Cr.) 137, 164 (1803).

[4] *Id.*

[5] *Id.* at 170.

[6] Louis Fisher, *Presidential War Power* (2d ed., University Press of Kansas, 2004), 17–32.

with World Wars I and II, the challenges took on an international cast. Only after the Korean War, in *Baker v. Carr* (1962), did the Supreme Court offer broad guidelines for the types of issues better left to the political branches: (1) when the Constitution textually commits an issue to another branch, (2) the lack of "judicially discoverable and manageable standards for resolving"[7] the dispute, (3) the impossibility of deciding a matter "without an initial policy determination of a kind clearly for nonjudicial discretion,"[8] (4) the impossibility of a court resolving an issue without expressing a lack of respect for another branch, (5) "an unusual need for unquestioning adherence to a political decision already made,"[9] and (6) "the potentiality of embarrassment from multifarious pronouncements by various departments on one question."[10]

A legal, political, and cultural turn during the 1960s and early 1970s stemming from the forces of globalism challenged the existing structures of social institutions that were spawned during the Enlightenment. The Vietnam conflict could be interpreted within these broad changing social, political, and economic milieux. This broad shift was accompanied by more widespread applications of the political question doctrine. Since the early 1980s, coincident with the emergence of a single global economy, presidents have increasingly exercised warmaking directives. The federal government took on the function of safeguarding the global market. This position profoundly departed from the isolationist outlook of U.S. policies before the world wars. Modified economic and political forces converged to render a new social contract *vis-à-vis* the private sector, with new functions of foreign intervention assumed by the executive.[11]

Legal rulings are often challenged at generational intervals of twenty-five to thirty years. It takes about three decades for a generational cohort to come into leadership roles, and then about thirty years more to reach the point when it steps aside and makes way for the next generation. The next cohort takes over bearing its own cultural meanings.

Historical sociologist Immanuel Wallerstein argues for the approximately thirty-year social periods from 1914 until about 1943 and again to 1973.[12] Projecting this formula back, we can estimate that earlier generational changes ran roughly from 1794–1824, 1824–1854, 1854–1884, and 1884–1914. These periods correspond to heightened litigation over the political doctrine. Broad changes in the design of artifacts—such as houses, gravestones, and clothing fashion—also seem to change at generational intervals. Material culture thus provides an additional index of cultural change. In this sense, legal rulings are cultural artifacts of their times.

---

[7] *Baker v. Carr*, 369 U.S. 186, 217 (1962).

[8] 369 U.S. 186, 217 (1962).

[9] *Id.*

[10] 369 U.S. 186, 217 (1962).

[11] As argued by Francis Fukuyama, *The End of History and the Last Man* (London: Hamish Hamilton, 1992).

[12] Immanuel Wallerstein, *The End of the World as We Know It*, (University of Minnesota Press, 1999).

Our method of analysis follows anthropological structuralism (e.g.,Emile Durkheim, Claude Levi Strauss), in which legal rulings are either complementary or out of step with broad structures of society. For example, government and law tend to exhibit more balance or symmetry in their organizational setup in societies with mechanical solidarity.[13] Alternatively, if the law reflects balance and symmetry (e.g., all citizens ought to be equal before the law) but the society is heavily stratified and is one with organic solidarity, then social imbalance results. In another line of reasoning, if the executive exerts unilateral power in making war, which is a structural imbalance in the tripartite governmental arrangement, then a basic legal asymmetry results.[14]

Generation One, ca. 1790s–1820s: Balance and Symmetry in Government as in the Nature of the Enlightenment

The democracies of America and France circa 1789 embodied the assumptions of the Enlightenment in their constitutionally encoded principles and in the governments designed to carry them out. That is, government was by the people, who asserted inalienable rights. The philosophies of Locke, Rousseau, and Voltaire about humankind's place within the natural order called for citizens to govern in an inherent balance of humanity and nature, not for kings to make unilateral decisions as mandates from heaven. Wealth was availed to the common man within his national territory (as espoused by Hume) and not as directed from above by a king. This was a significant departure or structural realignment from the prevailing cosmology of the time, which had a fixed hierarchic order running from all beings up to the king as "God's appointed agent on earth," and then to God. In political views, citizens were to be self-employed workers (mechanical solidarity). Artefacts and communities manifested a similar symmetry in design. In the United States, the executive and legislature were elected by the citizenry. Checks and balances prevented one branch from distorting this basic symmetry of authority. The judiciary was appointed by the executive and confirmed by the legislature to maintain the inherent balance. Throughout society from 1760 on, houses, gravestones, gardens, food preparation, song, and religion exhibit basic symmetry in design. Not unlike the three forms of government, "a Georgian house is rigorously symmetrical, and left and right halves are appended to a central element."[15]

Symmetry organized the cosmos, society, and government. As the harbinger of "enlightened" reasoning, Isaac Newton first explained the physical symmetry

[13] Mechanical solidarity relates to society where there are people with similar statuses, roles, and jobs.
[14] Please bear in mind that these are broad categories of a structuralist argument and are presented for heuristic reasons.
[15] Henry Glassie, *Folk Architecture of Middle Virginia* (Knoxville: University of Tennessee Press, 1976).

of the universe by the natural laws of physics (e.g., for every action there is an equal reaction).[16] The basic symmetrical design in material culture and in political cosmology appeared in America by the 1760s, so that social and cultural change precipitated the quest for a "symmetry-like" government in the American War of Independence.[17] From this structuralist perspective, social changes precipitated political changes sought by war so that war was an attempt to realign the form of government with the structure of society.

In the year 1800, when the political question doctrine was first questioned, some eighty percent of the working population was self-employed bespeaking basic social structural egalitarianism.[18] As previously mentioned, this is mechanical solidarity—a community of fairly similar economic pursuits first characterized by Emile Durkheim (1893). Durkheim contrasts this economic sameness with the economic and social interdependencies of industrial society, which he termed *organic solidarity*. During much of the first century, the basic social fabric was largely mechanical with autonomous farmers or independent businesses. By contrast, only about six percent of the workforce is presently self-employed, with upwards of ninety percent working for large organizations (i.e., firms, government).

Early in the Republic, the political question stemmed from an inherent ambiguity when American commercial interests extended outside of the national borders of the U.S. and nevertheless represented the interest of its citizens to pursue wealth and happiness. These interests were threatened outside of the United States in foreign ports of call. Shipping by New England merchants was seized by privateers or by the British navy (which led to the War of 1812). John Adams tried to invoke presidential prerogatives in seizing private ships sailing to and from French ports. The Supreme Court—wary of use of unbridled presidential powers—decided against the president in this case.[19]

With the Neutrality Act of 1794, Congress prohibited American citizens from engaging in private military expeditions against "a foreign prince or state, with whom the United States are at peace."[20] This act was challenged by Col. William S. Smith, who was indicted for military actions against Spain. Smith claimed that his action "was begun, prepared, and set in foot with the knowledge and the approbation of the executive."[21] While Americans have liberties of individual action, they must abide by statutes enacted by Congress. The ultimate authority is the will of the representatives of the people and thus of the common good. A circuit court

---

[16] *Philosophiae Naturalis Principia Matematica* (1687).

[17] From a structuralist standpoint, the American Revolutionary War paralleled the English Civil War earlier and the French Revolution (1789) in which the *ancien regime* (monarchy, aristocracy, and gentry) were disempowered by an alliance of largely self-employed merchants, craftsmen, and yeomen farmers/peasantry.

[18] Bureau of Labor Statistics, U.S. Department of Labor, *Employment and Earnings* 46, no. 1 (2000).

[19] *Little v. Barreme*, 2 Cr. (6 U.S.) 170 (1804).

[20] 1 Stat. 384, § 7 (1794).

[21] *United States v. Smith*, 27 Fed. Cas. 1192, 1229 (C.C.N.Y. 1806) (No. 16,342).

rejected Smith's argument: "The president . . . cannot . . . authorize a person to do what the law forbids."[22]

Since Congress established national policy, the president had no constitutional authority to sanction military forays by private citizens.[23] The court distinguished between the president's "defensive" power to resist invasion and Congress's "offensive" authority for military actions against foreign countries. There was "a manifest distinction between our going to war with a nation at peace, and war. . . made against us by actual invasion. . . . [I]t is the exclusive province of congress to change a state of peace into a state of war."[24] In this early reasoning, the main impetus for military action came from the legislative branch.

Neutrality gave way to hostilities with France (1794–1800). As a result of French interference with American shipping, Congress suspended commercial activities with France and enacted legislation for armed operations. The Supreme Court decided three cases between 1798 and 1800 that addressed private citizens fighting against foreign countries, seizure of enemy property, calling forth the militia, imposing duties on foreign countries during and after hostilities, and protecting American lives and property abroad.

In 1800, the Court decided a claim by Captain Tingy for compensation for recapturing a U.S. merchant ship from the French. Was Tingy entitled to compensation based on a 1799 act of Congress on ships repatriated from the "enemy"? In the absence of a formal declaration of war, were hostilities legally a war? "If *France* was an enemy, then the law [entitled Tingy] to one half of the value of the ship and cargo for salvage at the time; but if *France* was not an enemy, then no more than one-eighth can be allowed."[25] The Court ruled that the conflict was de facto a war. "War could be either declared ("perfect") or undeclared ("imperfect")."[26] In this first war power decision, the Court decided that "France was *an enemy* of the *United States*."[27]

In 1801, Captain Talbot of a U.S. warship captured a French merchant ship during legal hostilities and was in turn sued by the ship owner. The Court ruled in favor of Talbot and ascertained that "The whole powers of war being, by the constitution of the United States, vested in congress, the acts of that body can alone be resorted to as our guides in this inquiry."[28] In other words, only Congress had the authority "to determine the scope of hostilities."[29]

In the statute, Congress authorized seizing ships sailing *to* a French port. Yet, could a president, in time of war, exceed statutory authority as when President John Adams ordered the seizing of ships sailing *to and from* French ports? The

---

[22] *Id.* at 1230.

[23] *Id.* at 1228–31.

[24] *Id.* at 1230.

[25] *Bas v. Tingy*, 4 Dall. (4 U.S.) 37, 43 (1800) (emphasis in original).

[26] *Id.* at 40.

[27] *Id.* at 37 (emphasis in original).

[28] *Talbot v. Seeman*, 5 U.S. (1 Cr.) 1, 28 (1801) (emphasis added).

[29] Geoffrey S. Corn, *Presidential War Power: Do the Courts Offer Any Answers?*, 157 Mil. L. Rev. 180, 208 (1998).

Court decided against the president. Chief Justice Marshall asserted that when national policy is defined by statute, presidential "instructions cannot . . . legalize an act which without those instructions would have been a plain trespass."[30]

Generation Two, ca. 1820s –1850s: American Expansionism and Sectionalism

In the second generation of the Republic, Americans forged into the interior, and shipping expanded into the Gulf of Mexico. Political questions arose over conflicts with France and Spain, which had territorial ambitions to expand their holdings in North America beyond the Louisiana tract and Florida.

During the War of 1812, could the president call up the widely scattered militias to engage the British in Washington, D.C., or in New Orleans when easily two-thirds of American territory lay west of the Appalachian Mountains? While some industrialism began in the Northeast about 1825, most production was undertaken by self-sufficient farmers. A new regionalism pitted sectional interests and cultural traditions of the freeholder North against the "plantation South" and was symbolized in the Webster-Clay debates. The principles of federalism, premised on a society of mechanical solidarity, became increasingly strained. Were slaves "men created equal" and thus protected by the Constitution, or were they property? Yankee entrepreneurs copied and improved upon the British iron and textile industries around 1830, which caused profits in Britain to plummet and spurred the first great depression, when three million Europeans immigrated to America.[31] Immigrants provided the inexpensive labor to work the factories and build national infrastructure in the privately owned turnpikes, canals, and railroads linking parts of the immense country.

In design, the Enlightenment symmetry was replaced by Greek symbolism, which resonated with Jeffersonian-Jacksonian democracy. The pastoral Greeks were metaphoric of the democratic and mechanical ideal of land-owning free holders. Greek Revivalism designed housing (about 1825), civic architecture of courthouses, universities, and clothing. The county state and federal government buildings were built with rotundas and pillars, like those found in Greek (and Roman) architecture. Greek urns and willows decorated gravestones.[32]

New political questions arose in the context of the vast, newly settled interior. In 1827, the Supreme Court queried whether the president possessed the legal authority to suppress internal insurrections (especially slave revolts). Speaking for the Court, Justice Story wrote: "the authority to decide whether the exigency has arisen belongs exclusively to the president."[33] Yet, such discretion-

---

[30] *Little v. Barreme,* 2 Cr. (6 U.S.) 170, 179 (1804).

[31] See Eric R. Wolf, *Europe and the People Without History* (University of California Press, 1982), 291.

[32] James Deetz, *In Small Things Forgotten* (Anchor Books, 1977), 72.

[33] *Martin v. Mott,* 25 U.S. (12 Wheat.) 19, 28 (1827).

ary power of the president required the Court to evaluate the statutory policy of Congress: "Whenever a statute gives a discretionary power to any person, to be exercised by him, upon his own opinion of certain facts . . . the statute constitutes him the sole and exclusive judge of the existence of those facts."[34] Nevertheless, the Court upheld the tenet of representational democracy that only when Congress delegates to the president power to "call forth the militia" would deployment of forces rest with the commander in chief.

With the looming divide between the North and South, in 1849 the Court ruled that "in case of an insurrection in any State against the government thereof, it shall be lawful for the President of the United States . . . to call forth such number of the militia of any other State or States . . . to suppress such insurrections."[35] The power to decide whether an exigency had arisen is thus "given to the president" and reflects some centralizing of political power. Suppose the court concluded that the president had acted incorrectly: would those arrested be discharged? However, the court noted some trepidation. While Justice Taney conceded that the president could abuse his power,[36] "it would be in the power of Congress to apply the proper remedy."[37] Thus, Congress was empowered to thwart the actions of a power-usurping president, if the balance between the branches extended too far. Ultimately, they had the power of impeachment.

Further questions arose as America annexed parts of Mexico. Texas was added to the Union in 1845, and the subsequent Mexican War (1846) resulted in the grafting of the northern half of Mexico onto the United States. The boundaries of the present continental United States were finalized with the Gadsden Purchase (1853) and the addition of California. These vast new holdings raised questions about war booty, both in foreign lands and of goods destined for a foreign state during war.

A challenge in 1846 arose from duty paid on goods imported *from a foreign country*.[38] When duties were imposed upon a schooner (*Catherine*), trading with Tampico, Mexico, the Court decided whether this location was temporarily part of the United States since it was then occupied by American military forces.[39] The Court ruled that the president had no independent authority to include Tampico within the boundaries of the United States, which "can be done only by the treaty-making power or the legislative authority." The president's "duty and his power

---

[34] *Id.* at 30.

[35] *Luther v. Borden,* 48 U.S. (7 How.) 1, 43 (1849).

[36] *Id.* at 44.

[37] *Id.* at 45.

[38] 9 Stat. 42 (1846).

[39] See *Fleming v. Page,* 50 U.S. at 614.

are purely military."[40] Tampico was ruled to have been "a foreign port when this shipment was made."[41]

In another Mexican War case, Chief Justice Roger Taney granted a U.S. civilian trader damages for the seizure of his property by the U.S. Army. The Court ruled that orders of a military field officer do not justify lawful seizure. While the army might lawfully take possession of the goods to keep them from the enemy, "in order to justify the seizure the danger must be immediate and impending, and not remote or contingent."[42] Taney urged that the Court should "determine under what circumstances private property may be taken from the owner by a military officer in a time of war."[43]

In 1850, the Supreme Court restricted the discretionary powers of the commander in chief. Chief Justice Taney opined that the president "is authorized to direct the movements of the naval and military forces placed *by law* at his command."[44] The United States' occupation of Mexico did "not enlarge the boundaries of the Union, *nor extend the operation of our institutions and laws beyond the limits before assigned to them by the legislative power*."[45] No military conquest initiated by the president may annex territory to the United States; the president's power must conform to what Congress establishes *by law*.

In 1852, the Court held that "[e]very court of the United States . . . must derive its jurisdiction and judicial authority from the Constitution or the laws of the United States."[46] Neither the president nor a military officer may establish a court in a conquered country "and authorize it to decide upon the rights of the United States . . . nor to administer the laws of nations."[47]

Generation Three, ca. 1850s–1880s: The Industrial North Triumphs

The greatest crisis in American history involved how the federal government would restore the secessionist southern states to the Union. After the nation's bloodletting and forced reunification from the Civil War (1861–1865), the Calvinistic North, with its emphasis on science and industry, came to dominate the nation.[48] Following the Civil War, virtually all regions of the nation were connected by railroad as a social whole, rather than the loosely federated states of

---

[40] *Id.* at 614–15.

[41] *Id.* at 616. It is important to note that this case was decided after the hostilities were over; timing is often an important factor in determining whether the courts decide to adjudicate a case.

[42] *Mitchell v. Harmony*, 54 U.S. (13 How.) 115, 133 (1851).

[43] *Id.* at 135.

[44] *Fleming v. Page*, 50 U.S. (9 How.) 603, 615, 618 (1850) (emphasis added).

[45] *Id.* (emphasis added).

[46] *Jecker v. Montgomery*, 54 U.S. (13 How.) 498, 515 (1852).

[47] *Jecker v. Montgomery*, 54 U.S. (13 How.) 498, 515 (1852).

[48] See David Fischer, *Albion's Seed* (New York: Oxford University Press, 1989).

earlier generations. Factory-produced commodities were distributed throughout the nation as a single zone of distribution. Much of the North became urbanized with row housing adjacent to factories separated from the holders of capital in suburbia. Jeffersonian ideals of rural and small town egalitarianism were eclipsed by social asymmetry and urban social stratification. This was the economic interdependence of organic solidarity. New political questions arose from the vast new society interconnected from coast to coast. The balanced, equal parts of the early Union had given way to clear social asymmetry.

Emergency actions by President Lincoln during the Civil War, followed by military rule of the South throughout Reconstruction, raised questions of authority to conduct the war in its myriad of applications. First, was the South enemy (i.e., foreign) territory or a rebellious part of the federation? Could Lincoln suspend civil liberties without an Act of War? If independent states agreed to confederate, shouldn't they also be able to decide to disassociate? The courts repeatedly ruled that decisions by the executive outweighed claims by individuals or secessionist states. This is asymmetry in which the national institutions, seemingly guided by industrial interests, gave the executive sufficient leeway to strengthen the government.

Lincoln's proclamation of April 1861, which blockaded the southern ports, was contested. The litigants also claimed that Lincoln had exceeded his constitutional authority by seizing neutral vessels trading with the Confederacy; war had not been declared by Congress.[49] The Supreme Court ruled that secession constituted war and that the use of force to counter this military challenge came from the Constitution. The magnitude of the conflict outweighed "a technical ignorance of the existence of a war, which all the world acknowledges to be the greatest civil war known in the history of the human race, and . . . [to] cripple the arm of the Government and paralyze its power by subtle definitions and ingenious sophisms."[50] "If a war be made by invasion of a foreign nation, the President is not only authorized but bound to resist force by force. He does not initiate the war, but is bound to accept the challenge *without waiting for any special legislative authority.*"[51] With the exigencies of the moment aside, though, the president has "no power to initiate or declare a war either against a foreign nation or a domestic State."[52]

Early in the war (1861), Attorney General Bates advised that he would suspend the writ of habeas corpus during the rebellion since the executive "is especially charged by the Constitution with the 'public safety,' and he is the sole judge of the emergency which requires his prompt action."[53] Which branch was to de-

---

[49] *The Prize Cases,* 67 U.S. (2 Black) 635 (1863).

[50] *Id.* at 669–71.

[51] *Id.* at 668 (emphasis added)

[52] *Id.*

[53] Op. Att'y Gen. 74, 90 (1861). "The power to do these things," the opinion goes on to say, "is in the hand of the President, placed there by the Constitution and the statute law, as a sacred trust, to be used by him, in his best discretion, in the performance of his great first duty—to preserve, protect, and defend the Constitution. And for any breach of

cide when public safety requires suspension of the writ? Had the presidency assumed inordinate powers during the crisis of union?

In a defining case, John Merryman had been imprisoned on treason and petitioned for a writ of habeas corpus, which was issued. In delivering the writ the federal marshal was denied access to the fort where Merryman was incarcerated, even though Chief Justice Taney ruled that the authority of suspending the writ belonged to Congress and not to the president.[54] Unable to enforce his order, Taney concluded that his judicial power was "resisted by a force too strong for me to overcome."[55] Taney asked Lincoln to "determine what measures he will take to cause the civil process of the United States to be respected and enforced."[56]

Since the Constitution bestowed upon Congress the power to raise and support an army and provide and maintain a navy, were the court-martials during the Civil War lawful? The authority for courts martial derives from Congress, which did not declare war.[57] If persons are subjected to "illegal or irresponsible courts martial," civil courts will give proper redress.[58] In the case of one seaman, the Court concluded that the naval court had jurisdiction.[59]

In *Ex parte Vallandigham* (1864), Clement L. Vallandigham contended that he could not be tried by a military court.[60] The Supreme Court cited a procedural flaw to decline a review of this military trial. Justice Wayne held that "[t]he appellate powers of the Supreme Court . . . are limited and regulated by the acts of Congress, and must be exercised subject to the exceptions and regulations made by Congress. . . . The petition . . . [is] not to be within the letter or spirit of the grants of appellate jurisdiction to the Supreme Court."[61]

However, in *Ex parte Benedict*, a district court ruled that the president could not suspend the writ unless authorized by Congress.[62] The court warned that "once it were left in the power of any, of the highest magistrate, to imprison whomever he or his officers thought proper . . . there would soon be an end of

---

that trust he is responsible before the high court of impeachment, and before no other human tribunal." *Id.* at 91.

[54] *Ex parte Merryman*, 17 Fed. Cas. 144, 148 (C.C.Md. 1861) (No. 9,487) at 148.

[55] *Id.* at 153

[56] *Id.*

[57] *Dynes v. Hoover*, 61 U.S. (20 How.) 79, 81.

[58] *Id.* at 81.

[59] *Id.* at 83–84.

[60] 1 Wall. (68 U.S.) 243 (1864).

[61] *Id.* at 251. "Whatever may be the force of Vallandigham's protest, that he was not triable by a court of military commission," Justice Wayne goes on to say, "it is certain that his petition cannot be brought within the 14th section of the [Judiciary Act of 1789]; and further, that the court cannot, without disregarding its frequent decisions and interpretation of the Constitution in respect to its judicial power, originate a writ of certiorari to review or pronounce an opinion upon the proceedings of a military commission." *Id.* at 251–52.

[62] *Ex parte Benedict*, 3 Fed. Cas. 159 (D.N.Y. 1862) (No. 1,292).

all rights and immunities."[63] Chief Justice Taney's decision in *Ex parte Merryman* was sufficient "to show that the power of suspension is a legislative and not an executive power."[64]

In 1862, a circuit court held that the War Department could not suspend the writ of habeas corpus, although President Lincoln had properly proclaimed martial law and suspended the writ on September 24, 1862.[65] *Martin v. Mott* and *Luther v. Borden* sustained the president's power to suspend the writ during martial law.[66] As to whether martial law was justified, "this is a question for the president, not for the court, to determine."[67]

New legal meanings were established after the court overturned the decision in *Ex parte Bollman* (1807) that only Congress can suspend the writ. As to *Ex parte Merryman* and *Ex parte Benedict*, the court noted that "both cases came up on an entirely different state of facts from that which now exists. The president had not then proclaimed martial law, and . . . the privilege of the writ may be legally suspended without an act of congress."[68] In sum, during the most threatening year of the Civil War, the president was able to marshal unusual power.

In 1863, two district courts upheld Lincoln's suspension of the writ as "valid and efficient in law."[69] Citing the act of Congress of March 3, 1863, one district judge stated: "That during the present Rebellion, the President of the United States, whenever in his judgment the public safety may require it, is authorized to suspend the privilege of the writ of habeas corpus in any case throughout the United States."[70] This granted complete statutory authority: "No case is excepted."[71]

After the hostilities ceased, the Court ameliorated its views. In *Ex parte Milligan* (1866), the suspending of due process for noncombatants is not permissible where the civilian courts are available.[72] A decade later (1876), the Court

---

[63] *Id.* at 163. Based on a precedent in Great Britain that Parliament alone could authorize the crown to suspend the habeas corpus act.

[64] *Id.* at 165. In *Ex parte Bollman* (1807), the Court declared that the Constitution had vested the right of suspending the privilege of the writ of habeas corpus exclusively in Congress, and that body was the sole judge of the necessity that triggered the suspension. Said Chief Justice Marshall: "If at any time the public safety should require the suspension of the powers vested by this act in the courts of the United States, it is for the legislature to say so. The question depends upon political considerations, on which the legislature is to decide. Until the legislative will be expressed, this court can only see its duty, and must obey the laws." 4 Cranch (8 U.S.) 75, 101 (1807). Building on the argument in *Ex parte Bollman* (1807), the judge concluded that the president, without authority from Congress, had no constitutional authority to suspend the writ.

[65] *Ex parte Field*, 9 Fed. Cas. 1 (C.C.Vt. 1862) (No. 4,761).

[66] *Id.* at 8.

[67] *Id.*

[68] *Id.* at 9.

[69] *In re Dunn*, 8 Fed. Cas. 93 (S.D.N.Y. 1863) (No. 4,171).

[70] *In re Fagan*, 8 Fed. Cas. 947, 949 (D. Mass. 1863) (No. 4,604).

[71] *Id.*

[72] *Ex parte Milligan*, 71 U.S. (4 Wall.) 2 (1866).

struck down a military order that annulled a decree by a civil court as "an arbitrary stretch of authority."[73] Once peace had resumed, the "unbending rule of law, [overrides] . . . the exercise of military power, where the rights of the citizen are concerned [and] shall never be pushed beyond what the exigency requires."[74]

The priority of civil law over military authority was invoked in an 1866 review of a trial by military commission in South Carolina.[75] Significantly, because the Confederate army had surrendered seven months before the trial, the court held on habeas corpus that the conviction was illegal. The military tribunal lacked jurisdiction, since the civil courts were in the full exercise of their judicial functions at the time of the trial.[76]

However, in shifting from executive/military authority to congressional/ statutory authority in the occupied South, ambiguities persisted. When the state of Mississippi sought to enjoin President Andrew Johnson in 1867 from enforcing two Reconstruction Acts, the Court invoked the political question doctrine. Chief Justice Chase rejected the claim that the Court lacked jurisdiction to enjoin President Johnson from carrying out the Reconstruction statutes. The president's duties were "purely executive and political,"[77] lying outside of "judicial interference with the exercise of Executive discretion."[78] The Court avoided the noncompliance of the president by claiming no jurisdiction.[79]

In 1870, the Supreme Court decided whether Congress, in enacting the Legal Tender Acts of 1862,[80] possessed the power to render U.S. notes "legal tender in payment of all debts . . . to carry on war."[81] It decided that Congress had acted unconstitutionally: "An expedient of this sort is [not] an appropriate . . . means for the execution of the power to . . . carry on war."[82] However, a year later the Court reversed itself.[83] The "weather vane of the law" was pressured by ex-General Grant, who had by then become president.

---

[73] *Raymond v. Thomas,* 91 U.S. 712, 716 (1876).

[74] *Id.*

[75] *Ex parte Milligan,* 71 U.S. (4 Wall.) 2 (1866).

[76] 71 U.S. 2, 61. In 1868, a district court held that Dr. Samuel A. Mudd could be tried by military commission as being an accessory to the murder of President Abraham Lincoln. Mudd's grandson contested the ruling to clear his grandfather's name. In 1998, a district judge held that the Assistant Secretary of the Army was "arbitrary and capricious" under the Administrative Procedure Act for failing to address certain arguments raised by Mudd's grandson. See *Ex parte Mudd,* 17 Fed. Cas. 954 (No. 9, 899) (D. Fla. 1868); *Mudd v. Caldera,* 26 F. Supp. 2d 113, 117 (D.D.C. 1998), and *Mudd v. Caldera,* 134 F. Supp. 2d 138 (D.D.C. 2001).

[77] *Mississippi v. Johnson,* 71 U.S. (4 Wall.) 475, 499 (1867).

[78] *Id.*

[79] *Id.* at 501.

[80] 12 Stat. 345, 370 (1862).

[81] *Hepburn v. Griswold,* 75 U.S. (8 Wall.) 603, 616–17 (1870).

[82] *Id.* at 621.

[83] *Legal Tender Cases,* 12 Wall. 457 (1871). In 1863, the Court had declined to tackle an issue arising from the Legal Tender Acts; adopting a narrow construction of

Taken together, are the beginnings and endings of war political questions? During these especially dire circumstances, the political factor takes precedence over the normative questions to pursue business under constitutional liberties and guarantees.

In 1870, in order to determine whether southerners were entitled, by the act of Congress of March 2, 1867, to reimbursement for their land sold by the federal forces during the war, the Supreme Court first established when the war had ceased. In a civil or domestic war, "some public proclamation or legislation would seem to be required."[84] It also noted that Congress "has [retroactively] determined that the rebellion closed the 20th day of August, 1866," (although histories generally consider the surrender by General Lee in 1865 the end of the Civil War).[85]

In 1872, the Court held that a public act by the elected branches fixed the beginning and ending dates of wars. In legitimizing the temporal parameters of the Civil War, the Court ruled that "The executive department . . . was, at the commencement of hostilities, obliged to act during the recess of Congress, [and this action] must be taken [as the reference date]."[86] Then, Lincoln's proclamation of the blockade legally began the war, while another proclamation ended it.[87] Yet, since the war did not begin or end at the same time in all the states, the Court decided to take the proclamations of blockade as ascertaining the commencement of "official hostilities."[88] Similarly, the termination of war was ascertained by two presidential proclamations.[89]

Generation Four, 1890s –1920s: National Interests Abroad

The 1890s saw a shift to economic expansion abroad in the quest for raw materials and markets. After the second great depression (1876–1880s), American steel production ranked first in the world.[90] Historians characterize the end of the agrarian demographic push west, when the Great Plains were settled in the 1890s, as the "end of frontier."[91] At this threshold, a revised cosmology of "manifest destiny" was redirected beyond the continent. The Spanish-American War of 1897 was the nation's first war outside of continental North America, and it signalled the entry of the U.S. into competition with the European indus-

---

section 25 of the Judiciary Act of 1789, it held that it lacked jurisdiction. *Roosevelt v. Meyer*, 1 Wall. 512, 517 (1863).

[84] *United States v. Anderson*, 76 U.S. (9 Wall.) 56, 70–71 (1870).

[85] *Id.* at 71.

[86] *The Protector*, 12 Wall. 700, 702 (1872).

[87] *Id.*

[88] *Id.*

[89] *Id.*

[90] Wolf, *Europe and the People Without History*, 311–13.

[91] Frederick Jackson Turner, *The Frontier in American History* (1893).

trial powers for international resources and markets.[92] The shift to extending American interests abroad was inconsistent with the ethos of citizens defending the natural territory, as envisioned in the Constitution. It took a full generation— until after World War II—to fully integrate the new nonisolationism into the national ideology as political questions.

In 1901, the Court held that the president may govern newly acquired territories by the "laws of war."[93] This significantly departed from rulings during the Civil War. Duties could be legally imposed by the military on goods shipped from the United States to Puerto Rico. The Court ruled that the duties were valid during war, whereas those collected after peace was ratified were unlawful.[94] After the peace treaty, Puerto Rico was entitled to free entry "until Congress otherwise constitutionally directed."[95]

The Court also considered whether the U.S. seizure of a Spanish-owned vessel was lawful. To decide if the enemy had used the vessel for war purposes, the Court determined that the war did not cease until the ratifications of the treaty in April 1899, and this dismissed the presidential proclamation ending the war in August 1898. [96] A suspension of hostilities "does not terminate the war, but . . . suspends its operations."[97] Since the ship owner's claim arose before the exchange of ratifications, damages were not awarded, so that presidential decree was overridden.[98] American participation in World War I forever changed the relationship

---

[92] With a shift to a broad-based industrial economy by the 1880s throughout the upper Midwest, factory-produced commodities began to be marketed abroad and international competition for resources, colonies, and markets resulted in foreign wars. The United States surpassed both Britain and Germany in steel production by the late 1880s (Wolf at 312). The Spanish American War of 1898 is seen as one of the imperial aggrandizements, when the U.S. acquired Cuba, Puerto Rico, the Philippines, and Guam.

[93] *Dooley v. United States,* 182 U.S. 222, 231 (1901).

[94] *Id.* at 234.

[95] *Id.* at 235, 236. In a case arising from the Mexican War, the Court decided that military commanders could impose duties on imports during the conquest, but after the treaty such duties are illegal. The power of Congress to make rules and regulations respecting territory belonging to the U.S. prevailed over military decisions. *Cross v. Harrison,* 57 U.S. (16 How.) 164 (1854).

[96]*Hijo v. United States,* 194 U.S. 315, 323 (1904).

[97] *Id.* (citing Kent's Commentaries).

[98] At about the same time, President McKinley sent 5,000 U.S. troops to China in 1900 to protect threatened American citizens and intents. (Fred Hamilton was a U.S. serviceman found guilty of murder by a military court, under the 58th article of war, which required that a general court martial be assembled in "time of war." A circuit court in Arkansas had therefore to determine whether the Boxer Rebellion was a war.) While the president declared this initiative to "involve no war against the Chinese nation," (13 Messages and Papers of the Presidents 6423 (December 3, 1900) the court noted that "the existence of a condition of war must be determined by the political department of the government; that the courts take judicial notice of such determination and are bound thereby." (*Hamilton v. McClaughry,* 136 Fed. 445, 449 (C.C. Kan. 1905). While a formal declaration of war "is an unnecessary . . . condition of war," to recognize "a condition of war" by Congress, the "payment to the officers and men . . . there . . . (was) on a war

between political questions and the defense of national territory. In reviewing cases from this first multination war in a foreign theatre, the Supreme Court declared that "[t]he war power of the United States, like its other powers and like the police power of the States, is subject to applicable constitutional limitations."[99] Cases concerned the use of the war power to control private economic activity (rates, prices, and rents), to seize enemy-held property, and to prohibit the trafficking in liquor.

Even after the armistice, Congress prohibited the sale of liquor, under the guise of demobilization.[100] Liquor companies sued, charging that the statute was inoperative and was intended for domestic electioneering. The companies argued that the Constitution does not confer police powers upon Congress, and that its power to regulate the traffic in liquors must be found in "the implied war powers."[101] The companies argued that between the dates of enactment and the lawsuits "hostilities would not be resumed; [and] that demobilization had been effected; that thereby the war emergency ceased [and] . . . the statute became void."[102] However, in a second case, the Court sustained the statute that "Congress has the power 'to make all laws which shall be necessary . . . in the Federal Government."[103] "Since Congress has power to increase war efficiency by prohibiting the liquor traffic . . . it should [not] be denied the power to make its prohibition effective."[104]

Other war-related cases concerned governmental controls of pricing. The Lever Act of 1917 stipulated criminal penalties for companies that charged "unjust or unreasonable"[105] rates or exacted "excessive prices."[106] The Cohen Grocery Company sued, objecting that the law was ambiguous and could not be equitably enforced, especially since the country was then at peace.[107] Since the Supreme

---

basis." The engagement in armed hostilities thus was "as with intent of the fifty-eighth article of war." In this case, thus, de facto hostilities took precedence over a formal and legal declaration. *Id.*

While the president declared this initiative to "involve no war against the Chinese nation," the court noted that "the existence of a condition of war must be determined by the political department of the government; the courts take judicial notice of such determination and are bound thereby." While a formal declaration "is an unnecessary condition of war," to recognize "a condition of war" by Congress, the "payment to the officers and men there . . . (was) on a war basis." The engagement in armed hostilities thus was "as with intent of the fifty-eighth article of war." In this case, thus, de facto hostilities took precedence over a formal and legal declaration.

[99] *Hamilton v. Kentucky Distilleries Co.*, 251 U.S. at 146, 156 (1919).

[100] 40 Stat. 1046 (1918).

[101] *Hamilton v. Kentucky Distilleries Co.*, 251 U.S. at 155.

[102] *Id.* at 159.

[103] *Ruppert v. Caffey*, 251 U.S. 264, 300–01 (1920).

[104] *Id. at* 300–01.

[105] *United States v. Cohen Grocery Co.*, 255 U.S. 81, 86 (1921).

[106] *Id.*

[107] *Id.* at 86–87.

Court concluded that the "existence of a state of war"[108] could not suspend the Fifth and Sixth Amendments,[109] the Lever Act was thus "void for repugnancy to the Constitution."[110] America's traditional isolationism ended when President Wilson pressed detente and partnerships with allies. Such multilateral agreements extended the notion of confederation among war parties (countries) to the European countries on the other side of the Atlantic. From the 1920s on, most of the political questions cases involved foreign affairs. From this point forward, foreign relations was increasingly a political question.[111]

Generation Five, 1920s–1950s: World War II and Korea

The Second World War mobilized the nation after industrial capitalism had dramatically collapsed (1929–1940), and America went on to dominate the world's economic production (seventy-five percent) in the postwar years. Federal courts evaluated a variety of war power issues, including the extent to which the president could usurp statutory power to pursue the war, the detention of Japanese-Americans, and constitutional rights in military trials. The generational interval ended in the late 1950s when the "military complex-industrial complex" increasingly influenced the affairs of state and executive power during the Cold War.

In 1942, the Supreme Court decided that the military trial of eight German saboteurs was lawfully constituted. The defendants were lawfully in custody and had not shown cause for discharge by writ of habeas corpus.[112] Three months after the ruling the Court released its full opinion as *Ex parte Quirin* for the per curiam decision.[113]

In 1942, the Court upheld the government's power to "draft business organizations to support the fighting men."[114] Two years later, price-fixing by the Office of Price Administration under the Emergency Price Control Act was found legitimate, as was the rent control power of the administration.

In 1948, the Court confirmed that the executive could determine and recover excessive profiteering from the war effort. "In time of crisis nothing could be more tragic and less expressive of the intent of the people than so to construe

---

[108] *Id.* at 88–89.

[109] *Id.* at 88.

[110] *Id.* at 93.

[111] Linda Champlin and Alan Schwarz, *Political Question Doctrine and Allocation of the Foreign Affairs Power,* 13 Hofstra L. Rev. 215, 216–17 (1985): "[T]he political question doctrine . . . is thriving and growing in its application to the foreign relations power."

[112] *Ex parte Quirin,* 63 S.Ct. 1–2 (1942). The per curiam is also reproduced in a footnote in *Ex parte Quirin,* 317 U.S. 1, 18–19 (1942).

[113] *Ex parte Quirin,* 317 U.S. 1 (1942). In 1953, the Court heard the espionage case of Ethel and Julius Rosenberg, which cited *Ex parte Quirin.*

[114] *United States v. Bethlehem Steel Corp.,* 315 U.S. 289, 305 (1942).

their Constitution [so] that . . . it would substantially hinder rather than help in defending their national safety."[115] However, Justice Jackson warned about the ever-widening scope of war powers: "Particularly when the war power is invoked to do things to the liberties of the people, or to their property or economy that only indirectly affect conduct of the war and do not relate to the management of the war itself."[116] Generally, the Court deferred during the war to the political branches.

By upholding the legality of detaining 120,000 Japanese-Americans from the West Coast,[117] the Court "effectively engaged in the prudential surrender of its review power to the political branches. . . . [These cases] exercise[d] . . . the political question doctrine in everything but name."[118] "The Constitution has placed the responsibility of war-making [in the political branches of government, and] it is not for any court to sit in review of the wisdom of their action[s]."[119] In 1944, the Court upheld the constitutionality of the evacuation of Japanese-Americans and of their curfew.[120] Thus, the Court failed to independently review the facts upon which the political branches deemed the move a military necessity: "We cannot say that the war-making branches of the Government did not have ground for believing that in a critical hour such persons . . . constituted a menace to the national defense and safety."[121] In dissent, Justice Jackson offered that:

> A judicial construction of the due process clause that will sustain this order is a far more subtle blow to liberty than the promulgation of the order itself. A military order, however unconstitutional, is not apt to last longer than the military emergency. . . . But once a judicial opinion rationalizes such an order to show that it conforms to the Constitution, . . . the Court [has permanently] . . . validated the principle of racial discrimination . . . and of transplanting American citizens [in criminal procedure].[122]

The Court, nonetheless, held that the War Relocation Authority could not intern citizens whose loyalty was proven. A Japanese-American citizen whose loyalty had been verified was therefore entitled to "an unconditional release by the War Relocation Authority."[123]

---

[115] *Lichter v. United States*, 334 U.S. 742, 778–80 (1948).

[116] *Woods v. Miller Co.*, 333 U.S. 138, 146–47 (1948) (citing *Hamilton v. Kentucky Distilleries Co.*, 251 U.S. 146, 161).

[117] *Hirabayashi v. United States*, 320 U.S. 81 (1943), *Yasui v. United States*, 320 U.S. 115 (1943), and *Korematsu v. United States*, 323 U.S. 214 (1944).

[118] See Martin H. Redish, *Judicial Review and the "Political Question,"* Nw. U. L. Rev. 1031, 1032–33, 1037, 1039 (1984–85).

[119] *Hirabayashi v. United States*, 320 U.S. at 93.

[120] *Korematsu v. United States*, 323 U.S. at 217–18.

[121] *Id.* at 218.

[122] *Id.* at 246.

[123] *Ex parte Endo*, 323 U.S. 283, 304 (1944).

Following the war, the Court generally curtailed the latitude given to political questions. In 1946, the Court rejected the position of continued military rule in Hawaii.[124] The Court also ruled that the military trial of civilians unconstitutionally overrode the civil courts. Thus, during martial law, the Hawaiian Organic Act did not grant the power to substitute military proceedings for civil trials.

Nationalizing steel mills contradicted the inherent American value of pursuing wealth and happiness. Thus the unilateral decisions by the executive during the Korean conflict did not have widespread support, especially since the war did not threaten American domestic interests. In 1952, the Court decided that President Truman did not act within his constitutional purview when the Secretary of Commerce took control of most of the nation's steel mills. "Believing that a threatened strike would jeopardize national defense . . . the president was acting . . . [as] the Commander in Chief."[125] In this reasoning, the presidential power was inherent, plenary, and not subject to judicial scrutiny. Yet, negative public opinion caused this legal strategy to backfire. In popular sentiment, the government cannot nationalize the private sector.

"There was [also] a profound ambivalence on the part of much of the public about the Korean War"[126] as a foreign war on foreign soil. The government's arguments in district court challenged Truman's credibility, and populism factored in since the plaintiffs were private citizens. Justice Rehnquist remarked: "In *Youngstown*, private litigants brought a suit contesting the President's authority under his war powers to seize the Nation's steel industry. . . . Here, by contrast, we are asked to settle a dispute between coequal branches of our Government, each of which has resources available to protect and assert its interests, resources not available to private litigants outside the judicial forum."[127] The interests of private citizens prevailed over "unlimited and unrestrained Executive power."[128] Moreover, Truman's action was found to contravene the Taft-Hartley Act: "The President's order does not direct that a congressional policy be executed in a manner prescribed by Congress."[129]

Federal courts also decided whether the hostilities in Korea amounted to a "war" for validating life insurance claims, since Truman termed it a "police action." One district judge remarked: "We doubt very much if there is any question in the minds of the majority of the people of this country that the conflict now raging in Korea can be anything but war."[130] Another district judge supported a policy payment to a combatant who died as "a result of an act of war."[131] "The commitments formally made by the President, the Secretary of State and Congress

---

[124] *Duncan v. Kahanamoku*, 327 U.S. 304 (1946).

[125] *Youngstown Co. v. Sawyer*, 343 U.S. 579, 582 (1952).

[126] William H. Rehnquist, *The Supreme Court, How It Was, How It Is* (1987), 96.

[127] *Goldwater v. Carter*, 444 U.S. 996, 1004–05 (1979).

[128] *Youngstown Sheet & Tube Co. v. Sawyer*, 103 F. Supp. 569, 577 (D.D.C. 1952).

[129] *Id.* at 587–88.

[130] *Weissman v. Metropolitan Life Ins. Co.*, 112 F. Supp. 420, 425 (D. Cal. 1953).

[131] *Gagliormella v. Metropolitan Life Ins. Co.*, 122 F. Supp. 246 , 250 (D. Mass. 1954).

recognized that the Korean hostilities . . . were . . . full proportions of a war."[132] Large-scale combat financed by Congress was de facto war.

Generation Six 1960s–1990s: Executive Authority Challenged During Vietnam and Reasserted, ca. 1980

The end of the Vietnam conflict coincided with a broad shift to globalism in 1972–1973. Many of the assumptions of the Enlightenment were challenged in the political and academic worlds. New models emerged in the early 1970s to explain the new social order, such as the "world systems" approaches.[133] The authority of the executive was challenged (e.g., President Nixon was forced to resign or be impeached).

In the early 1970s, some former colonies organized economic and political blocs (e.g., OPEC, Coffee Cartel) to challenge western economic hegemony. Also contemporaneously, Milton Friedman (1972) presented the principles of the power of capital, which since have become the guiding principles of the global market. Global competition reorganized institutional and economic life. Business corporations restructured following the recession of 1974–1980 (1974 marked the largest decline in the stock market: twenty-four percent). Microchip and satellite-based telecommunications proliferated to interconnect the world market by the 1980s, and idea production (informationalism) distributed ideas of consumerism via the electronic media to a nascent global market. Computers reduced time between production and sales.[134]

The war in Southeast Asia gave rise to a number of lawsuits challenging the constitutionality of presidential authority to wage protracted hostilities in the absence of a declaration or authorization of war by Congress. During the first half of the Vietnam conflict, the courts avoided questioning the war invoking-powers of the executive. The political and cultural turnaround period was 1968–1970, when an increasingly vocal public opposition to the war was met by intensified efforts by the executive to "win with honor."

The early legal challenges were dismissed by district and appellate federal courts on grounds of (1) the political question, (2) unconsented suit against the United States, and (3) the plaintiffs lacking standing as members of the armed forces. The Supreme Court denied petitions seeking review, citing the political question doctrine. Thus, the courts implicitly supported the pursuit of the war as a political question. The federal courts noted the concurrence between the two political branches in prosecuting the war.

However, two new positions emerged between 1970 and 1973: (1) willingness to acknowledge the justiciability of the war, and (2) the increasingly nar-

---

[132] *Id.*

[133] E.g., Braudel 1973, Wallerstein 1974, Hayden White 1973.

[134] Manuel Castells, *The Rise of the Network Society* (Blackwell Publishers, 1996), 432–37.

rowed scope of the political question doctrine to reflect the increasing populist opposition to the war. As the war began to draw to a close in 1973, some courts reversed earlier opinions. One district court stated that congressional and executive actions did not constitute valid expressions of the doctrine. Another court issued an injunction to stop military involvement in Cambodia. Both rulings were reversed on appeal, however, and the Supreme Court continued to deny certiorari.

Let us now examine step-by-step the changing judicial climate throughout the Vietnam conflict, which was the nation's longest war. First, in 1967, an army private sought to enjoin military officials from sending him to Vietnam. He claimed that U.S. military action in Vietnam was unconstitutional and illegal and that the government had no lawful authority to send him there.[135] A district court dismissed the suit as "a political question . . . outside of the judicial function."[136] The courts "may not substitute themselves for the Commander in Chief . . . and determine the disposition of members of the Armed Forces."[137] On appeal, the court opined that resorting to the courts in political questions "is futile."[138]

It is difficult to think of an area less suited for judicial action than that into which Appellant would have us intrude. The fundamental division of authority and power established by the Constitution precludes judges from overseeing the conduct of foreign policy or the use and disposition of military power; these matters are plainly the exclusive province of Congress and the executive.[139]

In another case, three soldiers sought a ruling to prevent being ordered to Vietnam. The political question was affirmed per curiam by the Court of Appeals, and continued to certiorari by the Supreme Court. Justice Douglas remarked that "the suit is political is little more than a play upon words."[140] The political question doctrine was seen by some to be increasingly discordant with the body politic, whose interests the justices were sworn to protect.

In a habeas corpus case, reservists who were ordered to active duty were denied relief. When the Supreme Court denied certiorari, Justice Douglas noted that the underlying constitutional question was left unresolved: "Whenever the Chief Executive of the country takes any citizen by the neck and either puts him in prison . . . or sends him overseas to fight in a war, the question is a justiciable one."[141]

The federal courts continued their unwillingness to question the legality of the war:

---

[135] *Luftig v. McNamara*, 252 F. Supp. 819, 819 (1966).

[136] *Luftig v. McNamara*, 252 F.Supp. 819, 819 (1966).

[137] *Id.* at 821.

[138] *Luftig v. McNamara*, 373 F.2d 664, 665 (1967).

[139] *Id.* at 665–66.

[140] *Mora v. McNamara*, 387 F.2d 862 (D.C. Cir. 1967), cert. denied, 389 U.S. 934, 939 (1967).

[141] *McArthur v. Clifford*, 402 F.2d 58 (4th Cir. 1968), cert. denied, 393 U.S. 1002 (1968).

[T]his Court concludes that the distinction between a declaration of war and a co-operative action by the legislative and executive with respect to military activities in foreign countries is the very essence of what is meant by a political question. It involves just the sort of evidence, policy considerations, and constitutional principles which . . . are far more suitable for determination by coordinate branches.[142]

In 1970, an appellate court held that a plaintiff's status as a federal taxpayer did not entitle him to challenge the constitutionality of war expenditures. A general interpretation of decisions of war and peace remained outside of judicial review. The court stated, "There is a myriad of conceivable reasons why Congress might undertake a course of action which sanctions and implements executive action but which falls short of a formal declaration of war."[143] In *Orlando v. Laird*, the court ruled that if there is one political question in the fabric of government of the Republic, "it is whether or not to maintain a war. . . . Into this seamless web of national and international politics, the courts should not intrude."[144]

During the final years of the conflict, opposition to the executive increased. The earlier unequivocal stance of the courts seemed incongruent in the new social contexts. Members of Congress increasingly voiced opposition. As its sixth year began, the war was no longer simply a political question but one that seemed inconsistent with the time-honored notion of self-determination of the Vietnamese people. Thus, governmental action was seen to be contrary to hallmark American values.

In 1970, another army private challenged the order requiring him to report for duty in Vietnam on grounds that the war had never been declared or properly authorized by Congress. An appellate court decided that the issue met the standard of justiciability but that sufficient probability was not shown and considered the constitutionality of the conflict. The issue was "not whether the courts are empowered to 'second-guess' the President in his decision to commit the armed forces to action, but whether they have the power to make a particular kind of constitutional decision involving the division of powers between legislative and executive branches."[145] Six years of undeclared war and significant public opposition had undermined the political discretion of the executive. "[I]f the executive branch engaged the nation in prolonged foreign military activities without any significant congressional authorization, a court might be able to determine that this extreme step violated a discoverable standard for *some* mutual participation by Congress in accordance with Article I section 8."[146] How-

---

[142] *United States v. Sisson*, 294 F.Supp. at 515.

[143] *Davi v. Laird*, 318 F.Supp. 478, 481 (W.D. Va 1970).

[144] *Id.* at 484.

[145] *Berk v. Laird*, 429 F.2d 302, at 304 (2d Cir. 1970). "Since orders to fight must be issued in accordance with proper authorization from both branches under some circumstances, executive officers are under a threshold constitutional 'duty [which] can be judicially identified and its breach judicially determined.'" *Id.* at 305 [quoting *Baker v. Carr*, 369 U.S. 186, 198 (1962)].

[146] *Id.* at 305 (emphasis in original).

ever, it was determined that Congress "definitely has acted . . . through the Gulf of Tonkin Resolution and . . . through appropriation . . . of the project over a period of years."[147] Thus, the constitutional requirement of legislative consent for "mutual participation"[148] was met. With "a lack of judicially discoverable and manageable standards," the conflict remained a political question. Therefore, since Congress supported the war, and showed "mutual participation," it conformed to a political question.

Following *Berk*, the court considered that the political question doctrine did not preclude addressing whether military duty was justiciable. It determined that the test is "whether there is any action by the Congress sufficient to authorize or ratify the military activity in question."[149] Thus, in examining monetary appropriation for the war, the draft extension acts, and the Tonkin Gulf Resolution, the court concluded that "Congress and the Executive have taken mutual and joint action in the prosecution and support of military operations in Southeast Asia."[150] However, "[t]he means by which Congress has chosen to . . . approve the protracted military operations in Southeast Asia is a political question, [and therefore] . . . outside the power and competency of the judiciary."[151] In 1971, an appellate court held that the legislative action extending the Selective Service Act and appropriating billions of dollars to carry on military and naval operations "winding down the conflict and disengaging the nation from it, is also a political question."[152]

The court asserted, however, that if the executive was "now escalating the prolonged struggle instead of decreasing it, *additional supporting action by the Legislative Branch* . . . might well be required."[153] When President Nixon ordered on May 8, 1972, the mining of the ports and harbors of North Vietnam, which was clearly re-escalation, the same plaintiff sought a declaratory judgment that such operations were unlawful in the absence of explicit congressional authorization. The Second Circuit dismissed the case as still political in nature: "Here, however, the appellant invites us to extend the reach of judicial inquiry with respect to the Vietnam war into the domain of tactical and strategic military decisions ordered by the . . . Commander-in-Chief."[154] The court considered that "[t]he gravamen of this appeal must be, therefore, that the president's conduct has so altered the course of hostilities in Vietnam as to make the war . . . different from the war which we held [earlier] to have been constitutionally ratified and authorized by the Congress, or that congressional ratification and authoriza-

---

[147] *Id.*

[148] *Id.*

[149] *Orlando v. Laird*, 443 F.2d 1039, 1042(2d Cir.), cert. denied, 404 U.S. 869 (1971) (emphasis added).

[150] *Id.* (emphasis added)

[151] *Id.* at 1043.

[152] *DaCosta v. Laird*, 448 F.2d 1368, 1370 (2d Cir.1971), cert. denied, 405 U.S. 979 (1972).

[153] *Id.* (emphasis added).

[154] *DaCosta v. Laird*, 471 F.2d 1146, 1147 (2d Cir. 1973).

tion has terminated." Relying on the court's "now escalating" language, the appellant argued that the president's order to mine North Vietnam's harbors was unsupported by additional legislative authorization. Nevertheless, the appellate court considered that "the district court's limited inquiry was improper"[155]

> [T]his case is compounded by a lack of discoverable and manageable judicial standards. . . . Judges, deficient in military knowledge, lacking vital information upon which to assess the nature of battlefield decisions, and sitting thousands of miles from the field of action, cannot reasonably or appropriately determine whether a specific military operation constitutes an "escalation" of the war or is merely a new tactical approach within a continuing strategic plan.[156]

> [T]his Court is without power to resolve the issue narrowly presented in this case. . . . Those two coordinate branches of government—the Executive by military action and the Congress, by not cutting off the appropriations . . . have taken a position that is not within our power, even if it were our wish, to alter by judicial decree.[157]

Thus, instead of refusing to decide the war power issue on the merits, the courts did admit standing and did reach the merit. However, they dismissed the issue as lying outside the scope of their jurisdiction. The cooperation between the executive and legislative branches attested to the constitutionality of the war. In 1970, a district court held that men enlisted in the reserves had standing to challenge the constitutionality of the war. The "narrow legal question"[158] was whether the war was "being waged . . . under the authority of the branch of . . . government in which such power is constitutionally vested"[159] "To shy away on 'political question' grounds from interfering with a presidential war, itself, would be to strain at a gnat and swallow a camel."[160] The court also noted "Whatever the ultimate decision on the merits of the constitutional question may be, we are of opinion that the courts, eschewing indecision, inaction or avoidance on such grounds as 'no standing,' 'sovereign immunity,' and 'political question,' should discharge their traditional responsibility for interpreting the Constitution of the United States."[161] The decision was reversed on appeal. Members of reserves who were not ordered to Vietnam lacked the standing of military personnel to challenge the constitutional legality of the war.

---

[155] *DaCosta v. Laird*, 471 F.2d 1146, 1155 (2d Circ. 1973).

[156] *Id.* Referring to the court's language that an escalation would require an "additional supporting action of the Legislative Branch" [*DaCosta v. Laird*, 448 F.2d 1368, 1370 (2d Cir.1971), cert. denied, 405 U.S. 979 (1972)] the "onus was on litigants raising such a claim for proper judicial resolution of the issue." However, no such standards have been presented by the appellant in the case at hand.

[157] *DaCosta v. Laird*, 471 F.2d 1146, 1157 (2d Cir. 1973). *Id.* at 1157.

[158] *Mottola v. Nixon*, 318 F. Supp. 538, 540 (N.D. Cal. 1970).

[159] *Id.*

[160] *Id.* at 550.

[161] *Id.* at 553–54.

In a class action suit to stop the war in Vietnam, a three-judge district court decided that was a political question. The issues considered were whether (1) the involvement in Southeast Asia met the standards of a "war," (2) Congress had taken sufficient action to authorize the war, and (3) the president was justified in maintaining American forces there. While the federal courts are not deprived of jurisdiction, courts are hesitant to venture into foreign relations, since military actions underway could be undermined and affect domestic *contracts*.

Generation Seven, 1980 Onward: Presidential Wars and the Stability of the Global Economy

Political questions arose from the small-scale wars undertaken by the United States, or in conjunction with allies, to stabilize flash points that could destabilize the global market. Intervention was concentrated in both Central America and the Middle East as well as in Yugoslavia. The Middle East had been especially strategic, as well as volatile, since the Arab-Israel War of 1973 and the ensuing oil embargo. We have already noted the broad social changes that arose of out of the recessionary 1970s and the formation of a single global market by the early 1980s.[162]

The social contract between government and citizen, or between management and labor, was rechartered (e.g., who works where, job security, minimum health and living standards, the rights of citizenship). Income distribution became increasingly concentrated toward the top end of the social spectrum.[163] As Bauman observes, the private sector has increasingly "subordinated the structures of representative democracy to the service of [its] own interests. . . . Emancipation of capital from labor makes possible the emancipation of the state from legitimization . . . with a gradual erosion of democratic institutions."[164] Thus, we may consider the shift to globalism to be profound, comparable to the shift to industrialism in the latter 19th century. Both shifts were accompanied by new interpretations of the political question doctrine. In the latter shift, some of the basic functions of safeguarding the interest of the nation appeared to have eroded in favor of safeguarding the value in growth of capital. The state has largely ceased to protect its na-

---

[162] A third great awakening in religious revivalism, as manifested in fundamentalism and new ageism, reflected broad changes in beliefs. Evangelical religions grew at the expense of mainstream Protestant denominations, which dropped in membership by more than fifty percent. See Stephen Robert Warner, *Work in Progress toward a New Paradigm for the Sociological Study of Religion in the United States*, Amer. J. of Soc. 106, no. 5 (1993) 1044–93.

[163] Between 1980 and 2000 income increased sixty percent for the top twenty percent of the U.S. households, about twenty-five percent for the second and third highest quintiles, and between ten to fifteen percent for the bottom quintiles (Table F-1, "Income Limits for Each Fifth and Top 5 Percent of Families," U.S. Census Bureau, 2001).

[164] "Is There a Postmodern," in *The Transmodern Turn*, ed. Steven Seidman, 187–204 (Cambridge: Cambridge University Press, 1994) at 202.

tional industries with tariffs and to regulate what was admitted through communication within the state borders, and has generally reduced the social services provided to its citizens.[165] These policies have reorganized the functions of the state to better serve global capital.

The revised social contract between government and citizen bespeaks a wider shift from idealized social symmetry to one in which social asymmetry is accepted as the norm. From a structuralist standpoint, this departs from social symmetry identified in the values and material designs of the Enlightenment. As we have seen, the symmetrical design became widespread a generation before the democracies emerged during the 18th century. Thus, a significant departure from the notions of inherent social equality (symmetry) would signal the acceptance of social inequalities (in the asymmetries inherent in globalism). In his *New State Spaces*, Brenner points out how the ideational symmetries of democratic egalitarianism were borne out spatially: "During the Fordist-Keynesian period (1920s–1970s) state institutions sought to alleviate intra-national territorial inequalities, which were viewed as an impediment to balanced, stabilized macroeconomic growth. . . . As of the 1980s, a new growth-oriented competitiveness-driven approach to . . . governance was consolidated. . . . State institutions . . . began actively to intensify uneven development by promoting strategic cities . . . within each national territory and privileged sites for transnational capital investment."[166] This leads to splintered (asymmetrical) institutional landscapes rather than landscapes with a more equitable redistribution of national resources (symmetrical). Thus, the basic social contract between the governed and government realigned with the principles of monetarism and supply-side economics.[167] The political question doctrine is sufficiently ambiguous to broadly gauge the changed social context and the changed cultural values.

In this perspective, the overarching goal of the American state has changed from protecting the citizen to protecting capital. Does the political question doctrine give the executive greater latitude to insure the protection of transnational investments throughout the world and to insure the flow of labor and goods?

From 1980 to the early 1990s, lawsuits challenged presidential authority to conduct military operations abroad. Interestingly, members of Congress initiated some of these suits, which were dismissed on the doctrines of ripeness, mootness, political question, equitable discretion, and standing. The reasoning was that unless the legislative branch demonstrated a willingness to act, the courts would

---

[165] See Peter Dicken, *Global Shift*, (New York: Guiford Press, 1996); Immanuel Wallerstein, *The End of the World as We Know It* (University of Minnesota Press, 1999). Since the early 1980s, the average world tariff has decreased from about thirty percent to about four percent, foreign investment per year has quadrupled, and multinational corporations generate more than seventy percent of world trade in goods and services. G. DeMartino, *Global Economy, Global Justice: Theoretical Objections and Policy Alternatives to Neoliberalism* (Routledge, 2000).

[166] Neil Brenner, *New State Spaces* (Oxford: Oxford University Press, 2004), 259.

[167] See Milton Friedman and Rose Friedman, *Free to Choose: A Personal Statement* (New York: Harcourt Brace and Javanovich, 1980).

not intervene. Courts would adjudicate a war power dispute if the clash was clear and resolute, where the political branches reached a constitutional impasse, and a majority of the legislative body needed to clearly oppose the particular action.

In 1980, former crewmen of a privately owned cargo vessel, the *Mayaguez*, brought a suit against the United States seeking damages for personal injuries sustained when the American military's seizure of the vessel provoked action by Cambodian gunboats. The crewmen claimed negligence by the United States in executing the military operation and in failing to warn the *Mayaguez* of the danger of capture.[168] A district court held that the rescue operation involved a judgment of national interest and, therefore, was exempt under the Admiralty Act.[169] The claim of negligence was interpreted as a nonjusticiable political question,[170] since a rescue operation fell within foreign relations. The court may not scrutinize "the underlying factual or legal determinations on . . . which the President conducts the foreign relations of the United States."[171]

Several cases of American military involvement in El Salvador and Nicaragua were disposed on the grounds that the plaintiffs were members of Congress who could not challenge the president in the courts but should rather exhaust their own institutional channels. In 1982, Congressman George Crockett, along with twelve other House members and sixteen senators sought declaratory judgments that the supplying of military equipment to El Salvador by President Reagan's order violated the War Powers Clause of the Constitution, the War Powers Resolution (WPR), and the Foreign Assistance Act. The court concluded that the case was nonjusticiable since only fact-finding would "determine whether U.S. forces have been introduced into hostilities or imminent hostilities in El Salvador."[172] Questions as to the "nature and extent of the United States's presence in El Salvador and whether a report under the WPR is mandated . . . are appropriate for congressional, not judicial, investigation and determination."[173]

In a suit involving U.S. involvement in Nicaragua, twelve members of Congress alleged that the president had violated the neutrality laws, the WPR, the National Security Act, and the Boland Amendment. Members of Congress contended that atrocities committed by the U.S.-sponsored "Contra" forces were against the intent of the various acts, but the judiciary held these to be nonjusticiable political questions. The case involved "significant factual and policy questions for which there are no judicially discoverable and manageable standards."[174] Any judicial resolution could "seriously impinge"[175] on the Congress and the president to conduct foreign and national security.

---

[168] *Rappenecker v. United States*, 509 F.Supp. 1024, 1025 (N.D. Cal. 1980).

[169] *Id.* at 1027.

[170] *Id.* at 1028–29.

[171] *Id.* at 1028–29.

[172] *Crockett v. Reagan*, 558 F.Supp. 893, 898 (D.D.C. 1982).

[173] *Id.*

[174] *Sanchez-Espinoza v. Reagan*, 568 F.Supp. 596, 597–98 (D.D.C. 1983).

[175] *Id.*

The court also regarded covert CIA operatives in Nicaragua, Honduras, and El Salvador as nonjudicially discoverable participation by U.S. military person-nel.[176] Furthermore, the court considered that the ongoing congressional debate on the validity of the president's initiatives might unduly influence "the delicate dip-lomatic balance that is required in the foreign affairs arena."[177]

In a concurring opinion in the D.C. Circuit,[178] the court stated "[i]f the Con-gress chooses not to confront the President, it is not our task to do so."[179] The "war power[s] clause"[180] by the congressional plaintiffs was dismissed as "not ripe for judicial review."[181] Congress "has formidable weapons at its disposal—the power of the purse and investigative resources far beyond those available in the Third Branch. . . . [Yet], Congress expressly allowed the President to spend federal funds to support paramilitary operations in Nicaragua."[182] The will of the majority in Congress would equate, in this reasoning, with the will of the people.

In 1984, eleven other members of Congress challenged the executive order to invade Grenada, a foreign nation, which violated the War Powers Clause of the Constitution. The district court considered that it "would be unwise to intrude in [this] 'political' controvers[y]."[183] Citing the doctrine of equitable/remedial discre-tion, the plaintiffs had sufficient "in-house remedies available to them,"[184] such as the War Powers Resolution, appropriations bills, independent legislation, and even impeachment.[185] The case was dismissed when it finally reached the court, since the military action had terminated.[186]

Increasing numbers of suits were brought by members of Congress against the executive as American interests accelerated in the Gulf region. For example, 110 members of the House of Representatives sought a declaration that the War Powers Resolution required President Reagan to file reports on incidents in the Gulf in 1987.[187] A district court held that the equitable discretion and the political

---

[176] *Id.* at 600.

[177] *Id.*

[178] *Sanchez-Espinoza v. Reagan,* 770 F.2d 202 (D.C. Cir. 1985).

[179] *Id.* at 211, citing *Goldwater v. Carter,* 444 U.S. at 998 (Powell, J., concurring).

[180] Id. at 210

[181] *Id.*

[182] *Id.* at 211.

[183] *Conyers v. Reagan,* 578 F.Supp. 324, 326 (D.D.C. 1984) (citing *Vander Jagt v. O'Neill,* 699 F.2d 1166, 1174 (D.C. Cir. 1982)).

[184] *Id.*

[185] *Id.* at 327.

[186] *Conyers v. Reagan,* 765 F.2d 1124 (D.C. Cir. 1985).

[187] The plaintiffs contended that the reporting requirement of section 4(a)(1) of the War Powers Resolution was triggered by the July 22, 1987, initiation of U.S. escort op-erations in the Persian Gulf and by the September 21, 1987, attack on an Iranian navy ship laying mines in the Persian Gulf. They claimed that the U.S. Armed Forces had been introduced without a declaration of war "into hostilities or into situations where imminent involvement in hostilities is clearly indicated by the circumstances." 50 U.S.C. § 1543 (a) 1.

question doctrine made jurisdiction inappropriate.[188] Injunctive relief would allow "a plaintiff to circumvent the processes of democratic decision making."[189]

After the collapse of the Soviet bloc in 1990, foreign policy directed by the executive was increasingly unilateral. Thomas M. Franck noted that some federal judges refrained from examining the constitutionality of actions if the president "acted in the name of foreign policy or national security. According to this line of reasoning, courts may not inquire whether soldiers are being sent lawfully into combat or whether members of Congress have been deprived of their constitutional role in the decision to go to war."[190]

In 1990, fifty-three members of the House of Representatives and one senator filed an injunction to prevent President Bush from going to war against Iraq without congressional authorization.[191] The Justice Department claimed that only the political branches could determine whether the country was at war, since judicially discoverable and manageable standards to apply were absent. "If the Executive had the sole power to determine that any particular offensive military operation . . . does not constitute war . . . [then] the congressional power to declare war will be at the mercy of a semantic decision by the Executive."[192] Courts have "the power and the ability to make the factual and legal determination of whether this nation's military actions constitute war for purposes of the constitutional War Clause."[193] Yet, Congress did not assert its constitutional authority. It would be "both premature and presumptuous"[194] to decide whether a declaration of war is required when Congress "has provided no indication whether it deems such a declaration either necessary, . . . or imprudent."[195]

The judiciary should not decide the allocation of power between the political branches unless they reach "a constitutional impasse."[196] Otherwise, a decision

---

[188] *Lowry v. Reagan,* 676 F.Supp. 333 (D.D.C. 1987), aff'd, No. 87–5426 (D.C. Cir. 1988).

[189] *Id.* at 338 (citing *Riegle v. Federal Open Market Committee,* 656 F.2d 873, 881 (D.C. Cir. 1981).

[190] Thomas M. Franck, *Political Question/Judicial Answers: Does the Rule of Law Apply to Foreign Affairs?* 4 (1992). Federal judges, says Franck, routinely decide such "hot-potato issues" as reapportionment and affirmative action, yet "these same jurists tend to turn coy when challenged to decide whether a military conflict, such as the one in Vietnam, ultimately involving the expenditure of tens of thousands of lives and hundreds of billions of dollars, is lawful when waged by the president on his sole authority without a formal congressional declaration of war." *Id.* at 10.

[191] *Dellums v. Bush,* 752 F.Supp.1141 (D.D.C. 1990).

[192] *Id.* at 1145.

[193] 752 F.Supp. at 1146. The court said it "has no hesitation in concluding that an offensive entry into Iraq by several hundred thousand United States servicemen under the conditions described above could be described as a 'war' within the meaning of Article I, Section 8, Clause 11, of the Constitution." *Id.*

[194] *Id.* at 1149–50.

[195] *Id.*

[196] *Id.* at 1150 (quoting Justice Powell's concurrence in *Goldwater v. Carter,* 444 U.S. at 997–98).

might be without support from the elected branches. It is only if the majority of the Congress seeks relief from an infringement on its constitutional war-declaration power that it may be entitled to receive it.[197]

The discretion of the president to commit U.S. forces to the war in Yugoslavia was based on *Campbell v. Clinton*.[198] Judge Silberman concluded that courts lack "judicially discoverable and manageable standards"[199] for addressing war power issues. In opposition, Judge Tatel stated that the "courts are competent to judge . . . the allocation of war powers between the president and Congress."[200]

Rulings during the last two centuries do not automatically associate war power with the political question. Not only did courts decide war power issues, but they spoke against the authority of the president to venture into war-making activities against the express will or the silence of Congress. Some of the earliest of these decisions were written by justices who had been members of the Constitutional Convention or participated in state ratifying conventions.

In 1999, lawmakers again sought a declaration that President Clinton violated the War Powers Clause and the resolution by conducting air strikes in Yugoslavia without congressional authorization.[201] The district court held that the plaintiffs lacked standing, which would require that they needed to show a "constitutional impasse" or "actual confrontation" between the elected branches. Otherwise, small groups of legislators could seek a judicial remedy instead of using the available political process.[202] The case would have been ripe for judicial determination had Congress directed the president to remove U.S. forces and he refused, or if Congress had withheld funds and the president had decided "to spend that money . . . anyway."[203] Yet, the court acknowledged that any case involving coordinate and coequal branches of government raises separation of powers concerns: "To the extent that the President is arguing that *every* case brought by a legislator alleging a violation of the War Powers Clause raises a nonjusticiable political question, he is wrong."[204]

---

[197] *Id.* at 1151. No appeal was taken from the district court decision.

[198] 203 F.3d 19 (D.C. Cir. 2000).

[199] See Martin S. Sheffer, *The Judicial Development of Presidential War Powers* ix (1999). The courts, says Sheffer, "lie back, seeking to avoid having to rule on questions of the conduct of commander-in-chief [and war] powers, and when they are forced to rule, they usually uphold presidential action" (p. x). 203 F3d 19, 24-25 (D.C. Cir. 2000) [quoting *Baker v. Carr*, 369 U.S. 186, 217 (1962)].

[200] *Id.* at 37, 39.

[201] *Campbell v. Clinton*, 52 F.Supp.2d 34 (D.D.C. 1999).

[202] *Campbell v. Clinton*, 52 F.Supp. 2d at 43 (quoting *Goldwater v. Carter*, 444 U.S. at 997–98 (Powell, J., concurring)).

[203] *Id.*

[204] *Id.* n. 5 (emphasis in original).

Recent Developments

Because of the judicial record of avoiding war power cases from the Vietnam years to the 9/11 terrorist attacks on the United States, it was uncertain whether federal courts would be wholly deferential to the Bush administration or would exercise an independent check. The answer (at least partial) came on June 28, 2004, when the Supreme Court decided the case of *Hamdi v. Rumsfeld*. At issue was the authority of President Bush to designate a U.S. citizen, Yaser Esam Hamdi, as an "enemy combatant" and detain him indefinitely without formal charges, access to an attorney, or trial.

The Court was so divided that it could not muster a full majority. Instead, a plurality of four justices decided certain issues and were joined by a combination of other justices: Justices Souter and Ginsburg concurring in part and dissenting in part, Justices Scalia and Stevens dissenting, and Justice Thomas dissenting. These "dissents" actually agreed with certain parts of the plurality's decision.

The press paid particular attention to certain statements made by the plurality, written by Justice O'Connor. Some examples: "We have long since made clear that a state of war is not a blank check for the President when it comes to the rights of the Nation's citizens."[205] "Whatever power the United States Constitution envisions for the Executive in its exchanges with other nations or with enemy organizations in times of conflict, it most assuredly envisions a role for all three branches when individual liberties are at stake."[206]

These statements found their way extensively into newspaper editorials. However, the plurality's decision was marred by so many ambiguities that the Court's action offered little guidance to the lower courts. At most, and this was of some value, it was a signal to the lower courts that they have a part to play on war power issues. Similarly, on the same day, the Court decided *Rasul v. Bush*, setting forth some general guidelines on the treatment of detainees at the Guantanamo naval base in Cuba.[207] The task of district courts and circuit courts since that time has been to define the boundaries of presidential power and the rights of enemy combatants and detainees. The process has not been even or clear, but the courts once again understand that they have an institutional duty to clarify statutory questions and give meaning and life to constitutional rights.

Conclusions

The political question doctrine has allowed the political branches certain discretionary powers—especially during crises where innovative and quick measures were deemed necessary. Yet, what seems appropriate in one set of circumstances may be interpreted as excessive in other circumstances. In the broad

---

[205] *Hamdi v. Rumsfeld*, 542 U.S. 507, 536 (2004).
[206] *Id.*
[207] *Rasul v. Bush*, 542 U.S. 466 (2004).

sweep of two centuries, we note that contesting the political question doctrine has clustered at approximate generational intervals. The matter of who is covered by constitutional protections during war looms significant time and time again, especially in the dual and often contradictory purposes between the right of free enterprise and defeating the enemy. It has been during those wars when the nation itself was most threatened that the greatest latitudes were taken in the political question doctrine. For example, during the Civil War, World War II, and the Vietnam War the president was permitted especially wide discretionary powers by the Supreme Court.

In fact, at the height of the Civil War in 1863, Congress authorized the president complete statutory authority to suspend the writ of habeas corpus whenever he deemed necessary. These discretionary powers were curtailed as the crises began to abate. Generally, legal opinions shifted in the latter war years along with public sentiment. The courts decided a broad range of issues such as the statutory meaning of "enemy," distinctions between declared and undeclared wars, and conflict between presidential proclamations and congressional statutes. However, private individuals sued seeking redress on constitutional merits. Let us consider that the Constitution is a broad guideline and interpretations varied depending on the political and cultural pressures of the day. Most broadly, the judiciary recognized the constitutional basis that allowed the president to take defensive actions but reserved for Congress the right to initiate offensive actions against other countries.

As originally envisioned, the political question doctrine fit the national ideology of a fairly isolated nation expanding west following the Revolutionary War (1783) and the Louisiana Purchase (1803). Courts deferred to presidential judgment in calling forth the militia to repel imminent invasions and suppressing internal insurrections.[208] However, as commander in chief, the president had no authority to annex territory through military occupation.[209]

Taken as a whole, the three branches of government mirrored the balance inherent within the populace of largely self-employed farmers, artisans, and traders during the nation's first century. In *United States v. Smith* (1806), a circuit court ruled that neutrality policy was defined by statute or legal agreement among the states. Executive privilege to undertake military actions bespoke all too familiarly of the right of kings, which was an anathema in the national ethos. In 1814, the Supreme Court held that British property seized in the United States at the commencement of hostilities was not "enemy's property" unless Congress specifically authorized war by statute.[210]

The territorial extent of the continental United States was pretty much established by the 1850s. The courts held that the rights of the citizens in the newly annexed territories from Mexico were equally valid under the Constitution. From the 1850s through the Civil War, the preeminence of the values of an urban indus-

---

[208] *Martin v. Mott,* 25 U.S. (12 Wheat.) 19, 30 (1827); *Luther v. Borden,* 48 U.S. (7 How.) 1, 43 (1849).

[209] *Fleming v. Page,* 50 U.S. (9 How.) 603, 615 (1850).

[210] *Brown v. United States,* 12 U.S. (8 Cr.) 109, 129 (1814).

trial core against the cultural values and the political interests of the agricultural South was established. During the Civil War, the courts increasingly granted the president authority to act unilaterally.

A second phase of reinterpreting the doctrine to perform new functions coincided with the emergence of the United States as an international player following the Spanish American War. The courts reversed themselves from rulings during the Mexican War, and stated that the newly conquered territories acquired from Spain and outside of North America could be ruled by military law. The national cosmology came to distinguish between the American homeland with its ideas of government of the citizens on the one hand, and distant overseas posts for government functionaries, military bases and branch offices of business on the other hand. From then on, courts recognized that during hostilities, presidents have authority to determine the rates of duties in occupied territory to generate needed revenues. However, the courts also regarded this executive power as temporary and looked to statutory action by Congress to decide whether duties imposed upon goods after hostilities have ended are legally established.[211] In *Dooley v. United States* (1901), the Supreme Court ruled that the presidential power to exact duties upon goods being transported from the United States to Puerto Rico ceased with the ratification of a peace treaty.

The shift in national thinking from isolationism within the vast continent of North America to a contender in the world arena, competing for markets, colonies, and raw materials abroad developed only begrudgingly. The inherent contradiction between isolationism and the "heartland" versus commercial expansionism abroad was variously contested throughout the 20th century. In most cases, the need for commercial and industrial growth drove national policy. Only following World War II did the United States accept an ongoing international leadership role. The single generation between the world wars saw the whole-scale shift from the mechanical solidarity of agrarian landscapes to one of organic solidarity within urban landscapes. The nature and cultural values of the body politic was forever changed.

It was only after this shift to organic solidarity that new meanings of political questions emerged. An urban-based economy of mass production necessitated world markets to distribute the products. The shift to political and economic world leadership necessitated new legal interpretations. For example, although the Truman administration was loath to call hostilities in Korea a "war" for reasons of national ideology, federal judges readily could make that determination.

From *Little v. Barreme* (1804) through about 1952, courts overturned actions taken by the president as commander in chief. While courts acknowledged the president's broad discretionary powers in foreign policy and military actions, they usually did so only after establishing what Congress had authorized by statute. Even at the height of judicial unwillingness to reach the constitutional merits of the Vietnam War, the courts repeatedly looked for evidence of congressional ratification of the presidential initiatives in one way or another.

---

[211] *Fleming v. Page*, 50 U.S. at 614–15.

Although courts often decided war power disputes involving private citizens and their corporations, they reluctantly heard cases brought by members of Congress, which opened a Pandora's box in interpreting the doctrine. The judiciary dismissed the cases unless there was a clear conflict between the political branches, and unless Congress *en masse* confronted the president. When Congress decides to press a war power issue in the courts, it must do so as a body, and only after a majority voted to oppose the presidential actions.

Popular support diminished for actions by the president as both the Korean and Vietnam Wars became prolonged. The court decisions appeared to correlate with the increasing public opposition and thus cultural values within the context of the times. For example, the courts may have factored in the negative public reaction to President Truman's broad claims of executive power. Later, the sentencing of Vietnam War resisters seemed to decline as public opinion against the war increased.[212] It was only during the waning years of the Vietnam War that courts challenged war power questions.

Therefore, the judicial review of the Vietnam era rulings may be placed in the wider context of broad cultural, political, and economic changes. The legal meaning of the political question doctrine was reinterpreted during the early 1970s to more closely mesh with how the three branches interrelated. This mirrored how the United States related with the new global order, the increased investment of capital abroad, and the increased appearance of transnational corporations to influence American foreign policy and judicial review. Small wars abroad became increasingly more frequent from the 1970s on. This time period coincides with the global market beginning to take hold with an acceleration and full crystallization in the early '80s. The executive prerogative to wage undeclared war also became more fully established during the early 1980s. The once timeless balance between the three branches began to weigh more heavily in favor of the executive.

Terrorism as "post-nation state" warfare to undermine the penetration of global capital is germane to consideration as a political question. To what extent can new strategies for countering terrorism, such as the detention of suspects without the usual due process, be legally justified in thwarting terrorist organizations? Strategies for combating terrorism intersect with a trend to grant the holders of capital greater power in an increasingly stratified American state, and correlate with greater discretionary powers assumed by the executive. From the early 1980s to the present, the United States witnessed more presidentially initiated wars, although members of Congress filed lawsuits (unsuccessfully) to enjoin the wars in Iraq and Yugoslavia.

Commencing during the 1990s and continuing to the events following September 11, 2001, the unilateral power of the president to engage in limited wars

---

[212] Herbert M. Kritzer, *Federal Judges and Their Political Environment*, 23 Am. J. Pol. Sci. 194 (1979); Herbert M. Kritzer, *Political Correlates of the Behavior of Federal District Judges: A "Best Case" Analysis*, 40 J. Pol. 25 (1977); Dianne Bennett Graebner, *Judicial Activity and Public Attitude: A Quantitative Study of Selective Service Sentencing in the Vietnam War Period*, 23 Buff. L. Rev. 465 (1973–74).

accentuates the adoption of a neoclassical economic policy. Thus, thirty years after Vietnam and the cultural and social changes of the "postmodern/global turn" (1973), President Bush ordered a large-scale offensive in Iraq (2003). This executive unilateralism may signify an important redirection in American foreign policy along with rebuffing traditional European allies.[213] In this sense, the alliance of "like" nation states basic to arrangements of equals has been replaced by top-down commands and "going it alone" by a single remaining super power.

In the context of this new global order, issues of war and peace may lie beyond the scope of judicial scrutiny. What is different in this thirty-year cycle after Vietnam is that members of the military are not citizen conscripts, which typified American soldiers in the decades immediately before 1973. An argument may be made that policy may correlate with business interests (e.g., the contracts of Halliburton in reconstructing Iraq). The military initiatives of the president and his vice president, while diminishing civil liberties domestically and for international "detainees," may foster and protect capital flows worldwide.

The opportunities for unilateral decisions of the president to wage war for the benefit of safeguarding the global market, the flow of oil from the Middle East, or to combat terror would be structurally consistent with an increasingly stratified society with an international class of the holders of capital. The framers of the Constitution expected the decision to go to war to be made after thorough debate among congressional representatives who synthesized the collective judgments of lawmakers and the president. James Wilson spoke for other framers when he said it would not be in the power "of a single man" to involve the nation in war.[214]

In no area of federal authority is the decision to go to war more constrained. Without judicial and legislative controls, this exercise of presidential power exhibits shades of a monarchy that the framers of the Constitution clearly aspired to put behind them. Thus, one might ask whether, within this longitudinal look at two centuries, the power of the executive has outgrown the judicial and legislative checks envisioned in the Constitution. For the critics, the principles of government were laid out as one by and for the citizens rather than by and for the purveyors of capital within a global market.

In overview, the Constitution originally encoded the social, ideological, and economic principles of the Enlightenment with their inherent social symmetries. In the analytical mode of structuralism used in this essay, the power between the branches of the government became unbalanced, so that the Constitution seems increasingly out of sync in the contexts of globalism and heightened social stratification in a world integrated by market forces and militarily enforced by America. Alternatively, does the exceptional longevity of the United States reflect an inor-

---

[213] Nevertheless, in *Dellums* v. *Bush* (1990), Judge Greene rejected sweeping claims by the Justice Department that a president could mount offensive military operations bereft of congressional review.

[214] 2 The Debates in the Several State Conventions on the Adoption of the Federal Constitution 528 (Jonathan Elliot, ed. 1836).

dinately flexible Constitution that allows governmental adjustments to major social transformations (i.e., industrialism, informationalism, and the three major depressions of 1830s, 1870s, 1930s)? Is the Constitution sufficiently elastic to accommodate redefined functions of the executive to safeguard the global market, which is outside of the territorial United States and thus outside of the purview of its laws?

A Political Question by Any Other Name: Government Litigation Strategy in the Enemy Combatant Cases of *Hamdi* and *Padilla*

Nancy Kassop

Within two years after the terrorist attacks of September 11, 2001, legal challenges to the most controversial antiterrorism policies of the Bush administration began to wend their way through the federal courts, landing right on the doorstep of the United States Supreme Court. In April 2004, the Court heard oral argument in three cases challenging the administration's various detention policies: *Rasul v. Bush* and *Al Odah v. U.S.* (Guantanamo detainees), *Hamdi v. Rumsfeld* (citizen enemy combatant captured on the battlefield), and *Rumsfeld v. Padilla* (citizen enemy combatant arrested on U.S. soil), and it handed down decisions in them on June 28, 2004.[1] There was never much doubt that these cases would ultimately come before the Court. What was less certain was the litigating posture the government would take and the role the Court would assume for itself in national security matters that blend aspects of both military policy and law enforcement. Would the government claim that these matters were political questions, and would the Court accept such a claim? This essay argues that although the government has not formally argued that the Court should declare nonjusticiability of these issues as political questions, its refusal

---

[1] See *Rasul v. Bush*, 124 S.Ct. 2686 (2004); *Hamdi v. Rumsfeld*, 124 S.Ct. 2633 (2004); and *Rumsfeld v. Padilla*, 124 S.Ct. 2711 (2004).

to acknowledge a meaningful role for courts amounts to the same practical outcome.

The Issue for the Courts and for the Administration

The federal courts found themselves by mid-2002 faced with the task of determining the constitutionality of some of the extraordinary measures that were put in place after September 2001 to pursue persons suspected of terrorist activities and to forestall planning for future attacks. They were caught in the crossfire: in the past, they either deferred to the executive or sidestepped entirely cases that challenged *military* judgments, and, thus, one could presume that they might have little enthusiasm for deciding on the constitutionality of such policies during a period of heightened national security threat. Alternatively, monitoring *law enforcement* to insure consistency with due process protections is exactly what courts do.

The administration comes to the courts in an inherently defensive posture when these measures are challenged. Determining how to respond and how to fashion its strategy are key decisions. The Department of Justice must argue the government's position, defend against critics who charge that the administration is trampling on individual rights in the name of furthering national security, and define the legal context for the courts. Because the backdrop for these controversies is a blend of both military necessity and law enforcement, the administration's rationale for its policies, also, needs to consider elements from both of these spheres (although administration officials have contended repeatedly that the law enforcement paradigm is no longer appropriate, as it once was during the 1990s, for combating terrorism). Consequently, the federal courts need to navigate their way carefully through the uneasy interplay between these two environments.

These are classic separation of powers conflicts, pitting judicial power against executive authority. Both branches have choices: the president could argue, on constitutional and prudential grounds, that these are issues that should be left to the exclusive determination of the chief executive, and that courts are ill-positioned to decide such matters; or he could defend his positions vigorously on the merits and hope to persuade the courts to rule broadly in his favor. The courts, for their part, also face strategic choices: they must choose between abstaining on the basis of judicial avoidance doctrines or wading in and claiming the judicial ground to decide the issues on the merits.

Strategy is at the core of this dilemma for both the president and the courts, and there is keen awareness that the precedents produced by these cases will leave a substantial legacy. Both sides are equally mindful of these high stakes. The matrix of possible strategic positions consists of: (1) the president arguing and the courts deciding on the merits; (2) the president arguing on the merits and the courts deferring to him through judicial abstention; (3) the president arguing that an issue is a political question that only the president can determine and that courts have no role to play in these matters, and the courts agreeing with this position; or (4) the president asserting that these issues are political questions, but the courts deciding to engage the issue directly and rule on the merits.

As of April 2006, the record of both branches has developed sufficiently to allow for deducing some preliminary conclusions, and these make clear that the positions of the president and the courts do not conform neatly to any of the four possible alternatives proposed here. Rather, the administration has argued consistently that courts have no role in these matters, while simultaneously putting forth substantive arguments on the merits. Among the lower federal courts in *Hamdi, Rasul,* and *Padilla,* there was a mix of decisions, some deferring to the president as commander in chief (e.g., the Fourth Circuit's January 2003 decision in *Hamdi* and its September 2005 decision in *Padilla*),[2] but others claiming every ounce of judicial power belonging to them and issuing clear decisions on the merits, amounting to strong rebukes to the administration in its interpretation of presidential power (e.g., the Second Circuit's December 2003 decision in *Padilla*).[3] On June 28, 2004, the Supreme Court handed down decisions in all three cases, again, with a mix of outcomes, though leaving no doubt that it would not relinquish its role to interpret the law and the scope of the president's power during times of war. These decisions and subsequent developments will be examined later in this essay.

Two Lines of Precedents

What guidance might we gain from history? In fact, there are two lines of decisions from which the branches could have chosen. One line of cases represents Supreme Court decisions on civil liberties issues during wartime where the Court reviewed the arguments on the merits and ruled expansively for the president (e.g., the World War II era cases of *Quirin, Hirabayashi,* and *Korematsu*).[4] The other line is comprised of foreign policy cases from more recent decades where presidents placed heavy reliance on judicial avoidance doctrines such as ripeness, equitable discretion, and political question, and where courts were quite willing to accede to those claims in such cases as those challenging the constitutionality of the Vietnam war (e.g., *Massachusetts v. Laird, Holtzman v. Schlesinger*), or determining treaty termination powers in *Goldwater v. Carter,* or the constitutional allocation of war powers in *Dellums v. Bush,* and in the spate of War Powers Resolution cases challenging Reagan-era policies in Cen-

---

[2] *Hamdi v. Rumsfeld,* 316 F.3d 450 (4th Cir. 2003); *Padilla v. Hanft,* 423 F.3d 386 (4th Cir. 2005).

[3] *Padilla v. Rumsfeld,* 352 F.3d 695 (2d Cir. 2003).

[4] *Ex parte Quirin,* 317 U.S. 1 (1942); *Hirabayashi v. U.S.,* 320 U.S. 81 (1943); *Korematsu v. U.S.,* 323 U.S. 214 (1944).

tral America and the Persian Gulf (e.g., *Lowry v. Reagan, Crockett v. Reagan, Sanchez-Espinoza v. Reagan*).[5]

What might explain the difference in administration approach—and in judicial response—between these two eras? One likely candidate as the basis for this distinction is the Court's 1962 decision in *Baker v. Carr*.[6] It opened the door for presidents to assert nonjusticiability claims in the later cases, despite Justice Brennan's protestation to the contrary in his majority opinion that "it is error to suppose that every case or controversy which touches foreign relations lies beyond judicial cognizance."[7] Thus, there seems to be a clear break between the approach in the World War II-era cases and in the later ones, with *Baker* as one intervening variable that may offer a plausible explanation for the difference.

The argument for *Baker's* significance is strengthened when one considers that all of the cases involving wartime policies of military detention were *pre-Baker*, leaving the courts no opportunity since World War II until now to apply *Baker* to those policies. Presidents did *not* argue for judicial avoidance in *Quirin, Hirabayashi*, and *Korematsu*, whereas Brennan's list in *Baker* of the criteria that determine political questions, such as "a textually demonstrable constitutional commitment of the issue to a coordinate political department, or a lack of judicially discoverable and manageable standards . . . , or the impossibility of a court's undertaking independent resolution without expressing lack of the respect due coordinate branches of government . . . ," handed presidents a virtual road map of claims they could use to make the case for nonjusticiability in foreign affairs.[8] It should come as no surprise, then, that presidents *would* use these cues as defenses in the later group of foreign policy cases. However, none of these later cases really compares, in nature or in scope, to the World War II military detention cases. Thus, since the 1940s, the Court has not had to address, until now (with one exception), the same types of profoundly fundamental national security vs. individual liberties issues during wartime that it did during that earlier, pre-*Baker* time. The exception is the Pentagon Papers case, *New York Times Company v. U.S.*,[9] where the Court, in a three-paragraph per curiam opinion, held that the government needed to meet, which it did not here, a heavy burden to overcome a presumption against prior restraint. The president argued that he had inherent power to obtain a court injunction ordering newspapers to cease publication of the top security Department of Defense report on the history of U.S. involvement in the Vietnam War, but six justices rejected that view without proof that disclosure would "surely result in direct, immediate and ir-

---

[5] *Massachusetts v. Laird*, 400 U.S. 886 (1970); *Holtzman v. Schlesinger*, 484 F. 2d 1307 (2d Cir. 1973); *Goldwater v. Carter*, 444 U.S. 996 (1979); *Dellums v. Bush*, 752 F. Supp. 1141 (D.D.C. 1990); *Lowry v. Reagan*, 676 F. Supp. 333 (D.D.C. 1987); *Crockett v. Reagan*, 558 F. Supp. 893 (D.D.C. 1982); *Sanchez-Espinoza v. Reagan*, 568 F. Supp. 596 (D.D.C. 1983).
[6] 369 U.S. 186 (1962).
[7] 369 U.S.186, 211 (1962).
[8] *Id.* at 217.
[9] 403 U.S. 713 (1971).

reparable damage" to the nation, and even then, it would be for Congress to enact a specific law and not for the president to claim inherent power to ask the
courts to issue an injunction. This was a strong show of support for First
Amendment freedoms in conflict with a claim of potential harm to national security, but even this is on a different, or more abstract, plane than the current
constitutional disputes arising from antiterrorism policies.

"A Different Kind of War"

Moreover, the Bush administration emphasizes frequently that this war on terrorism is different from past wars, that its duration is uncertain though expected
to last for years, that the enemy consists of nonstate actors, and that the tactics
needed to win this conflict may be unconventional, unorthodox, and will include
far more than military ones.[10] Because some of the judicial precedents relied
upon by the administration are drawn from the World War II era (e.g., *Quirin*),
the contrast between a declared war and an undeclared war, and the legal ramifi-
cations of that distinction, are also implicated here. Presidents have far greater
latitude to act in times of declared war, yet, declarations of war have fallen out
of favor and have been replaced with specific statutory authorizations to use
military force, which provide presidents with the authority *only* to use the military, without lending foundational "cover" to broader, nonbattlefield policies
(e.g., suspension of writ of habeas corpus, military detentions in the U.S., or
military tribunals of detainees) that presidents were able to implement in the past
with greater ease when acting under a formal declaration of war from Congress.

One other consideration that frames any discussion of the administration's
policies in its war on terrorism is the degree to which those policies muddy the line
between military and criminal justice. John Yoo, a former Justice Department official, could not have put it more clearly when he said that the administration's
"whole theory of fighting the war on terrorism . . . was to move it out of the criminal justice system and treat it as a war."[11] This, too, is another way of disabling the
civilian court system from ruling on administration policies without ever having to
even invoke the "political question" doctrine. The administration calculated that
using the "war" analogy would enhance its latitude to act domestically, whereas
proceeding through the criminal justice system would impose substantial obstacles
that could impede the progress of its policies.[12]

[10] President George W. Bush, remarks at the Republican Governors Association fall
reception, September 19, 2002, http://www.whitehouse.gov/news/releases/2002/09/
20020919-14.html.
[11] Charles Lane, "War on Terrorism's Legal Tack is Rejected," *Washington Post*,
December 19, 2003, at 22.
[12] See, for example, a set of coordinated remarks by administration officials who defended the government's need to approach the war on terrorism on the basis of a military
paradigm rather than through a traditional law enforcement approach. See "Remarks by
the President at Bush-Cheney 2004 Reception," Houston, Tex., March 8, 2004,

Strategically, presidents understand only too well the dominant litigating posture they assume when claiming nonjusticiability of an issue as a "political question." Presidential assertion of a judicial incapacity to rule on a matter, when affirmed by the courts, automatically returns that issue to the *status quo ante*, i.e., the challenged policy that is the target of the suit (the president's position) prevails and remains undisturbed, though without the force of judicial precedent. The pattern of judicial reluctance to interfere with national security policy since *Baker* has left presidents with a fair degree of confidence that they have broad discretion to make policy in this area with minimal fear of judicial intervention.

Choices—For Presidents and for Courts

Presidents, then, face a dual legacy when it comes to deciding on the most effective strategy for litigating present-day national security cases. They can either (1) argue on the merits, as they did in the World War II cases, or they can (2) argue on some judicial avoidance doctrine, as they did in the later cases. Either way, the president, as Harold Koh reminds us in his aptly titled article, "(almost) always wins in foreign affairs."[13] The choice hinges on whether presidents wish to establish substantive precedents for the office by doing the legwork necessary to present reasoned constitutional arguments or whether they wish to assert automatic institutional dominance by preempting the field entirely and by disqualifying the judiciary's right to participate in deciding fundamental issues of constitutional law.

Courts, also, face this same legacy and same choice, and they, too, understand the consequences of selecting one strategy over the other. Thus, the current state of institutional relations between the executive and the judiciary is a vital part of this mix. In her analysis of the potential match-up between these two branches on those national security cases that, at the time, were likely to come before the Supreme Court, Linda Greenhouse cast this as "the imperial presidency vs. the imperial judiciary"[14]—and as "two inherently powerful institutions that for the last sev-

---

http://www.whitehouse.gov/news/releases/2004/03/20040308–21.html; "Remarks by Alberto R. Gonzales, Counsel to the President before the American Bar Association Standing Committee on Law and National Security," Washington, D.C., February 24, 2004, http://www.abanet.org/natsecurity/judge_gonzales.pdf; "Remarks by Secretary of Defense Donald H. Rumsfeld at Greater Miami Chamber of Commerce," Miami, Fla., February 13, 2004, http://www.defenselink.mil/transcripts/2004/tr20040213–0445.html; "Briefing on Detainee Operations at Guantanamo Bay," Department of Defense, Washington, D.C., February 13, 2004, http://www.dod.mil/faq/comment.html; "Remarks by the Vice-President at Bush-Cheney '04 Event," Minneapolis, Minn., February 23, 2004, http://www.whitehouse.gov/news/releases/2004/02/20040223–9.html.

[13] Harold Hongju Koh, *Why the President (Almost) Always Wins in Foreign Affairs: Lessons of the Iran-Contra Affair*, 97 Yale L.J. 1255, June 1988.

[14] Linda Greenhouse, "The Imperial Presidency vs. the Imperial Judiciary," *New York Times*, September 8, 2002, at 4.3

eral years have been in alpha mode, each intent on exercising its power to the maximum extent possible."[15] The question is whether the president will permit the courts to play *any* role at all and, presumably, establish judicial precedents for expansive presidential wartime authority in a post-World War II era, or whether the president will rule out the courts entirely in a post-*Baker* world, asserting that they have no role to play here. The president gets the first move, and the courts, as always, are in a reactive posture only. But Greenhouse noted that the courts (and *this* Supreme Court, in particular) will not be pushed aside lightly, and that even if the Court should rule that these issues do not meet threshold requirements, it will be the Court, not the president, who will make that determination.[16] The current Supreme Court, emboldened by its *Bush v. Gore* decision in December 2000 and by those where it has diminished the powers of Congress, sees itself as a player on the stage of national politics and is unlikely at this point to relinquish that spotlight and that influence. And, yet, the specific areas of military and national security policy are precisely the ones in which the Court, in its more recent cases, has restrained itself.

This brings us to the present cases and to an examination of whether the political question doctrine will play a role in the ongoing challenges to the administration's antiterrorism policies. That role, if it exists, would appear in government briefs and arguments and in court opinions. Justice Department officials would argue that the president should be unfettered in his ability to make national security policy, most especially, at a time when the nation is openly threatened by hostile forces and in the aftermath of a massive attack within its borders, and that courts should refrain from second-guessing in this policy area where they have no expertise or first-hand knowledge. For their part, courts adopting a political question doctrine approach would accept these executive branch arguments, and dismiss challenges to the president's policies without considering the merit of the arguments.

The focus of examination here will be on *Hamdi v. Rumsfeld* and *Padilla v. Rumsfeld* (later retitled *Padilla v. Hanft*, after being remanded by the Supreme Court back to the lower federal courts in South Carolina). These two cases address the detention of U.S. citizens as enemy combatants. The detention of foreign nationals at Guantanamo Bay, challenged in *Rasul v. Bush*, is an important issue, as well, but the fact of U.S. citizenship in the *Hamdi* and *Padilla* cases heightens the stakes to make these two cases slightly more critical.

If one searches the government briefs and court decisions to date in *Hamdi* and *Padilla*, one finds very few explicit references to the political question doctrine. Instead, there are Justice Department assertions of other judicial avoidance doctrines (e.g., jurisdictional challenges) and other expressions that urge the courts to rule that the president's power in this field is, of necessity, exclusive and not open to debate. Without relying on political question claims *overtly*, the executive

---

[15] Linda Greenhouse, "It's a Question of Federal Turf," *New York Times*, November 12, 2003 at 1
[16] *Id.*

branch has crafted a strategy that accomplishes the same objective by preempting the field and denying the courts much authority to rule. Effectively, then, civil liberties in wartime, according to the Bush administration, are what the president says they are.

The response in the lower federal courts in *Hamdi* and *Padilla* was somewhat mixed, with district court judges deciding on the merits and mostly against the government, and courts of appeals splitting—the Fourth Circuit ruling expansively for the government in *Hamdi* and in *Padilla v. Hanft*, primarily on the basis of deference to the executive, and the Second Circuit siding just as expansively with enemy combatant Padilla in the early round of this case. The pressure on courts to decide exactly how substantial a role they wish to play increases exponentially, as these cases go up the appellate court ladder to the next level, and once they are squarely inside the U.S. Supreme Court, it must determine whether it will use its judicial power to arbitrate between the executive and the Constitution. At issue here is nothing less than access to the courts when individual liberties are restricted by unilateral executive fiat.

The rest of this essay will address whether the political question doctrine has appeared so far a in the two citizen enemy combatant cases, *Hamdi* v. *Rumsfeld* and *Padilla* v. *Rumsfeld* (*Padilla* v. *Hanft*). It is first necessary to establish the basic factual underpinnings of the cases and the specific legal positions advocated by the government in its briefs and relied upon by the courts in their opinions. Although the major arguments urged by the government—and the responses by the courts to those arguments—will, of necessity, be examined here, this undertaking does not purport to be a thorough, detailed analysis of the nature and scope of the government's power to detain enemy combatants and the possible rights of such combatants. Rather, the intent of this chapter's inquiry is to consider more narrowly whether the political question doctrine has figured prominently in these arguments. Thus, the primary focus will be on identifying statements in case documents that shed light on whether the government or the courts conformed to a judicial avoidance posture.

Hamdi and *Padilla:* U.S. Citizens as Enemy Combatants

The cases of *Hamdi v. Rumsfeld* and *Padilla v. Rumsfeld* share the common issues of (1) whether the military may, based on its own criteria, designate American citizens as enemy combatants and detain them indefinitely, without charges and without access to counsel to contest their detention; (2) whether that designation may be challenged in the courts; and (3) if a challenge is permitted, what level of proof by the government is required to sustain it.

The two cases differ in that Yaser Esam Hamdi was captured overseas with a Taliban unit by the Northern Alliance in Afghanistan in late 2001 and then transferred by U.S. military authorities, first to Guantanamo Bay and later to a military brig in Norfolk, Virginia, and, ultimately, to one in Charleston, South Carolina. When his detention was challenged in court, the Department of Defense offered an affidavit, known as the Mobbs Declaration, as the sole evidentiary basis for capturing and holding him. This affidavit is a two-page (nine paragraphs) "declaration of facts," based on information from intelligence sources that establishes the facts surrounding the capture of Hamdi in Afghanistan.[17] Michael H. Mobbs is Special Advisor to the Under Secretary of Defense for Policy and heads the Detainee Policy Group.[18] Hamdi never saw this affidavit nor did he have any opportunity to discuss with his lawyers whether the facts contained in it were true.

Jose Padilla was arrested on a material witness warrant at O'Hare Airport in Chicago on May 8, 2002, and brought to New York City in connection with grand jury proceedings there. Based on a second, separate Mobbs Declaration from the Department of Defense, which described Padilla's associations with al Qaeda officials, the president determined on June 9, 2002 that Padilla was an enemy combatant and transferred him to military custody (and dropped the criminal charges) and moved him to a naval brig in Charleston, South Carolina. It was in this legal context that Padilla's case moved through the federal courts, up to and including the September 2005 decision at the Fourth Circuit Court of Appeals (*Padilla v. Hanft*, 05–6396), which reaffirmed the president's authority to hold him as an enemy combatant. His case took an abrupt turn in November 2005 when President Bush ordered him released from military custody, and the Department of Justice announced that he had been transferred to civilian jurisdiction and indicted in Florida on conspiracy charges.[19] He is scheduled to go on trial in fall 2006. One further attempt to get the U.S. Supreme Court to review the Fourth Circuit's 2005 decision in *Padilla v. Hanft* fizzled in April 2006, when the Court denied certiorari, based on "strong prudential considerations" that since Padilla was no longer in military custody, judicial consideration at this time of any possible rights he might assert under that status were only "hypothetical."[20] However, Justice Kennedy's statement that accompanied the denial of certiorari intimated that should Padilla be acquitted of criminal charges and returned to military custody once again as an enemy combatant, the Supreme Court would not hesitate to review his claims at that time.

---

[17] Brief submitted on behalf of the Center for Constitutional Rights . . . as Amici Curiae Supporting Yaser Esam Hamdi's Request for Affirmance, *Hamdi v. Rumsfeld*, 02–7338, U.S. Court of Appeals for the Fourth Circuit, October 24, 2002, at 11.

[18] Unclassified "Mobbs Declaration," August 27, 2002, on www.findlaw.com/legalnews/us/terrorism/cases.

[19] "Memorandum for the Secretary of Defense, Subject: Transfer of Detainee to Control of Attorney General," The White House, November 20, 2005; superceding indictment, *United States of America v. Adham Amin Hassoun, Mohamed Hesham Youssef, Kifah Wael Jayyousi, Kassem Daher, and Jose Padilla*, U.S. District Court, Southern District of Florida, Case No. 04–60001-CR-COOKE, November 17, 2005; and Unopposed Emergency Application and Notice of Release and Transfer of Custody of Petitioner Jose Padilla (05–6396, 4th Cir., Nov. 22, 2005). All of these documents are available on http://www.wiggin.com/practices/areainfo.asp?groupid=5&areaID=231.

[20] *Padilla v. Hanft* 547 U.S. __ (April 3, 2006).

Both defendants are American citizens, both were detained in military custody for an indefinite term, and both were denied access to counsel to challenge the basis for their detention. Both filed petitions for a writ of habeas corpus. Hamdi's petition was denied by the Fourth Circuit in January 2003, and Padilla's petition was affirmed by the Second Circuit in December 2003. The fact that one defendant was captured on foreign soil in the company of enemy forces during hostilities and the other was arrested within the territorial borders of the United States *is* a significant distinction, although both share overriding, broader legal questions.

One footnote to these cases is that, by February 2004, after both had been accepted for review by the U.S. Supreme Court, the Department of Defense announced that it would permit both Hamdi and Padilla to meet with their attorneys as "a matter of discretion and military authority" which "is not required by domestic or international law and should not be treated as a precedent."[21] These decisions were part of an evolving policy at the Defense Department for fashioning a review process for all detainees. Hamdi was offered the opportunity to meet with his counsel in December 2003, and the same offer was extended to Padilla in February 2004, after the military determined that such access "will not interfere with intelligence collection."[22] On May 18, 2004, the Department of Defense announced that it had ordered the establishment of annual administrative review procedures for enemy combatants housed at Guantanamo Bay, effective immediately.[23] Technically, this procedure did not apply to Hamdi or Padilla, since their ultimate detention location was not Guantanamo Bay. However, the broader issue of affording an annual review process to enemy combatants generally was, on its face, a welcomed and overdue step in the handling of all detainees captured in the war on terror.[24]

Additional updates in both cases are worth noting here. Following the June 28, 2004 Supreme Court decision in *Hamdi*, the government eventually released him from detention, and sent him back to Saudi Arabia in September 2004. The

---

[21] Thomas E. Ricks and Michael Powell, "Second Suspect Can See Lawyer," *Washington Post*, February 12, 2004, at A16.

[22] *Id.*

[23] Department of Defense, "Review Procedures Announced for Guantanamo Detainees," http://www.dod.gov/releases/2004/nr20040518-0806.html. The administrative review procedures may be found at http://www.defenselink.mil/news/May2004/d20040518gtmoreview.pdf.

[24] However, even this effort by the Defense Department to offer administrative hearings (to determine status initially and, then, review annually) to enemy combatants at Guantanamo has taken a controversial turn, with passage of the Graham-Levin-Kyl amendment, known as the Detainee Treatment Act of 2005, to the Defense Appropriations Act of 2006, P.L. 109–148, Secs. 1001–06). This amendment is currently under court challenge to determine the scope of its application of a sharply limited federal court jurisdiction to review only in the Court of Appeals, thus, effectively, denying a right of habeas corpus to detainees wishing to contest their detention. See *Al Odah v. U.S.* (05–5064, D.C. Cir.) and *Boumediene v. Bush* (05–5062, D.C. Cir.), both currently awaiting decision at the D.C. Circuit Court of Appeals.

case of Jose Padilla is still ongoing, refashioned and retitled as *Padilla v. Hanft* subsequent to the Supreme Court decision in June 2004, and in the government's opening brief filed in the Fourth Circuit in May 2005, new facts were submitted from an additional declaration (Rapp) that redefined the terms of the capture of Padilla by U.S. agents. The government no longer described him as being captured "on U.S. soil," but, rather, it argued that because he was *almost* captured by U.S. forces in Afghanistan in November 2001 but managed to escape into Pakistan, that his status was no different than Hamdi's (i.e., a battlefield combatant) because the Rapp affidavit now claimed that Padilla had been present *at one time* on a foreign battlefield. The government also offered other arguments to support its position at the Fourth Circuit stage that Padilla's status could no longer be distinguished from Hamdi's, once it produced evidence and arguments that Padilla's capture at O'Hare Airport did not qualify as "on U.S. soil."[25]

Summary of Legal Proceedings: *Hamdi v. Rumsfeld*

Hamdi's petition for a writ of habeas corpus, filed on May 10, 2002 in the District Court of the Eastern District of Virginia, was met with several rulings from that court ordering access to counsel. The government appealed each order and obtained stays from the district court and the Fourth Circuit Court of Appeals. On August 16, 2002, the district court found that the Mobbs Declaration was not sufficient for "meaningful judicial review" of Hamdi's detention. The court ordered the government to produce additional documentary information, whereupon the government appealed the order to the Fourth Circuit Court of Appeals for interlocutory review. On January 8, 2003, a Fourth Circuit panel reversed the district court order and ruled that the Mobbs Declaration was sufficient to sustain Hamdi's detention, and that the petition should be dismissed. The panel found that "because it is undisputed that Hamdi was captured in a zone of active combat in a foreign theater of conflict . . . the submitted declaration is a sufficient basis upon which to conclude that the Commander in Chief has constitutionally detained Hamdi pursuant to the war powers entrusted to him by the United States Constitution."[26] Thus, the capture of an American citizen in a combat zone was the only justification the government needed to offer in order

---

[25] See *Padilla v. Hanft*, Opening Brief for the Appellant, No. 05–6396, U.S. Court of Appeals for the Fourth Circuit, May 6, 2005. Among the arguments advanced in this brief are (1) that the entire world, including the U.S., is a "battlefield" in the war on terror, (2) that "locus of capture" is not a relevant fact, and (3) even if it is, Padilla's detention in the "secure customs area" at O'Hare Airport did not constitute "entry" into the U.S., since he was "never free from official restraint," and thus, had not "entered" the U.S. Therefore, the government now maintained in this brief that Padilla had not been "captured on U.S. soil," and that he was a "classic battlefield combatant."

[26] 316 F. 3d 450 (4th Cir. 2003).

to convince the court that the president had the power to detain a citizen indefinitely.

Hamdi's public defender, Frank Dunham, sought rehearing en banc, and on July 9, 2003, the Fourth Circuit, by an 8–4 vote, denied rehearing. Dunham petitioned the U.S. Supreme Court for a writ of certiorari in the October Term of 2003, which granted the petition and heard argument on April 28, 2004.

Government's Arguments: *Hamdi v. Rumsfeld*

The government's briefs in *Hamdi* are filled with cautions to the court "to act with special care in reviewing the challenge in this case."[27] The following passage is a crisp articulation of its position.

> . . . courts have an extremely narrow role in reviewing the adequacy of the government's return in a habeas action, such as this, challenging the quintessentially military judgment to detain an individual as an enemy combatant in a time of war. A court's inquiry should come to an end once the military has shown in the return that it has determined that the detainee is an enemy combatant. Although counsel may argue that that status is not a legally sufficient reason to justify the individual's detention . . . , the Court may not second-guess the military's enemy combatant determination. At the very most, given the separation of constitutional powers in this unique area, a court could only require the military to point to some evidence supporting *its* determination. Either way, no evidentiary hearing is required to dispose of a habeas petition in this military context.[28]

In short, the government argued in the Fourth Circuit that the concerns that arise in entertaining habeas petitions on behalf of enemies in time of hostilities as identified in *Johnson v. Eisentrager* are very much alive in this case, quoting from *Eisentrager*, "It would be difficult to devise a more effective fettering of a field commander than to allow the very enemies he is ordered to reduce to submission to call him to account in his own civil courts and divert his efforts and attention from the military offensive abroad to the legal defensive at home."[29] Acknowledging that the issues in *Eisentrager*, where the Court upheld the use of military commissions for German soldiers who were captured and tried for war crimes by the U.S. in China, were not fully analogous, the government still maintained that the same concern for judicial interference with military operations that was operative in *Eisentrager* was equally valid here, as well as the added risk in Hamdi's case of possible interference with intelligence-gathering if he were permitted to consult with counsel. "Thus, no evidentiary proceedings are required to resolve a habeas petition filed on behalf of such a detainee and no access between the de-

---

[27] Brief for Respondents-Appellants, 02–6895, *Hamdi v. Rumsfeld*, U.S. Court of Appeals for the Fourth Circuit, June 19, 2003, at 10.

[28] *Id.* at 12, emphasis in original.

[29] 339 U.S. 763, 779 (1950).

tainee and counsel for the next-friend is necessary."[30] All a court needed to do was to accept the military's determination that a detainee was an enemy combatant. "Going beyond that determination would require the courts to enter an area in which they have no competence, much less institutional expertise, intrude upon the constitutional prerogative of the Commander in Chief (and military authorities acting at his control), and possibly create 'a conflict between judicial and military opinion highly comforting to enemies of the United States.' *Eisentrager*, 339 U.S. at 779."[31] To the government, "a court's proper role would be solely to confirm that there was some factual basis to support that determination (that an individual is an enemy combatant)."[32]

In the government's response brief to the petition for a writ of certiorari in the Supreme Court, it argued that the Fourth Circuit's decision was correct on three grounds: the president's wartime authority to seize and detain enemy combatants (1) was consistent with prior rulings of the Supreme Court that recognized such authority (relying on *Quirin*), and that authority was not affected by the fact that Hamdi was a citizen; (2) was authorized by Congress when it had enacted express statutory authorization to the president on September 18, 2001 to use "all necessary and appropriate force" to respond to the terrorist attacks; and (3) was supported by "the time honored laws and customs of war."[33]

The government supported its argument that "the president's constitutional authority to capture and detain enemy combatants is at its height with respect to the detainee in this case"[34] by (1) interpreting Congress's September 2001 authorization as satisfying the first category of Justice Jackson's matrix of presidential emergency powers ("when the President acts pursuant to an express or implied authorization of Congress")[35], and (2) by claiming that when a person is captured in an active combat zone, the determination by the president that this person is an enemy combatant is "a quintessentially military judgment," citing *Hirota v. MacArthur*[36] that "the military—unlike Article III courts—has a unique institutional capacity to make enemy combatant determinations," and that a court's proper role in these circumstances is to confirm only that a factual basis exists for the military's determination of enemy combatant status.[37] Third, the government explained that the president's detention authority here did not violate 18 U.S.C. 4001 (a) because that statute applies only to civilian detentions, not military ones, as

---

[30] Brief for Respondents-Appellants, 02–6895, *Hamdi v. Rumsfeld*, U.S. Court of Appeals for the Fourth Circuit, June 19, 2003, at 30.

[31] *Id.* at 31, quoting from *Eisentrager*.

[32] *Id.* at 34.

[33] Brief for Respondents in Opposition, *Hamdi v. Rumsfeld*, U.S. Supreme Court, 03–6696, December 2003, at 13.

[34] *Id.* at 15.

[35] *Youngstown Sheet and Tube Co. v. Sawyer*, 343 U.S. at 635 (1952) (Jackson, J., concurring).

[36] 338 U.S. 197, 215 (1949) (Douglas, J., concurring).

[37] Brief for Respondents in Opposition, *Hamdi v. Rumsfeld*, U.S. Supreme Court, 03–6696, December 2003, at 16–17.

Section 4001was placed in Title 18 of the United States Code governing "Crimes and Criminal Procedure," and even if 18 U.S.C. applied to military detentions, there were two acts of Congress authorizing the president's authority in this case[38] and Defense Department appropriations for "prisoners of war" and for individuals "similar to prisoners of war"[39] that exempted it from coverage.[40] Finally, the government rejected Hamdi's lawyers' argument that hostilities in Afghanistan had concluded by noting that U.S. troops were still on the ground in that country, and that "the determination as to when hostilities have ceased is for the political branches and not appropriate for judicial resolution," citing *Ludecke v. Watkins*.[41]

A footnote on pages 25–26 in the government's response brief to the certiorari petition in the Supreme Court in December 2003 heralded the first announcement of a change in policy.[42] The government commented on the damaging consequences that could arise if an enemy combatant were afforded immediate access to counsel as a matter of right, as Hamdi's lawyers had argued, in that such access would impermissibly interfere with the gathering of intelligence by the military in its pursuit of the ongoing war. But, it also stated for the first time that "as a matter of discretion and military policy, the Department of Defense has adopted a policy of permitting access to counsel by an enemy combatant who is a United States citizen and is detained by the military in the United States, when DOD has determined that such access will not compromise the national security of the United States, and when DOD has determined either that it has completed intelligence collection from the enemy combatant or that granting access to counsel would not interfere with such intelligence gathering. In accordance with DOD's policy and the military's ongoing evaluation of Hamdi's detention, DOD has determined that Hamdi may be permitted access to counsel subject to appropriate security restrictions."[43] However, the government asserted that this new willingness to provide Hamdi with access to counsel did not impact the Fourth Circuit's decision, since that ruling did not reach the question of whether Hamdi's detention without access to counsel was justified by an intelligence-gathering need.

District Court Opinion in *Hamdi v. Rumsfeld*

The key issue in the district court was whether the Mobbs Declaration was sufficient as the factual basis for purposes of "meaningful judicial review" in a habeas corpus petition. Judge Doumar of the Eastern District of Virginia ruled on

---

[38] Pub.L. 107–40 (2001).

[39] 10 U.S.C. 956(5) and 10 U.S.C. 956(4).

[40] Brief for Respondents in Opposition, *Hamdi v. Rumsfeld*, U.S. Supreme Court, 03-6696, December 2003, at 26-27.

[41] *Id.* at 30; *Ludecke v. Watkins*, 335 U.S. 160 (1948).

[42] See page 10, infra.

[43] Brief for Respondents in Opposition, Hamdi v. Rumsfeld, U.S. Supreme Court, 03-6696, December 2003 at 25-26, n. 11; see http://dod.gov/releases/2003/nr20031202–0717.html.

July 31, 2002, that it was not, in part, because the information included in it was based on hearsay supplied by the Northern Alliance.[44] The district court, however, did not order access to counsel for Hamdi, but, instead, ordered the government to produce more evidence for in camera review. The government refused to comply with the order for more documents, and petitioned the Fourth Circuit for interlocutory review, where, on August 8, 2002, the Fourth Circuit directed the district court to "consider the sufficiency of the Mobbs Declaration as an independent matter before proceeding further."[45] The District Court then ruled on August 16, 2002, that, again, the Mobbs Declaration did not satisfy even minimal criteria for meaningful judicial review, and that "it leads to more questions than it answers."[46] The court, once again, ordered the government to submit to the district court the materials requested in its July 31 order so that the court may determine if the Mobbs Declaration is sufficient.

While Judge Doumar expressed respect for executive deference in military matters in his August 16 opinion, he also forcefully defended the power of the judiciary to protect individual rights, even when juxtaposed in a national security context. Doumar explained that:

> While it is clear that the Executive is entitled to deference regarding military designations of individuals, it is equally clear that the judiciary is entitled to a meaningful judicial review of those designations when they substantially infringe on the individual liberties, guaranteed by the United States Constitution, of American citizens. . . . The standard of judicial inquiry must . . . recognize that the "concept of 'national defense' cannot be deemed an end in itself, justifying any exercise of (executive) power designed to promote such a goal. Implicit in the term 'national defense' is the notion of defending those values and ideals that set this nation apart. . . . It would indeed be ironic if, in the name of national defense, we would sanction the subversion of one of those liberties . . . which makes the defense of the Nation worthwhile."[47]

He then examined the requirements of the Fifth Amendment Due Process Clause and noted that the government conceded at argument that Hamdi was entitled to access to counsel (since the government analogized Hamdi to the American defendant in *Quirin*—and then recognized that the *Quirin* defendant *was,* indeed, entitled to counsel). Thus, Doumar ruled that Hamdi's indefinite detention on U.S. soil entitled him to due process under the Fifth Amendment, although he (and Hamdi's lawyers, also) noted that the initial detention in a foreign land during ongoing hostilities was *not* properly subject to a due process challenge. Under that due process standard, Doumar ruled that the Mobbs Declaration was not sufficient

---

[44] Petition for Writ of Certiorari, *Hamdi v. Rumsfeld,* U.S. Supreme Court, October 1, 2003, at 9.

[45] August 8, 2002 order at 2.

[46] *Hamdi v. Rumsfeld,* Civil Action No.2:02cv439, August 16, 2002, at 9.

[47] *Hamdi v. Rumsfeld,* Civil Action No. 2:02cv439, August 16, 2002 at 8, quoting from *U.S. v. Robel,* 389 U.S. 258, 264 (1967).

to allow a court to determine if Hamdi's Fifth Amendment rights had been violated.[48]

Fourth Circuit Court of Appeals Decision in *Hamdi v. Rumsfeld*

A three-judge panel of the Fourth Circuit ruled on January 8, 2003, that Hamdi's detention was lawful and "virtually immune from factual inquiry by the judiciary," based largely on the fact that he was seized in a zone of active combat.[49] The panel reversed the District Court's August 16 production order, ruled that the Mobbs Declaration was sufficient as "some evidence" supporting the government's seizure and detention of Hamdi, and remanded to the district court with instructions to dismiss the habeas petition.[50]

The panel opinion took special care in examining the role of the judiciary during wartime. It started by noting that Articles I and II were quite specific in the expressed powers they allocated to the executive and legislative branches to address military and foreign policy matters, while Article III contained no analogous powers of such precision. It explained that such deference to the warmaking powers of the president and Congress was warranted because the executive had "expertise and experience" and because it was most appropriate to leave fundamental decisions regarding protection and sacrifice to the "branches most accountable to the people. . . . "[51] But it also stated that "judicial deference to executive decisions made in the name of war is not unlimited," and that "the duty of the judicial branch to protect our individual freedoms does not simply cease whenever our military forces are committed by the political branches to armed conflict," and that, therefore, "the detention of United States citizens must be subject to judicial review."[52]

On their face, these last three pronouncements constituted broad acknowledgement of the role of courts in reviewing wartime executive decisions. But the remainder of the opinion is a paean to executive power, and forcefully rejects the right of an enemy combatant to challenge his status and detention and, by extension, denies any substantive role for the courts in the protection of individual liberties in such circumstances. It acknowledges the inability to transfer the criminal law to the arena of armed conflict, and it recognizes the need for the executive branch to maintain "adaptability" in dealing with the evolving nature of threats to America. It views the designation of enemy combatants as "the closest imaginable connection to the president's constitutional responsibilities during the actual con-

---

[48] Id. at 8.
[49] Petition for Writ of Certiorari, *Hamdi v. Rumsfeld*, U.S. Supreme Court, October 1, 2003, at 3.
[50] *Hamdi v. Rumsfeld*, 316 F. 3d 450 (4th Cir. 2003).
[51] *Hamdi v. Rumsfeld*, 316 F.3d 450 (4th Cir. 2003).
[52] *Id.*

duct of hostilities."[53] It is also acutely aware of the burdens on government when legal challenges arise, as reflected in its pointed rebuke to the district court for overreaching in its production order: "The military has been charged by Congress and the executive with winning a war, not prevailing in a possible court case."[54]

The opinion concludes by noting that "the constitutional allocation of war powers affords the President extraordinarily broad authority as Commander in Chief and compels courts to assume a deferential posture in reviewing exercises of this authority. And, while the Constitution assigns courts the duty generally to review executive detentions that are alleged to be illegal, the Constitution does not specifically contemplate any role for courts in the conduct of war, or in foreign policy generally. . . . The privilege of citizenship entitles Hamdi to a limited judicial inquiry into his detention, but only to determine its legality under the war powers of the political branches. At least where it is undisputed that he was present in a zone of active combat operations, we are satisfied that the Constitution does not entitle him to a searching review."[55]

Hamdi filed a petition for rehearing in the Fourth Circuit, and one member of the court requested a vote for rehearing en banc. On July 9, 2003, the court voted eight to four to deny rehearing.[56] Judge Wilkinson and Judge Traxler wrote opinions, concurring in the denial of rehearing en banc. Judge Motz and Judge Luttig wrote opinions, dissenting from the denial of rehearing en banc, although for vastly different reasons.

Judge Luttig's concern was that the panel's opinion was "unpersuasive" and had not been sufficiently deferential to the government, while Judge Motz was the only judge on this court to maintain that the Mobbs Declaration *was* insufficient to justify Hamdi's enemy combatant status.

Judge Luttig wanted the court to rest its decision not on Hamdi's concession of the "undisputed" nature of the circumstances under which he was seized but rather on the deferential judicial standard urged by the government ("some factual basis," in contrast to the panel's "meaningful judicial review") when a president makes wartime decisions, such as designation of enemy combatants. In fact, Judge Luttig pierced through the panel's decision and scolded his fellow judges for their inconsistent result.

> The panel promised the Executive that the Judiciary would not sit in full review of his judgments as to who is an enemy combatant of the United States, but it adopted a rule that will henceforth do just that, cast the Judiciary as ultimate arbiter, in each and every instance, of whether the Executive has properly classified a detainee . . . it is apparent that the rule of law that was fashioned by the panel professedly in the name of deference to the Executive, and that now binds us, is, in application, a rule of no deference at all. For counsel must now be provided and judicial review had of the Executive's determination that one is an enemy com-

---

[53] *Id.*
[54] *Id.*
[55] *Id.*
[56] *Id.*

batant in every instance in which the petitioner but refrains from affirmative concession that he was seized in a foreign combat zone.[57]

Judge Motz chastised her brethren in the opposite direction, remarking that:

> the panel's decision marks the first time in our history that a federal court has approved the elimination of protections afforded a citizen by the Constitution solely on the basis of the Executive's designation of that citizen as an enemy combatant, without testing the accuracy of the designation. Neither the Constitution nor controlling precedent sanction this holding. . . . Without any acknowledgement of its break with precedent, the panel embarks on a perilous new course—approving the Executive's designation of enemy combatant status not on the basis of facts stipulated or proven, but solely on the basis of an unknown Executive advisor's declaration, which the panel itself concedes is subject to challenge as 'incomplete [ ]' and 'inconsisten[t]' hearsay. *Hamdi*, 316 F.3d at 473. . . . This is a thin reed on which to rest abrogation of constitutional rights.[58]

Judge Motz concluded her dissent with emotional appeals to the Court to "be vigilant in guarding Constitutional freedoms, perhaps never more so than in time of war" and to "not forget the lesson of *Korematsu*," where the Court deferred to a report by a member of the military, not so unlike the Mobbs Declaration, that explained the executive's actions.[59]

Summary of Legal Proceedings: *Padilla v. Rumsfeld*

Padilla's attorney filed a petition for a writ of habeas corpus on June 11, 2002, in the District Court of the Southern District of New York. On December 4, 2002, the court denied the government's motion to dismiss Padilla's habeas corpus petition, and ordered that he be permitted access to counsel for the purpose of challenging the factual basis of his enemy combatant designation. The court ordered further proceedings to establish conditions for access to counsel that would minimize any national security concerns. The government motioned for reconsideration of the order on the basis that affording Padilla access to counsel would compromise intelligence gathering. On March 11, 2003, Judge Michael Mukasey issued an opinion and order that reconsidered but rejected the government's arguments, and on April 9, he certified his previous orders for interlocutory appeal to the Second Circuit Court of Appeals. The Second Circuit heard oral arguments on November 17, 2003, and a three-judge panel issued a 2–1 decision on December 18, 2003, granting Padilla's request for a writ of habeas corpus and ordering the government to either bring criminal charges

---

[57] *Hamdi v. Rumsfeld*, 337 F. 3d 335 (4th Cir. 2003) [(Luttig, J., dissenting).

[58] *Id.* (Motz, J., dissenting).

[59] *Id.*

against him, arrest him as a material witness, or release him from custody within thirty days. The court held that the president does not have inherent constitutional authority to detain as an enemy combatant an American citizen seized within the country's borders and out of a zone of combat and that any such detention of American citizens must be expressly authorized by Congress. The Joint Resolution passed by Congress in September 2001 to authorize the use of military force against persons responsible for the September 11 terrorist attacks does not qualify as express authorization for detention of U.S. citizens in the domestic context and does not constitute the necessary statutory authorization for detention of U.S. citizens as an exception to the requirements of 18 U.S.C. 4001(a). The government appealed the ruling, petitioning the Supreme Court for a writ of certiorari. The Court granted the petition, and heard argument on April 28, 2004.

Government's Arguments: *Padilla v. Rumsfeld*

The government responded to Padilla's petition for a writ of habeas corpus in the district court with both procedural and substantive claims. Procedurally, it motioned to dismiss for lack of jurisdiction on the basis that (a) attorney Donna Newman did not satisfy the standards for "next friend" status in a habeas action; (b) that the proper respondent was Commander M. A. Marr, not President Bush, Secretary of Defense Cheney, or Attorney General Ashcroft, as named in the petition; and (c) that none of these named respondents is within the court's territorial jurisdiction.[60]

A summary of the key substantive points made by the government in its arguments on the merits to the district court and to the Second Circuit includes the following:

1. "[T]he authority of the United States to seize and detain enemy combatants is well-settled—and vital to our core military objectives, including preventing enemies from rejoining the conflict and gathering intelligence to prevent attacks on Americans and U.S. interests."[61] The government cited *Ex parte Quirin, In re Territo, Ex parte Toscano,* and *Colepaugh v. Looney* for support.[62]

2. "The capture and detention of enemy combatants during wartime falls within the President's core constitutional powers as Commander-in-Chief, which, in the present conflict, are exercised with the specific support of Congress. See *Hamdi v. Rumsfeld,* 296 F. 3d 278,281-282 (4th Cir. 2002). The Supreme

---

[60] Motion to Dismiss, Amended Petition for Writ of Habeas Corpus, 02 Civ. 4445, June 26, 2002, at 2.

[61] Motion to Dismiss, June 26, 2002, at 5.

[62] *Ex parte Quirin,* 317 U.S. 1, 31, 35 (1942); *In re Territo,* 156 F.2d 142, 145 (9th Cir. 1946); *Ex parte Toscano,* 208 F. 938, 940 (S.D. Cal. 1913); and *Colepaugh v. Looney,* 235 F.2d 429, 432 (10th Cir. 1956).

Court has 'stated in no uncertain terms that the President's wartime detention decisions are to be accorded great deference from the courts,' id. at 282 (citing *Ex parte Quirin*, 317 U.S. 1, 25 [1942])."[63] The government expanded on the issue of judicial deference to the president by quoting again from the Fourth Circuit's July 12, 2002 opinion in *Hamdi* that the petition in *Padilla*, as in *Hamdi*, "'arises in the context of foreign relations and national security, where a court's deference to the political branches of our national government is considerable.'"[64] The government referenced *U.S. v. Curtiss-Wright Export Corp.*, *The Prize Cases*, *Able v. U.S.*, and *Rostker v. Goldberg* to bolster its point that the courts have exhibited consistent deference to military judgments and have repeatedly refrained from entertaining challenges to military decisions.[65]

3. Judicial review of the president's determination that Padilla is an enemy combatant should, if at all, extend no further than in assessing whether there was "some evidence" supporting that determination, and the Mobbs Declaration is sufficient as factual evidence for the president's determination. "To the extent that the courts conclude that judicial review may be had of an executive determination during a war that an individual is an enemy combatant, such review is limited to confirming based on some evidence the existence of a factual basis supporting the determination. . . . The President's determination of June 9, 2002, and the attached Mobbs Declaration more than amply demonstrate the existence of a factual basis to support the determination that Padilla is an enemy combatant. . . . The reasons for limiting judicial second-guessing of the factual basis for an executive determination are at their most compelling in the circumstances of this case, which involves a challenge to the President's determination in a time of war that a particular individual is an enemy combatant who came to the United States as an al Qaeda affiliate to advance the enemy's terrorist campaign against United State citizens. Such determinations involve highly sensitive intelligence information and judgment calls about the credibility of foreign intelligence sources. The President's determination as commander in chief that an individual is an enemy combatant should, at a bare minimum, be accorded effect by the courts as long as some evidence supports that determination. . . . A more demanding inquiry would invite the 'special hazards of judicial involvement in military decision-making,' and 'would stand the warmaking powers of Articles I and II on their heads (*Hamdi*, 296 F. 3d at 284).'"[66]

4. In addition to the president's Article II Commander-in-Chief power, the government noted that two acts of Congress further supported the executive's authority to detain enemy combatants: the Authorization for the Use of Military

<hr>

[63] Respondents' Response to and Motion to Dismiss, the Amended Petition for a Writ of Habeas Corpus, 02 Civ. 4445, August 27, 2002, at 7.

[64] 296 F.3d at 281.

[65] 299 U.S. 304, 319-321 (1936); 67 U.S. (2 Black) 635, 670 (1862); 155 F.3d 628,633 (2d Cir. 1998); and 453 U.S. 57, 66 (1981).

[66] Respondents' Response, August 27, 2002, at 8-9.

Force, Pub. L. No. 107–40 (September 18, 2001), where they stated that Congress's express authorization to the president "to use force against those 'nations, organizations, or persons he determines' were responsible for the September 11 terrorist attacks" encompasses the detention of enemy combatants; and appropriations for the Department of Defense under 10 U.S.C. 956(5) to provide for "the maintenance, pay, and allowances of prisoners of war [and] other persons in the custody of the Army, Navy, or Air Force whose status is determined by the Secretary concerned to be similar to prisoners of war."[67] However, the government noted that "The President's exercise of his constitutional powers as commander in chief does not require the authorization of Congress."[68] The government claimed that the president had sufficient Article II constitutional authority to detain enemy combatants in a time of war, and that congressional authorization simply provided additional, though unnecessary, authority. Furthermore, the government explained that since the Authorization for Use of Military Force, Pub. L. 107-40 (2001) gave express authority to the president to use armed force, it only followed naturally that the greater encompassed the lesser, i.e., that "the authority to use force in an armed conflict necessarily embraces an attendant authority to capture and detain enemy combatants."[69]

5. The government responded to plaintiff's claim that presidents may detain enemy combatants only in a declared war between two nation states by quoting from *The Prize Cases* and *Johnson v. Eisentrager* and noting that "whether a state of armed conflict exists to which the laws of war apply is a political question for the President, not the courts to decide."[70] Again, the government borrowed from the Fourth Circuit's *Hamdi* decision[71] for its argument against a more searching review by the judiciary of the factual basis supporting the president's determination, stating that such a review "would entangle the judiciary in highly sensitive judgments about the reliability of foreign intelligence sources and the assessment of military justifications. . . . The judiciary is ill-equipped to conduct that manner of second-guessing of sensitive executive judgments, which lie at the heart of the President's exercise of his authority as Commander-in-Chief in wartime."[72]

6. In its January 9, 2003, filing of a Respondent's Motion for Reconsideration in Part of District Court Judge Mukasey's December 4, 2002, order to require the government to permit counsel to meet with Padilla, the government narrowed its argument to one focused on the needs of intelligence gathering and on Padilla's potential value as a source in this effort. It submitted to the court

---

[67] *Id.* at 11–12.
[68] Respondents' Reply in Support of Motion to Dismiss the Amended Petition for a Writ of Habeas Corpus, 02 Civ. 4445, October 11, 2002, at 12.
[69] *Id.* at 13.
[70] *Prize,* 67 U.S. (2 Black) 635, 670 (1862) and *Johnson,* 339 U.S. 763, 789 (1950); Respondents' Reply, October 11, 2002, at 7.
[71] 294 F. 3d at 284.
[72] Respondents' Reply, October 11, 2002, at 24.

the Jacoby Declaration, which assessed Padilla's potential intelligence value as "very high" and predicted that "providing Padilla access to counsel risks loss of a critical intelligence resource, resulting in a grave and direct threat to national security."[73] Judge Mukasey was not persuaded of these dire consequences, and in his March 11, 2003, opinion, rejected the government's motion to reconsider the court's December 2002 holding that Padilla be permitted to consult with counsel.

7. The government's brief in the Court of Appeals for the Second Circuit reprised many of the same arguments that had appeared in its district court filings. Again, there were motions to dismiss on jurisdictional grounds, and, similarly, the primary issue on the merits on appeal was whether the district court erred in ordering that Padilla be permitted to meet with counsel to contest the facts on which the president determined him an enemy combatant. Once more, the government argued that neither the Constitution nor the laws or customs of war afford enemy combatants the right to counsel for the purpose of challenging their detention. And, once more, the government turned to the Fourth Circuit's *Hamdi* decision, which rejected the right of an enemy combatant to contest the factual basis for his detention, and urged the Second Circuit here to adopt the same ruling. The government argued here that since an enemy combatant is not entitled to present facts to challenge the basis of his detention nor entitled to counsel for that purpose, the district court's order is in error as a matter of law. The Fourth Circuit in *Hamdi* noted that in an ordinary habeas proceeding, there is a normal expectation of factual development, whereas when the government detains on the basis of its warmaking powers, as it did in both *Hamdi* and *Padilla*, any effort to develop the facts "only *begs the basic question* in this case whether further factual exploration would bring an Article III court into conflict with the warmaking powers of Article I and II. Here, the specific interests asserted by the government flow directly from the warmaking powers . . . (*Hamdi III*, 316 F. 3d at 470 [emphasis added])."

In essence, the government urged that the proper standard for courts to review a president's determination of an enemy combatant designation consists, at most, of whether there was "some evidence" to support the president's decision. But because that standard depends solely on the facts presented by the president, there is no need for a right to counsel to contest those facts. Quoting from *Hamdi*, it further argued that "the determination that Padilla is an enemy combatant 'bears the closest imaginable connection to the President's constitutional responsibilities during the actual conduct of hostilities' (*Hamdi III*, 316 F. 3d at 466). That determination turns on considerations uniquely within the authority and expertise of the Commander in Chief." A quote here from Douglas's concurring opinion in *Hirota v. MacArthur* provides the clearest statement indicating that the government saw this issue as a political question: "The capture and control of those who were re-

---

[73] Declaration of Vice Admiral Lowell E. Jacoby [USN], Director of the Defense Intelligence Agency, January 9, 2003.

sponsible for the Pearl Harbor incident was a political question on which the President as Commander-in-Chief, and as spokesman for the nation in foreign affairs, had the final say."[74]

Similarly, the government expressed its concern that permitting Padilla to have access to counsel to contest the Mobbs Declaration "would risk entangling the judiciary in highly sensitive judgments lying at the heart of the Commander-in-Chief power."[75] It would also impose on the court the need "to weigh that (Padilla's) evidence against the Mobbs Declaration and assess the relative reliability of each. That would require the court to . . . ascertain the nature of Padilla's activities and associations while in Afghanistan and Pakistan . . . and the reliability of foreign intelligence sources and information. Those sorts of 'fine' judgments in evaluating whether a particular activity is linked to the war efforts of a hostile power are judgments the executive branch is most competent to make' *Hamdi III*, 316 F. 3d at 474. Any effort to ascertain the facts concerning (Padilla's) conduct while amongst the nation's enemies would entail an unacceptable risk of obstructing war efforts authorized by Congress and undertaken by the executive branch. Id. at 474–75."[76]

District Court Decision in *Padilla*

District Court Judge Mukasey issued opinions and orders on December 4, 2002, March 11, 2003, and April 9, 2003. Below is a summary of his rulings on the issues and some of his comments on the role of the courts in these matters.

He agreed that the commander in chief has wartime authority to detain enemy combatants, even when they are U.S. citizens captured on U.S. soil, as Padilla was.[77] Citing heavily from *The Prize Cases*, he asserted that commander-in-chief authority was not confined to circumstances involving a formal declaration of war or a conventional conflict between nation-states, and he commented that, in *Prize*, "the Court made it plain that what military measures were necessary was a political and not a judicial decision."[78] At a later point in his opinion, Mukasey emphasized that "the 'political branches,' when they make judgments on the exercise of war powers under Articles I and II, as both branches have here, need not submit those judgments to review by Article III courts. Rather, they are subject to the perhaps less didactic but nonetheless searching audit of the democratic process."[79]

---

[74] 338 U.S. 197, 215 (1949).

[75] Brief of Respondent-Appellant, 03–2235, July 24, 2003, at 46.

[76] Id.

[77] *Padilla v. Rumsfeld*, 02 Civ. 4445, December 4, 2002, at 92.

[78] *Id.* at 50; *Prize*, 67 U.S. (2 Black) 635.

[79] *Id.* at 95.

He also agreed that the proper standard of review for the courts of the president's determination of enemy combatants is a deferential one of whether there is "some evidence" supporting that determination.[80]

But he disagreed with the government that the Mobbs Declaration was sufficient as "some evidence."[81] Additionally, the court ruled that Padilla should be afforded access to counsel for the purpose of presenting facts in support of a habeas corpus petition as a matter of discretion under the All Writs Act, and to determine whether the evidence supporting the president's finding has been mooted by subsequent events.[82]

He held that Padilla's detention is not barred by 18 U.S.C. 4001(a), and that the Authorization for Use of Military Force, Pub. L. 107–40 (2001) satisfies the requirement under 18 U.S.C. 4001(a) as an "act of Congress" under which American citizens may be detained.[83]

He addressed the issue of whether a court may define at this point the conditions that will determine when the current conflict has ended, characterizing the issue as one that "defies the basic concept of Article III jurisdiction. Federal courts, it will be recalled, are not permitted to deal with any but actual 'cases' and 'controversies' . . . as opposed to those disputes that live only on the agendas of interested parties."[84] As for whether Padilla may claim that a court should be able to decide when he may be released, either because he has been detained excessively or because hostilities have ended, the court left that issue for another day, noting that "I do not understand Padilla to be making that claim now, and therefore see no need to face that issue now."[85]

Below are some comments about the scope of executive and judicial power by Second Circuit judges and government attorneys during the November 2003 hearing that are worth noting.

1. Judge Parker: "It (the case) implicates our powers as Article III courts to advise our coordinate branches on what the Constitution means."[86]
2. Judge Parker: "And . . . were we to construe the Constitution as permitting this kind of power in the Executive with only the modest—according to the government's proposal—kind of judicial review, we would be effecting a sea change in the constitutional life of this country."[87]
3. Paul Clement, Deputy Solicitor General: "in these realms of foreign policy and president's commander in chief authority, the power of the courts is at its limit."[88]

---

[80] *Id.* at 3.
[81] *Id.* at 75.
[82] *Id.* at 3.
[83] *Id.* at 71–72.
[84] *Id.* at 56.
[85] *Id.* at 56–57.
[86] Transcript, *Padilla v. Rumsfeld*, 2d Cir., November 17, 2003, at 69.
[87] *Id.* at 116.
[88] *Id.* at 69.

4. Paul Clement: "If one is not going to defer to the Executive's judgment (on combatant determination), what you would do is almost have to bring in the individuals that are referenced in Footnote 1 of the Mobbs declaration on page 5."[89]

Second Circuit Opinion—*Padilla v. Rumsfeld*

The Second Circuit issued its two to one ruling on December 18, 2003.[90] It was a significant victory for Padilla and, more generally, for critics of the government's policy of detaining U.S. citizens on domestic soil. The majority opinion of Judges Pooler and Parker drew extensively from Justice Jackson's famous concurring opinion in *Youngstown Sheet and Tube Co. v. Sawyer* and emphasized that a president had no inherent constitutional power to detain citizens on U.S. soil without express statutory authorization.[91] The majority rejected the application of *Ex parte Quirin* and *The Prize Cases,* as urged by the government, and relied, instead, on the limiting principles in *Ex parte Milligan* and *Ex parte Endo.*[92]

This decision was the most substantial defeat to date of the government's arguments, and key elements of it are contrary to the Fourth Circuit's decision in *Hamdi,* setting in place a conflict between the circuits that can only be resolved by Supreme Court review. The Second Circuit ruling was limited to capture and detention of citizens on U.S. soil, and, thus, is not directly applicable to capture of citizens on the battlefield and subsequent detention, as in Hamdi's case. Lower court decisions in both *Hamdi* and *Padilla* are careful to keep clear the factual distinctions in the two cases: still, there are some principles that may be applicable to both and some that are clearly not. The fact that Padilla was caught inside the borders of the U.S. and that Hamdi was caught on a battlefield in Afghanistan is an important difference. Because the Second Circuit relied so heavily on the domestic context of a president's powers, plaintiffs in *Hamdi* can take little comfort in that part of the Second Circuit decision. Of more help to Hamdi, however, would be the court's interpretation of the Non-Detention Act,[93] (18 U.S.C. 4001[a]), which prohibits the detention or imprisonment of any citizen unless pursuant to an act of Congress.

The majority opinion constitutes a vigorous affirmation of judicial power by federal court judges to interpret the scope of executive power, to engage in statutory construction, and to "say what the law is."[94] All three judges who participated in this case addressed the issues on the merits, exercised their judicial authority

[89] *Id.* at 114.
[90] *Padilla v. Rumsfeld,* 352 F. 3d 695 (2d Cir. 2003).
[91] *Youngstown,* 343 U.S. 579, 635–38.
[92] *Ex parte Quirin,* 317 U.S. 1; *Prize* 67 U.S. (2 Black) 635; *Ex parte Milligan,* 71 U.S. (4 Wall.) 2; and *Ex parte Endo,* 323 U.S. 283.
[93] 18 U.S.C. 4001(a).
[94] *Marbury v. Madison,* 5 U.S. (1 Cranch) 137 (1803).

with confidence, and understood well the historic dimensions of the power they were asked to interpret and the conflicting constitutional legacies from which they needed to choose. Because both the majority opinion and Judge Wesley's opinion, which concurred in part and dissented in part, were robust examples of judicial interpretation, there was little mention of any reference to doctrines of judicial avoidance or self-restraint. The only passage that acknowledges the judiciary's need to approach with some care issues of the president's authority as commander in chief is:

> We agree that great deference is afforded the President's exercise of his authority as commander in chief. See *Dept. of the Navy v. Egan.* . . . We also agree that whether a state of armed conflict exists against an enemy to which the laws of war apply is a political question for the President, not the courts. See *Johnson v. Eisentrager.* . . . Because we have no authority to do so, we do not address the government's underlying assumption that an undeclared war exists between al Qaeda and the United States.
>
> However, it is a different proposition entirely to argue that the President even in times of grave national security threats or war, whether declared or undeclared, can lay claim to any of the powers, express or implied, allocated to Congress. The deference due to the Executive in its exercise of its war powers therefore only starts the inquiry; it does not end it. Where the exercise of Commander-in-Chief powers, no matter how well-intentioned, is challenged on the ground that it collides with the powers assigned by the Constitution to Congress, a fundamental role exists for the courts. See *Marbury v. Madison.* . . . To be sure, when Congress and the President act together in the conduct of war, "it is not for any court to sit in review of the wisdom of their action or substitute its judgment for theirs" *Hirabayashi v. U.S.* But when the Executive acts, even in the conduct of war, in the face of apparent congressional disapproval, challenges to his authority must be examined and resolved by the Article III courts. See *Youngstown* (Jackson, J., concurring).[95]

Briefs and Oral Arguments in the Supreme Court

The arguments presented to the U.S. Supreme Court in *Hamdi* and *Padilla* differed little from the ones that had been used in the lower courts. In responding to the adverse decision of the Second Circuit, the government argued in its *Padilla* brief that the president had both constitutional and statutory authority to seize and detain enemy combatants wherever they were found, even inside the domestic borders of the United States, based on Article II's commander-in-chief power, *The Prize Cases* and on the Authorization for Use of Military Force (P.L. 107–40) which "necessarily embraces the capture and detention of enemy combatants."[96] Attorneys for Hamdi argued in their brief that the Fourth Circuit's reliance upon

---

[95] *Padilla v. Rumsfeld*, 352 F. 3d 695 (2d Cir. 2003).

[96] Brief for the Petitioner, *Padilla v. Rumsfeld*, 03–1027, March 17, 2004, at 38–39.

the Authorization for Use of Military Force and its interpretations of 4001(a) and *Quirin* were incorrect and were at odds with the Second Circuit's decision. In particular, Dunham noted that the Fourth Circuit's reliance upon *Quirin* was undermined by the fact that it predated passage of 4001(a), and that approval by the Court of the president's authority to establish military tribunals for trials of enemy combatants in *Quirin* was based on specific congressional authorization for tribunals and on a formal declaration of war, both conditions which are lacking in Hamdi's case.[97]

Oral Arguments in the Supreme Court in *Hamdi* and *Padilla*

There was no mistaking on the morning of April 28, 2004, inside the courtroom of the United States Supreme Court that the nine justices understood that these were historic cases that would lay the constitutional foundation for what could be an indefinite conflict with an unorthodox enemy. How the Constitution—and the courts—figure into the process for pursuing and defeating that enemy is still a "work in progress," but whatever systems and procedures that the government adopts to pursue the war and its combatants will speak volumes about whether, in critical times, it can continue to adhere to deeply held, fundamental American values, or whether the executive is willing to jettison the Constitution—and the courts—in order to maximize and stretch presidential power beyond all previous bounds. In short, is the Constitution equal to any crisis confronting the country, or must it be set aside in times of danger?

Hamdi

Deputy Solicitor General Paul Clement's argument in *Hamdi* included the following points: (1) the government possesses long-established authority to detain combatants, including citizens, on the battlefield and to hold them as long as necessary for their intelligence value; (2) the president does not need congressional authorization to seize and detain combatants, but even if he did under an arguable interpretation that 4001(a) requires it, the Authorization for Use of Military Force satisfies that requirement; (3) that some sort of preliminary military hearing *could* be instituted to determine the initial status of captured combatants, as Article V of the Geneva Convention provides; however, the Geneva Convention does not apply to the conflict in Afghanistan and, therefore, is inapplicable to *Hamdi*; and (4) he conceded slightly that "there is a continuing modest role for the courts" here, but only to determine if the length of detention had exceeded reasonable limits. But Clement noted that if someone raised that claim, "we would be in court vehemently saying that there is no role for the habeas court there. There are troops still on the ground in Afghanistan. It makes no

---

[97] Supplemental Brief for Petitioners, *Hamdi v. Rumsfeld*, 03-6696, January 5, 2004, at 8–9.

sense whatsoever to release an individual detained as an enemy combatant in Afghanistan while the troops are still on the ground."[98]

Among the justices, there were some interesting lines of questions. Justices Souter and Stevens raised an issue regarding timing, and Justices Breyer and Ginsburg pursued the possibility of offering some sort of neutral hearing to determine a combatant's status. Souter suggested that one could concede that a president would have broad unilateral authority to detain at the outset of a conflict, but that such authority might lose force over time, and, certainly, could not be legitimate two years after the start of hostilities, without some authorization from Congress.[99] Breyer and Ginsberg pressed Clement on the possibility of some neutral hearing. Breyer exclaimed,

> Wait. You're also—the words (in Pub. L. 107–40) are 'necessary and appropriate.' And also the words in the Constitution are 'due process of law.' And also the words in the Magna Carta were 'according to law.' And whatever the form of words in any of those documents there are, it seemed to refer to one basic idea that's minimum. That a person who contests something of importance is entitled to a neutral decision maker and an opportunity to present proofs and arguments.[100]

Clement conceded the point but then countered that the Army regulations used in past conflicts to interrogate combatants were for the purpose of complying with the Geneva Convention, which is inapplicable here.

In short, these two areas of questioning seemed to suggest openings for the Court, first, to try to find some middle ground for a satisfactory process to determine at an initial stage an enemy combatant's status, and second, to consider the issue of the length of detention, where a president's authority, at its broadest at the outset of a conflict, could not continue for an unlimited amount of time without some authorization from Congress.

Padilla

After lengthy consideration of the jurisdictional question, the arguments in *Padilla* brought key issues to the fore, and the justices and the attorneys grappled with the most fundamental principles for a government of limited powers: the respective roles of the courts, the executive, and Congress. What emerged from the arguments was a clear contrast between Clement for the government and Stanford

---

[98] Oral argument in the U.S. Supreme Court in *Hamdi v. Rumsfeld,* 03-6696, April 28, 2004, at 53, http://www.supremecourtus.gov/oral_arguments/argument_transcripts/03–6696.pdf.

[99] *Id.* at 31–32.

[100] *Id.* at 35–36.

University law professor Jenny Martinez as attorney for Padilla over their understanding of these roles.

Justice Breyer asked Clement why it would be "necessary and appropriate," using the wording of the Authorization for Use of Force, for the government to "proceed by other than a normal court procedure" when it has seized and detained a citizen enemy combatant.[101] Clement responded that he did not view "necessary and appropriate" as "an invitation for sort of judicial management of the executive's war-making power. I would have viewed it as a delegation to the executive to use its traditional authority to make discretionary judgments in finding what is the necessary appropriate force."[102] Thus, Breyer saw "necessary and appropriate" as a standard that *limited* the president's actions to nothing beyond what was "necessary and appropriate," while Clement viewed it as a permissive standard, without limits. Clement continued: "You have to recognize that in situations where there is a war—where the government is on a war footing, that you have to trust the executive to make the kind of quintessential military judgments that are involved in things like that."[103] Following that logic, one justice asked, "But if the law is what the executive says it is, whatever is necessary and appropriate in the executive's judgment . . . and it leads you up to the executive, unchecked by the judiciary. So what is it that would be a check against torture?"[104] Clement's reply was that "the Court in *Ludecke vs. Watkins* made clear that the fact that executive discretion in a war situation can be abused is not a good and sufficient reason for judicial micromanagement and overseeing of that authority."[105] Clearly, the government's position was that the executive should have unfettered power in war circumstances, unreviewable by the courts.

Martinez joined the issue by asking the Court to reject a claim by the executive to an unlimited power to imprison indefinitely any person he deems an enemy combatant, a claim that she described was "a departure from our nation's traditions" and one that, "at a minimum, Congress would have to clearly and unequivocally authorize."[106] And Congress did *not* authorize indefinite detention, she continued, when it passed the Authorization for Use of Military Force, nor was there any indication or any debate that they thought that the legislation they were passing at the time would include the authority to detain.[107] Martinez emphasized that Section 4001(a) was passed by Congress in 1971 to repeal the Emergency Detention Act and to ensure that "the executive should not be able to rely on that general declaration of war . . . to lock up citizens."[108] Section 4001(a) requires

---

[101] Oral argument in the U.S. Supreme Court in *Padilla v. Rumsfeld*, 03–1027, April 28, 2004 at 16, http://www.supremecourtus.gov/oral_arguments/argument_transcripts/03-1027.pdf.

[102] *Id.* at 17.

[103] *Id.* at 23.

[104] *Id.* at 22.

[105] *Id.* at 23.

[106] *Id.* at 29.

[107] *Id.* at 43.

[108] *Id.* at 45–46.

specific authorization for any executive detention, and it was that level of specificity that was lacking in the Authorization for Use of Force.

A common theme emerged across both the *Hamdi* and *Padilla* oral arguments—that Congress, as the lawmaking institution, could and should have entered this debate at the outset, and should have stepped in to provide specific authorization, including guidelines and limits, for detentions, if that is what the circumstances warranted. Martinez noted, "Congress is the body of our government . . . that was entrusted by the Founders for making law to deal with new situations. And Congress is fully capable of considering the various parameters of any sort of scheme of detention that might be necessary.[109] "And," she continued, "certainly this Court would have the power to review, to determine whether that system established by Congress were constitutional."[110]

Analysis

The documentary record in the *Hamdi* and *Padilla* cases is rich with references to the heavy constitutional significance these cases—and their ultimate judicial resolution—embody. The legal professionals on both sides of both cases understand the impact that the final decisions will have on constitutional history and the legacy they will leave for this and future generations, just as we depend at this time on the World War II precedents as a starting point for current analysis. Are there any patterns we can discern in the positions presented in the briefs and opinions reviewed here that might give us a clue as to how presidents and courts view their respective roles and powers in this most critical and deeply symbolic area of public policy? And is there evidence here, as might be reasonably anticipated, of a political question doctrine at work—either on the part of the president's lawyers or by the courts?

The Government's Position

As for the administration, one could posit that it is trying to have it both ways: on the one hand, it may be employing a "quasi" or, perhaps, a "sub silentio" political question doctrine that finds little room for courts to review the executive's position, but, in the alternative, if courts, in fact, take the plunge and review the issues on the merits, the administration wants to be sure that it has made its strongest substantive case to them. The government makes only a few overt references to a "political question" analysis, but, rather, argues most often for limited, circumscribed judicial review that extends substantial deference to the executive. Of the two competing legacies of cases noted at the outset of this article addressing war

[109] *Id.* at 42.
[110] *Id.*

powers or military policies, the government here unquestionably sides with the World War II era cases that are so evident throughout their filings.

The Position of the Courts

a. The District Courts

The courts offer a much more varied and, thus, more interesting but less cohesive picture. The two district court decisions differed in a few ways. Judge Mukasey's decision in *Padilla* was a nuanced one that drew from *The Prize Cases* to support considerable deference to the executive to make wartime decisions but also held that courts had a role, though limited, to determine the sufficiency of the administration's justification for its enemy combatant designation (a "some evidence" standard). Moreover, he was not persuaded that the Mobbs Declaration was sufficient to meet even the deferential "some evidence" standard, and he ruled that Padilla was entitled to have access to counsel as a matter of discretion, though not as a matter of a Fifth or Sixth Amendment right, for the purpose of contesting his enemy combatant status under conditions agreed to by both parties (except that the government refused to agree to *any* conditions). Thus, Mukasey in the *Padilla* district court decision examined the substantive issues thoughtfully, and ruled in a way that gave some, but not total, comfort to the executive.

Judge Doumar in *Hamdi* was much more assertive in his rulings against the government and provided a deeper protection for the enemy combatant than Mukasey had in *Padilla*. Doumar not only raised the standard for the Mobbs Declaration up to a more muscular "meaningful judicial review," as opposed to Mukasey's "some evidence" standard of review, and determined that that stronger standard was not met by the government here, but he also held that Hamdi was entitled to a Fifth Amendment Due Process right that encompassed access to counsel to competently challenge his status, in contrast to Mukasey's discretionary right of access to counsel for Padilla.

b. The Courts of Appeals

The decisions at the circuit court level were even more split and more opposite—and more substantive—than those at the district court level. The Fourth Circuit's panel decision paid lip service to a limited role for the judiciary in wartime decisions but then proceeded to reinforce the broadest possible power to presidents, at least in the circumstances here where Hamdi was initially captured and detained in an active combat zone.

The Second Circuit's panel opinion was, among all of the opinions here, undoubtedly, the most far-reaching and most protective of individual rights *and* of a court's authority to monitor the government's interference with those rights during wartime. The slightly different facts here gave this case an exclusively domestic context, which accounts for some of the greater expansiveness the court was able to bring to it, in contrast with Hamdi's "active combat zone" context, but one is struck by just how far from the other court opinions in both cases this one is. In fact, it rejects *Quirin*, which the Fourth Circuit embraces. It rejects *The Prize Cases*, and relies, instead, on the underpinnings of *Milligan*. It uses *Curtiss-Wright*, but in an extraordinarily rare reading of it, rather than the usual "sole organ" recitation (which the Fourth Circuit uses) underlying almost unlimited executive power in foreign affairs. The Second Circuit actually interprets *Curtiss-Wright correctly*, as a delegation of powers case, turning Sutherland's assertion of the need for less statutory restriction in the foreign affairs field to its advantage by positing that, in the domestic sphere here, *greater* and *more explicit* statutory restriction is required—and it is precisely that explicit statutory restriction that is lacking in this instance.

Jackson Lives—But Which One?

Turning to a different part of the analysis, an intriguing feature between the *Hamdi* and *Padilla* cases was the dueling contest for the soul of Justice Jackson in his *Youngstown* concurrence. In its *Hamdi* briefs, the government placed the president's authority to designate enemy combatants in Jackson's *first* category, supported by explicit statutory authorization from Pub. L. 107–40 and an appropriations statute. The Second Circuit panel opinion placed considerable reliance for the foundation of its decision on the fact that the president's authority to designate enemy combatants was squarely in Jackson's *third* category, "when a president takes measures incompatible with the express or implied will of Congress" (here, in violation of 18 U.S.C. 4001[a]), and that a court could uphold a president's designation authority only with the explicit authorization of Congress, which Pub. L. 107–40 did not satisfy.

Clearly, the courts in all opinions at both levels, but to varying degrees, were not at all inclined to relinquish their authority to decide the substantive issues here. Concededly, the issues were sufficiently narrow and, at times, technical, and addressed through reference to established precedents and standard statutory construction. There is potential, however, for questions of constitutional interpretation that are far more subjective and of far greater magnitude to edge their way into the courts in their consideration of antiterrorism cases, questions such as "what constitutes war?", "where is the battlefield?", and "when is war terminated?". If these questions are not "political" and not *inappropriate* for courts, then it may be argued that few others are.

June 28, 2004: The U.S. Supreme Court Decides *Hamdi* and *Padilla*

The final day of the Supreme Court's 2003–2004 term brought with it decisions in *Hamdi* and *Padilla*, as well as in the other high-profile case on antiterrorism policies, *Rasul v. Bush*, where the Court upheld, six to three, the jurisdiction of federal district courts to hear habeas challenges from foreign nationals captured abroad and detained at Guantanamo Bay. A basic scorecard here would be that:

the government lost "big" in *Rasul*, received a mixed result in *Hamdi*, and found that a definitive outcome in *Padilla* would be postponed for a later day. Speculation about Supreme Court decisions is always risky, at best, but there are some factors to consider here. First, as noted earlier by Linda Greenhouse, this is a Supreme Court that wants to be not only *a* player but the *dominant* player in constitutional interpretation.[111] Second, this particular collection of justices has little history together as a body on separation of powers matters. The last major cases on those topics, such as *U.S. v. Nixon, INS v. Chadha, Buckley v. Valeo, Bowsher v. Synar, Morrison v. Olson,* and *U.S. v. Mistretta,* all pre-date this specific group of justices sitting as a whole, and it may be difficult to handicap even those who participated in those earlier decisions, although one might presume a solid threesome in support of executive power (Rehnquist, Thomas, and Scalia) and a foursome supportive of individual rights and of the Court's authority to protect those rights (Breyer, Stevens, Souter, and Ginsburg), and, as usual, O'Connor and Kennedy as the swing votes.[112]

What is now clear from the decisions the Court handed down in June 2004 on the Bush administration's antiterrorism policies is that the political question doctrine played no role for the Court, while it received nominal respect from the government as part of its litigation strategy. The temptation for courts to protect their interpretive role, either to affirm executive primacy or to carefully monitor governmental intrusion into individual rights, is hard for them to ignore or override. At least, at the Supreme Court level, these justices wanted to be "players" in these disputes, and found no reason to revive the political question doctrine for these foreign and military policy matters. Indeed, it would have been hard for the Court to justify use of the political question doctrine on these issues, since there were so many precedents already available from which to choose. The question which then loomed largest was whether, in fact, they would place reliance on World War II era decisions, such as *Quirin* and *Eisentrager,* where executive branch policies received broad support from the Court of that time, or whether they would fashion a different, and restrictive, response to presidential initiatives during a national security crisis, such as in the 1952 Steel Seizure Case of *Youngstown Sheet and Tube Company v. Sawyer.* The answer is a mixed one which, moreover, is not yet the final one. There are still more rounds—and more decisions—to come.[113]

---

[111] Greenhouse, 2002, at 4.3.

[112] *U.S. v. Nixon,* 418 U.S. 683 (1974); *INS v. Chadha,* 462 U.S. 919 (1983); *Buckley v. Valeo,* 424 U.S. 1 (1976); *Bowsher v. Synar,* 478 U.S. 714 (1986); *Morrison v. Olson,* 487 U.S. 654 (1988); and *U.S. v. Mistretta,* 488 U.S. 361 (1989).

[113] As noted above, Padilla now faces criminal trial in Florida in Fall 2006, but the possibility persists that the government could, at some future date, redesignate him as an enemy combatant, and this entire process would begin anew. Two other high-profile challenges to antiterrorism policies are currently pending, *Hamdan v. Rumsfeld* in the Supreme Court and *Al Odah v. U.S./Boumediene v. Bush* in the D.C. Circuit Court. The Supreme Court heard arguments in *Hamdan v. Rumsfeld,* 05–184, on March 28, 2006, on appeal from the D.C. Circuit Court, where the July 15, 2005 decision there (No. 04–5393, D.C. Cir.) dismissed a challenge to the November 13, 2001 military order issued by

Hamdi

Justice O'Connor, writing for a plurality of four in *Hamdi v. Rumsfeld*, penned the words that the media would use to explain the decision to a waiting public, words that left no doubt that these justices were not willing to relinquish a role for the judiciary, even during times of war: "we necessarily reject the Government's assertion that separation of powers principles mandate a heavily circumscribed role for the courts in such circumstances. . . . We have long since made clear that a state of war is not a blank check for the President when it comes to the rights of the Nation's citizens. . . . Whatever power the United States Constitution envisions for the Executive in its exchanges with other nations or with enemy organizations in times of conflict, it most assuredly envisions a role for all three branches when individual liberties are at stake."[114]

At bottom, O'Connor's opinion made crystal clear that, in matters of individual rights during wartime, the president's policies were not immune from judicial review. The decision in *Hamdi*, however, did not produce a neat conclusion, and it consisted of a variety of opinions on two basic questions: (1) did the president have authority to detain U.S. citizens as enemy combatants picked up on the battlefield?; and (2) if so, were these combatants entitled to contest the evidence that gave rise to their designation and detention?

The plurality of Justices O'Connor, Kennedy, Breyer, and Rehnquist held, on the broadest issue before them, that Congress, in its authorization to use military force enacted in the wake of the September 11 attacks, provided the president with authority to detain enemy combatants. Such detention of U.S. citizens did not violate Section 4001(a), which prohibited the detention of any U.S. citizen "except pursuant to an Act of Congress," because, as the plurality concluded, "the AUMF is explicit congressional authorization for the detention of individuals in the narrow category we describe."[115] That "narrow category" comprised those individuals labeled as "enemy combatants," described as persons who were "part of or supporting forces hostile to the United States or coalition partners" in Afghanistan and who "engaged in an armed conflict against the United States" there;[116] because Hamdi was apprehended in Afghanistan by the Northern Alliance and was alleged

---

President Bush that authorized the use of military tribunals for detained foreign nationals. A decision is expected from the Supreme Court by early summer. Two post-*Rasul* cases that addressed procedures instituted at Guantanamo Bay to provide for status hearings for foreign national detainees there resulted in opposite rulings by two federal district court judges in Washington, D.C. (Judge Leon in *Khalid v. Bush*, 355 F. Supp. 2d 311 [D.D.C. 2005], and Judge Green in *In re Guantanamo Detainees*, 355 F. Supp. 2d 443 [D.D.C. 2005]), and these cases were appealed to the D.C Circuit, which heard arguments on March 22, 2006 in *Al Odah v. U.S*, 05-5064, and *Boumediene v. Bush*, 05–5062. A decision is expected from the D.C. Circuit Court in Spring 2006.

[114] *Hamdi v. Rumsfeld*, 124 S. Ct. 2633, 2650 (2004).

[115] *Id.* at 2638.

[116] *Id.* at 2639.

to have taken up arms with the Taliban against U.S. forces there in late 2001, he fit this description.

Two other pairs of justices disagreed with this part of the decision. Justices Souter and Ginsburg did not agree that the AUMF authorized Hamdi's detention, while Justices Scalia and Stevens concluded separately that the government had only two options before it when it confronted U.S. citizens aiding an enemy, and those were to either criminally charge the person (most likely, with treason), or to utilize the Suspension Clause in the Constitution, providing for the suspension of the writ of habeas corpus "when in Cases of Rebellion or Invasion the public Safety may require it." Scalia noted that the clause did not specify that suspension required an act of Congress, but he was careful to say that "it has been so understood, consistently with English practice and the Clause's placement in Article I."[117]

On the second issue, the plurality was joined by Souter and Ginsburg who agreed that, once detained by the government, enemy combatants such as Hamdi must be afforded the opportunity to rebut the evidence for that detention before a neutral decisionmaker, and that this opportunity must be "meaningful" and must comport with the "core elements" of due process, that is, the right to notice of charges and to confront the evidence against him with the assistance of counsel before an impartial magistrate.[118] The plurality was emphatic here in concluding that Hamdi was entitled to basic procedural protections and, also, that the government's standard of "some evidence" was constitutionally inadequate, but it was equally willing to permit other procedures that catered to the government's interests, such as hearsay evidence and a presumption favorable to the government, as long as it was a rebuttable one.

Thus, the outcome in *Hamdi* allowed both sides to claim some ground: the president, who now had judicial confirmation that capture and detention of enemy combatants (and U.S. citizens in that category) was authorized by Congress (although the Court did not reach the far more compelling question of whether the president would have had such authority in the absence of congressional action); and civil liberties advocates, who pointed to the plurality's concern for due process protections during times of military conflict and its sharp language putting the executive branch on notice that wartime policies were subject to judicial review and that courts would not shrink from scrutinizing those policies with care.

Padilla

The Court did not reach the merits of Padilla's case, ruling, instead, five to four, that the case had been brought in the wrong jurisdiction. He should have, according to the majority, filed his suit in the district court in South Carolina against the commander at the naval brig in Charleston, where he was ultimately

---

[117] *Id.* at 2665.
[118] *Id.* at 2660.

housed and detained in military custody, upon the president's designation of him in June 2002 as an enemy combatant, rather than filing it in the southern district of New York, where he had been brought and jailed in May 2002 as a material witness after being apprehended in Chicago. The majority rejected Padilla's and the dissent's argument that because of the "unique facts" of this case, the Court should treat the "immediate custodian" rule flexibly.[119] For the Court, a relaxation of the rules, under the 1973 *Braden* precedent, would be appropriate only where there was no immediate physical custody with respect to the custody being challenged, a circumstance that did not exist in Padilla's case, where Commander Marr, in her position as commander of the Consolidated Naval Brig in Charleston, South Carolina, exercised immediate custody over Padilla.[120]

The effect of the Supreme Court's decision in *Padilla* was to reverse the Second Circuit's December 2003 ruling (1) that Secretary of Defense Rumsfeld was the proper respondent to Padilla's request for habeas corpus relief, and (2) that the district court for the southern district of New York had jurisdiction over the Secretary under New York's long-arm statute. The high court did not reach the merits of the Second Circuit's decision that the president did not have authority from either Article II's commander-in-chief clause or the AUMF to capture and detain an American citizen as an enemy combatant on U.S. soil. This issue is clearly at the heart of the case, and it is, perhaps, the most dramatic one in the antiterrorism cases so far. The Court sidestepped it temporarily here, but it is arguably the most fundamental and most wrenching issue among all of the post-9/11 policies.

The second round of *Padilla*, refashioned as *Padilla v. Hanft* (Hanft replaced Marr as the commander of the Naval Brig in South Carolina), proceeded through the federal district court in South Carolina (No. Civ A.2:04–2221–26A, 2005 WL465691 [D.S.C. Feb. 28, 2005]) and the Fourth Circuit (423 F.3d 386 [4th Cir. 2005]) but ended abruptly with the April 3, 2006, denial of certiorari in the U.S. Supreme Court and the transfer of Padilla to criminal jurisdiction in Florida.[121] This case is ongoing, and if its unpredictable history to date is any guide, we may continue to be surprised at how it will unfold in the future.

In the 2004 Supreme Court case, Justice Stevens' dissent, joined by Justices Souter, Ginsburg, and Breyer, was especially forceful in its rejection of the majority's opinion and, also, in its characterization of this case as "an exceptional" one that these dissenters believed the Court should have decided because it raised

---

[119] 124 S.Ct. 2711, 2716 (2004).

[120] *Braden v. 30th Judicial Circuit Court of Kentucky*, 410 U.S. 484, 498 (1973).

[121] *Padilla v. Hanft*, 547 U.S. ___ (April 3, 2006); "Memorandum for the Secretary of Defense, Subject: Transfer of Detainee to Control of Attorney General," The White House, November 20, 2005; superceding indictment, *United States of America v. Adham Amin Hassoun, Mohamed Hesham Youssef, Kifah Wael Jayyousi, Kassem Daher, and Jose Padilla*, U.S. District Court, Southern District of Florida, Case No. 04–60001-CR-COOKE, November 17, 2005; and Unopposed Emergency Application and Notice of Release and Transfer of Custody of Petitioner Jose Padilla (05–6396, 4th Cir., Nov. 22, 2005). All of these documents are available on http://www.wiggin.com/practices/areainfo.asp?groupid =5&areaID=231.

questions "of profound importance to the nation."[122] They noted that the Court had created numerous exceptions to the immediate custodian rule previously, and that there were "special circumstances" here that would have justified an exception in this case.[123] Above all, these justices used strong language to leave no doubt that they viewed the issue here of executive detention of U.S. citizens on U.S. soil without access to counsel or a hearing to contest the detention as amounting to "nothing less than the essence of a free society."[124] They deemed the case "singular" in its importance, "not only because it calls into question decisions made by the Secretary himself, but also because those decisions have created a unique and unprecedented threat to the freedom of every American citizen."[125]

Round Two: *Padilla v. Hanft*

It came as no surprise, then, that Padilla's lawyers would refile the case in the district court in the Fourth Circuit on July 2, 2004, merely days after the U.S. Supreme Court's decision. On February 28, 2005, U.S. District Court Judge Henry Floyd issued his opinion in a ruling that declared that the AUMF did not constitute, under 4001(a), the explicit congressional authorization necessary for the president to detain militarily on domestic soil a U.S. citizen, and that, absent congressional approval and consistent with the Court's analysis in *Youngstown*, the president had no inherent authority to order such action. His opinion was critical of the government's willingness to defer so fully to the president, and he had harsh retorts to the government for the arguments it was advancing. To have accepted the government's arguments, in Floyd's words, would have been "a betrayal of this Nation's commitment to the separation of powers that safeguards our democratic values and individual liberties."[126]

Moreover, Floyd included two pointed comments in his opinion that were aimed straight at the administration. Given the administration's public statements of its opposition, generally, to "judicial activism," Floyd said first that "For the court to find for Respondent would also be to engage in judicial activism. This Court sits to interpret the law as it is and not as the Court might wish it to be."[127] And, finally, as the clearest and most direct rebuke to the administration's ap-

---

[122] *Id.* at 2727.

[123] *Id.* at 2728. These exceptions included the fact that Padilla's attorney had not been officially notified by the government of his removal from prison in New York to his military custody in South Carolina until after his departure from New York. The dissenters note that, had she known of his pending removal prior to his departure, she could have filed his habeas petition in the southern district of New York while he was still there, and that the immediate custodian at that time would have been Secretary of Defense Rumsfeld, since he maintained control over Padilla at that point.

[124] *Id.* at 2732.

[125] *Id.* at 2730.

[126] *Padilla v. Hanft*, 2005 WL 465691 (D.S.C. 2005)

[127] *Id.*

proach to its antiterrorism policies, in referring to Padilla's case, he said, "Simply stated, this is a law enforcement matter, not a military matter."[128]

After an unsuccessful attempt to ask the U.S. Supreme Court to hear the case on an expedited basis in April 2005, Padilla's attorneys appealed the case to the Fourth Circuit, which heard oral argument in mid-July 2005. The most significant feature of the government's argument was that "Padilla is a classic battlefield combatant subject to military detention under *Hamdi*," as a result of new facts introduced in August 2004 in the Rapp Declaration.[129] The government argued that this new evidence indicates that Padilla's activities in Afghanistan in 2001–2002 "fall precisely within that definition of enemy combatant" that the Court used in the *Hamdi* decision, that is, of "an individual who . . . was part of or supporting forces hostile to the United States or coalition partners in Afghanistan and who engaged in an armed conflict against the United States there."[130] With this new evidence that U.S. forces had spotted Padilla on the battlefields in Afghanistan but that he had "escaped capture on the battlefield but came to the United States intent on committing further hostile acts here," the government intended to change the issue from the thorny and highly sensitive one of capture of a citizen enemy combatant *on U.S. soil* (emphasis added) to one that was on judicially sanctioned ground, after *Hamdi*, of battlefield capture authorized by the AUMF. The government repeatedly noted in its briefs and argument that "the place of capture" should not be dispositive, while the hostile acts in which a person engages are what determine whether he meets the definition of an enemy combatant.[131] In addition to reliance on *Hamdi*, once the government stated that, as an enemy combatant, Padilla was no different than Hamdi, it also rested its position equally on *Quirin*, on the basis that Padilla's actions were not distinguishable from those of the Nazi saboteurs, who entered the country "bent on hostile acts."[132] As the final leg of its argument, the government asserted that, despite the sufficiency of *Hamdi* and *Quirin* as ample precedents for its legal position here, it also maintained that "the president has inherent authority as Commander in Chief to detain Padilla as an enemy combatant," and brushed away Padilla's opposing arguments based on *Youngstown* and *Milligan*.[133]

---

[128] *Id.*

[129] See Respondent's Answer to the Petition for the Writ of Habeas Corpus, *Padilla v. Hanft*, CA No. 02:04–2221-26AJ (District Court for the District of South Carolina), August 30, 2004, where the Rapp Declaration (dated August 27, 2004) was first introduced in evidence as Exhibit B.

[130] Reply Brief for the Appellant, *Padilla v. Hanft*, CV 05–6396 (D.C. Cir.), June 21, 2005, at 5.

[131] *Id.* at 1–2, 12–13, 23–25. See also Respondent's Answer to the Petition for the Writ of Habeas Corpus, *Padilla v. Hanft*, CA No. 02:04–2221-26AJ (District Court for the District of South Carolina), August 30, 2004.

[132] Reply Brief for the Appellant, *Padilla v. Hanft*, CV 05–6396 (D.C. Cir.), June 21, 2005, at 20, quoting *Quirin* at 37–38.

See generally Reply Brief at 19-23 for argument based on *Quirin*.

[133] *Id.* at 23–24.

For their part, Padilla's attorneys continued to rely on their position that (1) the AUMF does not authorize indefinite detention of citizens arrested in the United States, (2) Section 4001(a) (the Non-Detention Act) applies to *all* detentions, including military ones, and the AUMF does not satisfy the requirement of 4001(a) for an act of Congress that authorizes detentions, (3) the Court's decisions in both *Hamdi* and *Quirin* do not support a position of congressional approval for presidential power to detain citizens seized in the U.S., (4) the president has no inherent power to detain citizens seized in civilian settings in the U.S., and (5) the new evidence introduced by the government in the Rapp Declaration, for a variety of procedural reasons, is not admissible here.[134]

The Fourth Circuit handed down its decision in *Padilla v. Hanft* on September 9, 2005, in which Judge Luttig, for a unanimous three-judge panel, agreed with every element of the government's argument, and soundly reversed the district court's decision.

> We conclude that the President does possess such authority (to detain militarily a citizen of this country who is closely associated with Al Qaeda, an entity with which the U.S. is at war) pursuant to the Authorization for Use of Military Force Joint Resolution.[135]
>
> As the AUMF authorized Hamdi's detention by the President, so also does it authorize Padilla's detention. . . . Under the definition of 'enemy combatant' employed in *Hamdi*, we can discern no difference in principle between Hamdi and Padilla.[136]

Efforts to gain Supreme Court review of this decision began in October, but by November 22, the Department of Justice petitioned the Fourth Circuit for release and transfer of Padilla to the Federal Detention Facility in Miami, Florida, at the same time that it announced the criminal indictment, a move by the government that appeared calculated to avoid Supreme Court review.[137] Judge Luttig issued a stinging opinion for the Fourth Circuit in December, rejecting the government's application for transfer and denying their request for withdrawal of the Fourth Circuit's September opinion, making palpable his displeasure with the government's apparent willingness to jettison his court's strong opinion endorsing the president's authority to detain. He castigated the government for its failure to provide reasons for its changed position, and went so far as to state openly that the government's actions here suggest "an appearance that the government may be

---

[134] Brief of Petitioner-Appellee, Appeal from a Final Judgment of the United States District Court for the District of South Carolina, *Padilla v. Hanft*, CV 05–6396 (D.C. Cir.), June 6, 2005.

[135] *Padilla v. Hanft*, 423 F.3d 386 (4th Cir. 2005) at 6.

[136] *Id.* at 11.

[137] See Unopposed Emergency Application and Notice of Release and Transfer of Custody of Petitioner Jose Padilla (05–6396, 4th Cir., Nov. 22, 2005). The indictment was dated November 17, 2005, but released publicly on November 22, at the same time as the petition for release and transfer. For an excellent listing of *Padilla* case documents, see: http://www.wiggin.com/practices/areainfo.asp?groupid=5&areaID=231.

attempting to avoid consideration of our decision by the Supreme Court . . . ,"[138] and that it has left "impressions that . . . may ultimately prove to be (at a) substantial cost to the government's credibility before the courts."[139]

Appeal of this opinion to the Supreme Court resulted in a reversal of Luttig's opinion denying transfer, and an order granting Padilla's release from military custody (January 4, 2006).[140] For the next eight weekly conferences of the Court, Padilla's petition for certiorari appeared on the list of cases distributed for consideration at each of them. On April 3, Justice Kennedy, for Justice Stevens and Chief Justice Roberts, filed an opinion concurring in the denial of certiorari. Justice Ginsburg filed an opinion, on behalf of Justices Souter, Breyer, and herself, dissenting from the denial of certiorari, and noting that she would grant the petition. Thus, ended the three-and-a-half year effort to gain Supreme Court review of this important issue. The government succeeded in winning authorization from the Supreme Court to transfer Padilla to civilian authorities in Florida for criminal prosecution, and it also won, perhaps, more importantly for its own strategies, a "reprieve" from Supreme Court review that commentators viewed as unlikely to be favorable to the government's arguments on the merits.

Conclusions

What can we say, in conclusion, about whether the political question doctrine has been evident in the Bush administration's antiterrorism policies, either in the government's litigation strategy or in the response of the federal courts, as they build a record of decisions on these issues?

Perhaps, it may be fair to say that the government *had* advanced, however subtly, a dual position in its arguments in the early stages of litigation, allowing it to hedge its bets—that is, one that suggested a minimal, if any, role for courts in battlefield matters (a "political question" doctrine approach without asserting it explicitly), but one that also posited that, *if* the courts took up the challenge and began to rule on the merits in these cases, the government wanted to be fully prepared to make strong arguments supporting unrestrained executive power. In essence, the government waited to take its cue from the courts.

With the exception of the Fourth Circuit opinions in *Hamdi*, there has been little inclination on the part of the courts to deal themselves out of a substantive role here. (Even the most recent Supreme Court denial of certiorari in *Padilla v. Hanft* was explained as based on "prudential considerations" of timing, where the Court preferred to await the outcome in the criminal case in Florida before undertaking what it described as a case where the petitioner's "claims raise fundamental issues respecting the separation of powers, including consideration of the role and

---

[138] *Padilla v. Hanft*, 05–6396 (CA4, Dec. 21, 2005) at 2.
[139] *Id.* at 13.
[140] Order Granting Release from Military Custody (05A578, USSC, Jan. 4. 2006).

function of the courts.")[141] Although there are occasional murmurings by courts of the need to respect the power of the executive in times of military conflict, the judicial decisions so far, at least, in the *Hamdi* and *Padilla* (round one) cases, have demonstrated that, when faced with the stark realities of the antiterrorism policies whose constitutionality they are asked to determine, most federal judges have zeroed in immediately on the substantive questions presented. There has been no mention whatsoever by federal judges of political question doctrine. Consequently, the government realized that even the hint of a reduced judicial role in these cases was not going to advance its chances. Thus, it turned subsequently to a strategy of presenting the strongest arguments it could muster on the merits.

This essay began by noting that both sets of parties in the cases examined here were cognizant of the enormous historical impact the decisions in these cases would carry. That position has not changed, even though we are now slightly closer to having a picture of some of those decisions, as a result of the first wave of Supreme Court rulings in June 2004. But more rulings are yet to come, and perhaps, the forthcoming ones may be even more historically significant than those already decided.[142] What is no longer in doubt is that when it comes to issues of individual rights during wartime, federal courts, including the U.S. Supreme Court, have cast aside any reluctance they may have had from earlier times to address these issues directly, and they stand ready to exercise judicial power, even in the face of governmental assertions of grave national security implications. What may have once been a political question for the courts is "political" no more—and is, instead, a vibrant part of their judicial function.

---

[141] 547 U.S.___(2006), Kennedy, concurring.
[142] See note 113, infra, for references to specific cases.

Political Questions in France

Pierre Avril[1]

The idea that there might be questions that are "political" in nature, and which would therefore be nonjusticiable, naturally shocks a jurist's mind. It is a basic tenet of jurisprudence and the code of ethics that a jurist assumes there to be universality under the law. As such, major exceptions of nonlaw that are political in nature render cognitive and professional discordance with the notion that all decisions are legal or illegal; there should not be a murky area of exceptions—but there is.

When the jurist examines the issue a little less abstractly, however, she/he notices that such political questions involve often the exercise of a discretionary power. That is, a power in which no legal rule governs the merits, and in such cases, the judiciary can legitimately only verify whether, in the challenged decision, the procedures were followed or properly adhered to. If the jurist probes further, he/she will encounter principles very general in nature that he/she might declare applicable in the case at hand. At this point, the emphasis shifts from the norms of accepted actions within their contexts to the actors who carry out the decisions. As such, what legitimate authority could the judge invoke to impose his/her own appreciation (which will inevitably be colored with covert or overt opportunism) to the appreciation or judgment of leaders that are democratically invested with the task of deciding in such circumstances? To the control (judicial

---

[1] Professeur à l'Université de Paris II, membre du conseil supérieur de la magistrature, France.

review) of the judge is then opposed the political responsibility of the leaders, which is ultimately played before the people.

Political questions are at the heart of this inherent antagonism between governmental branches that are coordinated yet rivals (to draw upon the formula put forth by Robert Dahl). They are associated or coordinated insofar as their functions are inscribed in the Constitution and are usually exercised in different arenas. Yet, they are rivals when their respective scopes directly overlap. If two branches have jurisdiction to resolve an issue, and they differ, which one is correct? While the relationship between the coordinate branches is in principle determined by the Constitution, what happens when this relationship is sufficiently ambiguous to require interpretation?

Following a dynamic understanding of the built-in conflict among the coordinate branches, the reader will conclude that it is settled, in practice, through political means, i.e., in a mode that recognizes the concurrence of the legitimacy and purview of the various branches (*sur un mode politique, à savoir la concurrence des légitimités*). In the broad, contextual perspective, the legitimacy of the judge is expanding in our societies, whereas that of the political authorities is increasingly on the defensive. Evoking the "subordination of politics to the law" (*soumission de la politique au droit*) as one of the ideas that characterizes the strong trends nowadays, Philippe Raynaud notes that the concept underlying the modern state used to very closely link individual rights and political power.[2] He also points out that this very concept now faces a crisis. Pierre Manent adds that "the civil rights (*les droits*) have invaded all of the fields of analysis, and even, so to speak, our conscience. As such, they broke their alliance with power, and have even become unwavering enemies. From the alliance between the power and the law, we have now moved to a power of the law, in which the rule of the judges would be the empirical or phenomenalogical manifestation of laws."[3] Manent concludes that "we now face with this one of the main problems of contemporary democracy."

For the French jurist whom the constant reference to the rule of law ("État de droit") leaves rather perplexed, one of the equivocal aspects revealed by these reflections stems from the fact that the term *droit*, in French designates two distinct concepts in the English language, which distinguishes (and rightly so) between: (1) "le droit" (*law*), and (2) "les droits subjectifs," i.e., the individual rights (*rights*). The result is that the well-established principle according to which the political authorities should respect the law has evolved, moving from the idea of a necessary reinforcement of judicial review of the actions of these political authorities to ensure their conformity to the law to the generalized intervention of the judge to protect individual rights.

---

[2] Philippe Raynaud, "Le droit, la liberté et la puissance," *Revue européenne des sciences sociales*, XXXVIII, no. 118, 75.

[3] Pierre Manent, "Les problèmes actuels de la démocratie," *Commentaires*, no. 98 (Été 2002).

To briefly examine the case in France, with its traditions of public law and of the jurisdictional organization that ensues from it, three phases could be identified or distinguished within this general movement.

First, the separation of administrative and judicial authorities, since 1790, has led, as we know, to the establishment of the administrative jurisdiction (at the top of which is the Conseil d'État). This is the sole jurisdiction or instance competent to determine the legality of actions of the executive branch, as well as the responsibility of states *vis-à-vis* individuals.

Second, the revolutionary sovereignty of the law "expression of the general will" prohibited until 1958 any judicial review of the law. The Conseil Constitutionnel has thus been established to ensure the respect by the Parliament of the limits defined for its scope by the new Constitution. However, since a famous decision, (*Liberté d'association*), rendered on July 16, 1971, often compared to *Marbury v. Madison*,[4] it extends its control to ensuring the respect of the rules on the merits, by integrating in its norms of reference those which the Preamble of the Constitution mentions—namely the "Declaration of the Rights" (*declaration des droits de l'homme et du citoyen* of 1789, "the fundamental principles recognized by the laws of our Republic" and the "principles necessary to our era," proclaimed in 1946.

Third, the criminal responsibility (*responsabilité pénale*) of members of government for actions undertaken in the exercise of their functions falls since 1993 within the ambit of the *Cour de justice de la république*. This tribunal decides of the judicial pursuits against ministers.

The Acts of Government (*actes du gouvernement*)

Historically, the question of justiciability of political questions in France involved the "acts of government" (*actes du gouvernment*) for which the Conseil d'État recognized a jurisdictional immunity. This transpired once the minister justified his decision by the political motivation that inspired the particular action in question. This justification of the act of government was abandoned in 1875 through the decision *Prince Napoléon*. This occurred just three years after the adoption of the "delegated justice" instead of "justice retained" (*justice retenue, justice déleguée*). Until then, the Conseil d'État would propose to the minister the solution of litige or contentious questions that might occur between the administration and private individuals. It was the minister who made the decision. Following a process close to the conventions of the British Constitution,[5] the established practice was for the minister to follow the advice given to

---

[4] *Marbury v. Madison*, 5 U.S. (1 Cranch) 137, 170 (1803).

[5] On the transposition of this notion in French constitutional law, see Pierre Avril, *Les Conventions de la Constitution—Normes non écrites du droit politique* (Presses Universitaires de France, coll. Leviathan, 1997).

him, though he was not bound to do so by the law. Henceforth, the Conseil d'État reaches decisions rendered in the name of the French people.

The decision *Prince Napoléon* did not put an end to the acts of government, but it relegated the justification of the political aspect that contradicted its jurisdictional vocation. The Conseil d'État now simply states that the actions do not fall within its purview. In the absence of an explicit justification, the commentators were compelled to establish a list of such acts (*actes du gouvernement*) based on the jurisprudence: What transpired is that the Conseil d'État refused to pronounce itself on actions that involved the relationship of the government with Parliament or with foreign states.

The question of the acts of government[6] has generated a substantial literature of interpretation. Some commentators view it as a survival of political motivation, while others see that the acts do not depend on the strict exercise of executive function, i.e., the application of the law, and are therefore not administrative acts. The *commissaires du gouvernement* presented them at times as mixed actions (*actions mixtes*) that fell outside the scope of the Conseil d'État by virtue of the rules of competence whenever they concerned the Parliament or foreign states.[7]

Eventually, the Conseil d'État developed control through the "*actes détachables*" theory, so that the acts of government were well on their way to extinction (*une catégorie en voie d'extinction*). While the term *acte du gouvernment* seemed to be disappearing from judicial decisions, it was resurrected with the decision *Rubin de Servens*. This decision pertained to the decision of the president of the Republic to resort to the exceptional powers of article 16 of the Constitution, during the *putsch des généraux* (generals putsch) in Algeria. Since then, the decisions explicitly cite the term for the presidential decision to resort to a referendum, the dissolution of the National Assembly, or the nomination of a member of the Conseil Constitutionnel. However, two qualifications need mention: Since 1981, the Conseil Constitutionnel has declared itself competent, as judge of elections, to determine the conformity with the Constitution of certain actions that the Conseil d'État refused to decide (with the notable exception of the decree dissolving of the National Assembly). On the other hand, the Conseil d'État limited the scope of the acts of government, and it has even deemed illegal the refusal of the prime minister to initiate the procedure of declassifying certain material according to article 37 alinea 2 of the Constitution, so as to determine the nature of a legislative provision (*en vue de faire reconnaitre la nature reglèmentaire d'une disposition de forme legislative*). This was a discretionary decision, especially since it concerned the relationship of government with the legislative body.[8]

---

[6] On this question, see M. Long, P. Weil, G. Braibant, P. Delvolve, and B. Genevois, Dalloz, *Les grands arrêts de la jurisprudence administrative* (14th ed., 2003).

[7] Contrary to what his title seems to indicate, the commissaire du government presents his conclusions *independently*, taking into account the legal viewpoint and the general interest.

[8] The decision *Association ornithologique et mammalogique de Saone-et-Loire* (December 3, 1999) justifies this invalidation on the ground that the clause in question ignored a directive of the European Union pertaining to the protection of birds and to the

This evolution is marked by an episode that is particularly revealing as to the evolving relationship between law and politics. More precisely, this shows the relationship between the judge and those who govern (politicians and governments). The referendum of April 8, 1962, which approved the Evian agreements, *Accords d'Evian*, recognizing the independence of Algeria, ascribed to the president of the Republic the authority to undertake, by decree, measures necessary to implement these agreements. President De Gaulle established on these grounds the military Court of justice in order to judge the members of the OAS (*organisation armée secrète*), who were responsible for assassinations. The Conseil d'État, which was appealed to against this decree (*ordonnance*), invalidated it by its *Canal* decision, on October 19, 1962, on the grounds that it limited seriously the rights of the defense. The reaction to this decision was very vivid, with General De Gaulle asserting that the Conseil d'État had "gone beyond the scope of administrative contentieux."[9] It has to be borne in mind that the decision *Canal* was rendered at a time of political crisis, after the National Assembly had been dissolved, and before the referendum about the election of the president of the Republic by universal suffrage, so that the Conseil d'Etat appeared as if it was siding with the opposition.[10] After the victory of the Gaullists, the government had the new Assembly vote a law validating all the decrees (*ordonnances*) and therefore restoring the military court of justice. A reform of the Conseil d'Etat was announced with the purpose of combating the politicization for which it was taken to task. In the final analysis, the decree of reorganization of the Conseil d'Etat ended up being limited to essentially technical dispositions, now that the serenity had been restored. This episode highlights and illustrates the interaction between the general movement of the jurisprudence, which tends to reinforce the control of judges, and the political responsibility of the governors (*gouvernants*) and political leaders, whose arbiter is the universal suffrage at the polls. When the people have confirmed the leaders, the judge should defer. Judges are therefore incited to be more restrained when the exercise of their control is likely to engage them in an open conflict with the political leaders invested with popular trust or vote of confidence. This is confirmed by the experience of the Conseil Constitutionnel.

---

dates of hunting periods. This decision has been strongly criticized by commentators: See *Revue française de droit administratif* 3 (2000).

[9] Pierre Avril, *La Ve République, Histoire Politique et Constitutionnelle*, Presses Universitaires de France, 1994, 94.

[10] From a judicial/legal viewpoint, the Conseil d'Etat had transposed to the authorization given by the referendum of April 8, 1962, the reasoning that it applies to the decrees (*ordonnances*) made by the government on the authorization of Parliament by virtue of article 38 of the Constitution. Even though they pertain to the realm or domain of the law, these decrees are administrative acts, insofar as they have not been ratified by Parliament.

Constitutional Jurisprudence

Established in 1958, the Conseil Constitutionnel is both a political and jurisdictional body. Comprised of nine members nominated by the president of the Republic, the president of the National Assembly and the president of the Senate
for a nine-year nonrenewable term, the Conseil Constitutionnel is called upon
either by one of the three nominating authorities or by the prime minister, or,
since 1974, by sixty members of the Assembly (*députés*) or by sixty senators, to
determine the conformity to the Constitution of the laws adopted by Parliament
before they are ratified. This is an abstract review or review a priori (*controle
abstrait ou a priori*). The Conseil Constitutionnel is also the arbiter for parliamentary elections, presidential elections, and referendums. This avenue, which
gives the minority the opportunity to challenge a newly adopted law, is analyzed
judicially as the verification of the conformity to the Constitution of a given law.
If there are doubts in this regard, however, it is politically the equivalent of one
additional step of the parliamentary procedure analogous to the optional passage
in some sort of third chamber composed differently. The analogy with a third
reading is, of course, denied by the Conseil Constitutionnel, which emphasizes
the exclusively judicial character of this review that is grounded on the bringing
together of the clauses for the law in question to the relevant constitutional principles and rules.

   Under the influence of Dean George Vedel, who served on the Conseil Constitutionnel from 1980 and 1989, and in order not to lend itself to the accusation of
representing a "government of judges," the Conseil made a point to ground its
decisions on clauses that figured expressly in the texts, avoiding resorting to arbitrary nonwritten principles that it could create. Of course, this strict approach does
not eliminate the classical controversies pertaining to the interpretation of the Constitution—particularly with regard to the old texts to which its preamble refers,
because the choice of a principle of interpretation is inevitably a choice of a political nature—both in terms of the preferences that it implies and the consequences
that result from such choice. But in addition to the "political" character inherent to
constitutional justice to the extent that it applies to the law, which is the work of
the representatives of the people, the most delicate point concerns the questions
that are political "by nature," that is the decisions that depend on the discretionary
appreciation of the legislator, and express a political choice (i.e., decisions that the
sheer and pure application of the law cannot fully determine in a decisive manner).
The judge is then well inspired to exercise his/her competence only with prudence
and moderation.

   The decision of January 16, 1982, on the law of nationalizations[11] offers a
good example about the manner in which the Conseil Constitutionnel faced these
difficulties. On the judicial or legal level, the difficulty lay in the interpretation of
texts pertaining to property right that went back to 1789 and 1946. On the political

---

   [11] On the jurisprudence, see Louis Favoreu and Loïc Philip, *Les grandes décisions
du Conseil Constitutionnel* (12th ed., Dalloz, 2003).

level, the difficulty resulted from the fact that what was in question was the application of the socialist program platform after the election of François Mitterand and the overwhelming victory of the French left. The opposition saw in the Conseil Constitutionnel a defense against collectivism (*le collectivisme*), while the new majority in government warned it by invoking the example of the Supreme Court and its resistance to the New Deal in 1938.

The problem of interpretation was raised by the contradiction between, on the one hand, the Declaration of 1789, which affirms that property is one of the natural and inalienable rights, at the same level as liberty and security, and, on the other hand, the Preamble of 1946, which proclaims that every business with the characteristics of a public service or a monopoly must become the property of the community. In order to surmount the difficulty, the Conseil undertook to restore the matter in a historical perspective: it recognized the legitimacy of nationalizations, the principle of which had been most recently affirmed, but it delineated the limits of such nationalizations, given that the Declaration of 1789 had been confirmed by the French people on several occasions. In this fashion, it avoided a direct confrontation with the new majority in power without capitulating before it.

On the political level, it was indeed asserting that the appreciation by the legislator of the necessity of nationalizations could not be invalidated (except in case of manifest error—we shall come back to this) insofar as the scope of these nationalizations did not undermine property right to an extent such as to put in question the natural and inalienable right proclaimed in 1789. However, the decision declared unconstitutional certain modes of indemnifying or compensating that did not meet the character of "fairness" required by the Declaration of 1789 in case of expropriation with the purpose of general interest.

The appreciation of the appropriate character of a certain law by the legislator was therefore sovereign, and the Conseil could not oppose its appreciation or judgment to it in this regard; it reserves only the right to verify the conformity to the Constitution of the way it was implemented. It cannot control the opportune character of a certain law—except in case of a manifest error, as the decision of 1982 specifies. The notion of "*erreur manifeste*" or "manifest error" is a notion borrowed from the jurisprudence of the Conseil d'Etat, which uses it to exercise its control on the acts that are matters for the discretionary appreciation of the administration when this appreciation is evidently erroneous. In such cases it is indeed the facts themselves that contradict this appreciation.

The Conseil Constitutionnel resorted to this approach with regard to the apportionment (*electoral decoupage*) in New Caledonie, which revealed a flagrant overrepresentation of electoral districts with a majority of kanak. This overrepresentation was deliberate, and it responded to the political will to satisfy the demands of the indigenous people, who were a minority, but it lead to a difference in representation that was as big as the double. Called upon by the opposition, the Conseil affirmed on August 8, 1985, that the representation should rest on "essentially demographic bases." It admitted, however, that it might not be strictly proportional to the population of each district because of other imperatives or constraints of general interests such as the ones invoked by government: namely, allowing the *kanak* minority to express itself. But these considerations could intervene only to a certain extent, and this extent had been, in the case at hand, "manifestly exceeded." The reasoning is therefore three-fold and consists of first affirming the judicial legal principle of equality; second, of recognizing that the circumstances justified departing from the rule; and third, concluding that such an exception to the principle should not be so significant or important that it undermines the principle itself. It is therefore an approach analogous to that which was adopted in the case of the nationalizations and property rights in order to reconcile the law with the political objectives of the majority in power at the time. This jurisprudence was confirmed in 1986 after the change in political majority, when the right came back to power and drastically reformed the mode of elections to the National Assembly. The continuity of its jurisprudence thus allowed the Conseil Constitutionnel to face political changes by affirming the same principles *vis-à-vis* the contradictory initiatives of the political right and the political left, successively in power. This was namely the case in matters of the press and television, particularly sensitive realms, because of their political implications.

We have, however, to note that this equilibrium requires a very strong prudence on the part of the judge. Thus, the decision of August 13, 1993, the law on immigration and the right of asylum, was too overtly in opposition to the political right, which had once again gained the majority at the National Assembly. Indeed, the Conseil Constitutionnel had been more demanding in its criteria and exigencies, compared to that which it had formulated in its previous decisions rendered on the same topic and the reaction was brutal: The Constitution was revised on the 25th of the following November in order to validate the law that had been rejected. This process cannot but evoke the episode of the *Canal* decision in 1962: in both cases, the judge ventures imprudently beyond what is politically acceptable at a time when the legitimacy of the political leaders was confirmed by the people.

Political Penalization

Does the repression of crimes or misdemeanors committed by members of government in the exercise of their functions raise a "political question"? This question has for long been ignored because of the jurisprudence adopted by the Cour de Cassation (the highest jurisdiction of the judiciary). Indeed, article 68 of the Constitution provided that members of government were justiciable in such cases by the High Court of Justice (*Haute Cour de Justice*) without specifying whether the competence of the latter Court was exclusive or whether it was to be exercised concurrently with the regular tribunals (*tribunaux de droit commun*) that could thus be presented with the claims of the victims in case the members of Parliament decided not to send the ministers before the High Court. This last interpretation was adopted by the judges on the merits (*les juges du fond*), who considered that they were competent to judge members of government, when the offence that they were reproached had been committed in the exercise of their functions. In the decision *Frey v. de Blignieres*, the criminal chamber of the

Cour de Cassation decided on March 14, 1963, that the interpretation of article 68 that had been retained by the Court of Appeal of Paris was erroneous and that the High Court was the only one competent in such cases. Thus, this privilege of jurisdiction reserved to the sole members of Parliament the appreciation of the infraction that was being reproached, and its judgment by the High Court, itself comprised of members of Parliament. Therefore, the ordinary justice (tribunals) should not determine cases which, by virtue of being related to the exercise of governmental functions raised a political question.

The practical inconvenience of this solution was that the cumbersome character of the procedure provided for in article 68 made it in fact inapplicable, and resulted in an impunity of the members of government. The High Court was never able to function, even in cases of blatant corruption, as in the Nucci case in 1987. The question was to rise again in the 1990s, with the case of the contaminated blood (*affaire du sang contaminé*). It was discovered that persons who had undergone blood transfusion had been contaminated with the AIDS virus, and the health authorities were taken to task for not having reacted in due time by taking the necessary measures. Doctors who were in charge of organizing the blood transfer, which comes under the health administration, were indicted in 1992. In addition, attempts were made to submit the minister and the secretary of state to public health, as well as the prime minister, to the Haute Cour de Justice. Press campaigns accused them of gross negligence and of delays that led to the contamination of a certain number of people, many of whom passed away. For reasons of political solidarity first, and then of procedure, these indictments did not come before the High Court.

In order to respond to the emotions of public opinion, the Constitution was revised on July 27, 1993, and the Cour de Justice de la Republique (*Court of Justice of the Republic*) was established to look into crimes and misdemeanors committed by members of government in the exercise of their functions, including those committed before 1993. Henceforth, the victims could instigate legal proceedings (*poursuites pénales*) by referring their case to a commission of claims (*commission de requêtes*) comprised of judges. If the commission deems the request justiciable and not grounded in a willingness of judicial harassment, it transmits it to the commission of instruction (*commission d'instruction*), which plays the role imparted in the ordinary procedure to the *juge d'instruction* (which is referred to as the inquisitory procedure, distinct from the accusatory procedure of the Anglo-Saxon legal system). This commission, comprised of three judges of the Cour de Cassation, decides whether to send the accused before the Cour de Justice. The public interest (*ministère public*) is represented by the attorney general of the Cour of Cassation (*le procureur général près la Cour de Cassation*) throughout the procedure.

All of the preliminary phase is therefore inspired by a concern or willingness to come closer to the ordinary judicial procedure, both with regard to the persons concerned and with regard to the application of criminal law (*droit pénal*), with the exception of the filter by the *commission des requêtes* (commission of requests). On the other hand, the political nature inherent to the persons accused, and to the relation of the facts with their governmental functions, has led to compose the Court by Members of Parliament, with three adjunct judges from the Cour de Cassation, one of whom presides over the Court. This compromise between the political and the judiciary, which seemed an appropriate synthesis to the specific character of this new jurisdiction, was to reveal itself as a false compromise or an apparent compromise ("compromis apparent" in the sense given to this expression by Carl Schmitt), that is an apparent solution that in fact delays to a subsequent time the decision: is there a political or a legal responsibility involved? This is an ambiguity that the decision of March 9, 1999, was to raise.

The ministers were taken to task for their delay in reacting to evidence that the AIDS virus was being transmitted by transfusion: they should have immediately treated the stocked blood in order to render it safe. First of all, the Court had to characterize this behavior. The crime of poisoning, which was considered for a short while, was abandoned in favor of the crime of "involuntary breach of the life and physical integrity of persons," a characterization that elicited a double criticism. On the one hand, the interpretation of article 68, according to some, could not be directed at unintended crimes of members of government but only to a guilty intention on their part. To this, the decision responded that when the text is silent on this matter, the penal law, which speaks to nonintentional crimes, must apply. On the other hand, the public attorney (*procureur géneral*) considered that since article 68 pertained to "actions," it could only pertain to crimes that were committed (crimes par commission) and not "crimes by omission." What was in question, in his view, was a defective functioning of the state system, and thus the political responsibility of the ministers. They might have committed mistakes but these did not come under the competence of the Court of Justice because "the judicial authority should not institute itself as a controller of the executive power." He therefore dropped the charges. The Court refused to follow his view, and asserted the autonomy of the criminal responsibility *vis-à-vis* the political responsibility, but it concluded that the crime was not committed (*le crime n'était pas constitué*) in the case of the prime minister and of the minister of health. On the other hand, it found that the secretary of state, who was directly in charge of the file, was guilty of the crime, while dispensing him, however, of a penalty. Such a compromise reflects the equivocal nature of the accusation, since it was obvious that there had been an avoidable delay. But, this delay (which was a limited delay anyway) resulted from the slowness inherent in governmental bureaucracy, for which the ministers were accountable but which did not constitute criminal activity. It was necessary to respond to the indignation of public opinion on the legal level, given that the negligence of the ministers did not lead to the natural consequence of their resignation. The difficulty in this case stemmed from the fact that the negligence did not appear perfectly clear until after the change of the political majority, and hence of the government.

The contaminated blood affair has revealed on this occasion that the judges of the commission of instruction (contrary to the general attorney) were sensitive to the pressure of the media and of public opinion, as much as the parliamentary judges were sensitive to the ambiguous character of the mission that was ascribed to them. Besides, the position of the Cour de Cassation has changed as compared to its previous jurisprudence prior to the creation of the Cour de Justice de la Republique. It considers that the acts committed by the ministers in the exercise of their functions do not concern those that were committed "on the occasion" of these functions, which come henceforth under the competence of the judiciary (*droit commun*), but only those "that have a direct relation with the conduct of state business (*conduite des affaires de l'Etat*) for which the Cour de justice de la Republique was competent. This last formulation translates very clearly the penalization of bad or incompetent administration, and the confusion that is henceforth established between penal responsibility and political responsibility. It poses in new terms the definition of "political questions" in a generalized movement of juridicization of political life, which is indeed, as Pierre Menent observed, "one of the major problems of contemporary democracy."

Who Should Be the Authoritative Interpreter of the Constitution?
Why There Should Not Be a Political Question Doctrine

Erwin Chemerinsky[1]

Who should interpret the U.S. Constitution? The obviously correct answer is that all government officials and institutions are required to engage in constitutional interpretation. All elected officeholders take an oath to uphold the Constitution. Therefore, legislators—federal, state, and local—are obliged to consider the constitutionality of bills before ratifying them. The executive must consider constitutionality in deciding what laws to propose, which bills passed by the legislature to veto, and what executive policies to implement. The judiciary, at the very least, must consider the constitutionality of laws before applying them to decide cases and controversies. In short, the decision that society shall be governed by a constitution necessitates that all branches and levels of government interpret the Constitution.

The real question to be addressed is not who should interpret the Constitution but, more specifically, who should be the authoritative interpreter of the Constitution? When there is a disagreement over how the Constitution should be interpreted, who resolves the conflict? Who gets the final say in determining the mean-

[1] Sydney M. Irmas Professor of Public Interest Law, Legal Ethics, and Political Science, University of Southern California, Los Angeles, California.

ing of a constitutional provision (final, that is, until the interpretation is overruled in a constitutional amendment or the interpreter changes its mind.)? Disagreements over the meaning of the Constitution are inevitable. For example, Congress enacts a statute that it implicitly or explicitly declares to be constitutional. The judiciary, in considering the law, concludes that it is unconstitutional. Whose view triumphs? The president claims a right to keep certain documents secret because of executive privilege. The Court rules that executive privilege does not apply. Whose view triumphs? The president rescinds a treaty and asserts inherent constitutional authority to do so. The Senate believes that such recision without its advice and consent is unconstitutional. Whose view triumphs?

Ultimately, the question of whether there should be a political question doctrine turns on the answer to these questions. In this volume, I argue that the judiciary should be the ultimate interpreter of the Constitution and thus conclude that there should not be a political question doctrine. Part I considers possible answers to the question of who should be the authoritative interpreter of the Constitution. Part II argues that the judiciary should play this role. Based on this, Part III argues that there should not be a political question doctrine.

My central thesis is a simple one: the Constitution exists to restrict what the government may do. As *Marbury v. Madison* recognized long ago, the limits of the Constitution have little meaning if they are not enforced.[2] The effect of the political question doctrine is to eliminate the possibility of judicial enforcement of key constitutional provisions. I believe that this is inconsistent with the very purpose of the Constitution and with the judiciary's role in our democratic society.[3]

I. Who is the Authoritative Interpreter?

There are three possible answers to the question of who should be the authoritative interpreter of the Constitution. One approach is for no branch of government to be regarded as authoritative in constitutional interpretation. Each branch of government would have equal authority to determine the meaning of constitutional provisions, and conflicts would be resolved through political power and compromise. If Congress and the president believe that a law is constitutional, and they could implement it without assistance from the Court, they could disregard a judicial ruling of unconstitutionality. If the president believes a law to be unconstitutional, he or she could refuse to enforce it, notwithstanding declarations of its constitutionality from the legislature and judiciary.

---

[2] 5 U.S. (1 Cranch) 103 (1803).

[3] A similar position is advocated in Martin Redish, *Judicial Review and the Political Question*, 79 Nw. U. L. Rev. 1031 (1985). For a defense of the political question doctrine, see Rachel E. Barkow, *More Supreme Than Court?: The Fall of the Political Question Doctrine and the Rise of Judicial Supremacy*, 102 Colum. L. Rev. 237 (2002).

This approach to constitutional interpretation finds support early in U.S. history from presidents such as Thomas Jefferson and Andrew Jackson. Jefferson wrote:

> But nothing in the Constitution has given . . . [the judges] a right to decide for the Executive, more than to the Executive to decide for them. Both magistracies are equally independent in the sphere of action assigned to them. The judges, believing the law constitutional, had a right to pass a sentence of fine and imprisonment because that power was placed in their hands by the Constitution. But the Executive, believing the law to be unconstitutional, was bound to remit the execution of it because that power is confided to him by the Constitution. That instrument meant that its coordinate branches should be checks on each other. But the opinion which gives to the judges the right to decide what laws are constitutional, and what not, not only for themselves in their own sphere of action, but for the Legislature and Executive also, would make the judiciary a despotic branch.[4]

Similarly, Andrew Jackson declared in vetoing a bill to recharter the Bank of the United States:

> The Congress, the Executive, and the Court must each for itself be guided by its own opinion of the Constitution. Each public officer who takes an oath to support the Constitution swears that he will support it as he understands it, and not as it is understood by others. It is as much the duty of the House of Representatives, of the Senate, and of the President to decide upon the constitutionality of any bill or resolution which may be presented to them for passage or approval as it is of the supreme judges when it may be brought before them for judicial decision. The opinion of the judges has no more authority over Congress than the opinion of Congress has over the judges, and on that point the President is independent of both. The authority of the Supreme Court must not, therefore, be permitted to control the Congress or the Executive when acting in their legislative capacities, but to have only such influence as the force of their reasoning may deserve.[5]

Under this first approach, there is no authoritative interpreter of the Constitution. Support for this approach is found not only in proclamations of long-dead presidents. The Reagan administration articulated and advocated the view that each branch has equal authority to interpret the Constitution, and that the executive and legislature are not bound by the judiciary's rulings. In October 1986, Attorney General Edwin Meese gave a highly publicized speech in which he explicitly at-

---

[4] Thomas Jefferson, letter to Abigail Adams, September 11, 1804, 8 *The Writings of Thomas Jefferson* 310 (Ford ed. 1897).

[5] Andrew Jackson, *Veto Message,* 2 Messages and Papers of the Presidents 576, 581–83 (Richardson ed. 1896).

tacked the view that the judiciary is the ultimate arbiter of constitutional questions. Meese argued that each branch has equal authority to decide for itself the meaning of constitutional provisions. Meese remarked: "The Supreme Court, then, is not the only interpreter of the Constitution. Each of the three coordinate branches of government created and empowered by the Constitution—the executive and legislature no less than the judiciary—has a duty to interpret the Constitution in the performance of its official functions. In fact, every official takes an oath precisely to that effect."[6]

There is a second, distinct approach to the question of who is the authoritative interpreter of the Constitution. In this approach, one branch of government is assigned the role of final arbiter of disputes for each part of the Constitution, but it is not the same branch for all parts of the Constitution. Thus, each branch would be the authoritative interpreter for some constitutional provisions. Because the Constitution does not specify who should interpret the document, some institution would need to allocate interpretive authority among the branches of government.

Arguably, the second approach is the one that best describes the current system of constitutional interpretation. The judiciary has declared that cases arising under certain parts of the Constitution pose political questions and are matters to be decided by branches of government other than the courts. For example, the courts frequently have held that challenges to the president's conduct of foreign policy—such as whether the Vietnam War is unconstitutional—pose a political question not to be resolved by the judiciary.[7] By declaring a matter to be a political question, the Court states that it is for the other branches of government to interpret the constitutional provisions in question and decide whether the Constitution is violated. The effect is the second approach: for each part of the Constitution, there is a final arbiter, but it is not the same branch for all constitutional provisions.

A third approach is to assign to one branch of government final authority for all constitutional interpretation. Although every governmental institution interprets the Constitution, one branch is assigned the role of umpire; its views resolve disputes and are final until reversed by constitutional amendment. Arguably, *Marbury v. Madison* endorses this approach. Chief Justice Marshall declared that "[i]t is emphatically the province and duty of the judicial department to say what the law is."[8] Similarly, in *United States v. Nixon,* the Supreme Court held that it was the judiciary's duty to determine the meaning of the Constitution. In rejecting the president's claim that it was for the executive to determine the scope of executive privilege, Chief Justice Warren Burger, writing for the Court, stated: "The President's counsel [reads] the Constitution as providing an absolute privilege of confidentiality for all Presidential communications. Many decisions of this Cowl, how-

---

[6] Edwin Meese, "The Law of the Constitution: A Bicentennial Lecture," Tulane University Citizens Forum on the Bicentennial of the Constitution, October 21, 1986, 11.

[7] I describe these cases in detail in Erwin Chemerinsky, *Federal Jurisdiction*, 4th ed., 155–59 (New York: Aspen Publishers, 2003).

[8] 5 U.S. (1 Cranch) at 177.

ever, have unequivocally reaffirmed the holding of [*Marbury* v. *Madison*] that 'it is emphatically the province and duty of the judicial department to say what the law is.'"[9]

Marbury v. Madison and *United States v. Nixon*, however, could be viewed as ambiguous and as not resolving the question of which of these three approaches is preferable. *Marbury* could be read narrowly as holding only that the Court is the final arbiter of the meaning of Article III of the Constitution, which defines judicial power. The specific issue in *Marbury* was whether a section of the Judiciary Act of 1789 was inconsistent with Article III. Accordingly, *Marbury* could be interpreted, consistent with the second approach described above, as assigning to the judiciary only the responsibility for interpreting Article III. In fact, *Marbury* could even be seen as consistent with the first approach—that there is no final interpreter of the Constitution. By this view, *Marbury* simply holds that the judiciary may interpret the Constitution in deciding cases—it is one voice—and that it is not required to defer to legislative or executive interpretations. *Marbury*, according to this argument, says nothing about whether other branches of government are bound to follow the Court's interpretation. Chief Justice Marshall's declaration could be understood as emphatically declaring that the courts do get a say. Under this approach, *Marbury v. Madison* says nothing about who is the authoritative interpreter of the Constitution.

Likewise, *United States v. Nixon* could be viewed as a limited ruling that the judiciary has the final say in cases raising the question of access to evidence necessary for criminal trials. The Court in *Nixon* emphasized the judiciary's special role in ensuring fair trials:

> The impediment that an absolute, unqualified privilege would place in the way of the primary constitutional duty of the Judicial Branch to do justice in criminal prosecutions would plainly conflict with the functions of the courts under Article III . . . [T]o read the Article II powers of the President as providing an absolute privilege as against a subpoena essential to enforcement of criminal statutes on no more than a generalized claim of the public interest in confidentiality of non-military and non-diplomatic discussions would upset the constitutional balance of a 'workable government' and gravely impair the role of the courts under Article III.' The right to the production of all evidence at a criminal trial similarly has constitutional dimensions. [I]t is the manifest duty of the courts to vindicate [the Sixth and Fifth Amendment] guarantees and to accomplish that it is essential that all relevant and admissible evidence be produced.[10]

Thus, *United States v. Nixon* can be viewed as a narrow holding that the Court is the final arbiter in matters relating to the judiciary's powers under Article III.

Therefore, in determining who is the authoritative interpreter of the Constitution, it is necessary to choose among three approaches: (1) that there is no final

---

[9] 418 U.S. 683, 703–05 (1974).

[10] *Id.* at 709.

arbiter over cases presenting questions as to the Constitution's meaning, (2) that each branch is the final arbiter for some constitutional provisions, and (3) that one branch should be the final arbiter in all disputes over constitutional interpretation. Each of these has some support. The next section considers why the judiciary is better suited to engage in constitutional interpretation than Congress or the president. The final section discusses why the judiciary should be the authoritative interpreter of all constitutional provisions—that is, why the third approach described above is preferable.

II. The Need for Judicial Interpretation

The federal courts, and especially the Supreme Court, are best suited to engage in constitutional interpretation for two separate, although interrelated, reasons. First, the judiciary is the institution most able to protect the Constitution's structure and values from majoritarian pressures. Second, the judiciary's decision-making method is preferable for constitutional interpretation and evolution.

A. Judicial Protection from Majoritarian Pressures

The Constitution exists to protect certain matters from majoritarian decision making. A society chooses to have a constitution, rather than just to be governed by statutes, in order to safeguard the structure of government and fundamental values from majority rule. In large part, the decision to be governed by a constitution is animated by fear that a political majority could gain control of government and disenfranchise, and perhaps persecute, the minority. A constitution is unique primarily because of the difficulty of amending or altering it.

Accordingly, in deciding who should be the authoritative interpreter of the Constitution, a primary criterion should be determining which branch of government can best enforce the Constitution against the desires of political majorities. Under this criterion, the federal judiciary is the obvious choice. The judiciary is the institution most insulated from political pressures. Article III of the Constitution provides that federal court judges have life tenure, unless impeached, and that their salary may not be decreased during their terms of office. Unlike legislators or the president, federal judges never face reelection.

Furthermore, the method of federal judicial selection reinforces its anti-majoritarian character. Unlike the House of Representatives, whose members are elected at the same time, or the Senate where one third of the members are chosen at each election, the Court's members are appointed one at a time, as vacancies arise. Therefore, generally, no single administration is able to appoint a majority of the Court or of the federal judiciary. The result is that the Court reflects many political views, not just that which is dominant at a particular time.

Certainly, it is not original or profound to observe that the judiciary's political insulation makes it well-suited to uphold the Constitution. If anything is clear from the structure of the Constitution and the language of Article III, it is that the federal judiciary was given life tenure and salary protection precisely to ensure its independence. It, however, is worth elaborating why this insulation is so important in the process of constitutional evolution and interpretation.

First, the judiciary is the only institution obligated to hear the complaints of a single person. For the most part, the federal judiciary's jurisdiction is mandatory. Although the Supreme Court has discretion in choosing which cases to hear, with rare exceptions, a lower federal court must rule on every case properly filed with it. Long ago, Chief Justice Marshall wrote, "[I]t is most true that this Court will not take jurisdiction if it should not but it is equally true that it must take jurisdiction if it should. . . We have no more right to decline the exercise of jurisdiction which is given, than to usurp that which is not given."[11]

In contrast, the legislature and the executive are under no duty to hear the complaints of a single person. An individual or small group complaining of an injustice to a legislator or the president could be ignored easily. If only a few constituents care about something, and if acting to help them would consume more time than it seems worth to get their votes in the future, they may be ignored. Moreover, if helping the few will hurt more constituents, the few are likely to be disregarded, no matter how just their cause. For example, prisoners are a constituency with relatively little political power. In many states, felons are permanently disenfranchised from voting, meaning that elected officials need worry little about meeting their demands.[12] Providing adequate resources for prisoners—sufficient money for their shelter, food, medical care, and training—requires expenditures unlikely to be popular with taxpayers. With no constituency to pressure for their humane treatment, the political process tends to ignore the rights and needs of prisoners.

The courts, however, are obligated to rule on each person's properly filed complaint. It does not matter whether the litigant is rich or poor, powerful or powerless, incarcerated or not. The Constitution's purpose of protecting the minority from the tyranny of the majority is best fulfilled by an institution obligated to listen to the minority. Groups such as prisoners and mental patients are most likely to have their rights protected through an institution such as the judiciary that is required to address their complaints. Similarly, the judiciary is much more likely than the legislature to listen to criminal defendants' claims that their rights were violated or to poor individuals' objections that they are denied equal justice.

Second, the judiciary not only is most likely to listen to complaints, but it is also most likely to respond to them and apply the Constitution. The judiciary is supposed to decide each case on its own merits, subject only to the accepted norm that like cases should be treated alike. Therefore, in every case where there is an allegation that the Constitution is being violated, the judiciary is obligated, if it has

---

[11] *Cohens v. Virginia*, 19 U.S. (6 Wheat.) 264, 404 (1824).
[12] See *Richardson v. Ramierez*, 418 U.S. 24 (1974).

jurisdiction and if there is no way to decide the case on nonconstitutional grounds, to issue a constitutional ruling. The legislature, by contrast, need not decide each matter before it on its own merits. Logrolling and voting trade-offs are accepted parts of the legislative process. Although legislators are forbidden by their oath of office to enact laws that they believe to be unconstitutional, they are not required to provide a remedy every time someone complains that government is doing something unconstitutional. Only the judiciary is obligated to respond to unconstitutional practices—something that makes the courts an ideal forum for ensuring that the Constitution is upheld.

Third, the judiciary is most willing to enforce the Constitution when faced with strong pressures from political majorities. Even if the legislature and executive would listen to all claims and respond on the merits, they are still less likely to uphold the Constitution when faced with intense reactions from their constituents. The judiciary's insulation from politics makes it best suited to enforce the Constitution. It is this insulation that caused Alexis de Tocqueville to remark that "the power vested in the American courts of justice of pronouncing a statute unconstitutional forms one of the most powerful barriers that have been devised against the tyranny of political assemblies."[13]

The argument is not that legislators are likely to act in bad faith and disregard their oath to uphold the Constitution (although there may be cases where this does occur). Rather, the point is that constitutional interpretation inherently requires choices as to what the Constitution should mean. Constitutional interpretation requires decisions as to how the abstract values stated in the Constitution are best applied in specific situations. These choices are best made by an institution whose primary commitment is to the Constitution, not to gaining reelection. Owen Fiss observes that "[l]egislatures are not ideologically committed or institutionally suited to search for the meaning of constitutional values, but instead see their primary function in terms of registering the actual, current preferences of the people."[14] The judiciary, much more than the political branches of government, is to be trusted in deciding whether the Constitution should protect the speech activities of a politically unpopular group, such as the Nazi party. The judiciary, committed to upholding the First Amendment and not faced with intense pressure from constituents, is in a better position to decide whether school prayer violates the Constitution. The judiciary, relatively insulated from intense lobbying, is better suited to deciding whether the right of privacy includes the right of a woman to decide whether to have an abortion.

The best institution for interpreting the Constitution is thus not the one that most reflects the current preferences of the majority. Rather, constitutional interpretation is best done by a politically insulated body. Harry Wellington explains:

If society were to design an institution which had the job of finding society's

[13] Alexis de Toqueville, *Democracy in America*, ed. Bradley 103 (New York: A. A. Knopf, 1945).
[14] Owen Fiss, *Foreword: The Forms of Justice*, 93 Harv. L. Rev. 1, 10 (1979).

set of moral principles and determining how they bear on concrete situations, that institution would be sharply different from one charged with proposing policies. The latter institution would be constructed with the understanding that it was to respond to the people's exercise of political power. . . . The former would be insulated from pressure. It would provide an environment conducive to rumination, reflection and analysis. [15]

Constitutional interpretation is a process of deciding what values are so fundamental that they should be safeguarded from political majorities. It makes little sense to allow the majoritarian process to decide what should be protected from itself. No matter what the appropriate process of identifying constitutional values, the judiciary's insulation and commitment to decisions based on the merits make it best suited for such interpretation. Alexander Bickel remarked that "courts have certain capacities for dealing with matters of principle that legislatures and the executive do not possess. Judges have, or should have, the leisure, the training, and the insulation to follow the ways of the scholar in pursuing the ends of government. This is crucial in sorting out the enduring values of a society."[16] Constitutional interpretation requires an institution to serve as the nation's moral conscience—an institution responsible for identifying values so important that they should not be sacrificed and reminding the country when it is violating its own most cherished values. The Supreme Court frequently has defined its role in exactly these terms, as a moral conscience.

Finally, the legislature is to be trusted least when the question is the constitutionality of a statute that it enacted. Constitutional values will not be protected from majority rule if the legislature can both enact laws and determine their constitutionality. Allowing review by another branch of government creates a check that otherwise would not exist. The executive veto provides something of a check; however, Congress can override a veto. Moreover, the president is electorally accountable and may reflect the same pressures as Congress. Thus, the judiciary is most detached and has the least involvement in the enactment of laws or the implementation of policies. The Court's only self-interest is in enhancing its long-term powers. Certainly, the judiciary's institutional self-interest justifies fear of its deciding cases to aggrandize its own powers. I would argue, however, that in resolving specific controversies it is better to trust an institution with only long-term interests than one with immediate interests in the outcome of the matter.

In sum, once it is decided that society should be governed by a constitution in order to make certain matters less amenable to majoritarian control, judicial review is a desirable mechanism for interpreting and enforcing the document.

---

[15] Harry Wellington, *Common Law Rules and Constitutional Double Standards: Some Notes on Adjudication,* 83 Yale L. J. 221, 246–47 (1973).

[16] Alexander Bickel, *The Least Dangerous Branch* (Indianapolis: Bobbs-Merrill, 1962), 26.

B. The Judiciary's Decision-Making Methods

In addition to the conclusion that the courts are most able to protect the Constitution from majoritarian pressures, the methods of judicial decision making make it the best institution for constitutional interpretation. The judiciary is unique in that it is the only institution committed to arriving at decisions based entirely on arguments and reasoning. Executive and legislative officials frequently offer no formal explanations for their decisions, and even when they provide statements, they usually do not purport to be comprehensive. The judicial method is a process of hearing arguments (written and oral) from the parties, reaching decisions based on the arguments, and justifying the results with a written opinion stating reasons for the decision. Although neither the Constitution nor any statute compels a court to write and publish opinions, publicly stated reasons for decision are embedded in the U.S. legal system. In fact, it has long been recognized that the "traditional means of protecting the public from judicial fiat . . . [are] that judges give reasons for their results."[17]

The Court must write an opinion demonstrating that its decision is not arbitrary. It must explain both why the values it is protecting are worthy of constitutional status and how those values are embodied in legal principles. Additionally, the Court must explain why its decision is consistent with prior holdings, is legitimately distinguishable from precedents, or justifies overruling conflicting cases.

In contrast, the legislature and the executive need not follow any particular decision-making process. Neither Congress nor the president is required, either by law or by tradition, to state reasons for decisions. Although Congress produces legislative histories and the president issues executive proclamations, only the judiciary is committed to reaching all decisions by logical reasoning from principles rather than results based on political considerations. A legislature is allowed, even expected, to make arbitrary choices unsupported by a guiding principle. Even if all the Supreme Court's constitutional decisions are merely hunches or reflections of personal predilections, the Court must still justify those conclusions in legally acceptable terms. Moreover, only the judiciary is committed to following precedent in reaching its decisions.

III. Why the Judiciary Should Be the Final Arbiter: Against the Political Question Doctrine

For the most part, government operates without a need for constitutional interpretation. Many provisions of the Constitution are sufficiently clear and specific to provide adequate instructions for the conduct of government. For example, there is usually no dispute as to how federal government officials are elected, the

---

[17] G. Edward White, The Evolution of Reasoned Elaboration: Jurisprudential Criticism and Social Change, 59 Va. L. Rev. 279, 299 (1973).

length of their terms of office, or the procedures they are to follow in enacting laws. There are, however, many constitutional provisions that are ambiguous and lack the degree of specificity found in sections of the Constitution dealing with the selection process. Because of constitutional provisions that are not completely clear, constitutional conflicts do arise, such as questions as to the proper meaning of specific constitutional provisions and questions about how to resolve conflicts among various sections of the document. The question posed at the beginning of this chapter is how these conflicts should be resolved. Put another way, who should be the authoritative interpreter of the Constitution?

The worst approach is if no branch of government is authoritative, with all constitutional questions resolved by political power and compromise. Under this approach, the executive and legislature would be under no obligation to follow judicial interpretations of the Constitution. Each branch could interpret the Constitution for itself, without regard to the others' views. As such, the legislature and executive could institute a policy of persecuting minorities and simply ignore judicial declarations invalidating their policy. The judiciary's functions as an antimajoritarian check would be lost if the politically accountable branches could disregard virtually all judicial rulings.

Furthermore, the Constitution would not have an articulated meaning. There would be a series of Court decisions, some followed, some not. The ultimate results would simply reflect the respective powers of the various branches and not the Constitution's mandates. The benefits of the judiciary's method of decision making would be lost, as the other branches would be authoritative for many constitutional decisions.

Constitutional crises would be commonplace if no branch of government were the authoritative interpreter of the Constitution. For example, what would happen if the judiciary declared an executive practice unconstitutional and enjoined it, but the executive steadfastly maintained it was constitutional and ignored the injunction? The example is not farfetched. If no branch were regarded as authoritative in constitutional interpretation, what would have happened after *United States v. Nixon* when the judiciary and the president disagreed over the proper scope of executive privilege? One possibility is that Congress could try to impeach the president for ignoring a judicial order. This option is obviously extreme, highly disruptive of government, and unlikely to be used except in rare circumstances. Alternatively, the Court could hold the president in contempt and impose judicial sanctions on the chief executive. It is unclear whether it is constitutional to impose such sanctions on a sitting president. Furthermore, because it is unlikely that the Court will implement its own punishment for contempt (having the Court marshal arrest the president and hold him or her in jail), the judiciary needs to depend either on the executive to act against the president or on impeachment. Any of these options would provoke major constitutional crises.

To develop the meaning of the Constitution in an orderly, coherent manner and ensure that its mandates are observed, society needs an authoritative interpreter of the Constitution. The previous section described why the Supreme Court, and the federal judiciary, is best suited to serve in this role. Now I argue that the

Court should be the authoritative interpreter of the meaning of *all* constitutional provisions.

Currently, there are many parts of the Constitution that the Court refuses to interpret. For these provisions, the political branches are the authoritative interpreters. For example, in a series of decisions the Supreme Court has said that certain constitutional challenges only state a "generalized grievance" and therefore no plaintiff has standing to sue. In *United States v. Richardson,* [17] the plaintiff claimed that statutes providing for the secrecy of the Central Intelligence Agency budget violated the Constitution's requirement for a regular statement and account of all government expenditures. The Court refused to rule on whether the challenged statute violated the Constitution. The Court held that the plaintiff's case only presented a "generalized grievance," and hence the plaintiff lacked standing to sue. The Court concluded that because the plaintiff could not show that his personal rights were violated, but instead only could claim injury as a citizen and taxpayer, the Court should not rule. The Court held that ultimately the statements and accounts clause was a part of the Constitution to be enforced not by the judiciary but rather by the political process. The Court declared: "It can be argued that if respondent is not permitted to litigate this issue, no one can do so. In a very real sense, the absence of any particular individual or class to litigate these claims gives support to the argument that the subject matter is committed to the surveillance of Congress, and ultimately to the political process."[18]

Similarly, in *Schlesinger v. Reservists Committee to Stop the War,* [19] the plaintiffs sued to enjoin members of Congress from serving in the military reserves. Article I, section 6, of the Constitution prevents a senator or representative from holding civil offices. Again, the Court refused to rule on the plaintiffs' claim of unconstitutionality, holding that the matter posed a generalized grievance; that is, plaintiffs could only allege injuries as citizens and taxpayers. The Court concluded that ultimately it was for the political process to enforce this constitutional provision. The Court stated: "Respondents seek to have the Judicial Branch to compel the Executive Branch to act in conformity with the Incompatibility Clause, an interest shared by all citizens. . . . [The] claimed nonobservance [with the Constitution adversely affects] only the generalized interests of all citizens in constitutional governance and that is an abstract injury. . . . Our system of government leaves many crucial decisions to the political process. The assumption that if respondents have no standing to sue, no one would have standing, is not a reason to find standing."[20]

The effect of decisions such as *Richardson* and *Schlesinger* is to assign to the political branches the responsibility for interpreting and enforcing certain constitutional provisions. Although the plaintiffs claim that the government is blatantly violating the explicit words of the Constitution, the Court concluded that the matter was for the political process and not the judiciary to decide.

---

[18] *Id.* at 179.
[19] 418 U.S. 208 (1974).
[20] *Id.* at 227.

In addition to these standing rules, the political question doctrine allocates interpretation of some constitutional provisions to the electorally accountable branches of government. By declaring certain subject matter to pose a political question, the Court states that it will not rule on claims of unconstitutionality. The political branches are given the ultimate say as to the meaning of those provisions. In other words, the political question doctrine is invoked by the courts to avoid ruling on a matter when it deems the resolution of the controversy to be committed to another branch of government. The whole point of placing something in a Constitution is to insulate it from the political process. In essence, some constitutional provisions are made meaningless when matters are deemed to be political questions.

The inappropriateness of allocating constitutional decision making to the political branches can be demonstrated by considering a proposal by Jesse Choper that all questions of separation of powers be deemed political questions and therefore not reviewable by the courts. Choper contends that the courts should declare that litigation contesting the constitutionality of presidential actions is nonjusticiable:

> The federal judiciary should not decide constitutional questions concerning the respective powers of Congress and the president vis-à-vis one another; rather, the ultimate constitutional issues of whether executive action (or inaction) violates the prerogatives of Congress . . . should be held to be nonjusticiable, their final resolution to be remitted to the interplay of the national political process.[21]

Choper's approach would leave all questions of separation of powers for resolution by the political branches. Such an approach is inconsistent with a Constitution committed to protecting separation of powers. The Constitution creates the structure of government, in part, to prevent those in power from increasing their authority. Yet Choper's approach would allow the president to be given almost unlimited authority, usurping virtually all power allocated to Congress in the Constitution, so long as Congress agrees. For example, under Choper's approach, the Court could not declare unconstitutional the president's seizure of steel mills or the president's impoundment of congressionally appropriated funds.[22] Unless Congress acted to stop the president, the executive could completely disregard the Constitution's allocation of powers to Congress.

Thus, Choper's approach sanctions an almost total transfer of legislative power to the executive so long as Congress does not object. Repeated congressional inaction would result in a tremendous shift of power to the White House. Such a growth in executive authority could threaten the entire system of checks and balances. As Justice Felix Frankfurter noted: "The accretion of dangerous

---

[21] Jesse Choper, *Judicial Review and the National Political Process* (University of Chicago Press, 1980), 263.

[22] See, e.g., *Youngstown Sheet & Tube Co. v. Sawyer*, 343 U.S. 579 (1952) (declaring unconstitutional presidential seizure of the steel mills).

power does not come in a day. It does come, however slowly, from the generative force of unchecked disregard of the restrictions that fence in even the most disinterested assertion of authority."[23]

Moreover, Choper's approach assumes that Congress has the authority to restrain unconstitutional presidential actions. If the president acts unconstitutionally, for example, by seizing an industry or impounding funds, what can Congress do? Congress could pass a statute directing the president to cease the unconstitutional activity. However, the president could veto the law. This means that Congress could stop the president only if two thirds of both houses of Congress were willing to act. Political realities, including support for a president from his or her own political party, might make such an override of a veto unlikely.

History shows that Congress is generally unwilling to restrain the president. "[C]ongressional review of executive policy-making is sporadic, and the executive frequently makes policy without Congress either taking responsibility for it or repudiating it. The result is a system sharply skewed towards executive policy-making."[24] Paul Gewirtz explains many reasons why Congress may not act even though a majority of its members disagree with the president: "[W]hen Congress is faced with an executive policy that is in place and functioning, Congress often acquiesces in the executive's action for reasons which have nothing to do with the majority's preferences on the policy issues involved. . . . In such a situation, Congress may not want to be viewed as disruptive; or Congresspersons may not want to embarrass the President; or Congress may want to score political points by attacking the executive's action rather than accepting political responsibility for some action itself; or Congresspersons may be busy running for reelection or tending to constituents' individual problems; or Congress may be lazy and prefer another recess."[25]

In short, Choper's approach permits separation of powers to be rendered nonexistent. The Constitution's function of preventing the accumulation of power in one branch of government would be undermined. I believe that the judiciary should resolve claims that the president is acting in excess of the Constitution's grant of power to the executive and unconstitutionally usurping legislative power. Judicial review exists to protect the Constitution—including the provisions defining the structure of government—from majority rule. To ensure that the Constitution is protected from majoritarian pressures, the judiciary should be the authoritative interpreter of all provisions. The judiciary should abandon the justiciability doctrines, such as the generalized grievance standing requirement and the political question doctrine, which allocate interpretation of certain parts of the Constitution

---

[23] *Id.* 594 (Frankfurter, J., dissenting).

[24] Arthur S. Miller, *An Inquiry into the Relevance of the Intentions of the Founding Fathers, with Special Emphasis Upon the Doctrine of Separation of Powers*, 27 Ark. L. Rev. 583, 600 (1973).

[25] Paul Gewirtz, *The Courts, Congress, and Executive Policy-Making: Notes on Three Doctrines*, 40 Law & Contemp. Problems 46, 79 (1976).

to the political branches. The courts should be the authoritative arbiters of the entire Constitution.

Several objections might be made to this conclusion. First, it might be argued that my approach is inconsistent with 200 years of judicial declarations that certain subjects pose a political question. Although I could respond by dismissing this objection as normatively irrelevant, I contend that it is Choper's approach that misconstrues the historical meaning of the political question doctrine when he claims that it should prevent the courts from deciding whether the president has usurped another branch's powers. The political question doctrine, as set forth in *Marbury v. Madison,* provides that the courts should not review an official's performance of duties in which he or she has discretion. Only the exercise of lawful discretion should be unreviewable. Claims that an official is acting without constitutional authority or violating a constitutional provision are not political questions.

Phrased differently, in each case involving a separation of powers issue, the question is whether the official has the power to act and, if so, whether the act is discretionary or mandated by some external authority. The inquiries of whether the official has the authority to act or an obligation to act in a particular manner are not political questions. Only if the act is discretionary is the official's conduct an unreviewable political question. As the Court declared in *Baker v. Carr:*

> Deciding whether a matter has in any measure been committed by the Constitution to another branch of government, of whether the action of that branch exceeds whatever authority has been committed, is itself a delicate exercise in constitutional interpretation, *and is a responsibility* of this Court as ultimate interpreter of the Constitution.[26]

Thus, the political question doctrine simply precludes review of the exercise of discretionary power; it does not prevent a court from determining whether the executive's conduct is an unconstitutional usurpation of judicial or legislative power. Justice William Brennan explained that the political question "doctrine does not pertain when a court is faced with the *antecedent* question whether a political branch has been constitutionally delegated as the repository of political decision-making power. The issue of decision-making authority must be resolved as a matter of constitutional law, not political discretion; accordingly it falls within the competence of the courts."[27]

Second, it can be argued that the political question doctrine and allocation of constitutional decision making to the legislature or executive is desirable because other branches of government have special expertise for some subject matters. For example, it is argued that the president has special expertise in the area of foreign policy. However, this only justifies deference to the executive's foreign policy choices and careful consideration of the president's expert opinions. There is no

---

[26] 369 U.S. 186, 211 (1962).
[27] *Goldwater v. Carter*, 444 U.S. 999, 1007 (1979) (Brennan, J., dissenting).

reason why the president's expertise requires complete abdication and total deference when there are allegations of unconstitutional actions.

Moreover, in most instances, the political question doctrine is invoked in situations where expertise is completely irrelevant. The question of whether the Vietnam War was unconstitutional because the president was waging war without a congressional declaration does not turn on foreign policy expertise. Rather, it poses a fairly standard constitutional question concerning the meaning of two abstract provisions: the president's power as commander in chief and the congressional power to declare war. Similarly, expertise does not justify judicial abdication in the generalized grievance cases where the Court defers to the political process. The question of whether it is unconstitutional for members of Congress to serve in the army reserves, the issue in the *Schlesinger* case, turns on an interpretation of a constitutional provision, not factual information possessed by an expert.

Third, it can be argued that there are some instances where the stakes are too high and the basis for judicial decisions are too unclear to permit court involvement. An example of this would be impeachment. If a president were impeached, should the Court review the case to determine if there were a "high crime or misdemeanor" or whether the proper procedures specified in Article I were followed? The argument is that the Court would exacerbate, not solve, a constitutional crisis if it declared unconstitutional the impeachment of a president. It is a nightmare to imagine a situation where the House impeached a president and the Senate voted for conviction, but the Court ruled that the president should remain in office. Thus, to avoid this possibility, it could be argued that the judiciary should deem itself to lack authority to review all impeachment cases.

Yet, I would argue that this is an argument for great caution and judicial deference, not for total noninvolvement no matter what the circumstances. What if a president were impeached for an act that was completely lawful and within his constitutional powers? Although perhaps unlikely, probability of occurrence is not the relevant test because it also is unlikely that the Court would declare an impeachment unconstitutional in the absence of compelling circumstances. Also, it must not be forgotten that Andrew Johnson was impeached and almost removed from office for exercising the chief executive's prerogative to remove cabinet officers. Or what if the Senate declared a president to be convicted by less than a two-thirds vote, for example, on the basis of a committee's determination?

In such circumstances, judicial review is essential. It is primarily necessary to uphold the Constitution. The provisions dealing with impeachment become meaningless if the legislature can impeach by whatever procedures or standards it desires. Judicial involvement is also necessary to uphold the separation of powers. If the legislature could disregard the Constitution and impeach whenever it chooses, there is a danger of a great shift in power toward the legislature and a threat to the structure of government.

Again, to say that there is a judicial role does not speak to the substantive standards of review that the Court should use. Especially in situations like impeachment, great judicial deference on the merits is appropriate. But there is an enormous difference between automatically denying review in every case and, in contrast, hearing the case with a strong presumption in favor of the legislature's action.

Finally, it might be argued that judicial restraint, such as that described by Choper, is necessary to protect the Court's legitimacy and credibility. Choper argues that the judiciary should not become involved in separation of powers or federalism issues so as to reserve its institutional influence for individual rights cases. Choper's position follows the views of those, such as Alexander Bickel and Felix Frankfurter, who contend that the courts must preserve their institutional credibility by avoiding decisions that will draw the ire of the other branches of government. They argue that owing to the judiciary's limited power to implement its decisions the courts must depend on voluntary compliance by the legislature and executive.

Choper apparently assumes that judicial decisions in separation of powers cases lessen the Court's credibility and legitimacy. Yet there is absolutely no evidence supporting this conclusion. To the contrary, the Court's ruling in cases such as *Youngstown Sheet and Tube v. Sawyer* and *United States v. Nixon* likely enhanced the Court's credibility. The decisions were highly respected and viewed as necessary checks on the president.

Additionally, Choper assumes that the degree of lessened credibility will translate into disregard for judicial decisions. Although Choper offers examples where the judiciary was ignored, there is no evidence that the decreased credibility from separation of powers or federalism rulings will be sufficient to cause increased disregard of Court decrees. In short, Choper offers no evidence that the Court's credibility is so fragile that a few unpopular separation of powers decisions will undermine its authority. Nor is there any evidence that the Court's separation of powers decisions undermine its institutional legitimacy more than its decisions in other areas.

Finally, Choper assumes that maintaining credibility is more important than upholding separation of powers or federalism. He must be assuming either that separation of powers is relatively unimportant or that the long-term benefits of Court rulings in other areas outweigh the need for judicial protection of the structure of government. Neither of these assumptions is supported.

Conclusion

This discussion has attempted to establish that the judiciary should be the authoritative interpreter of all constitutional provisions. For the Constitution to serve its function as a restraint on political majorities, there is a need for Court enforcement of its strictures. Furthermore, judicial elaboration is the best means for constitutional interpretation. It is undesirable to allocate constitutional decision making to other branches of government through the political question doctrine. The Constitution is best upheld if one branch, the judiciary, is the authoritative interpreter.

Bush v. Gore: Too Political?

Louis Fisher[1]

Few Supreme Court decisions have been hammered as hard as *Bush* v. *Gore* (2000), which decided twenty-five crucial electoral votes in Florida. The ruling closed the curtain on an extraordinary legal process, featuring decisions by lower state courts in Florida, federal district courts, a federal appellate court (the 11th Circuit), the Florida Supreme Court (four times), and the U.S. Supreme Court (twice). Within a day, Al Gore gave his concession speech, and on January 6, 2001, a joint session of Congress officially tallied the electoral votes that made George W. Bush the next president. Many professors of law and political science condemned the Court for deciding a dispute that should have, they said, been left to political institutions.[2]

The Academic Assault

There is much in the Court's handling of the case that invites and deserves criticism, but professors relied too much on hyperbole rather than close analysis.

---

[1] Senior Specialist in Separation of Powers, Congressional Research Service, Library of Congress.
[2] This article draws on the author's *35 Frenzied Days: The Florida Election*, 18 Journal of Social Affairs 35–71 (2001).

Reason, facts, balance, objectivity, and thoughtfulness all went out the window.
Judge Richard Posner referred to "the naked partisanship of intellectuals."[3] Academics regarded it as insightful to describe *Bush* v. *Gore* as the worst decision
since *Dred Scott*. Law professors cranked up the rhetoric. Jamin Raskin called
the decision "quite demonstrably the worst Supreme Court decision in history. . . . *Dred Scott* was, by comparison, a brilliantly reasoned and logically
coherent decision."[4] Some professors compared the decision to *Plessy v. Fergu-
son* (1896), which upheld the "separate but equal" doctrine for segregating
blacks and whites. Articles came adorned with cutesy titles: "Not as Bad as
Plessy. Worse."[5] A snide, supercilious tone crept into law reviews. Jack Balkin,
writing for the eminent *Yale Law Journal*, opened with this paragraph:

> Shortly after the Supreme Court's 5-4 decision in *Bush v. Gore*, one member of
> the majority, Associate Justice Clarence Thomas, addressed a group of students in
> the Washington, D.C., area. He told them that he believed that the work of the
> Court was not in any way influenced by politics or partisan considerations. This
> speech was widely reported in the press. Afterwards the question on many legal
> scholars' minds was not whether Justice Thomas had in fact made these state-
> ments. The question was whether he also told the students that he believed in
> Santa Claus, the Easter Bunny, and the Tooth Fairy.[6]

In a full-page ad in the *New York Times* on January 13, 2001, 554 law professors charged that the U.S. Supreme Court had acted as "Political Partisans, Not
Judges of a Court of Law."[7] As did Balkin, the law professors highlighted the five-
to-four split: "when a bare majority of the U.S. Supreme Court halted the recount
of ballots under Florida law, the five justices were acting as political proponents
for candidate Bush, not as judges." Although these academics found the five-to-
four margin abhorrent, they managed to say nothing about a similar division (four-
to-three) on the Florida Supreme Court, which ruled favorably to Gore. By adding
their names to ads of this nature, academics parade not their expertise but their
"partisanship and self-interest."[8]

More recent scholarship has taken to task the academic ranting hurled at *Bush
v. Gore*. To David Ryden, "it is difficult to recall another instance in which the
scholarly opinions and analysis appeared to derive directly from commentators'

---

[3] Richard A. Posner, *Breaking Deadlock: The 2000 Election, the Constitution, and
the Court* (Princeton, N.J.: Princeton University Press, 2001), viii.

[4] Max Boot, "Law Professors v. the Supreme Court," *The Wall Street Journal*, August 13, 2001, A13.

[5] Jed Rubenfeld, *Not as Bad as Plessy. Worse, in* Bush v. Gore: *The Question of Legitimacy* (Bruce Ackerman ed. Yale University Press, 2002), 20.

[6] Jack M. Balkin, Bush v. Gore *and the Boundary Between Law and Politics,* 110
Yale L. J. 1407 (2001).

[7] *The New York Times*, January 13, 2001, A7.

[8] Neal Devins, *Bearing False Witness: The Clinton Impeachment and the Future of
Academic Freedom*, 148 U. Penn. L. Rev. 165 (1999).

respective partisan or ideological disposition."[9] Similarly, Jeff Polet remarked that for "all the charges of partisanship that have been leveled against the Court, one would be hard-pressed not to conclude that the same can be said of virtually all of the commentary."[10]

Critics of the Court typically derided the positions of the majority while overlooking the unusual principles promoted by the minority. Both the conservative and liberal blocs in *Bush v. Gore* presented some strange configurations. As Ryden notes, the majority "exhibited a newfound fondness for the Equal Protection Clause, creatively manipulating it to stop the recounts," while the liberals "were transformed into the new caretakers of federalism and judicial restraint; their new best friends were legislatures rather than courts."[11] Similarly, critics rebuked the Court for deciding a "political question" while accepting without complaint the participation of the Florida Supreme Court.

The Political Question Issue

Ryden argues that *Baker v. Carr* (1962) represented the "piercing of the 'political question' barrier."[12] That reapportionment case did much to sketch out the various categories of political questions, but the barrier (if it ever existed) was pierced long before 1962. A majority of the Supreme Court in 1946, and again in 1948, was prepared to adjudicate reapportionment disputes, but the shortness of time remaining before the election (a few months off) convinced the Court not to decide the case.[13]

Samuel Issacharoff claimed that until the "breakthrough reapportionment cases of the 1960s, the Court refused to immerse itself in any claim implicating the political process."[14] "Immerse" is a verb of uncertain content, but it is not true to suggest that the Court stayed away from political process cases before the 1960s. In 1875, a unanimous Court denied that women were entitled to vote as a privilege

[9] David K. Ryden, *Out of the Shadows:* Bush v. Gore, *the Court, and the Selection of a President,* in *The U.S. Supreme Court and the Electoral Process* (David K. Ryden ed. Georgetown University Press, 2002), 224.

[10] Jeff Polet, *The Imperiousness of* Bush v. Gore, in *The U.S. Supreme Court and the Electoral Process* (David Ryden, ed., Georgetown University Press, 2002), 263.

[11] David K. Ryden, *What* Bush v. Gore *Does and Does Not Tell Us About the Supreme Court and Electoral Politics,* in *The U.S. Supreme Court and the Electoral Process,* 251.

[12] *Id.* at 249.

[13] *Colegrove v. Green,* 328 U.S. 549 (1946); *MacDougall v. Green,* 335 U.S. 281 (1948). See Louis Fisher, *American Constitutional Law* (Durham, N.C.: Carolina Academic Press, 2005), 984.

[14] Samuel Issacharoff, *Political Judgments,* in *The Vote: Bush, Gore & the Supreme Court* (Cass R. Sunstein and Richard A. Epstein, eds., University of Chicago Press, 2001), 57.

and immunity protected by the Constitution.[15] An 1886 decision, seemingly at odds with the ruling on women, referred to voting as "a fundamental political right, because preservative of all rights."[16] Other rulings during this period offered guidance on the right to vote.[17] In 1927, Justice Oliver Wendell Holmes, Jr., heard a litigant say that a question concerning a party primary was nonjusticiable because of its political character. He dismissed the objection as "little more than a play upon words."[18]

If ever there was a political question for the Court to duck it was *Dred Scott v. Sandford* (1857).[19] Yet the justices not only took and decided a slavery case that helped drive the country toward civil war, they urged President James Buchanan in his inaugural address to tell the nation that the case "legitimately belongs to the Supreme Court of the United States, before whom it is now pending, and will, it is understood, be speedily and finally settled."[20] The case, speedily decided, settled nothing.

In *Marbury v. Madison* (1803), Chief Justice John Marshall bravely asserted that "Questions in their nature political . . . can never be made in this court."[21] Nevertheless, Marshall first chided President Thomas Jefferson for his refusal to deliver a judicial commission to William Marbury, while conceding, at the end of the opinion, that the Court had no jurisdiction to grant relief. Having declined to help Marbury, the Court proceeded to claim the right to tell the other branches what is and what is not constitutional. That wasn't political? It is hard to conceive of a purer form.

Just as it is incorrect to date the political question doctrine back to 1962, so is it a misconception to call the doctrine "a dead letter, and has been for some time."[22] The political question doctrine is so diffuse and elusive that it difficult to gauge how alive, or dead, it is. Certainly there are cases, and issues, that the courts will avoid either in large part or entirely. A recent example is a decision in 2001 by a federal appellate court that was asked to decide whether the North American Free Trade Agreement (NAFTA) was a "treaty" requiring Senate ratification pursuant to the Treaty Clause. It had been passed as a regular bill and submitted to the president for his signature. The court held that there were no standards available to the judiciary to decide whether one procedure (treaty vs. statute) was mandatory

[15] *Minor v. Happersett*, 88 U.S. 162, 178 (1875).

[16] *Yick Wo v. Hopkins*, 118 U.S. 356, 370 (1886).

[17] E.g., *United States v. Reese*, 92 U.S. 214 (1876); *United States v. Cruikshank*, 92 U.S. 542 (1876); Ex parte *Siebold*, 100 U.S. 371 (1880); Ex parte *Yarbrough*, 110 U.S. 651 (1884).

[18] *Nixon v. Herndon*, 273 U.S. 536, 540 (1927).

[19] 60 U.S. (19 How.) 393 (1857).

[20] Fisher, *American Constitutional Law*, 756.

[21] 5 U.S. (1 Cr.) 137, 170 (1803).

[22] Ryden, *What Bush v. Gore Does and Does Not Tell Us*, 260.

over the other. The issue raised was a nonjusticiable political question, beyond the competence of the court to decide.[23]

Notwithstanding the protean nature of the political question doctrine, critics of the Court had little hesitation in insisting that the justices should have sidestepped *Bush v. Gore* as too political for judicial disposition. Elizabeth Garrett argued that the Court "should have . . . left the matter to the political sphere."[24] If that test applies to the U.S. Supreme Court, what about the Florida Supreme Court? Should it also have deferred to the political sphere, or was it somehow acceptable for the Florida Supreme Court to jump in with both feet but inappropriate for the U.S. Supreme Court to get involved?

Howard Gillman, in his study of *Bush v. Gore*, concluded that "in light of the partisan nature of the request to intervene, it should have been the easiest thing for our Supreme Court justices to just say no, even if they believed that there were problems with the Florida Supreme Court's decisions."[25] Why? As Judge Posner has noted, if it was strange for the U.S. Supreme Court to select the president, "for the Florida Supreme Court to pick the president of the United States is even weirder."[26]

Alan Dershowitz advised courts not "to jump into controversies that are political in nature and are capable of being resolved—even if not smoothly or expeditiously—by the popular branches of government. Judges have no special competence, qualifications, or mandate to decide between equally compelling moral claims (as in the abortion controversy) or equally compelling political claims (counting ballots by hand or stopping the recount because the standard is ambiguous)."[27] This position has much to commend it, but it doesn't belong to Dershowitz, who has supported the judicial disposition of many liberal causes.

Garrett, Gillman, and Dershowitz are in the liberal camp, but some conservative critics also argued that the Court should have sidestepped the Florida case. Steven Calabresi, who calls himself a "staunch supporter" of George W. Bush, writes that the problem with *Bush v. Gore* "is that the case raised a political question that ought to have been decided by Congress on January 6 when it counted the votes in the electoral college."[28] There is much to recommend about this position, but giving Congress the final say on January 6 did not necessarily exclude the Su-

---

[23] *Made in the USA Foundation v. United States*, 242 F.3d 1300 (11th Cir. 2001), cert. denied, sub nom. *United Steelworkers of America, AFL-CIO, CLC, et al.*, 534 U.S. 1039 (2001).

[24] Elizabeth Garrett, *Leaving the Decision to Congress*, in *The Vote: Bush, Gore & the Supreme Court* (Cass R. Sunstein and Richard A. Epstein, eds., University of Chicago Press, 2001), 39.

[25] Howard Gillman, *The Votes That Counted: How the Court Decided the 2000 Presidential Election* (Chicago: University of Chicago Press, 2001), 205.

[26] Posner, *Breaking Deadlock*, 143.

[27] Alan M. Dershowitz, *Supreme Injustice: How the High Court Hijacked Election 2000* (New York: Oxford University Press, 2001), 194.

[28] Steven G. Calabresi, *A Political Question*, in *Bush v. Gore: The Question of Legitimacy*, 137–38.

preme Court. The two remedies are not mutually exclusive. The Court could have legitimately intervened to nullify or block the decisions of the Florida Supreme Court, while allowing the dispute to find a political answer in Congress.

No Role for Congress?

Judge Posner defends the Court's decision in part because he has no faith in Congress. On that point I find him quite unpersuasive. He argues that Congress "is not a competent forum for resolving such disputes" because conflicts about "the lawfulness of competing slates of presidential electors call for legal-type judgments rather than for raw exercises of political power."[29] Posner advises that "[w]e should endeavor to keep Congress out of the picture, so far as that is possible to do. It is a large, unwieldy, undisciplined body (actually two bodies), unsuited in its structure, personnel, and procedures to legal dispute resolution. . . ."[30]

First, *Bush v. Gore* had more to do with the raw exercise of political power than "legal-type judgments." Those who defend the Court's decision see little merit in its equal protection analysis. Their argument is more about the need to settle the matter quickly, even if on legally shaky grounds.[31] Second, Congress is indeed a competent forum for resolving disputes about presidential elections. Both the Constitution[32] and statutory law contemplate situations in which decisions about presidential elections are placed exclusively in Congress.

Some of these congressional decisions may not be what Posner calls "legal-type judgments." In 1800, for example, the House of Representatives had to choose between Thomas Jefferson and Aaron Burr, who ended up with the same number of electoral votes. In 1824, electoral votes were divided among four candidates: Andrew Jackson, William Crawford, John Quincy Adams, and Henry Clay. The House picked Adams on the first ballot. In the 1876 election, neither Rutherford B. Hayes nor Samuel J. Tilden had a majority of electoral votes. To resolve the matter, Congress created an Electoral Commission, including five justices of the Supreme Court. Through this procedure Hayes gained twenty disputed electoral votes and won the presidency.

The role of the five justices, split along partisan lines, convinced Congress to adopt a different procedure for future problems. Congress passed legislation in 1887 to create a system that encouraged states to pass legislation for the appointment of electors. If the states followed specified procedures, their decisions would be treated as "conclusive" by Congress when it met to receive electoral votes.[33] Statutory procedures explain what would happen in disputes over the counting of

---

[29] Posner, *Breaking Deadlock*, 145.

[30] *Id.* at 250.

[31] E.g., Cass R. Sunstein, *Order Without Law,* 68 U. of Chicago L. Rev. 757 (1991).

[32] U.S. Const. art. II, sec. 1; amend. 12 and 20.

[33] 24 Stat. 373, sec. 2 (1887); 3 U.S.C. sec. 5 (2000).

electoral votes in Congress. The two houses, acting separately, need to concur on a series of questions.[34] If they cannot concur, the matter goes to the House of Representatives, with each state having one vote.[35] Through these processes, Congress legitimately makes "legal-type judgments."

Cass Sunstein agrees with Posner that the Court needed to decide the matter because Congress was the wrong body to resolve the dispute. The decision, Sunstein says, "brought a chaotic situation to an abrupt end. From the standpoint of constitutional order, it is reasonable to speculate that any other conclusion would have been far worse. In all likelihood, the outcome would have been resolved in Congress, and here political partisanship might well have spiraled out of control."[36] Spiral out of control? The matter would have gone to Congress, where a deadlock would have occurred between the Republican House and the Democratic Senate. In such situations, where the two houses cannot concur, the matter then goes to the House. Because of Republican control over state delegations, the House would have selected Bush. Too "partisan"? That is the procedure provided by law.[37]

What Happened in Florida

On the evening of election day, November 7, 2000, television networks first projected Gore as the winner in Florida (and therefore president). By early morning, the networks switched to announce Bush as the winner. Gore called Bush to concede defeat but then called back with a retraction. Bush's lead on November 8 stood at 1,784 votes. Because that margin was less than one-half of one percent of the total votes cast, state law mandated an automatic machine recount in all sixty-seven counties. The recount cut Bush's lead to 327 votes.

Florida law offers candidates two ways to challenge election results. One approach takes place before certification of the election results, the other after. Under Section 102.166, candidates may file a "protest" with the canvassing board, which has authority to call for a manual recount. An initial test recount is conducted in at least three precincts. Under Section 102.168, covering the period after certification, unsuccessful candidates may "contest" an election by filing a lawsuit in circuit court. The complaint must establish grounds to show that the result of the election can be changed or "place[d] in doubt."

On November 9, the Florida Democratic Executive Committee exercised the protest option by requesting manual recounts in four counties: Miami-Dade, Broward, Palm Beach, and Volusia. This marked mistake number one for the Gore team. In a disputed election, it makes no sense for candidates to insist on recounts in certain districts that had gone heavily for them. If this were allowed,

---

[34] 3 U.S.C. sec. 15 (2000).
[35] Amend. 12.
[36] Sunstein, *Order Without Law*, 772–73.
[37] 3 U.S.C. sec. 15 (2000).

Bush could have ordered a recount of four Republican-rich counties. New totals would have come from these recounts, possibly electing Gore or Bush, but the controversy would have continued, eventually pushing the demand for a state-wide recount, which is what happened.

Bush and some of his supporters went to federal district court to bar the manual recount. They argued that a manual recount might diminish the accuracy of the vote count because of ballot degradation and varying methods used by county canvassing board to determine a voter's intent. On November 13, the court denied their motion, holding that the Florida statute authorizing a manual recount did not violate the First Amendment, the Due Process Clause, or the Equal Protection Clause. Manual recounts, said the court, were not so unreliable that their use would rise to the level of constitutional injury. Further, plaintiffs' alleged injuries and public interest did not weigh in favor of preliminary injunctive relief.[38]

Democrats filed a separate action to challenge the counting of absentee ballots in Seminole County. With the manual and machine recounts underway, Florida law required that all county returns be certified by 5 p.m. on the seventh day after an election, unless the secretary of state exercised statutory discretion to accept ballots (such as those received from overseas) counted after the deadline. On November 13, Florida Secretary of State Katherine Harris announced that she would ignore returns of manual recounts received after the statutory deadline of November 14 at 5 p.m.

Conflicts existed between federal and state law regarding absentee ballots received from members of the armed services. Florida law required that the envelopes containing the ballots be postmarked. Following that standard, many votes from the military (expected to favor Bush) would have been thrown out. However, federal law, which was controlling on this issue, provided that balloting materials by the armed services be carried "free of postage."[39]

The Volusia County Canvassing Board filed suit in Florida court, claiming that it was not bound by Harris's decision. The Palm Beach County Canvassing Board and the Florida Democratic Party joined as intervenors. On November 14, Judge Terry Lewis ruled that the deadline was mandatory and that he had no authority to "rewrite the statute" creating another deadline. However, he said that the Volusia Board could amend its returns at a later date and that Harris could exercise her discretion (but "not do so arbitrarily") in determining whether to ignore the amended returns.[40] Subsequent to his order, Harris instructed Florida's Supervisors of Elections to submit to her by 2 p.m. on November 15 why they should be allowed to amend certified returns previously filed. After considering their reasons in light of specific criteria, Harris announced on November 15 that the amended

---

[38] *Siegel v. Lepore*, 120 F.Supp.2d 1041 (S.D. Fla. 2000), aff'd, 234 F.3d 1163 (11th Cir. 2000).

[39] 39 U.S.C. sec. 3406 (2000).

[40] *McDermott v. Harris*, Case No. 00–2700 (Cir. Ct., 2d Judicial Dist., Leon County, Fla., November 14, 2000).

returns would not be accepted and that she would certify the results of the presidential election on November 18.

Bungling by the Florida Supreme Court

After Judge Lewis denied Gore relief, the Florida Supreme Court issued a unanimous ruling on November 21 to extend the certification date. This was supposedly a win for the Democrats, but it created two problems for Gore. First, the more time spent on the protest phase, the less time for the contest period. Second, the decision by the Florida Supreme Court was properly viewed as highly partisan. Of the seven justices, six had been appointed by Democrats and the seventh was an appointment agreed to by outgoing Democrat Lawton Chiles and the incoming governor, Republican Jeb Bush. The televised oral argument revealed a stunning performance of partisan conduct by the justices.

Guided in part by "the will of the people" as the "guiding principle in election cases," the court looked to language in the Florida Constitution providing that "[a]ll political power is inherent in the people." It called the right to vote "the pre-eminent right" in the Declaration of Rights of the Florida Constitution. The court also examined two conflicting sections of Florida law, concluding that Harris was required to accept returns after the seven-day deadline set forth in Florida law. This moved the November 14 certification deadline to 5 p.m. on November 26.[41] The court produced no evidence that Harris had abused the discretion granted her by law. Richard Epstein has pointed out that "if the canvassing boards and the secretary of state did not abuse their discretion, then it seems as though the Florida Supreme Court abused its."[42]

Three days later, the U.S. Supreme Court granted Bush's motion for expedited consideration of a cert petition to consider two questions: (1) whether the Florida Supreme Court, by effectively changing elector appointment procedures after the election day, violated the Due Process Clause or 3 U.S.C. sec. 5, and (2) whether the Florida Supreme Court changed the manner in which the state's electors are to be selected, in violation of the state legislature's power under the U.S. Constitution, Art. II, sec. 1, cl. 2, which provides: "Each State shall appoint, in such Manner as the Legislature thereof may direct, a Number of Electors, equal to the whole Number of Senators and Representatives to which the State may be entitled in the Congress."

In addition, the Court added another question: (3) what would be the consequences of finding that Florida Supreme Court's decision does not comply with 3 U.S.C. sec. 5? That provision of federal law offers a guarantee (or "safe harbor") if states appointed electors in a certain manner. To be entitled to the safe harbor, states had to enact laws to appoint electors six days before the time fixed for the

---

[41] *Palm Beach County Canvassing Bd. v. Harris,* 772 So.2d 1220 (Fla. 2000).

[42] Richard A. Epstein, *"In Such Manner as the Legislature Thereof May Direct,"* in *The Vote: Bush, Gore & the Supreme Court,* 36.

meeting of the electors. Such appointments are then "conclusive" on Congress. For the year 2000, states had to appoint by December 12, six days before the electors met on December 18. Here is the language from 3 U.S.C. sec. 5:

> If any State shall have provided, by laws enacted prior to the day fixed for the appointment of the electors, for its final determination of any controversy or contest concerning the appointment of all or any of the electors of such State, by judicial or other methods or procedures, and such determination shall have been made at least six days before the time fixed for the meeting of the electors, such determination made pursuant to such law so existing on said day, and made at least six days prior to said time of meeting of the electors, shall be conclusive, and shall govern in the counting of the electoral votes as provided in the Constitution, and as hereinafter regulated, so far as the ascertainment of the electors appointed by such State is concerned.

The Florida Supreme Court's decision on November 21 deeply troubled a number of justices of the U.S. Supreme Court. Indeed, had the Florida Supreme Court handled the matter with greater restraint and professionalism, it is unlikely that the U.S. Supreme Court would have intervened. During oral argument on December 1, several justices sharply questioned the Florida Supreme Court's extension of the statutory deadline for certification. To be eligible for the safe harbor, state law had to be in effect before an election. How could the Florida judiciary change the deadline after the election?

Justice Anthony Kennedy asked about the extension: "Isn't that such an amorphous, general, abstract standard that it can't possibly be said to be law that was enacted and in place at the time of the election?" Also on altering the deadline, Justice Sandra Day O'Connor remarked: "Well, but certainly the date changed. That is a dramatic change. The date for certification. Right?" She later asked: "Who would have thought that the [Florida] Legislature was leaving open the date for change by the court? Who would have thought that?" Gore's attorney, Laurence Tribe, appeared to make light of the change in deadlines, saying, "it is part of the popular culture to talk about how unfair it is to change the rules of the game." He dismissed the change in deadlines as "nothing extraordinary. It's not like suddenly moving Heartbreak Hill or adding a mile or subtracting a mile from a marathon." Kennedy jumped in with some sarcasm: "In fact, we can change the rules after the game; it's not important. Popular culture."

When the Deputy Attorney General of Florida argued that 102.166 authorizes manual recounts, Justice Antonin Scalia was ready with a correction: "That's different from requires." On a different point, Scalia asked Tribe: "Can I ask you why you think the Florida Legislature delegated to the Florida Supreme Court the authority to interpose the Florida Constitution?" Chief Justice William Rehnquist made the same point: "It seems to me a federal question arises if the Florida Supreme Court, in its opinion, rather clearly says that we're using the Florida Constitution to reach the result we reach in construing the statute," referring to *McPherson v. Blacker*, 146 U.S. 1 (1892), for the proposition that art. II, sec. 1, cl. 2, gives plenary power to the state legislature to appoint electors.

Some justices were inclined to leave the matter to other political institutions. Justice Ruth Bader Ginsburg argued that the Court has generally deferred to state courts when they interpret state law: "I mean, in case after case, we have said we owe the highest respect to what the State Supreme Court says is the state's law." Justice David Souter suggested it might be better to let Congress resolve the dispute under 5 U.S.C. sec. 15, which authorizes Congress and eventually the House of Representatives to select the president. Justice Stephen Breyer wondered whether the issue was too speculative to warrant intervention by the Court.

Instead of batting the Florida Supreme Court over the head, the U.S. Supreme Court tried subtlety. A per curiam order on December 4 vacated the judgment of the Florida Supreme Court and sent some gentle hints. Acknowledging that the U.S. Supreme Court generally defers to a state court's interpretation of a state statute, the per curiam noted that in the selection of presidential electors the Florida Legislature was not acting solely under state authority but also by virtue of authority granted under Art. II, sec. 2, cl. 2, of the U.S. Constitution. The per curiam found considerable uncertainty as to the grounds used by the Florida Supreme Court, particularly the extent to which it saw the Florida Constitution as circumscribing the authority of the Florida Legislature under Article. II. The Court was also unclear how much consideration the Florida Supreme Court had given to 3 U.S.C. sec. 5.[43]

The underlying message was, "Try again, but this time be more careful." Interestingly, nothing in the grant of cert on November 24 or in the per curiam of December 4 mentioned what would later be the key issue: the Equal Protection Clause. If the Court hoped that gentle warnings would have an impact on the Florida Supreme Court, it would soon be disappointed. But the general, cautious language of the per curiam was all that could hold the justices together for a unanimous statement. Unanimity often cloaks serious divisions, and certainly that was true here.

Round Two in Florida

While the U.S. Supreme Court was considering the per curiam, Judge N. Sanders Sauls of Leon County Circuit Court presided over a case brought by Gore, who challenged the state certification of Bush as erroneous. Gore claimed that the vote totals wrongly included illegal votes and failed to include legal votes that had been improperly rejected. Much of the two-day trial focused on the legitimacy of counting indented ("dimpled") ballots, where the voter had not punched through the ballot. If election officials counted these ballots, did this mean that votes were being discovered or manufactured?

---

[43] *Bush v. Palm Beach County Canvassing Board*, 531 U.S. 70 (2000).

On December 4, Sauls announced that he found "no credible statistical evidence, and no other competent substantial evidence to establish by a preponderance of a reasonable probability that the results of the statewide election in the State of Florida would be different from the result which had been certified by the State Elections Canvassing Commission." He found no evidence of illegality, dishonesty, gross negligence, improper influence, coercion, or fraud in the balloting and counting procedures. He also concluded that Gore's request for a partial recount would create "a two-tier situation within one county, as well as with respect to other counties." A two-tier system, he said, would treat voters differently depending upon the county they voted in. Voters in a county with a manual count would have a better chance of having their votes counted. Any remedy requested by a plaintiff would require "a review and recount of all ballots, and all of the counties in this state."[44]

In reviewing this ruling, the Florida Supreme Court agreed with Sauls that any recount would have to be done statewide, not just the counties selected by Gore. However, a four-to-three court on December 8 reversed Sauls by granting Gore a manual recount in all Florida counties. The court held that Sauls had failed to apply the proper standard in determining Gore's burden under the contest statute. Sauls required a "preponderance of a reasonable probability," but under 102.168 it was enough for Gore to show that the results of the election had been "placed in doubt."

Florida Supreme Court Chief Justice Charles T. Wells and two other justices issued strong dissents. Wells flagged a serious problem with the majority's opinion. By failing to provide a meaningful standard for counting ballots, the majority created equal protection problems: "Continuation of this system of county-by-county decisions regarding how a dimpled chad is counted is fraught with equal protection concerns, which will eventually cause the election results in Florida to be stricken by the federal courts or Congress."[45] To Wells, the direction to the trial court to conduct a manual recount "violates article II, section 1, clause 2 of the United States Constitution, in that neither this Court nor the circuit court has the authority to create the standards by which it will count the under-voted ballots."[46] Wells also argued that the Florida Supreme Court should give "deference to decisions made by executive officials charged with implementing Florida's election laws," but that is precisely what he and his colleagues failed to do with their unanimous decision of November 21, overriding Secretary of State Harris.

On the evening of December 8, Judge Terry Lewis ordered the counting of ballots to begin at 8 a.m. the following day (Saturday) and be concluded by 2 p.m. on Sunday, December 10. He left it up to the canvassing boards to determine the standards for judging the "clear indication of the intent of the voter." Any disagreements would be returned to him for final determination.[47] In this manner,

[44] *Gore v. Harris*, Case No. CV 00–2808 (December 4, 2000).
[45] *Gore v. Harris*, 772 So.2d 1243, 1267 (Fla. 2000).
[46] *Id.* at 1268.
[47] *Gore v. Harris*, Case No. 00–2808 (December 9, 2000).

Judge Lewis promised to supply a single, impartial standard to review these contested ballots. However, this uniform standard would be imposed *afterwards*, not before.

No More Ducking and Weaving

With the issue headed back to the U.S. Supreme Court, the justices could no longer hide behind vague and enigmatic utterances. Either it had to assert its authority or let the Florida Supreme Court win the day. Early on the afternoon of December 9, while ballots were being segregated into different categories in Florida and some votes counted, the U.S. Supreme Court ordered a stay to the recount process. In a concurrence, Scalia spoke forthrightly about the issue that had troubled a number of his colleagues: "the propriety, indeed the constitutionality, of letting the standard for determination of voters' intent—dimpled chads, hanging chads, etc.—vary from county to county, as the Florida Supreme Court opinion, as interpreted by the Circuit Court, permits." He also expressed concern that "each manual recount produces a degradation of the ballots, which renders a subsequent recount inaccurate."[48]

The sharp divisions within the Court now became visible. Stevens, joined by Souter, Ginsburg, and Breyer, dissented. Stevens said that the majority, by stopping the vote count, departed "from three venerable rules of judicial restraint that have guided the Court throughout its history." On questions of state law, he said that the Court had "consistently respected the opinions of the highest courts of the States." This sentence was artfully drafted. While it may be generally true that the U.S. Supreme Court treats with respect the opinions of state supreme courts, that does not mean that the Court consistently sustains those rulings. Second, Stevens said that on questions committed in large measure to another branch of the federal government, "we have construed our own jurisdiction narrowly and exercised it cautiously." Again, whatever generalization might be made about the Court's relationship with Congress and the president has little to do with the fact that the Court on many occasions has struck down the actions of the legislative and executive branches. As a third point, Stevens said that on federal constitutional questions "that were not fairly presented to the court whose judgment is being reviewed, we have prudently declined to express an opinion." That is generally true, but certainly throughout its history the Court has not always been so "prudent."

The case was set for oral argument on Monday, December 11, at 11 a.m. During the argument, O'Connor said she found it "troublesome" that the Florida Supreme Court had not responded to the remand by the U.S. Supreme Court on December 4: "It just seemed to kind of bypass it and assume that all those changes and deadlines were just fine and they'd go ahead and adhere to them." Later that day, the Florida Supreme Court released its opinion in response to the remand. It

---

[48] *Bush v. Gore*, 531 U.S. 1046 (2000).

reviewed its arguments on the "shall" versus "may" statutory conflict and maintained that the November 26 deadline it established on November 11 "was not a new 'deadline' and has no effect in future elections." Footnote 17 indicated that manual recounts were circumscribed by 3 U.S.C. sec. 5, "which sets December 12, 2000 as the date for final determination of any state's dispute concerning its electors in order for that determination to be given conclusive effect in Congress."[49] If December 12 was indeed the deadline, how could the Florida Supreme Court on December 8 have set in motion a recount procedure that was almost certainly impossible (given inevitable appeals) to complete by December 12?

As oral argument continued, six justices expressed concern about the inadequate standards for recounting votes in Florida: Breyer, Kennedy, O'Connor, Rehnquist, Scalia, and Souter. Because Thomas had joined the stay order, he was likely the seventh justice troubled by the lack of standards. When Kennedy asked whether the "intent of the voter" standard could vary from county to county, Gore attorney David Boies admitted it "can vary from individual to individual." With concessions of that nature, there was little doubt about what the Court would decide.

At about 10 p.m. on December 12, the Court released its opinion reversing the Florida Supreme Court. The per curiam opinion, finding a violation of the Equal Protection Clause because of the standardless manual recounts, said a state "may not, by later arbitrary and disparate treatment, value one person's vote over that of another." The Court held that no recount procedure in place under the Florida Supreme Court's order would both comply with minimal constitutional standards and meet the December 12 date. Seven justices found constitutional problems with the recount ordered by the Florida Supreme Court, but Souter and Breyer would have returned the matter to Florida with instructions to establish uniform acceptable standards.

Rehnquist's concurrence, joined by Scalia and Thomas, cited other grounds for reversing the Florida Supreme Court. Rehnquist emphasized that the Court was not dealing with an ordinary election, "but with an election for the president of the United States."[50] Whatever "comity and respect for federalism" might cause the court to defer to state courts on issues of state law had no application to the case at hand. Article II, sec. 1, cl. 2, provides that "[e]ach State shall appoint, in such Manner as the Legislature thereof may direct," electors for president and vice president, and it was that language that prompted Rehnquist to say that a "significant departure from the legislative scheme for appointing presidential electors presents a federal constitutional question."

Moreover, Rehnquist said that the Florida Legislature had delegated to the secretary of state and to state circuit courts the authority to run the elections and oversee election disputes. That general legislative scheme could not be altered by the Florida Supreme Court "so as to wholly change the statutorily provided appor-

---

[49] *Palm Beach County Canvassing Bd. v. Harris*, 772 So.2d 1273, 1286 (Fla. 2000).
[50] *Bush v. Gore*, 531 U.S. 98, 112 (2000).

tionment of responsibility among these various bodies."[51] Rehnquist remarked that in any election except a presidential election the Florida Supreme Court could give as little deference to Florida's executive officials as it chose, "and this Court will have no cause to question the court's actions." Yet for presidential elections "the court must be both mindful of the legislature's role under Article II in choosing the manner of appointing electors and deferential to those bodies expressly empowered by the legislature to carry out is constitutional mandate." Rehnquist met the federalism issue head-on by saying that the Court's inquiry "does not imply a disrespect for state *courts* but rather a respect for the constitutionally prescribed role of state *legislatures*." As to language in Florida statute 102.168 authorizing a trial judge to provide relief that is "appropriate under such circumstances," Rehnquist said that it must have been the intent of the Florida Legislature that the relief would become final by the cut-off date of 3 U.S.C. sec. 5.

The Four Dissenters

Justices Stevens, Souter, Ginsburg, and Breyer issued separate dissenting opinions. Stevens began by saying that the U.S. Constitution assigns to the states "the primary responsibility for determining the manner of selecting the presidential electors." So it does, but which branch at the state level has the primary responsibility: the state judiciary, or the state legislature? Claiming that it was "settled practice" to accept the opinions of the highest courts of the states as providing the final answers, he acknowledged that on "rare occasions" either federal statutes or the Federal Constitution "may require federal judicial intervention in state elections. This is not such an occasion." To Stevens, the federal questions resulting from the Florida elections were "not substantial."

Stevens denied that there was a constitutional problem in determining the "intent of the voter." That standard, he said, was no less sufficient than the standard used in courtrooms to determine the guilt of the accused: "beyond a reasonable doubt." Even if aspects of the remedial scheme for counting votes were found to violate the Equal Protection Clause, the solution for Stevens was not to stop the recount but to return the matter to Florida "to allow more specific procedures for implementing the legislature's uniform general standard to be established." As for the deadline established in 3 U.S.C. sec. 5, he pointed to precedents of states delivering electoral votes beyond the deadlines and having them counted by Congress. For example, in 1960 Hawaii appointed two slates of electors. Congress selected one of them on January 4, 1961.

At the end of his dissent, Stevens sharply denounced the majority for failing to show confidence in the "impartiality and capacity" of the Florida judiciary. That was a cheap shot. No member of the Court, including Stevens, automatically defers to state court decisions. Still, Stevens charged: "It is confidence in the men and women who administer the judicial system that is the true backbone of the rule

---

[51] *Id.* at 114.

of law. Time will one day heal the wound to that confidence that will be inflicted by today's decision. One thing, however, is certain. Although we may never know with complete certainty the identity of the winner of this year's presidential election, the identity of the loser is perfectly clear. It is the nation's confidence in the judge as an impartial guardian of the rule of law." How "impartial" was Stevens in making this statement? Moreover, if reversing the Florida Supreme Court did damage to "the nation's confidence in the judge as an impartial guardian of the rule of law," the U.S. Supreme Court does that every time it reverses a federal district court, a federal appellate court, or one of its own decisions. Judge Posner said Stevens' accusation "is what is called fouling one's own nest."[52]

In his dissent, Souter said that the Court should not have reviewed either case coming up from Florida and should not have stopped the recount. Instead, the state should have followed the opinions of the Florida Supreme Court, "and political tension could have worked itself out in the Congress following the procedure provided in 3 U.S.C. sec. 15." Under that procedure, in order to reject the electoral votes from a state, both houses must agree. If under this process Congress is unable to select a president, the dispute moves to the House of Representatives, where each state casts a single vote. Because of the makeup of the 50 states' delegations in Congress on January 6, 2001, Bush would have been chosen president. Souter presents a legitimate alternative, giving neither the U.S. Supreme Court nor the Florida Supreme Court the final say, but shifting the decision to the political process and established constitutional and statutory procedures.

Souter concedes in his dissent that the conduct of the election in Florida presented serious questions of equal protection. Although states may use a variety of voting mechanisms, and those mechanisms will differ in their effectiveness in recording a voter's intent, the results in Florida suggested to Souter that "a different order of disparity" existed for identical types of ballots and identical brands of machines. Members of the canvassing boards adopted different techniques for counting "hanging" or "dimpled" chads. Souter could not conceive of any legitimate state interest in allowing these different treatments "of the expressions of voters' fundamental rights." The differences seemed to Souter "wholly arbitrary." To fix this problem, Souter would have returned the case to the Florida courts with "instructions to establish uniform standards" for counting the ballots. He thought the process could be completed by December 18, but gave no indication of what "instructions" the Court would deliver: merely general instructions or more specific guidelines. Either way, it is virtually certain that Florida could not have adopted timely, adequate instructions that would have survived court challenges. As a result, the selection of the president would have been thrown into Congress, which I think would have been fine.

Ginsburg's dissent criticized the majority for not respecting "the state high court's province to say what the State's Election Code means." While citing precedents that restraint on the part of the U.S. Supreme Court "helps build a co-

[52] Posner, *Breaking Deadlock*, 175.

operative judicial federalism," none of the examples she offered for independent state analysis came close to justifying the magnitude of Florida's role in selecting a president. Ginsburg did an effective job in criticizing the Court's acceptance of December 12 as the deadline for bringing Florida into compliance with 3 U.S.C. sec. 5. If Florida were to miss that date, it "would still be entitled to deliver electoral votes Congress *must* count unless both houses find that the votes 'ha[d] not been . . . regularly given'" (citing language in 3 U.S.C. sec. 15). Under 3 U.S.C. sec. 12, if Congress has not received a state's electoral votes by "the fourth Wednesday in December" (for the year 2000, December 27), it shall request that the state secretary of state send a certified return immediately.

Breyer, in the fourth dissent, said that the Court "was wrong to take this case. It was wrong to grant a stay." He agreed with the majority that the equal protection problem with the Florida recount "does implicate principles of fundamental fairness," but would have returned the case to Florida "with instructions that, even at this late date, would permit the Florida Supreme Court to require recounting *all* undercounted votes in Florida" and to do so "in accordance with a single uniform standard." Like Souter, Breyer dodged the central issue by not suggesting at least some of the ingredients that would constitute a single uniform standard. If the U.S. Supreme Court was wary of creating new standards, what would give the Florida courts (after being bopped in the head twice) the confidence to devise standards? There was scarcely any incentive to do that.

Breyer recognized that the selection of the president "is of fundamental national importance" but regarded the importance as "political, not legal," counseling that "this Court should resist the temptation unnecessarily to resolve tangential legal disputes, where doing so threatens to determine the outcome of the election." That doesn't make much sense. If Breyer encouraged Florida to adopt new standards, and those standards were challenged in court, those lawsuits were likely to come back to the U.S. Supreme Court, where the justices would again be involved in "tangential legal disputes," either by affirming or nullifying the standards. In fact, the importance was both political and legal. In recommending that the issue be returned to Florida, Breyer was inviting the Florida Supreme Court to make legal determinations in developing the single uniform standard. The issue was also political in the sense that the dispute was most likely to end up in Congress. Breyer concluded that when Congress in 1887 wrote the statute governing the procedures to be followed in counting electoral votes for the president, it attempted to minimize the role of the U.S. Supreme Court. That is true. Breyer said it was left to Congress, as a political body, to express the people's will "far more accurately than does an unelected Court. And the people's will is what elections are about." That point is weak because the "unelected" Florida Supreme Court had already intervened.

The per curiam suggests that the December 12 deadline came from the Florida Supreme Court: "The Supreme Court of Florida has said that the legislature intended the State's electors to 'participat[e] fully in the federal electoral process,' as provided in 3 U.S.C. sec. 5." The per curiam contains conflicting statements about whether the Florida Supreme Court, or a Florida trial judge, could

have issued uniform standards. In one place, the per curiam states that for purposes of resolving the equal protection challenge, "it is not necessary to decide
whether the Florida Supreme Court had the authority under the legislative
scheme for resolving whether disputes to define what a legal vote is and to mandate a manual recount implementing that decision." A few pages later, however,
the per curiam remarks: "we are presented with a situation where a state court
with the power to assure uniformity has ordered a statewide recount with minimal procedural safeguards. When a court orders a statewide remedy, there must
be at least some assurance that the rudimentary requirements of equal treatment
and fundamental fairness are satisfied." This seems like a pretty clear rebuke to
the Florida judiciary, and yet, given the remand of December 4 by the U.S. Supreme Court, Florida courts were no doubt leery of crafting standards that might
be taken as the creation of "new law" and thus invite further reversals.

A Summing Up

The U.S. Supreme Court was compelled to intervene because of serious issues
created by the Florida Supreme Court, which (1) established a new deadline for
issuing the certification, (2) performed a strained statutory interpretation of the
conflict between "shall" and "may," and (3) called for a statewide manual recount without uniform standards. Changing the statutory deadline from November 14 to November 26 looked too much like the creation of a new law. On
statutory interpretation, it is true that there was a conflict between two statutory
provisions. 102.111 directed that the secretary of state "shall" ignore county
returns not received by 5 p.m. of the seventh day following an election; 102.112
said that late returns "may" be ignored. It was proper for the court to treat
102.112 as controlling, because it was added in 1989 while 102.111 dates back
to 1951. However, the court concocted a third category: the secretary "must"
accept late returns up to the court's November 26 deadline. It thus transformed
statutory discretion ("may") into a mandate. Regarding the lack of uniform standards, the Florida Supreme Court may have been gun-shy about "creating new
law" and running afoul of 3 U.S.C. sec. 5.

   In reversing the Florida Supreme Court, the U.S. Supreme Court relied
heavily on the December 12 deadline. For several reasons, this analysis was
artificial and unconvincing. First, states can forgo the "safe harbor" of 3 U.S.C.
sec. 5 and submit their results on December 18 and even later. Second, the ballots probably could have been counted by December 12 had the Court not issued
its stay. Of course, any result of the manual recount announced by December 12
would have been subject to legal challenges, with the case going back to the
Florida Supreme Court and probably to the U.S. Supreme Court.

   It might have been more persuasive if the U.S. Supreme Court had issued
this ruling: "The standardless manual recount provisions in place in Florida for
the presidential election violate fundamental principles of equal protection. We
have no authority to create new standards in the middle of the game. Neither

does the Florida Supreme Court, a Florida trial judge, or the Florida Legislature. The Florida Legislature has authority to create uniform standards that will satisfy equal protection guarantees, but those standards must necessarily govern future elections, not this one." Instead of relying on the December 12 deadline, the U.S. Supreme Court could have emphasized the inability of any political institution (judicial, executive, or legislative) to change the rules in the middle of an election contest. Moreover, by stating that it had no authority to issue such standards, it would have looked less "activist" and less intent on arrogating power that belongs in the hands of other political bodies.

Other options were available. The U.S. Supreme Court, by a seven-to-two margin, could have given Florida until December 18 to develop acceptable standards for the recount. Florida courts would have had to hear testimony in creating those standards, let the recount go forward, permit Gore and Bush to object to particular ballots, and then allow judicial review by the Florida Supreme Court and the U.S. Supreme Court. This process could not have been completed by December 18, but the spotlight would have been taken off the U.S. Supreme Court and redirected to the impossibility of Florida correcting inadequacies in its system.

On December 22, the Florida Supreme Court responded to the remand of December 12. It explained that the "intent of the voter" standard it ordered on December 8 was the legislative standard in place as of November 7, 2000, and that "a more expansive ruling would have raised an issue as to whether this Court would be substantially rewriting the Code after the election, in violation of article II, section 1, clause 2 of the United States Constitution and 3 U.S.C. sec. 5 (1994)." The Court laid out the immense technical and legal hurdles of trying to conduct a manual recount. First, it would be necessary to adopt (after opportunity for argument) adequate statewide standards for determining a "legal vote." Judicial review must then be available to decide objections raised by the candidates. Moreover, the secretary of state advised that the recount of only a portion of the ballots required that "undervotes" (when voters did not register a choice for president) be screened out. However, the voting machines were not designed for that function. If a recount of "overvotes" (when voters registered a choice for both presidential candidates) were required, a second screening would be necessary. In creating equipment and developing new software, Florida law requires that the secretary of state evaluate such changes for accuracy. Finally, the Florida Supreme Court conceded what Chief Justice Wells had said in his dissent on December 8: the development of standards to count ballots belongs to the Florida Legislature. The court now recognized that "the development of a specific, uniform standard necessary to ensure equal application and to secure the fundamental right to vote throughout the State of Florida should be left to the body we believe best equipped to study and address it, the Legislature."[53] Finally, on its fourth try, the Florida Supreme Court got it right.

Credit should be given to a number of judicial opinions, at both the federal and state level, that dealt expeditiously and competently with a number of issues

---

[53] *Gore v. Harris*, 773 So.2d 524, 526 (Fla. 2000).

that arose in the Florida election. On January 5, 2001, the U.S. Supreme Court denied cert on several issues that had been decided by lower courts. One involved an 11th Circuit decision that rejected a challenge to absentee ballots cast by overseas voters. The other concerned a suit arguing that George W. Bush and Richard B. Cheney were both "inhabitants" of Texas and thus in violation of the Twelfth Amendment, which prohibits the president and vice president from being inhabitants of the same state. The Fifth Circuit had ruled that Cheney, who had a home in Dallas, Texas, was a resident of Wyoming.[54]

Democratic voters filed suit to throw out nearly 25,000 absentee ballots in Martin and Seminole counties. They argued that the ballots, which favored Bush over Gore by about two to one, should be discarded because election officials allowed Republican workers to fix Republican ballot applications by adding voter identification numbers. Judges Terry Lewis and Nikki Clark agreed that the changes to the ballot applications violated state law but found no evidence of fraud, gross negligence, intentional wrongdoing, or partisan misconduct. Election officials treated Republicans and Democrats differently but that was because a number of Republican request forms had missing or incorrect voter identification numbers on them, while there were no similar problems with the Democratic request forms. Although there was not strict compliance with the election law, Florida case law only requires "substantial compliance." The two judges decided that the voters were qualified, registered, and had cast valid absentee ballots that should be counted.[55] Their rulings were affirmed by the Florida Supreme Court.[56]

Courts have a legitimate right to participate in election contests to review accusations of misconduct, fraud, and other charges. The Florida trial courts did an excellent job of airing complaints and educating citizens. Each side brought in experts and statisticians, trying to prove a case. Judges Lewis and Clark ventilated the dispute over absentee ballots, showing convincingly that the irregularities committed by elected officials did not invalidate the votes. Although Judge Sauls was reversed by the Florida Supreme Court, his position that manual recounts had to be done on a statewide basis—and not by selected counties—was accepted both by the Florida Supreme Court and the U.S. Supreme Court. Much of the work of the state judiciary was constructive and beneficial.

---

[54] *Harris v. Florida Elections Canvassing Commission,* 531 U.S. 1062 (2001); *Jones v. Bush,* 531 U.S. 1062 (2001).
[55] *Taylor v. Martin County Canvassing Board,* Case No. 00-2850 (Fla. 2000); *Jacobs v. Seminole County Canvassing Board,* Case No. CV-00-2816 (Fla. 2000).
[56] *Taylor v. Martin County Canvassing Board,* 773 So.2d 517 (Fla. 2000); *Jacobs v. Seminole County Canvassing Board,* 773 So.2d 519 (Fla. 2000).

Political Questions and Political Cases:
The Evolving Justifications for Judicial Involvement in Politics

Nathaniel Persily[1]

If we can learn one lesson from the most recent round of vocal attacks on the judiciary, the work of the federal courts and especially the Supreme Court is by nature political. Whenever a court declares a statute or other state action unconstitutional, it necessarily performs a political act by voiding the work performed by an elected branch of government. There is a difference between political questions and political cases, however, as many in this volume have recognized and as the Supreme Court emphasized as early as *Baker v. Carr,*[2] if not *Marbury v. Madison.*[3] The subset of political cases that attain the auspicious status of presenting political questions are unified by particular rationales given for judicial abstinence from what is otherwise a justiciable case or controversy. This chapter examines what is perhaps the most political subset of potential political ques-

---

[1] Professor of Law, University of Pennsylvania Law School. An earlier draft of this chapter appeared as *Suing the Government in Hopes of Controlling It: The Evolving Justifications for Judicial Involvement in Politics,* 5 Univ. of Penn. J. of Const'l L. 607 (2003).

[2] 369 U.S. 186 (1962).

[3] 5 U.S. (1 Cranch) 137, 174 (1803).

tions: lawsuits where plaintiffs turn to the judiciary in hopes of gaining greater representation, access, power, or control of government.

For most of our nation's history, courts viewed such suits as involving questions outside the province and beyond the capabilities of the judiciary. When the Supreme Court began to intervene, it did so based on the rationales found in the famous footnote four of *U.S. v. Carolene Products*[4]: namely, removing restrictions of the political processes that could bring about the repeal of undesirable legislation, or preventing discrimination against discrete and insular minorities. Specifically because federal judges are not elected and accountable, the argument goes, they are in the best institutional position to police politics to prevent majoritarian tyranny and to safeguard the processes that bring about democratic change.

Contrary to the hoary Supreme Court precedent that removed the political question hurdle from voters, candidates and parties seeking redress for this class of political rights violations, however, the most recent cases of this ilk reveal what I consider two disturbing trends. The first concerns the co-opting of the *Carolene Products* rationales for the adjudication of "normal" political conflict. Whereas once plaintiffs ran to the courthouse as a last resort when the structures of politics systematically closed them out of the legislature, now plaintiffs who have lost through the "normal" operation of democratic government routinely run to the judiciary for a second bite at the apple. The second trend involves the supplementing of the *Carolene Products* rationales with alternative justifications for judicial intervention into the political process. In a series of decisions, the Court has intervened in the political process in the name of what can best be described as "tradition," safeguarding processes and institutions from innovations that are themselves often justified as protecting minorities or providing greater political access. This chapter concludes by evaluating whether these unintended and perhaps inevitable consequences have served to undermine the justifications for even the initial judicial forays into politics that are normally viewed as crowning, progressive achievements of the modern Court.

Judicial Intervention into Politics—The Salad Days

Most would time the Supreme Court's intervention into politics with the 1962 decision in *Baker v. Carr*[5] and its progeny over the next decade that established the one-person, one-vote rule. Because of the vigorous disagreements the justices expressed in those cases as to whether they should descend into the "political thicket"[6] of redistricting, the one-person, one-vote cases appear as a watershed in the judiciary's conceptualization of its role in the political system. This first impression is somewhat misleading, however.

---

[4] *United States v. Carolene Products Co.*, 304 U.S. 144, 153 n. 4 (1938).
[5] 369 U.S. 186 (1962).
[6] See *Colegrove v. Green*, 328 U.S. 549, 556 (1946).

Prior to *Baker* the Court had intervened several times in the electoral process, sporadically protecting African-American voters by enforcing the guarantees of the Equal Protection Clause and the Fifteenth Amendment. As early as (or depending on your perspective, as late as) 1915, the Court struck down certain grandfather clauses as inconsistent with the Fifteenth Amendment.[7] And in the following forty years, it used the Fourteenth and Fifteenth Amendments in the *White Primary Cases* to strike down a series of attempts by the Texas Democratic Party to exclude African Americans from participating in both formal and informal candidate-nominating processes.[8] Just two years prior to *Baker*, the Court (with Justice Felix Frankfurter writing for it, no less) struck down the Tuskegee racial gerrymander on Fifteenth Amendment grounds, finding it to be merely a more sophisticated form of outright disfranchisement.[9]

Although prior to *Baker* the Court intervened (if ever) in only the most extreme cases of race-based disfranchisement, immediately after *Baker* the Court extended its reach into cases where the plaintiffs were not discrete or insular minorities. Indeed, the Court created the right to vote out of whole cloth—reading into the Equal Protection Clause a protection against discrimination in voting that made the Fifteenth, Nineteenth, and Twenty-Fourth Amendments superfluous.[10] The bounds of this newly discovered right were not limited to historically oppressed groups or even discrete or insular minorities; they extended even to thirty-one-year-old stockbrokers who lived with their parents and wanted to vote in school board elections.[11] And once the Court established the right to vote, the rights to run for office and to appear on the ballot, as a party[12] or a candidate,[13] represented the next logical jurisprudential steps. However, these post-*Baker* cases, like the one-person, one-vote cases themselves, could be justified by appealing to the first of the *Carolene Products* rationales, what John Hart Ely calls "clearing the channels of political change."[14] Judicial action was necessary, it was thought, because incumbent politicians had no incentive to redraw the favorable districts that elected them, to make the ballot more inclusive, or to expand the franchise to include voters that might be less reliable supporters.

Although the Court may have been the major agent of political change in the 1960s and early 1970s, Congress also played an influential role in expanding the franchise and attempting to prevent capture of the electoral process by the powerful. With the Voting Rights Act of 1965,[15] Congress eliminated literacy tests[16] and

---

[7] *Guinn v. United States,* 238 U.S. 347 (1915).

[8] See *Nixon v. Herndon,* 273 U.S. 536 (1927); *Nixon v. Condon,* 286 U.S. 73 (1932); *Smith v. Allwright,* 321 U.S. 649 (1944); *Terry v. Adams,* 345 U.S. 461 (1953).

[9] *Gomillion v. Lightfoot,* 364 U.S. 339 (1960).

[10] *Harper v. Va. Bd. of Elections,* 383 U.S. 663 (1966).

[11] *Kramer v. Unified Free Sch. Dist. No. 15,* 395 U.S. 621 (1969).

[12] *Williams v. Rhodes,* 393 U.S. 23 (1968).

[13] *Bullock v. Carter,* 405 U.S. 134 (1972).

[14] John Hart Ely, *Democracy and Distrust: A Theory of Judicial Review* (Harvard University Press, 1980), 105–34.

[15] 42 U.S.C. §§ 1971, 1973 (2000).

secured to African Americans, and later other groups, the promise of enfranchisement made in the Fourteenth and Fifteenth Amendments. Whereas Congress's principal concern with the Voting Rights Act was protection of discrete and insular minorities, the Federal Election Campaign Act (FECA), particularly as amended in 1974,[17] sought to release the political process from the supposed stranglehold of wealthy campaign contributors. At least before *Buckley v. Valeo*[18] mauled it beyond recognition, FECA represented for its supporters some hope for clearing the channels of political change by muting the corrupting effect of money on the political process.

Like Congress, the national political parties also played a role in pluralizing and invigorating the electoral process. Throughout this time period, the parties slowly expanded the number of states that nominated their candidates in direct primaries, as opposed to backrooms filled with much smoke and just a few powerful party apparatchiks. With the reforms of the early 1970s, the Democratic Party completely transformed the national party conventions that would follow: providing for proportional representation according to race and gender, and enacting a series of reforms that transferred power from party leaders to the mass party membership.[19]

The Co-optation of *Carolene Products*

The judicial and legislative innovations of the 1960s had several unintended, even if not entirely unforeseeable, consequences. In their dissents in *Baker v. Carr*[20] and *Reynolds v. Sims*,[21] Justices Felix Frankfurter and John Harlan warned of judicial entanglement in politics, fearing both the lack of administrable standards for redistricting and the erosion of confidence and credibility in the judiciary once it involved itself in the inherently political task of drawing district lines. History has vindicated them, for reasons even beyond those explicit in their predictions.[22] One of those reasons is the co-optation of the pro-minority and anti-entrenchment rationales in the service of normal partisan conflict.

The redistricting arena presents the most glaring examples of this co-optation. The Court has not yet taken the implicit anti-entrenchment rationale of the one-

---

[16] Not too long before *Baker* the Court had upheld literacy tests as constitutional. *Lassiter v. Northampton County Bd. of Elections*, 360 U.S. 45 (1959).

[17] 2 U.S.C. §§ 431–42 (2000).

[18] 424 U.S. 1 (1976) (per curiam).

[19] See Nelson W. Polsby, *Consequences of Party Reform* (Oxford University Press, 1983).

[20] 369 U.S. 186 (1962) (Frankfurter, J., dissenting).

[21] 377 U.S. 533 (1964) (Harlan, J., dissenting).

[22] See generally Nathaniel Persily, Thad Kousser and Patrick Egan, *The Complicated Impact of One Person One Vote on Political Competition and Representation*, 80 N.C. L. Rev. 1299 (2002).

person, one-vote cases to its logical conclusion and constructed a coherent constitutional constraint on partisan gerrymandering. Indeed, for those of us who thought the political question doctrine in this arena would be relegated to the history books, the four-justice plurality opinion in *Vieth v. Jubelirer*[23] echoed Frankfurter and suggested that the absence of judicially manageable standards justified judicial abstention from this thickest of political thickets. While not recognizing a partisan gerrymandering claim outright, the Court has instead supplied a set of claims distantly removed from either the malrepresentation or entrenchment rationales undergirding the initial redistricting cases. Partisan actors routinely appeal to such rules to force the redistricting process into court, regardless of the absence of inequity in the extant district map.

Claims of unconstitutional racial gerrymandering and race-based vote dilution in violation of the Voting Rights Act often serve as stealthy vehicles for the expression of partisan gripes. Whereas the *Gomillion* Court vindicated the rights of black voters fenced out of Tuskeegee in an artful scheme of disfranchisement, the nature of the harm the Court remedied in *Shaw v. Reno*[24] had nothing to do with protecting minority rights or removing restrictions on the political process. At most, the racial gerrymandering cause of action coming from *Shaw* arises out of a concern for expressive harms, not political handicaps, suffered by anyone experiencing a squiggly district drawn to help out minority voters.[25] More importantly, however, throughout the 1990s plaintiffs pigeonholed their partisan claims as racial gerrymandering or "wrongful districting" claims, hoping to strike down a politically undesirable district map by alleging that race was the predominant factor in the construction of one of its districts. To add insult to injury for *Carolene Products* values, the Court established in its last *Shaw* case of the 1990s round of redistricting that a desire to create a safe Democratic or Republican district would immunize that district from a charge of racial gerrymandering.[26]

Litigation under the Voting Rights Act has proven equally susceptible to partisan manipulation. For example, New Jersey Republicans brought a challenge under Section Two of the Voting Rights Act in an attempt to force the state's redistricting commission to go back to the drawing board on the state's legislative districting map. Noticing that several districts had lower percentages of African Americans than under the previous plan, the Republicans enlisted some African-American plaintiffs in an ultimately unsuccessful vote dilution lawsuit.[27] The Democrats adopted a similar strategy with minority plaintiffs in litigation challenging

---

[23] 541 U.S. 267 (2004).

[24] 509 U.S. 630 (1993).

[25] *See* Richard H. Pildes and Richard G. Niemi, *Expressive Harms, "Bizarre Districts," and Voting Rights: Evaluating Election-District Appearances After Shaw v. Reno*, 92 Mich. L. Rev. 483 (1993).

[26] *See* Easley v. Cromartie, 532 U.S. 234 (2001).

[27] *Page v. Bartels,* 144 F.Supp.2d (D.N.J. 2001) (three-judge court) (holding that a legislative reapportionment plan did not violate the Voting Rights Act).

New Mexico's congressional districts[28] and the re-redistricting of Texas's congressional districts.[29] Finally, in enforcing Section Five of the Voting Rights Act, which requires certain jurisdictions to get preclearance from the federal government that a contemplated legal change with respect to voting does not make minority voters worse off, the Department of Justice has allowed partisanship to creep into its decisions. In stalling the 2002 state court plan for Mississippi's congressional districts, for example, the DOJ successfully let a pro-Republican federal court plan go into effect.[30]

Even the one-person, one-vote rule, itself, has become unmoored from its original guiding principle of combating malrepresentation and political lockups. Whereas it originated in attempts to prevent the overrepresentation of rural areas at the expense of urban centers, it has evolved into just one more opportunity for partisan losers in the redistricting process to get a second bite of the apple in court. The requirement of perfect population equality for congressional districts that *Karcher v. Daggett*[31] codified has led to absurd results. For example, Democrats successfully (even if temporarily) upended the Pennsylvania congressional district map merely because one congressional district had nineteen people more than another.[32] They did this despite the fact that each district had over 600,000 people in it and that the margin of error for the census (let alone population movement between the census and the enactment of the plan) ensured that the districts had actual populations differing by thousands.

The co-optation of the *Carolene Products* rationales is not limited to redistricting fights. In its most significant, recent case concerning political parties, for example, the Court declared California's blanket primary, which allowed any voter to vote in any party's primary in any race, to be unconstitutional under the

---

[28] *Jepsen v. Vigil-Giron,* No. D-101-CV-200102177 (1st Jud. Dist. Santa Fe County Jan. 2, 2002) (holding that drawing a Hispanic-majority district is not required by the Voting Rights Act and that the establishment of this kind of district should be left to the legislature, not the courts).

[29] Session v. Perry, 298 F.Supp.2d 451, 498 (E.D. Tex. 2004) (per curiam), judgment vacated and remanded by Henderson v. Perry, 125 S.Ct. 351 (U.S.Tex. Oct 18, 2004)

[30] See Jeffrey Toobin, *Poll Position: Is the Justice Department poised to stop voter fraud—or to keep voters from voting?*, New Yorker (Sept. 20, 2004) ("The main business of the Voting Section is still passing judgment on legislative redistricting in areas that have a history of discrimination. Under Ashcroft, its actions have consistently favored Republicans—for instance, in Georgia, where the department challenged the Democrats' gerrymander, and in Mississippi, where the Voting Section stalled the redistricting process for so long that a pro-Republican redistricting plan went into effect by default.").

[31] 462 U.S. 725 (1983).

[32] See *Vieth v. Pennsylvania,* 195 F.Supp.2d 672 (M.D. Pa. 2002). See generally Pamela S. Karlan, *The Fire Next Time: Reapportionment After the 2000 Census,* 50 Stan. L. Rev. 731, 735–36 (1998) (discussing the partisan use of one person, one vote).

First Amendment.[33] Instead of campaigning against the initiative,[34] the established political parties (hardly discrete and insular minorities), as well as the minor parties, challenged the initiative in court, arguing that forcing them to accept "outsiders" in their primary elections violated their freedom of association. Analogizing political parties to other more-private associations,[35] the Supreme Court agreed with their position.[36] Contrast *Jones* with *Timmons v. Twin Cities Area New Party*[37] or *Clingman v. Beaver*,[38] in which the Court upheld ballot regulations effectively making it more difficult for minor parties (with a greater claim on minority status and *Carolene Products* values) to become significant electoral players. Indeed, in *Clingman*, the Libertarian Party of Oklahoma wanted to open up its primary to members of other parties with the aspiration that its eventual nominee might have a better chance in the general election. Although the *Jones* Court in the name of party autonomy upheld the right of parties to close themselves off when the state wanted to open up their primaries, it then denied this minor party in *Clingman* a similar right to open itself up when the state wanted it closed.

Bush v. Gore[39] represented the worst-case scenario of co-optation of the *Carolene Products* rationales. The per curiam opinion cited classic precedent largely justified through appeals to minority protection and entrenchment prevention. In support of the halting of recounts mandated by the new interpretation of the Equal Protection Clause, the Court cited its one-person, one-vote precedents (*Reynolds v. Sims, Gray v. Sanders*,[40] and *Moore v. Ogilvie*[41]) and its precedent in striking down the poll tax (*Harper v. Virginia Board of Elections*). That Bush was not a "discrete and insular minority"[42] or that political institutions, such as the Florida State Legislature or the United States Congress, were ready, willing, and able to vindicate his rights, played no role in the Court's opinion. The equal right to vote included the equal chance that identical ballots would be counted identically, the Court concluded, at least in the factual context presented at the time.

---

[33] *Cal. Dem. Party v. Jones,* 530 U.S. 567 (2000). See generally Nathaniel Persily, *Toward a Functional Defense of Political Party Autonomy*, 76 N.Y.U. L. Rev. 750 (2001) (discussing *Jones* and other party primary cases).

[34] See Richard L. Hasen, *Parties Take the Initiative (and Vice Versa)*, 100 Colum. L. Rev. 731 (2000) (explaining how California's parties sat out the political fight surrounding the initiative in favor of litigating against it).

[35] *Jones*, 530 U.S. at 574–75.

[36] I should note that I agree with the result in *Jones* and have argued in favor of substantial constitutional protection for party autonomy based largely on the *Carolene Products* rationales. See Persily, *supra* n. 32 (justifying party autonomy from the standpoint of protection of minorities and promoting electoral competition).

[37] 520 U.S. 351 (1997) (upholding fusion bans that prevented candidates from appearing on more than one party's line on the general election ballot).

[38] 125 S.Ct. 2029 (2005) (upholding a law that prevented parties from allowing members of other parties to vote in their primary election).

[39] 531 U.S. 98 (2000).

[40] 372 U.S. 368 (1963).

[41] 394 U.S. 814 (1969).

[42] *United States v. Carolene Products Co.,* 304 U.S. 144, 153 n. 4 (1938).

Despite the original intent of the Court that manufactured the right to vote, the right could not be constrained to its purposes: in *Bush v. Gore*, it morphed into a cause of action that was judicially cognizable regardless of the position of power, available alternative forums for resolution, or even the existence of the injury of the plaintiff.

The Court's Footnote to Footnote Four

In addition to expanding the constituency for the *Carolene Products* exceptions to judicial abstinence from political conflict, the Court has created new rationales for judicial forays into the political thicket. Although generalization obscures the jurisprudential subtleties and the differences among the coalitions that have formed to create this new justification for judicial involvement in politics, the various decisions might be summarized as protecting certain institutional and political "traditions." More troubling than the lack of constitutional justification for these moves is the Court's selective, or even made-up, notion of tradition in the recent political process cases.

The "wrongful-districting" cause of action, mentioned above, provides a case in point. In *Shaw v. Reno*[43] and its progeny, the Court established an "analytically distinct"[44] cause of action arising when a state subordinates "traditional districting principles"[45] to race in the construction of a legislative district. The Court has enumerated such principles as "compactness, contiguity, and respect for political subdivisions"[46] while recognizing that other variables, such as incumbency protection and respect for communities of interest, might make the list in an individual case. Although the Court originally justified the *Shaw* action in the name of preventing racial stereotyping and segregation, the subsequent cases established that this was not a cause of action particular to discrete and insular minorities. Indeed, any resident in the unconstitutional district, regardless of the resident's race or injury, could challenge these districts.[47] *Shaw*'s invocation of tradition is particularly inapt and selective, given that it leaves out some of the most truly traditional districting principles: namely, malapportionment and the use of districting to dilute minority votes and to entrench incumbent parties and candidates. One might have thought that the reapportionment revolution of the 1960s, let alone the later racial

---

[43] 509 U.S. 630 (1993).

[44] *Id.* at 652.

[45] *Id.* at 686 n. 8.

[46] *Id.* at 647.

[47] See *United States v. Hays,* 515 U.S. 737 (1995) (holding that any resident, regardless of race, has standing to bring a *Shaw* claim against his or her own district). On the problems of *Shaw* standing, see John Hart Ely, *Standing to Challenge Pro-Minority Gerrymanders*, 111 Harv. L. Rev. 576 (1997) (arguing in favor of the Court's holding in *Hays*); Samuel Issacharoff and Pamela S. Karlan, *Standing and Misunderstanding in Voting Rights Law*, 111 Harv. L. Rev. 2276 (1998) (responding to Ely).

vote dilution cases, had removed any presumption in favor of "tradition" in the redistricting process.

The political party cases also provide examples of the Court's explicit or implicit reliance on tradition, over minority rights or anti-entrenchment, to adjudicate political controversies. In *Jones*,[48] a majority of the members of both parties supported the law (i.e., the law was not one party's attempt to entrench itself at the other's expense), but the leaders of the party (again, hardly a discrete or insular minority) successfully argued the law violated the party's First Amendment associational rights. Indeed, proponents of the law justified it as a means of breaking the stranglehold party leaders held on the nomination process and a way of enfranchising independent voters that otherwise had no say in primary elections. The Court, however, viewed the associational rights claim as "consistent with [the] tradition" of political parties[49]—apparently overlooking the strong anti-party tradition stretching from Federalist No. 10 through the Progressive Era of enlisting the state in breaking up and controlling party machines.[50]

The reliance on the "traditional two-party system" in the ballot access cases also highlights the change in priorities regarding judicial intervention into the political process. In these cases, the Court has not established a new cause of action; rather, it has codified tradition as a state interest. In *Timmons v. Twin Cities Area New Party*,[51] the Court upheld a ban on "fusion" candidacies that prevented minor parties from nominating a candidate already nominated by a major party. As with the blanket primary, proponents of fusion viewed it as a means of increasing minority participation and challenging duopolistic control of the electoral process. Nevertheless, noting that the law favored the "traditional two-party system," the Court found the fusion ban tailored toward "temper[ing] the destabilizing effects of party-splintering and excessive factionalism."[52] To its credit, the Court in *Timmons* at least paid heed to the tradition of fusion candidacies in the late 19th century, although in most minor party ballot access cases the vibrant political tradition of smaller parties gets short shrift.

The Court's support for tradition in the political process cases is not limited to the predictable coalition of the five more conservative justices. In *U.S. Term Limits, Inc. v. Thornton*,[53] and *Cook v. Gralike*,[54] for example, Justice Stevens' opinions for the Court interpreted the Constitution as preventing states from indirectly or directly limiting the terms of its members of Congress. Indeed, it is hard to imagine a measure more friendly than term limits to the value of combating constriction of the political process in the *Carolene Products* tradition. Although the

---

[48] 530 U.S. 567 (2000).

[49] *Id.* at 574.

[50] See generally Adam Winkler, *Voters' Rights and Parties' Wrongs: Early Political Party Regulation in the State Courts, 1886–1915*, 100 Colum. L. Rev. 873 (2000) (describing early political party cases).

[51] 520 U.S. 351 (1997).

[52] *Id.* at 367.

[53] 514 U.S. 779 (1995).

[54] 531 U.S. 510 (2001).

debate in *U.S. Term Limits* concerns federalism more than tradition per se, the fundamental question there was whether states could innovate beyond the congressional qualifications listed in the Constitution to add a limit on terms. Consistent with its rejection of other political innovations, the Court said no to this departure from tradition in the electoral process.

Conclusion

What began as a judicial revolution to expand the franchise and break political lock-ups has matured into opportunities for partisan manipulation and judicial reinforcement of traditional power structures. It is worth considering whether this entire enterprise, on balance, has done more harm than good. To engage in the inquiry is, I admit, somewhat akin to asking how many angels can dance on the head of a pin. Judicial involvement in politics is here to stay, so time might be more fruitfully spent in justifying when courts should be involved rather than whether they should have ever waded into the political thicket. Moreover, all would admit that *some* judicial involvement is necessary to prevent the worst abuses by political actors: for example, outright disfranchisement, Soviet–style ballots, or draconian political speech codes.

Nevertheless, I think a good argument can be made that judicial involvement in politics—whatever its philosophic appeal—has disserved the values that formed its original justification. Although the one-person, one-vote rule may have led to greater representation of urban areas and temporary reshuffling of the political structure, decennial redistricting has allowed parties and incumbents to make elections less competitive, and has often created legislatures that are less representative. Although the Court's discovery of the right to vote led it to strike down poll taxes, most of the "important" moves in expanding the franchise were accomplished through constitutional amendments that prevented discrimination in the right to vote based on race, gender, age, and (even) failure to pay a poll tax. It was Congress, moreover, through the Voting Rights Act that eliminated literacy tests the Court had upheld earlier as constitutional and put teeth in federal protections of voting rights for racial minorities. Admittedly, the Court was indispensable in enforcing these pro-minority laws and amendments. In most cases, however, an interpretive regime that clung closely to the available text rather than dangerously expanding judicial authority in service of the *Carolene Products*-type values would have proven sufficient to prevent the disturbing types of laws that export political costs onto unrepresented and powerless groups.

Although no one can deny that judicial intervention has sometimes done wonders in the service of protecting minorities and breaking political lockups, the recent political process case law has placed a lot of weight on the other side of the balance. Plaintiffs have successfully used the Fourteenth Amendment precedents on behalf of partisan interests often completely at odds with the pro-minority and anti-entrenchment principles, and the courts have used their relatively new role in the political arena to shore up traditional power structures and even impose their own partisan preferences.

This balancing of the pros and cons of judicial involvement in politics is not merely an academic enterprise. It should serve as a warning shot to those who would expand judicial authority into uncharted territory.[55] The history of lawsuits brought against the government in order to control it teaches us lessons about the unintended consequences of constitutional innovation. It should caution us against further steps down the same or similar roads. With each new constitutional rule or judicial accretion of power comes the risk that the next Court will justify an incremental move in the direction ideologically opposite to its predecessor. Those of us who advocate such innovations should do so cautiously and humbly, for we may later need to bear the responsibility for providing the weapons our opponents use to injure the very groups we intended to help.

---

[55] See, e.g., Samuel Issacharoff and Richard H. Pildes, *Politics as Markets: Partisan Lockups of the Democratic Process*, 50 Stan. L. Rev. 643 (1998) (urging courts to become the equivalent of trustbusters of political cartels).

Termination of the ABM Treaty and the Political Question Doctrine:
Judicial Succor for Presidential Power

David Gray Adler

President George W. Bush's unilateral termination of the 1972 ABM Treaty between the United States and Russia,[1] an act overshadowed by the trauma, chaos and confusion that gripped the nation in the weeks and months following the September 11 outrage, renewed the long-standing and largely unresolved controversy over the constitutional repository of the authority to terminate treaties. President Bush's announcement on December 13, 2001, that he had given to Russia the requisite six-month notice of the United States intention to withdraw from the ABM Treaty in accordance with the treaty,[2] triggered a lawsuit, *Kucinich v. Bush,* in which thirty-two members of the House of Representatives challenged the constitutionality of Bush's action on grounds that the president may not terminate a treaty without congressional approval. The Federal District Court, however, refused to reach the merits of the case. It held that the congres-

---

[1] Entered into force on October 3, 1972. 23 UST 3435.

[2] Art. XV, cl. 2 provided: "Each party shall, in exercising its national sovereignty, have the right to withdraw from this Treaty if it decides that extraordinary events related to the subject matter of this Treaty have jeopardized its supreme interests. It shall give notice of its decision to the other Party six months prior to withdrawal from the Treaty."

sional plaintiffs lacked standing and dismissed the case as a nonjusticiable political question.[3]

The court's unwillingness to reach the merits in *Kucinich* reflects a troubling and increasing tendency among courts to elide the substantive issues involved in foreign affairs cases in which plaintiffs assert executive abuse of power and usurpation.[4] The result of this judicial abstention, typified by the invocation of the political question doctrine, is that presidential aggrandizement of foreign affairs powers remains uncurbed and unchecked. Worse, it lends, if not the imprimatur of law and authority, a certain unwholesome encouragement of the tendencies of the "Imperial Presidency."[5] Professor Louis Henkin has rightly stated: "By calling a claim a political question courts foster the perception that it is not a constitutional question and encourage the exercise of political power without regard to constitutional prescriptions and restraints."[6]

This article has three aims. First, it analyzes the application of the political question doctrine to the issue of treaty termination. It is argued here that the question of the constitutional repository of the authority to terminate treaties is, indeed, a justiciable issue. Second, it offers an account of the impact of judicial abstention on both the constitutional governance of American foreign policy and the enterprise of constitutionalism. Third, it argues that treaties should be terminated by the president and the Senate.

Treaty Termination and the Political Question Doctrine

The immediate backdrop against which to view *Kucinich* is, of course, *Goldwater v. Carter* (1979), in which the Supreme Court held that the issue of treaty termination constituted a nonjusticiable political question.[7] *Goldwater* arose out of President Jimmy Carter's unilateral termination of the 1954 Mutual Defense Treaty with Taiwan.[8] Senator Barry Goldwater and other members of the House and the Senate contended that President Carter was constitutionally required to obtain congressional consent before terminating a treaty. In his opinion for a plurality—not a majority—of the Court's members, Justice William Rehnquist wrote that the issue could not be resolved by the courts:

---

[3] 236 F.Supp. Id 1 (D.D.C. 2002).

[4] See, e.g., such war powers cases as *Crockett v. Reagan*, 720 F.2d 1355 (D.C. Cir. 1983); *Dellums v. Bush*, 752 F.Supp. 1141 (D.D.C. 1990); and *Campbell v. Clinton*, 52 F. Supp.2d 34 (D.D.C. 1999); and the first treaty termination case, *Goldwater v. Carter*, 444 U.S, 996 (1979).

[5] See generally the insightful work of Arthur Schlesinger, Jr., *The Imperial Presidency* (Boston: Houghton Mifflin, 1973).

[6] Louis Henkin, *Constitutionalism, Democracy and Foreign Affairs* (New York: Columbia University Press, 1990), 87.

[7] 444 U.S. 996 (1979).

[8] 6 UST 433. On December 15, 1978, Carter provided notice to Taiwan of the United States' intention to withdraw from the treaty.

[T]he basic question presented by the petitioners in this case is "political" and therefore nonjusticiable because it involves the authority of the president in the conduct of our country's foreign relations and the extent to which the Senate or the Congress is authorized to negate the action of the President.[9]

Justice Lewis Powell concurred, but on grounds of ripeness, and Justice Thurgood Marshall also concurred in the Court's holding, but filed no opinion.[10]

The *Kucinich* Court thoroughly embraced Justice Rehnquist's political question analysis which, Judge Bates observed in his opinion for the court, was "instructive and compelling.[11]

It is not at all clear why the question in both *Goldwater* and *Kucinich*— whether the president has the constitutional authority to terminate a treaty— should be viewed as nonjusticiable. In his dissent in *Goldwater*, Justice William Brennan wrote that plurality's perception of the issue of treaty termination as a political question "profoundly misapprehends the political question doctrine as it applies to matters of foreign relations."[12] Moreover, as Justice Powell, noted, the plurality's "reliance upon the political question doctrine is inconsistent with our precedents."[13] Justices Brennan and Powell had in mind as the controlling cases *Baker v. Carr*, the reapportionment case,[14] and *Powell v. McCormack*, which reversed the House of Representatives refusal to seat Adam Clayton Powell.[15] As we shall see, these cases do not afford support for the invocation of the political question doctrine by the *Goldwater* and *Kucinich* courts.

In his opinion in *Baker v. Carr*, Justice Brennan sought to draw order from the confusion that surrounded the political question doctrine. Justice Brennan set forth six alternative tests for identifying political questions:

Prominent on the surface of any case held to involve a political question is found a textually demonstrable constitutional commitment of the issue to a coordinate political department; or a lack of judicially discoverable and manageable standards for resolving it; or the impossibility of deciding without an initial policy determination of a kind clearly for nonjudicial discretion; or the impossibility of a court's undertaking independent resolution without expressing lack of the respect due coordinate branches of government; or an unusual need for unquestioning adherence to a political decision already made; or the potentiality of embarrassment for multifarious pronouncements by various departments on one question.[16]

In *Kucinich*, Judge Bates observed that "several" of the analytical threads of the political question doctrine were present in the treaty termination challenge,

---

[9] 444 U.S. at 1003.

[10] *Id.*, at 995–1001.

[11] 236 F.Supp.2d, 14.

[12] 100 S. Ct., 533, 539 (1979).

[13] Id., at 539.

[14] 369 U.S. 186 (1962).

[15] 395 U.S. 486 (1969).

[16] 369 U.S. at 217.

yet it has been widely acknowledged that Baker attached greatest importance to the textual "commitment" test. Professor set forth the "classical" view of the doctrine, and Herbert Wechsler wrote that, "all the doctrine can defensibly imply is that the courts are called upon to judge whether the Constitution has committed to another agency of government the autonomous determination of the issue raised."[17] Further, it has been widely assumed that *Powell v. McCormack* principally hinged on the commitment issue. In Powell, the House argued that by virtue of its constitutional powers as expressed in Article I, section 5, paragraph 1, it is to be the judge of the qualifications of its own members. The Court, however, said that the provision "is limited to the standing qualifications prescribed in the Constitution," meaning age, citizenship, and residence. In its exclusion of Powell, on the grounds of misconduct, the Court held, the House had gone beyond the authority vested in it.[18] Thus, Congress was not granted any authority to add "qualifications" to the provision.

In *Powell*, the Court rejected the claim that the case involved a political question because the issue turned on whether the claimed power had been committed to the House. Accordingly, the Court moved from the premise that it is the "ultimate interpreter of the Constitution," vested with the "responsibility" to decide "whether the action of another branch . . . exceeds whatever authority has been committed."[19] In *Kucinich*, Judge Bates acknowledged that there "is thus no textual commitment of the authority over treaty termination to any branch of government," for, indeed, the Constitution is silent on the locus of the authority to terminate treaties.[20]

The second criterion advanced in *Baker*—"a lack of judicially discoverable and manageable standards"—was not advanced by Judge Bates, although he did quote with approval the Court's acknowledgment in *Crosby v. National Foreign Trade Council* (2000), that "the nuances of the foreign policy of the United States . . . are much more the province of the Executive Branch and Congress than of this Court."[21] That is merely to state the obvious, for courts are not called upon to choose war or peace, or to determine which treaties ought to be negotiated or which nation ought to be recognized. In *Goldwater*, Justice Powell denied that the issue of treaty termination involved a "lack of judicially discovered and manageable standards." Powell stated: "We are asked to decide whether the president may terminate a treaty under the Constitution without congressional approval. Resolution of the question may not be easy, but it requires us to apply normal principles of interpretation to the constitutional provisions at issue."[22] Accordingly, the Court might seek "standards" in familiar places: the debates in

---

[17] Herbert Wechsler, Toward Neutral Principles of Constitutional Law, 73 Harv. L. Rev. 1, 7–8 (1969).

[18] *Id.*, at 550.

[19] *Id.*, at 521.

[20] 236 F. Supp. 2d., 15.

[21] *Quoted* in *id.*

[22] 100 S. Ct., 535.

the Constitutional Convention, judicial dicta, historical practice, and in the writings of eminent scholars and commentators.[23]

Judge Bates makes no attempt to adduce Justice Brennan's third test, "the impossibility of deciding without an initial policy determination of a kind clearly for nonjudicial discretion." For his part, Justice Powell found no application for this test in *Goldwater*. One cannot be sure about what Brennan had in mind when he proposed this test. Of course, the judicial branch may not undertake an initial policy determination to make or terminate a treaty, for this is nonjudicial in character. On the other hand, the determination of whether the appropriate department or branch of government has exercised that authority is within the province of the judiciary. In fact, in Goldwater, Justice Brennan addressed the point: "The issue of decision-making authority must be resolved as a matter of constitutional law, not political discretion; accordingly, it falls within the competence of the courts."[24] *Kucinich* required no "initial policy determination"; rather, it required a simple inquiry into the propriety of President Bush's termination of the ABM Treaty. The courts, it was emphasized in *Baker v. Carr*, "cannot reject as 'no law suit' a bona fide controversy as to whether some action denominated 'political' exceeds constitutional authority."[25] Moreover, history is replete with rulings from courts on lawsuits that have alleged abuse of power and usurpation by Congress or the president, as seen, for example, in cases ranging from *Marbury v. Madison* to *Youngstown Sheet and Tube Co. v. Sawyer*.[26]

In *Kucinich*, Judge Bates adduced Justice Brennan's fourth test, "the impossibility of a Court's undertaking independent resolution without expressing lack of the respect due coordinate branches of government," as grounds for invoking the political question doctrine. Patently, judicial deference to one of the coordinate branches cannot be meant to imply abstention from the exercise of judicial review itself. The Court, it should be said, does not commit a social solecism if it determines that the president has transgressed constitutional bounds. If that were the measure of legal etiquette, then the Court would have been precluded from ruling in Steel Seizure Case or the Watergate Tapes Case, among others.[27] Such rulings are pursuant to Chief Justice John Marshall's charge in *Marbury v. Madison* (1803), "to say what the law is."[28] As Marshall observed in *Marbury*, "to what purpose are powers limited, and to what purpose is that limitation committed to writing, if these limits may, at any time, be passed by those intended to be restrained?"[29] Due deference to the president does not prevent the

---

[23] David Gray Adler, *The Constitution and the Termination of Treaties* (New York: Garland Press, 1986) 84–247.

[24] 100 S. Ct. 539.

[25] 369 U.S., 217.

[26] 1 Cranch 137 (1803); 343 U.S. 579 (1952).

[27] In *Youngstown Sheet and Tube Co. v. Sawyer*, 343 U.S. 579 (1952), President Harry Truman's seizure of the steel industry was held invalid because, in the words of Justice Burton, the president "invaded the jurisdiction of Congress." *Id.*, 660.

[28] 1 Cranch 137, 177 (1803).

[29] *Id.*, at 176.

Court from scrutinizing the constitutional validity of his actions. If that were so, there would be no protection from an errant president. Moreover, the availability of the impeachment power is proof that the republic cannot be held hostage to a usurpations executive. Must the nation be forced to such extreme measures when a more modest remedy—judicial review—is at hand to rein in a president who abuses or usurps constitutional powers?

Judge Bates has sought to convert Justice Brennan's "respect" test into a prohibition of lawsuits brought by members of Congress. Judicial intervention by way of hearing legal challenges that are not authorized by Congress, or which run counter to the apparent will of that body, he reasoned, would exhibit "as lack of respect" owed to Congress. His position, however, overlooks the possibility, indeed, one might say, probability, that congressional plaintiffs might be the agents who better protect the institution of Congress from members who are indifferent toward their institutional powers and responsibilities. In fact, the refusal by a court to rule on the merits of a congressional lawsuit, on the order of the suit filed in *Kucinich*, may well reward the vice of congressional indifference and, even ignorance, of its institutional powers, while it denies an airing to the virtues of constitutional interest, concern, and knowledge, as exhibited in *Kucinich*, among other congressional lawsuits. Kucinich did not require review of the president's activities as commander-in-chief, and it did not involve interference in the area of foreign policy. "Such a case," Justice Powell noted in *Goldwater*, "would arise if we were asked to decide, for example, whether a treaty required the president to order troops into a foreign country."[30] Drawing on *Baker v. Carr*, Justice Powell added:

> But "it is error to suppose that every case or controversy which touches foreign relations lies beyond judicial cognizance." This case "touches" foreign relations, but the question presented to us concerns only the constitutional division of power between Congress and the president.[31]

"Some arbiter," wrote Justice Robert H. Jackson, "is almost indispensable when power is . . . balanced between different branches, as the legislative and executive . . . each unit cannot be left to judge the limits of its own power."[32] The Court need not shrink from its role as an arbiter; in fact, it has frequently resolved conflicting claims of competence between proponents of legislative and executive power. That was precisely the issue put before the *Kucinich* Court. Whatever risk existed of a "lack of respect due" the president, the overriding concern must attach to the defense and maintenance of integrity of the Constitution and its framework of limited government. "It is far more important," ob-

---

[30] 100 S. Ct, 535.

[31] *Id.*, quoting *Baker v. Carr*, 369 U.S., 211.

[32] Robert H. Jackson, *The Struggle for Judicial Supremacy* (New York: Knopf, 1949), 9.

served Justice William O. Douglas, "to be respectful to the Constitution than to a coordinate branch of the government."[33]

Judge Bates observed that the "circumstances" of the *Kucinich* case presented "an unusual need for unquestioning adherence to a political decision already made"—Brennan's fifth test in *Baker v. Carr*.[34] Judge Bates emphasized the uncertainty that might arise from a judicial ruling that overturned President Bush's announcement of his intention to terminate the ABM Treaty. Bates stated: "Foreign governments must be able to rely upon the pronouncements of the United States regarding its treaties." If the court were to hold Bush's action unconstitutional it would summon the mischief anticipated by Brennan's final test for "The potential of embarrassment from multifarious pronouncements by various departments on one question" would be undeniable."[35]

While it is not clear what kinds of cases might constitute "an unusual need for unquestioned adherence" outside, perhaps, a congressional declaration of war, it is hard to imagine that this test could encompass the termination of treaties. For if the *Kucinich* Court were to declare President Bush's termination of the ABM Treaty unconstitutional because there was no senatorial participation, the Senate, if it wished the termination to stay in effect could terminate the treaty.

Perhaps the "unquestioned adherence" test is intended to refer to those cases in which the court fears that its decision might be disobeyed. For example, if the *Kucinich* Court had ruled Bush's termination unconstitutional, how could it have compelled compliance with its decision?

This is a dangerous question for a constitutionally limited government, since the mere hint that the court's rulings would hinge on the likelihood of disobedience to its order would scuttle the rule of law and betray the very premise of constitutionalism. Early in the history of the Republic, Chief Justice Marshall was informed that "there was no means of compelling" the United States to pay costs, but he responded, "that would make no difference, because we are to presume that they would pay them, if bound by the law so to do."[36]

The results of a presidential refusal to enforce a Supreme Court decision are uncertain; there may be support for his refusal, there may be a political backlash, or perhaps it would render him impeachable for his contravention of the law. Whatever consequences flow from such a presidential action, they should not deter the Court from expounding the meaning of the Constitution or of maintaining "a strong American bias in favor of judicial determination of constitutional and legal "issues."[37]

---

[33] *Massachusetts v. Laird*, 400 U.S. 886, 894 (1970), dissenting opinion.

[34] 236 F. Supp. 2d, 16, quoting Baker v. Carr, 369 U.S. 217.

[35] 236 F. Supp. 2d, 16.

[36] *United States v. Hooe*, 3 Cranch 73, 90 (1805). In *Worcester v. Georgia*, 6 Pet. 515 (1832), Marshall ruled against Georgia despite a threat from President Andrew Jackson that he would not enforce the decision. Warren, 1926, 205, 212–19.

[37] Louis Jaffe, *Standing to Secure Judicial Review: Public Actions*, 74 Harv. L. Rev 1265, 1302 (1961).

Judge Bates's warning of the "potential embarrassment" that would result from "multifarious pronouncements by various departments" on the issue of treaty termination invokes an analytical thread that would undercut the practice of judicial review itself. Probably Justice Brennan had in mind the case of *Luther v. Borden* (1849).[38] There the Court was asked to decide whether the charter government that still existed in Rhode Island in 1841 or the rival Dorr government was the legitimate government of the state. In an opinion written by Chief Justice Roger Taney, it was held that the president, by taking measures to call out the militia at the request of the governor in the charter government, had recognized that government as legitimate and that his decision was binding on the courts. Yet Taney held that the president's decision was temporary and provisional; Congress had the final voice. Further, the separate houses, by seating members, might decide for themselves that one government or the other was legitimate. In spite of all this, the federal courts were bound by decisions of the state courts.[39] *Luther v. Borden* quite clearly represents the possibility of multifarious pronouncements by several departments on one question. The problem would seem to be beyond remedy; if the federal courts pass on the question, there are still five other agencies that may issue pronouncements on what constitutes a republican form of government.

But neither *Kucinich v. Bush* nor *Goldwater v. Carter* posed a comparable problem. In both cases only the president had acted. If either court had reached the merits of the case and had held that the president does not possess a unilateral authority to terminate treaties, that fact, no doubt, would be embarrassing to some and annoying to officials in Moscow and Peking, but it would not produce the chaos Justice Brennan had in mind.

The issue presented in *Kucinich*—whether the president may unilaterally terminate the ABM Treaty—does not conform to the analytical threads of the political question doctrine; indeed, the question of the constitutional repository of the authority to terminate treaties is eminently justiciable. In truth, the issue of whether the president has exceeded his constitutional authority goes to the issue of the scope of authority conferred on him by the Constitution. Accordingly, the question is simply one involving "jurisdiction." Treatment of treaty termination as a political question ignores the fundamental task of judicial interpretation of the scope of authority vested in the president. And where there is a serious, and well-founded assertion of usurpation—a great constitutional sin — there is all the more reason for the judiciary to reach the merits of the case.

Moreover, the application of the political question doctrine to treaty termination in particular, and to foreign affairs in general, is apt to generate confusion and mislead the public. The characterization or denomination of a foreign relations action as "political" is likely to engender the perception that the conduct of foreign relations is beyond constitutional prescription. Yet there is nothing in the architecture of the Constitution—text, design, and history—to support such a

---

[38] 7 How.1 (1849).
[39] *Id.*, at 40–44.

premise. On the contrary, the framers of the Constitution were at pains to apply the premises and principles of constitutionalism—the doctrine of separation of powers and checks and balances, and the rule of law—to the formulation, management, and conduct of foreign relations. Professor Henkin has rightly observed: "When the courts refuse to decide a claim of usurpation by the President of the legislative power, they abdicate their function of preserving constitutionalism as well as our democracy."[40] Judicial abdication will likely result in further executive lawlessness.

The assertion that a presidential violation of a statute or a constitutional provision is not justiciable is puzzling. The claim that presidential acts are deserving of judicial deference is not grounded in the intellectual scaffolding that sustains the principles of judicial self-restraint. The origins of that theory lay in the need to defer to Congress because of its status as the lawmaking branch of government. The president holds no comparable status. Moreover, the president's duty under the Take Care Clause, the clear demand for the president to "take care that the laws be faithfully executed," is a reminder of his high duty as the nation's administrator-in-chief to enforce all the laws, whether they pertain to domestic or foreign affairs. There is, then, no rationale for undue deference to a usurpatious executive under cover of the political question doctrine. More pointedly, we may say with Archibald Cox, that a "refusal to act would have the effect of legitimizing the evil."[41]

Since it is true that there is no textual commitment of the authority to terminate treaties, does that yield the conclusion that treaty termination defies manageable standards? Does the Constitution's silence on the locations of the authority to terminate treaties leave us without a map or a compass as we explore the constitutional landscape of treaty termination? On the contrary, there is strong and sufficient evidence to conclude that the president has no authority to terminate treaties. As we shall see, the constitutional design contemplates that treaties should be terminated by the treaty power—the president and the Senate—an approach that reflects the Constitutional Convention's commitment to collective decision making and the delegates' fear of unilateral executive power in the formulation and conduct of American foreign policy. The framers' aversion to unilateral presidential control of the nation's foreign relations was described by Alexander Hamilton in Federalist No. 75:

> The history of human virtue does not warrant that exalted opinion of human nature which would make it wise in a nation to commit interests of so delicate and momentous a kind, as those which concern its intercourse with the rest of the

---

[40] Henkin, *Constitutionalism*, 88.

[41] Archibald Cox, *The Role of the Supreme Court in American Society*, 50 Marquette L. Rev. 575, 591 (1967).

world, to the sole disposal of a magistrate created and circumstanced as would be a President of the United States.[42]

The framers' fears of unilateral executive control of foreign policy, fears manifested in their refusal to lodge either the treaty power or the war power in the hands of the presidency, would have precluded as well a grant to the president of authority to terminate treaties. The Convention, it is true, did not directly discuss the issue of treaty termination, perhaps because the framers assumed that the principle of symmetrical construction, characterized by John Calhoun as a basic rule of legal interpretation, would apply to the issue of termination: "when a power is given to do an act, the power to is also given to repeal it."[43] Accordingly, the powers which make treaties may rescind them as well.[44] This position was adopted by both John Jay and James Madison. In Federalist No. 64, Jay wrote that "they who make treaties may alter or cancel them."[45] In a letter of January 2, 1791, to Edmund Pendleton, Madison stated: "That the contracting parties can annul the treaty can not, I presume be questioned, the same authority, precisely, being exercised in annulling as in making a treaty."[46]

Madison's reference to the symmetry of treaty making and treaty termination, the combined wisdom and judgment of both the president and Senate, finds further support in both historical and policy concerns. Indeed, there are several reasons to believe that the framers might have applied this rule of symmetrical construction to the issue of treaty termination. Nothing less than this symmetry would have reached the concerns that lay at the core of the debate on the treaty power. The various regional interests and state jealousies required a mechanical solution in which the states would have an "equal" voice in the treaty power. Without it, the small states would not have agreed to support the Constitution. Those concerns, which stood at the center of the compromise reached by the Committee of Eleven, could not have been satisfied if the framers had not intended to provide the Senate with a voice in the termination of treaties. The felt need among southern delegates to the Convention to protect their regional interests through the treaty power provoked an intense debate among the framers, in which it became clear that the southern delegates were prepared to leave the Convention if their interests were not protected in the construction of the treaty power. In consideration of the intensity of that debate, it is inconceivable that the states would have left the door open to a treaty termination arrangement that might have ignored or sacrificed their interests. This symmetrical principle

---

[42] *The Federalist Papers,* Edward M. Meade, ed. (New York: Modern Library, 1937), 75: 487.

[43] Jonathan Elliot, *Debates in the Several State Conventions,* 5 vols. (Philadelphia: J. B. Lippincott, 1837), 4: 463.

[44] See, generally, David Gray Adler, *The Framers and Treaty Termination: A Matter of Symmetry,* Ariz. State L. J. 891 (1981).

[45] Federalist No. 64, 421

[46] The Writings of James Madison, Gaillard Hunt, ed. (New York: Putnam, 1900–1910), I: 523–24.

would also be consistent with the authority of the president and the Senate to affect the status of treaties at every other stage, in full service of the framers' belief that "the foreign relations of the new republic consisted largely of treaties to be concluded with other countries."[47] As Hamilton explained to the New York Ratifying Convention, the Senate, "together with the President, are to manage over concern with foreign nations."[48]

The proposition that the president and the Senate may terminate, as well as make treaties, derives support from policy concerns as well. The same sort of skill and experience involved in the negotiation of foreign affairs is needed in terminating treaties. In fact, it is arguable that greater dexterity, and more wisdom, are necessary in the termination of treaties because such an action might well be contemplated when relations are somewhat strained and anxiety and tension are high. Moreover, although the Constitution is silent on the matter of treaty termination, there also is no provision for repealing statutes. There seems never to have been any doubt among the framers that this requires action of precisely the same kind, by precisely the same authorities, for either enactment or the recession of a law. Thus, as Jay explained it in Federalist No. 64, the mechanics involved in the creation and termination of laws and treaties are analogous.[49]

There is, it should be noted, some judicial authority for the views that treaties are to be terminated by the same authority that makes them. In 1821, in The Amiable Isabella, Justice Joseph Story, in what was the first judicial holding that pertained to the termination of treaties, stated: "[T]he obligations of the treaty cannot be changed or varied but by the same formalities with which they were introduced; or at least by some act of as high an import, and of as unequivocal an authority."[50] Similarly, in *Techt v. Hughes* (1920), Judge (and later, Justice) Benjamin Cardozo, writing for the New York Court, stated that: "The president and the Senate may denounce the treaty, and thus terminate its life."[51]

Finally, two literary presidents—William Howard Taft and Woodrow Wilson—have weighed in on behalf of the principle of symmetrical construction as it pertains to the issue of treaty termination. Taft wrote: "The abrogation of the treaty involves the exercise of the same kind of power as the making of it" (Taft, 1916, 599, 610). Similarly, President Wilson, addressing the Merchant Marine

---

[47] Louis Henkin, *Foreign Affairs and the Constitution* (Mineola, N.Y.: Foundation Press, 1972), 129.

[48] Elliot, *Records*, 2: 291.

[49] *Federalist* No. 64, 421.

[50] 19 U.S. (6 Wheat.) 1 (1821).

[51] 229 N.Y. 222, 243, cert. Denied, 254 U.S. 643 (1920). Cardozo issued this ruling with respect to the general denunciation of treaties in a case involving the termination of treaties because of war. It would appear that he believed the whole field of termination by denunciation was within the scope of the treaty power. Cardozo's statement is cited with approval in Clark v. Allen, 331 U.S. 503, 509 (1942).

Act, objected to any interference by Congress in the denunciation of treaties, because this would be an infringement of the treaty power."[52]

Conclusion

The *Kucinich* case raised a simple question: May the president terminate the ABM Treaty without congressional approval? The court's unwillingness to reach the merits of the case and its characterization of the dispute as a political question reflect a deeply disturbing trend among lower court judges who refuse to exercise the power of judicial review to rein in usurpatious executives. The extraordinary judicial abdication of its duty "to say what the law is," has not been reserved for unimportant issues and cases. On the contrary, the acts of abdication have occurred in some of the most important areas of American life, including the question of the authority to choose between war and peace. The *Kucinich* court's refusal to rule on the constitutionality of President Bush's termination of the ABM Treaty leaves one to wonder whether this president, or a subsequent one, may feel authorized to remove the United States from other bedrock treaties and organizations, including the United Nations. Judicial abdication comes with a price. Above all, it undermines the constitutional preference for collective decision making, and it exalts executive unilateralism. There is no reason whatever to believe that this judicial behavior serves either the interests of constitutionalism or the broader interests of the nation. Indeed, there are a good many reasons to believe it does not.

---

[52] Jesse S. Reeves, *The Jones Act and the Denunciation of Treaties*, 33 Amer. J. of Int'l L. 33 (1921).

Political Questions and Political Remedies

Jonathan R. Siegel[1]

The puzzling and troubling feature of the political question doctrine is the potential it seems to have to render constitutional provisions meaningless. After armed struggle and tremendous political effort, our ancestors gave us the magnificent achievement of a written Constitution that limits the powers of government.[2] Under the political question doctrine, however, the principal enforcement mechanism for those constitutional limits—judicial review—is not available for certain constitutional provisions. At least at first blush, therefore, it might appear that some parts of the Constitution, though ostensibly constraining the behavior of government, cannot in fact do so, because of the lack of an enforcement mechanism for the constraint.

Defenders of the political question doctrine explain this apparently troubling fact in numerous ways. They point out that the lack of judicial enforcement does not automatically render a constitutional constraint meaningless. The political branches may successfully police themselves by obeying judicially unenforceable constitutional provisions.[3] Indeed, some scholars argue, the political branches may

---

[1] Professor of Law, George Washington University Law School. I would like to thank my colleague John Duffy for his helpful comments on an early draft of this essay.

[2] See *Marbury v. Madison,* 5 U.S. 137, 176 (1803) ("The powers of the legislature are defined and limited; and that those limits may not be mistaken or forgotten, the constitution is written.").

[3] J. Peter Mulhern, *In Defense of the Political Question Doctrine*, 137 U. Pa. L. Rev.

have institutional advantages that make them *better* suited to apply certain constitutional provisions than the judiciary.[4]

The main purpose of this essay is to critique one further argument used by defenders of the political question doctrine: that, even where a constitutional provision is not judicially enforceable, it is still susceptible to *electoral* enforcement.
When voters, this argument runs, have no judicial remedy for a perceived constitutional violation because of the political question doctrine, they can still take to the
polls and turn offending politicians out of office. Thus, this argument suggests, we
should not be overly concerned that the political question doctrine deprives the
courts of enforcement power over certain constitutional provisions, because the
electoral process provides an appropriate substitute.[5]

This essay calls attention to the flaws in this argument. The argument ignores
critical differences between the judicial and the electoral processes. Not only
might attempts to use the electoral process to remedy constitutional violations be
utterly impractical because of the cost and effort required, but the electoral process
lacks crucial structural elements provided by the judicial process that make the
latter a proper mechanism for the enforcement of constitutional constraints. The
judicial process is mandatory in nature; it focuses on particular issues; it provides a
statement of reasons for its decisions; it operates within a system of precedent; and
it operates according to law, not according to majoritarian preference. These features of the judicial process, this essay argues, are not found in the electoral process and are crucial to the appropriateness of the judicial process for resolving constitutional issues.

The primary purpose of this essay is to demonstrate the flaws in this one, particular argument used in defense of the political question doctrine. But beyond
that, the essay suggests that analyzing the flaws in the argument is of interest because it provides useful insight into the issue of the political question doctrine's
ultimate validity. In cataloging the differences between the judicial and electoral
processes, we see some of the important reasons why the judicial process is so
well suited to serving as the enforcement mechanism for constitutional constraints.
It is not just, as is often noted, that the judicial process is insulated from politics
because of the life tenure of federal judges. That point is critically important, to be
sure, but the other characteristics of the judicial process that distinguish it from the
electoral and political processes (its mandatory nature, focus on particular issues,
express articulation of reasons for decisions, operation within a system of precedent, and nonmajoritarian operation according to law) also play a vital role in ren-
dering constitutional provisions meaningful. Defenders of the political question
doctrine must explain why we should entrust our Constitution's enforcement to
processes that lack these vital characteristics.

97, 156–62 (1988).

   [4] Rachel Barkow, *More Supreme than Court? The Fall of the Political Question Doctrine and the Rise of Judicial Supremacy*, 102 Colum. L. Rev. 237, 329 (2002).

   [5] See *infra* Part II.

Part I of this essay prepares the ground for this argument by discussing what the political question doctrine actually is and, in particular, by rehearsing the well-known point of Professor Louis Henkin that the term "political question doctrine" should not be used when referring to cases in which a court merely holds that a challenged governmental action is not subject to legal constraint. The essence of the doctrine is that it may bar judicial enforcement of actual legal constraints on government behavior. Part II then puts forward the main argument: the electoral process cannot provide an appropriate substitute for judicial enforcement of constitutional constraints, because it lacks characteristics of the judicial process that are essential to the task of enforcing such constraints. In cataloging these characteristics, we see why the judicial process is so well suited to that task and why any doctrine that takes that task away from it bears an especially heavy burden of justification.

I. Hooray for Henkin

In coming to a view about the political question doctrine, one must begin by understanding what the doctrine actually is. Unfortunately, usage reveals that the doctrine has two quite different meanings. One of these, which I shall call the *real* political question doctrine, provides that, in some circumstances, the federal courts cannot enforce legal constraints on government action, even when the occasion for such enforcement arises in what, but for the political question doctrine, would be a proper Article III case or controversy. The other, which may be called the *bogus* political question doctrine, merely expresses the point that a plaintiff who challenges government action that is not subject to legal constraint must necessarily lose.

This observation is, of course, nothing new. In his justly famous 1976 article, *Is There a Political Question Doctrine?*, Louis Henkin pointed out that, in many cases, the political question doctrine serves no real function, but only provides a confusing and deceptive packaging of obvious principles such as that "[t]he courts are bound to accept decisions by the political branches within their constitutional authority," and that "[t]he courts will not find limitations or prohibitions on the powers of the political branches where the Constitution does not prescribe any."[6] Readers of the present volume will probably be well versed in this basic point, articulated by Henkin thirty years ago. Nonetheless, I do not ask the reader's pardon for taking a few pages to drive the point home, because the cases and the scholarly literature show that Henkin's point is still underappreciated, and because my main line of argument requires a clear understanding of what the real political question doctrine actually does.

---

[6] Louis Henkin, *Is There a Political Question Doctrine?* 85 Yale L.J. 597, 622 (1976).

A. The Bogus Political Question Doctrine

Imagine that a taxpayer brought a lawsuit in federal court asserting that income tax rates are just too high and asking the court to order that they be reduced. Such a lawsuit would of course deserve immediate dismissal. The Constitution gives Congress the power to tax incomes[7] and imposes no constraint that would prevent Congress from imposing the current set of income tax rates. Plaintiff would have failed to state a claim upon which relief could be granted.

A funny thing could happen, however, on the way to dismissing the plaintiff's frivolous case. Instead of simply pointing out that the plaintiff has not stated any legal reason why Congress is required to lower tax rates and therefore dismissing under Federal Rule 12(b)(6),[8] the court might invoke the political question doctrine. The court might remark that the choice of tax rates is "committed to the political process for resolution" and dismiss for lack of Article III jurisdiction.

Invocation of the political question doctrine in such a case would perhaps be harmless—it would not much matter precisely which label the court put on dismissal of such an obviously frivolous case—but it would surely be pointless. As Henkin observed long ago, we do not need a nebulous "doctrine" to tell us that when a plaintiff challenges a government action that is not subject to legal constraint, the plaintiff loses. Common sense and Rule 12(b)(6) tell us that. To the extent the doctrine calls for dismissal of cases *because* defendants' actions are legally unconstrained, it does not work at all.

Moreover, the principle of Occam's razor, applied to legal thinking, would warn us to avoid multiplying doctrines needlessly. Invocation of the political question doctrine where it serves no purpose is at least potentially dangerous. Because doctrines ought to do something, not nothing, courts are likely to imagine that the political question doctrine must do more than merely duplicate the concept of dismissal for failure to state a claim; they may struggle to give it content, and it may give government lawyers a weapon to dismiss lawsuits that courts should hear.[9] Courts should therefore avoid the doctrine in cases in which it serves no function.

All of this would be too obvious to be worth pointing out if some cases and scholarly articles did not still, almost thirty years after Henkin, use the political question doctrine to express the point that a plaintiff must lose when there is simply no legal constraint on the government action that plaintiff challenges (or when the plaintiff, at least, points to no applicable legal constraint). The Third Circuit's decision in *New Jersey v. United States* provides an excellent, recent example of

---

[7] U.S. Const., art. I, sec. 8, cl. 1; *id.* amend. XVI.

[8] See Fed. R. Civ. P. 12(b)(6) (permitting dismissal of a plaintiff's complaint for "failure to state a claim upon which relief can be granted").

[9] Cf. Jonathan R. Siegel, *Suing the President: Nonstatutory Review Revisited*, 97 Colum. L. Rev. 1612, 1649 (1997) (noting that, in their desire to win cases, government lawyers may urge courts to stretch jurisdictional doctrines to cover cases to which they should not really apply); Kenneth Culp Davis, *Suing the Government by Falsely Pretending to Sue an Officer*, 29 U. Chi. L. Rev. 435, 438–42 (1962) (same).

such pointless, or bogus, invocation of the political question doctrine.[10] The state of New Jersey alleged that the federal government's failure to enforce the immigration laws imposed unconstitutional costs on the state by compelling it to expend funds to educate illegal alien children and prosecute illegal aliens who commit crimes.[11] The court of appeals affirmed dismissal of the complaint.

The court's opinion was, however, curious: first it found the state's claims to be meritless, but then it held them to be political questions. For example, the court said that "there is no basis for a claim that the Constitution has been violated by the federal government's inaction, which allegedly has set in motion events that have indirectly caused the state to incur costs."[12] That is, the court explained why the state's claim failed on its *merits*: there is simply no legal requirement that the federal government implement the immigration laws so as to avoid imposing costs on states. Having said that, however, the court held the claim to be a nonjusticiable political question. Invoking the well-known list of political question factors given by the Supreme Court in *Baker v. Carr*,[13] the court held that the Constitution commits immigration to the political branches of government, that there would be no judicially discoverable and manageable standards for resolving the issues the case presented, and that resolving the issues would express a lack of respect for a coordinate branch.[14]

The case presents a particularly clear example of a court's invoking the political question doctrine when it really means to say that the plaintiff's claims failed on their merits. The court all but held that the claims were political questions precisely *because* they failed on their merits.[15] The court determined that the issues presented were committed to the political branches because it determined that the Constitution does not constrain the enforcement discretion of the political branches with regard to immigration matters. It seems particularly egregious to say that a court cannot interpret the Constitution and resolve the claims presented by a plaintiff when the court has just finished doing exactly that.

A similar example of bogus invocation of the political question doctrine occurred in the Tenth Circuit's decision in *Schroder v. Bush*,[16] a case rather like the

---

[10] 91 F.3d 463 (3d Cir. 1996).

[11] *Id.* at 465–66. The case was one of a spate of similar cases brought by several states at the time.

[12] *Id.* at 467.

[13] 369 U.S. 186, 217 (1962).

[14] 91 F.3d at 470.

[15] No one doubts that courts may hear constitutional challenges to immigration and naturalization laws when a plaintiff points to a legal constraint that at least might be applicable to them, such as the constraint arising from the Equal Protection Clause. See, e.g., *Miller v. Albright*, 523 U.S. 420 (1998) (upholding naturalization laws against an Equal Protection challenge). Here, the real problem was not that the judiciary may never consider attacks on the immigration laws but that the plaintiff state had not specified any legal constraint on Congress's ability to pass such laws that could even conceivably have formed the basis of such an attack.

[16] 263 F.3d 1169 (10th Cir. 2001).

income tax hypothetical posed above. The plaintiffs in *Schroder* were farmers suffering from difficult economic conditions. They sought an order requiring the president, cabinet secretaries, and the United States itself to "control United States currency and to maintain market conditions so as to be favorable to small farmers."[17] They also asked the court to order the U.S. Trade Representative to "cooperate in negotiating and implementing foreign trade agreements that would benefit small farmers."[18]

Needless to say, the court of appeals affirmed dismissal of this frivolous complaint. But rather than simply observe that plaintiffs had stated no reason why federal economic, farm, and international trade policy was unlawful, the court invoked the political question doctrine. Referring to the *Baker v. Carr* factors, the court determined that the case "presents textbook examples of political questions."[19]

The court's analysis was, however, more confusing than helpful. The court observed that the Constitution commits the regulation of commerce, the establishment of bankruptcy law, and the regulation of currency to Congress.[20] That is certainly true, but it has little to do with the reason the case was properly dismissed. Congress's regulation of commerce, bankruptcy, and currency comes before the courts all the time; courts regularly pass on whether Congress has exceeded the limits of its power in these areas.[21] The problem was not that regulation of these issues is unreviewably committed to Congress, but that the plaintiffs had not stated any basis for review; they had not stated any reason why Congress's actions were unlawful.

The court also said that the plaintiffs' requested relief would require "'initial policy determinations' in an area devoid of 'judicially discoverable and manageable standards' and where 'multifarious pronouncements by various departments' would lead to confusion and disaster."[22] This was somewhat more to the point, but was merely a long-winded way of saying, once again, that plaintiffs had not alleged the violation of any legal constraint on federal economic policy. The court's political question analysis added nothing to its decision and could provide dangerous ammunition for some future government lawyer to use in trying to get a court to dismiss a proper challenge to federal farm policy.

---

[17] *Id.* at 1172.

[18] *Id.* at 1173 (internal quotation omitted). As if that were not enough, plaintiffs also asked the court to declare that "sub-par agricultural commodity prices shall be allowed as an affirmative defense in any action for debt." *Id.*

[19] 263 F.3d at 1174.

[20] *Id.*

[21] See, e.g., *United States v. Lopez,* 514 U.S. 549 (1995) (holding that Congress exceeded its powers under the Commerce Clause); *Northern Pipeline Construction Co. v. Marathon Pipe Line Co.,* 458 U.S. 50 (1982) (holding provisions of the bankruptcy laws unconstitutional); *Richardson v. Sullivan,* 996 F.2d 311 (10th Cir. 1993) (Table, text in Westlaw) (holding that Congress did not violate the Constitution by taking the dollar off the gold standard).

[22] 263 F.3d at 1174 (quoting *Baker v. Carr,* 369 U.S. at 217).

Pointless invocation of the political question doctrine may also be observed in the scholarly literature. In a recent symposium about *Baker v. Carr*, for example, Robert Pushaw takes the Supreme Court to task for adopting a "cavalier attitude" under which the political question doctrine "has ceased to function as a meaningful jurisdictional restraint."[23] Professor Pushaw laments the impact of *Baker* and recommends reinstating the "Federalist approach" to political questions, under which, he says, constitutional provisions can rebut the presumption favoring judicial review.[24] In describing what questions would actually be political questions under such a Federalist approach, however, Professor Pushaw observes that the doctrine would apply where the people have "entrusted their federal government representatives with complete latitude" and where "by definition the exercise of such discretion cannot violate the Constitution."[25] Thus, for example, Professor Pushaw observes that, under his view, no court could hear a claim against the president's decision to veto a bill passed by the Congress because even though vetoes are occasionally misguided, the president's discretion with regard to the veto power is absolute.[26]

Such a formulation provides that the political question doctrine should apply precisely where it serves no purpose. We need no special jurisprudential doctrine to get rid of lawsuits challenging presidential vetoes as misguided. Such a challenge to a veto must fail on its merits, because, as Professor Pushaw observes, the president has plenary authority to veto any bill.

Once for all, courts and scholars should internalize Henkin's insight and cease invoking the political question doctrine for cases in which a court, having examined the relevant legal sources, concludes that there is no applicable legal constraint on the action that the plaintiff is challenging. The very fact that the court has reached that conclusion proves that the matter is not beyond judicial cognizance. The court has simply concluded, in the perfectly ordinary way, that the plaintiff has not stated a claim upon which relief can be granted. It is useful, even vital, to remember that our Constitution allows many important questions to be resolved by the untrammeled play of competing political forces, but this point should lead to the ordinary dismissal of cases on their merits, not to the invocation of a special and mysterious jurisdictional doctrine.

B. The Real Political Question Doctrine

It would be equally wrong, however, to carry Henkin's insight too far. Courts sometimes invoke the political question doctrine in cases in which they merely hold, in the ordinary way, that defendant's actions are not unlawful, but that does

---

[23] Robert Pushaw, *Judicial Review and the Political Question Doctrine: Reviving the Federalist "Rebuttable Presumption" Analysis*, 80 N.C. L. Rev. 1165, 1167 (2002).

[24] *Id.* at 1167–68.

[25] *Id.* at 1196–97.

[26] *Id.* at 1197.

not mean that they invoke the doctrine *only* in such cases. There really are cases in which a court dismisses the plaintiff's claim, not because the defendant's action is subject to no legal constraint, but because the court concludes (rightly or wrongly) that the legal constraint applicable to the defendant's actions is not judicially enforceable. Perhaps the best example of such a case—a case that very usefully illustrates the difference between bogus and real political question cases—is the D.C. Circuit's decision in *Morgan v. United States.*[27]

The case concerned an extremely close election for a seat in the House of Representatives in 1984. The Secretary of State of Indiana certified that the Republican candidate had won by a small margin. After making its own inquiry, however, a House committee concluded that the Democratic candidate had defeated the Republican by just four votes. By a party-line vote, the House seated the Democrat. A group of Republicans brought suit seeking an injunction requiring the seating of the Republican candidate.

There can be no doubt that when either house of Congress investigates a contested election and decides which candidate to seat, its action is subject to legal constraint. The house must seat the candidate who received more lawful votes. This requirement follows from the constitutional provisions that the House of Representatives "shall be composed of members chosen every second year by the people of the several states,"[28] and that the Senate "shall be composed of two senators from each state, elected by the people thereof."[29] For either house to seat as a member a candidate who actually lost the election would surely be unlawful, indeed, unconstitutional.

Nonetheless, when the *Morgan* case reached the D.C. Circuit, that court summarily held that it lacked jurisdiction. Then-Judge Scalia observed that the Constitution provides that "[e]ach House shall be the Judge of the Elections, Returns and Qualifications of its own Members."[30] The command that each house shall not only judge its own elections, but shall be "*the* Judge" of them, Judge Scalia determined, excluded anyone else, including federal judges, from judging such elections. "It is difficult," he said, "to imagine a clearer case of 'textually demonstrable constitutional commitment' of an issue to another branch of government to the exclusion of the courts."[31]

This case, then, illustrates the *real* political question doctrine: the challenged action was undoubtedly subject to legal constraint, but the court dismissed the case on the ground that the legal constraint was not judicially enforceable.[32] Notice the

---

[27] 801 F.2d 445 (D.C. Cir. 1986).

[28] U.S. Const., art. 1, sec. 2.

[29] U.S. Const., amend. XVII.

[30] U.S. Const., art. I, sec. 5, cl. 1.

[31] 801 F.2d at 447. Judge Scalia also relied on the history of the Elections Clause, which, in his view, was "entirely consistent with its plain exclusion of judicial jurisdiction." *Id.*

[32] Curiously, Judge Scalia, after citing the Elections Clause, concluded that "without need to rely upon the amorphous and partly prudential doctrine of 'political questions,' . . . we simply lack jurisdiction to proceed." 801 F.2d at 447. I am not sure why, in this unusual

difference from bogus political question cases. In this case, assuming the facts stated in plaintiff's complaint to be true, the challenged government action was unlawful; indeed, it was unconstitutional. The court needed special, unusual reasoning to explain why it declined to enforce a legal constraint on the defendant's actions.[33]

Morgan demonstrates the error of the view, taken by some scholars, that when a court dismisses a challenge to governmental action on the basis of the political question doctrine it is always necessarily holding "that there are no legal rules constraining the validity of [the] challenged action."[34] Sometimes, as *Morgan* shows, the action is subject to legal constraint. Similarly, it is not correct to say that the political question doctrine "applies *only* in cases in which, on the merits, the government action was constitutionally permissible in any event."[35] It is true that the political question doctrine is often, uselessly, invoked in such cases. Courts also, however, invoke the doctrine in cases in which it really does something: it prevents the courts from enforcing, in what would otherwise be a proper Article III case, an actual legal constraint on government conduct.

The Supreme Court's latest major political question doctrine case, *Nixon v. United States*,[36] is somewhat frustrating in that it fails to take a clear position as to whether it invokes the real or bogus political question doctrine. The case concerned the claim by impeached federal judge Walter Nixon that the Senate vio-

---

case actually involving the political question doctrine, Judge Scalia concluded that the doctrine was not involved!

[33] Henkin notes that even where government action is subject to legal constraint and violates that constraint, ordinary principles of equity may cause a court to deny injunctive relief. He regards some political question cases as being explainable on that ground (Henkin, *supra* n. 6, at 617–22). I cannot prove that ordinary principles of equity could not have explained the *Morgan* case, but it seems unlikely that equity would demand that a court tolerate the possibility that the losing candidate is holding a seat in Congress. Cf. *Powell v. McCormack,* 395 U.S. 486 (1969).

[34] Wayne McCormack, *The Political Question Doctrine—Jurisprudentially*, 70 U. Det. Mercy L. Rev. 793, 795 (1993); see also Wayne McCormack, *The Justiciability Myth and the Concept of Law*, 14 Hastings Const. L. Q. 595, 614, 623 (1987). Professor McCormack also says that the result of calling an issue a political question is that "there are not and never could be any judicially-enforceable constraints" on the action—a different, and tautologically true, statement. Professor McCormack equates "legal constraints" with "judicially-enforceable constraints," see 70 U. Det. Mercy L. Rev. at 822 ("[I]f a court is not willing to enforce a provision or principle, then that provision or principle is not law."), but *Morgan* illustrates the difference between them. The law—specifically, the law set forth in the Constitution—requires a house of Congress deciding a disputed congressional election to seat the winner, but the D.C. Circuit determined that law to be judicially unenforceable.

[35] Louis Seidman, *This Essay is Brilliant/This Essay is Stupid: Positive and Negative Self-Reference in Constitutional Practice and Theory*, 46 UCLA L. Rev. 501, 529 n. 60 (1998). In fairness, Professor Seidman may be referring only to the political question doctrine "in the form used in *Nixon v. United States*[, 506 U.S. 224 (1993)]," which could be construed as a bogus political question doctrine case. See *id.* But if the sentence quoted in the text above is meant to be unqualified, *Morgan* shows it to be incorrect.

[36] 506 U.S. 224 (1993).

lated its constitutional obligation to "try" his impeachment when it assigned the actual taking of evidence to a Senate committee.[37] The Supreme Court affirmed dismissal of Nixon's complaint on the basis of the political question doctrine.

Some of the statements in the Court's opinion suggest that the Court was invoking the real political question doctrine; that is, it held that the constitutional constraints imposed by the requirement that the Senate "try" impeachments are not judicially enforceable. The Court noted that the Constitution gives the Senate the "sole" power to try impeachments;[38] the Court held that the word "sole" has "considerable significance" and indicates that the Senate is to act "'independently and without assistance or interference.'"[39] The Court reasoned that impeachment could not properly serve as a check on the judiciary if judges could review and nullify impeachment trials.[40] The Court also determined that the difficulties in granting relief (difficulties that would be particularly severe following impeachment and conviction of the president) counseled against justiciability.[41] All of these arguments suggested that the Court was holding that even if the Constitution constrains the procedures that the Senate may use to "try" an impeachment, no court can enforce those constraints.

On the other hand, other statements in the Court's opinion suggest that the Court held that the constitutional provision that the Senate shall "try" impeachments simply does not impose any constraints on the procedures that the Senate may use in an impeachment trial. The Court looked at dictionary definitions of the word "try" and concluded that "we cannot say that the Framers used the word 'try' as an implied limitation on the method by which the Senate might proceed in trying impeachments."[42] It also noted the three specific, constitutionally imposed constraints on impeachment trial procedure[43] and concluded that their precise "nature suggests that the Framers did not intend to impose additional limitations on the form of the Senate proceedings by the use of the word 'try.'"[44] These statements suggest the possibility that *Nixon* is a bogus political question case that really just held that the plaintiff's claim was meritless.[45] Indeed, it is hard to see what business the Court would have had even investigating the meaning of the word "try" to the extent that it did if, as is suggested by the Court's other language, the selection of impeachment trial procedures is a political question wholly com-

---

[37] See U.S. Const., art. I sec. 3, cl. 6; 506 U.S. at 226–28.

[38] U.S. Const., art. I, sec. 3, cl. 6; 506 U.S. at 230–31.

[39] 506 U.S. at 231 [quoting *Webster's Third New International Dictionary* 2168 (1971)].

[40] *Id.*, at 234–35.

[41] *Id.*, at 236.

[42] 506 U.S. at 230.

[43] The senators must be on oath, a two-thirds vote is required for conviction, and, when the president is tried, the chief justice presides. U.S. Const., art. I, sec. 3, cl. 6; 506 U.S. at 230.

[44] 506 U.S. at 230.

[45] Some scholars interpret the *Nixon* case just this way. See, e.g., Seidman, *supra* n. 35, at 529.

mitted to the Senate for resolution. Thus, while it is possible that *Nixon* demonstrates the continued viability of the real political question doctrine, the case may also be a mere bogus political question case.[46]

C. The Importance of the Distinction

The foregoing discussion shows that the phrase "political question doctrine" covers two entirely different situations: in one, it is no more than a needlessly complicated way to say that any plaintiff must lose who does not state some reason why a defendant's challenged actions are unlawful; in the other, it states that courts must sometimes stay their hand even when the defendant's actions *are* unlawful. Two such different situations should have different names. Using the same name for both can only cause confusion.

Even worse, applying the same doctrine to both situations must confound attempts to decide whether we should have a political question doctrine or not. If some people understand the doctrine to mean that courts ought to dismiss cases in which plaintiffs challenge government actions that are not subject to legal constraint, then discussion of the doctrine is hopeless. Who could be against that? *Of course* a court should dismiss a case in which the plaintiff challenges the president's decision to veto a bill as misguided or claims that the government must run the economy for the benefit of farmers. There's nothing to discuss.

Moreover, arguments supporting dismissals in such bogus political question doctrine cases may be perfectly valid (since such cases should certainly be dismissed), yet have no application to real political question doctrine cases, because of the very different circumstances that such cases present. And yet, because the same name is used for both, one might easily be confused into thinking that an argument that supports dismissal in bogus political question cases shows that the real political question doctrine should be preserved. When this happens, the bogus political question doctrine becomes more than a complicated but harmless affectation; it is pernicious.

The political question doctrine should, therefore, be banished from cases where it does no work. It should be reserved for cases in which the challenged government action is, or at least might be, subject to a legal constraint on which the plaintiff relies, but in which a court believes that it cannot enforce the con-

---

[46] One final possibility is worth noting: perhaps the Court was saying that the word "try" *might* impose limitations on the procedures that the Senate may use in trying an impeachment, but that it would be inappropriate for the Court to decide the question one way or the other, because the legal constraints imposed by the word, if there are any, are not judicially enforceable. If that is what the Court is saying, I would characterize the case as a real political question case. Such a disposition would leave open the possibility that the Court is declining to enforce actual legal constraints on government action, which would distinguish the case from a bogus political question case, in which a court dismisses because the challenged government action is simply not subject to any legal constraints (or at least, any that the plaintiff has invoked).

straint. As to that conclusion, the court might be right or wrong, but at least there is an issue to discuss.

II. The Judicial Process and the Political Process

Once it is understood that the real political question doctrine forecloses courts from enforcing actual legal constraints on government behavior, the doctrine raises an obvious and pressing question: how will those constraints get enforced, if at all? The very essence of our Constitution is usually thought to lie in the constraints that it imposes.[47] As Chief Justice Marshall observed in *Marbury v. Madison*, "[t]o what purpose are powers limited, and to what purpose is that limitation committed to writing; if these limits may, at any time, be passed by those intended to be restrained?"[48] Alexander Bickel pointed out that Marshall's argument does not immediately prove that the Constitution's constraints must be *judicially* enforceable,[49] but still, the Constitution's constraints on the political branches are supposed to be real constraints, not mere hortatory admonitions. Under the American doctrine of judicial review, the normal enforcement mechanism for these constraints is for courts to treat the Constitution as law that courts may enforce in cases that come before them.[50] The political question doctrine's departure from this normal pattern is immediately troubling and demands a justification.

This essay focuses on one argument that courts sometimes use in addressing this difficulty. Courts sometimes suggest that the political question doctrine does not destroy the requisite enforceability of constitutional constraints, because the Constitution can still be enforced, as Bickel put it, "ultimately and finally [by] the people through the electoral process."[51] That is, if political actors should violate legal constraints on their behavior, the people are not without a remedy, even if the political question doctrine blocks a judicial remedy. The people can always vote the offending politicians out of office.

The Supreme Court articulated this view most clearly in *United States v. Richardson*, in which it declined to consider the plaintiff's claim that the Statement and Account Clause of the Constitution required the publication of the

---

[47] Courts sometimes apply the political question doctrine to nonconstitutional constraints on government behavior, e.g., *Smith v. Reagan,* 844 F.2d 195, 200 (4th Cir. 1988) (holding that plaintiffs' claim under the Hostage Act, 22 U.S.C. § 1732, presented a nonjusticiable political question), but this essay focuses on constitutional constraints.

[48] *Marbury v. Madison,* 5 U.S. 137, 176 (1803).

[49] Alexander Bickel, *The Least Dangerous Branch: The Supreme Court at the Bar of Politics* 3 (1962).

[50] E.g., Laurence Tribe, *American Constitutional Law* 367 (3d ed. 2000); Larry D. Kramer, *The Supreme Court, 2000 Term, Foreword: We the Court,* 115 Harv. L. Rev. 1, 8 (2001).

[51] Bickel, *supra* n. 49, at 3.

budget of the Central Intelligence Agency.[52] Although the Court based its dismissal on its determination that the plaintiff lacked standing to sue, the case is appropriately considered here because the Court's decision was so broad as to suggest strongly that no one could ever have standing to seek enforcement of the Statement and Account Clause.[53] As Professor Tushnet has observed, such a decision "blur[s] the lines between standing law and the political question doctrine" and "comes very close to asserting that the question presented was a political one."[54]

In justifying its decision that the Statement and Account Clause would effectively be insusceptible of judicial enforcement, the Court expressly suggested that the plaintiff, although debarred from suit, might use the electoral process to remedy what he perceived as a constitutional violation:

> It can be argued that if respondent is not permitted to litigate this issue, no one can do so. In a very real sense, the absence of any particular individual or class to litigate these claims gives support to the argument that the subject matter is committed to the surveillance of Congress, and ultimately to the political process. . . . The Constitution created a representative Government with the representatives directly responsible to their constituents at stated periods of two, four, and six years; that the Constitution does not afford a judicial remedy does not, of course, completely disable the citizen who is not satisfied with the 'ground rules' established by the Congress for reporting expenditures of the Executive Branch. Lack of standing within the narrow confines of Art. III jurisdiction does not impair the right to assert his views in the political forum or at the polls. Slow, cumbersome, and unresponsive though the traditional electoral process may be thought at times, our system provides for changing members of the political branches when dissatisfied citizens convince a sufficient number of their fellow electors that elected representatives are delinquent in performing duties committed to them.[55]

Other courts have echoed this suggestion that the electoral process provides the appropriate enforcement mechanism for legal constraints that cannot be judicially enforced and have applied it specifically to political question doctrine cases. The D.C. Circuit, for example, invoked this argument in its opinion in the Walter Nixon impeachment case. Judge Edwards, in his dissenting opinion, argued that if

---

[52] 418 U.S. 166 (1974). The Statement and Account Clause provides that "a regular Statement and Account of the Receipts and Expenditures of all public Money shall be published from time to time." U.S. Const, art. I, sec. 9, cl. 7. Richardson, a U.S. taxpayer, asserted that Congress had violated the clause by providing that expenditures of the Central Intelligence Agency need not be published. The Supreme Court ordered the case dismissed.

[53] *Id.* at 418 (quoted *infra*). But see *Halperin v. Central Intelligence Agency,* 629 F.2d 144 (D.C. Cir. 1980) (reaching merits of constitutionality of statute exempting CIA's budget from publication where the plaintiff had sought the budget under the Freedom of Information Act).

[54] Mark Tushnet, *Law and Prudence in the Law of Justiciability: The Transformation and Disappearance of the Political Question Doctrine,* 80 N.C. L. Rev 1203, 1214 (2002).

[55] 418 U.S. at 179.

impeachments pose nonjusticiable political questions, then the Senate might adopt a rule allowing it to convict and remove impeached officers by a mere majority vote.[56] The court replied that "if the senators try to ignore the clear requirement of a two-thirds vote for conviction, they will have to contend with public outrage that will ultimately impose its sanction at the ballot box."[57] Similarly, in affirming dismissal of the election challenge in *Morgan v. United States*, the D.C. Circuit noted that "a substantial degree of responsibility is still provided by regular elections, [and] the interim demands of public opinion."[58] Likewise, the Seventh Circuit, affirming dismissal in *Schroder v. Bush* (discussed above), approvingly quoted the district court's remark that "[p]laintiffs' remedies are at the polling place, not the courts."[59]

---

[56] *Nixon v. United States*, 938 F.2d 239, 256 (D.C. Cir. 1991) (Edwards, J., dissenting in part and concurring in the judgment), aff'd, 506 U.S. 224 (1993).

[57] *Id.* at 246. The court also remarked that "[i]t does not help establish justiciability to pose hypotheticals of outrageous behavior by a coordinate branch." *Id.* It is, of course, somewhat difficult to imagine that the Senate would blatantly ignore the two-thirds voting requirement for impeachment proceedings. It is not, however, impossible to imagine that nontrivial questions might arise in the requirement's application. What if, of 100 senators present for an impeachment vote, sisty-six vote "guilty," thirty-three vote "not guilty," and one votes "present" or declines to vote? The constitutional text would seem pretty clearly to preclude a conviction ("no person shall be convicted without the concurrence of two thirds of the members present," U.S. Const., art. I, sec. 3, cl. 6), but it is not impossible to imagine that the presiding officer would rule that a vote of sixty-six "guilty" and thirty-three "not guilty" is a two-thirds vote to convict. A question might also arise from a senator's unconventional vote, such as Senator Arlen Specter's vote of "not proven, therefore not guilty" on the impeachment of President Clinton. See Peter Baker and Helen Dewar, "Clinton Acquitted; 2 Impeachment Articles Fail to Win Senate Majority; Five Republicans Join Democrats In Voting Down Both Charges," *Washington Post* (Feb. 13, 1999), A1.

The D.C. Circuit left open the possibility that a claim that the Senate violated the two-thirds requirement would be justiciable (938 F.2d at 246 n. 2). Some language in the Supreme Court's opinion suggests that it too left that possibility open, but other language in the opinion suggests that the political question doctrine would foreclose such a claim. As discussed earlier, some passages in the Supreme Court's *Nixon* opinion contrast the clarity of the three specific constitutional requirements for impeachment trials with the open-ended nature of the word "try"; these passages hint that a claim that the Senate violated the specific requirements might be justiciable. Other parts of the opinion make arguments that are independent of the nature of the alleged defect in an impeachment trial (such as that judicial review would prevent impeachment from serving as a check on the judicial branch, that there is a compelling need for finality in impeachment cases, and that it would be difficult to fashion relief); these parts suggest that the courts could never review any judgment of conviction in an impeachment case, even if the Senate violated a clear rule such as the two-thirds requirement.

[58] *Morgan v. United States,* 801 F.2d 445, 450 (D.C. Cir. 1986).

[59] 263 F.3d 1169, 1171 (10th Cir. 2001). For more similar statements in political question doctrine cases, see, e.g., *Smith v. Reagan,* 844 F.2d 195, 200 (4th Cir. 1988) (holding that plaintiffs' claim under the Hostage Act, 22 U.S.C. § 1732, presented a nonjusticiable political question; "[a]ccountability lies in oversight by Congress or in criticism from the electorate, but not in the judgments of the courts."); *Flynn v. Shultz,* 748 F.2d 1186 (7th Cir.

Scholars, too, have invoked this argument in defense of the political question doctrine. Rachel Barkow, for example, asks, "are there not some constitutional questions that should be answered by the political branches precisely because these branches are accountable to the people?"[60] She notes statements from the Framing era suggesting that "[i]f the Congress makes laws inconsistent with the Constitution . . . [a] universal resistance will ensue," and that "[t]he ability to vote a member [of Congress] or the president out of office 'will prove a security to [the people's] liberties, and a most important check to the power of the general government.'"[61] By contrast, she notes, because Supreme Court Justices hold office for life, "the people cannot express their discontent or satisfaction at the ballot box" when the Court improperly asserts control over what ought to be a political decision.[62] Indeed, Larry Kramer, similarly relying on historical materials, suggests that the Constitution's framers conceived of popular measures, most particularly elections, and not judicial review, as the primary enforcement mechanism for the entire Constitution.[63]

Reliance on the electoral process forms but a small part of arguments made in defense of the political question doctrine. Courts typically use the argument as a mere fillip, with the main analysis going to the *Baker v. Carr* factors.[64] Professor Barkow, too, had many other more important arguments to offer.[65] Still, it is worth examining this argument in detail and seeing exactly what is wrong with it, because its refutation provides useful insights.

1984) (also holding that claims under the Hostage Act present nonjusticiable political questions; "the failure of the president to take any action after a finding of a wrongful detention is made is not remediable by the courts, nor, perhaps, even Congress, but solely by the electorate"). For similar statements not actually involving the political question doctrine, see *Troxel v. Granville*, 530 U.S. 57, 91–92 (2000) (Scalia, J., dissenting) ("[W]hile I would think it entirely compatible with the commitment to representative democracy set forth in the founding documents to argue, in legislative chambers or in electoral campaigns, that the State has *no power* to interfere with parents' authority over the rearing of their children, I do not believe that the power which the Constitution confers upon me as a judge entitles me to deny legal effect to laws that (in my view) infringe upon what is (in my view) that unenumerated right."); *Collinson v. Gott*, 895 F.2d 994, 1006 (4th Cir. 1990) (Wilkinson, J., concurring) ("[If the defendant] overstepped the boundary of sound judgment, he should be called to account, not under § 1983, but at the ballot box.").

[60] Barkow, *supra* n. 4, at 327.

[61] *Id.* (quoting 2 *Elliot's Debates* at 168; 4 *Elliot's Debates* at 71).

[62] *Id.*, at 297.

[63] See Kramer, *supra* n. 50, at 26–27, 72–73.

[64] See, e.g., *Schroder*, 263 F.3d at 1171–76; *Morgan*, at 801 F.2d at 447–50.

[65] Barkow, *supra* n. 4, at 300–35.

A. The Electoral Process as a Substitute for Judicial Remedies

The argument noted above suggests that the electoral process may provide an appropriate substitute for a judicial remedy. This suggestion cannot, however, be sustained. It ignores a host of problems that must inevitably arise in attempts to use the electoral process to enforce legal constraints on political behavior. Examination of these problems reminds us of the fundamental differences between political and judicial remedies—differences that go to the heart of our system of judicial review.

To begin with, the suggestion that citizens should use the electoral process to redress nonjusticiable constitutional grievances will often be entirely impractical. Perhaps Mr. Richardson, after being turned away by the judicial system, could stir up some political interest in the question of whether the United States should publish the CIA's budget, but the notion that he could use this issue to turn the president or members of Congress out of office is plainly untenable. The issue is simply not of sufficient importance; no substantial number of voters could ever be expected to cast their votes based on it. It would be equally difficult—even for one who agreed with the merits of his constitutional claim—to imagine former Judge Nixon's "convinc[ing] a sufficient number of [his] fellow electors that elected representatives [were] delinquent"[66] in failing to try his impeachment before the full Senate. As these cases show, violations of the Constitution may involve rather obscure issues that would not likely have much, if any, resonance in actual election campaigns.

Nor would the case necessarily be different for truly important issues. Even in the case of the most momentous constitutional violations, there may be no practical way to use a politician's unconstitutional actions to engineer his or her subsequent electoral defeat. Few constitutional claims could be more serious than the claim that the 2000 presidential election was stolen, but voters who believe that it was may have little chance of putting the issue to work electorally. Professor Barkow, in criticizing the Supreme Court's decision to resolve the *Bush v. Gore* case, argues that the Article II questions involved in the case may have been political questions that the Court should have left for Congress to resolve,[67] and she observes that the Court, by taking the decision away from the political process, left the people with no way to "express their discontent or satisfaction at the ballot box."[68] Suppose, however, that the Court had held the dispute nonjusticiable and left it for congressional resolution; would voters have used the ballot box to "express their discontent or satisfaction"? The earliest opportunity to do so was two years away, and the election dispute, momentous as it was, was subsequently drowned out by the even more momentous terrorist attacks of September 11, 2001.

---

[66] *Richardson*, 418 U.S. at 179.

[67] Barkow, *supra* n. 4, at 300. Professor Barkow does not quite conclude that the questions *were* political questions; she states that "the Article II question in the *Bush* cases presented a strong candidate for application of the political question doctrine." *Id.*

[68] *Id.*, at 297.

Even if Congress, rather than the Supreme Court, had resolved the 2000 election controversy, there seems little reason to believe that voters would have had any practical way to turn the 2002 or 2004 elections into a referendum on the validity of Congress's decision.

This impracticality of using the electoral process to air constitutional grievances is a symptom of several vital differences between the judicial and political processes. Some such differences are very practical in nature: for example, attempting to use the electoral process to redress a constitutional grievance would obviously require a tremendous investment of time, effort, and resources, probably orders of magnitude beyond the investment necessary for litigation. There are also, however, more theoretically significant differences that emphasize the unsuitability of the electoral process for the resolution of legal grievances no matter what resources might be put into the effort.

First, the judicial process is *focused*. A plaintiff comes to court with a specific claim of right, and the judicial process provides a proceeding for the resolution of that specific claim. By contrast, the electoral process is never focused on just one issue. Congressional and presidential elections are not referendums. Each candidate always embodies a package of positions on the numerous issues facing the electorate at any given time, plus general qualities such as trustworthiness, experience, skill, and charm. For this reason, even if voters wanted to use an election to express their views on alleged constitutional violations, the process of voting would not give them a clear opportunity to do so. Voters cannot vote on discrete issues; they can vote only on the whole package that a candidate represents.[69]

Indeed, what if two groups of voters were simultaneously attempting to use an election to remedy two different alleged constitutional violations, each of which had been held to involve a nonjusticiable political question? Each candidate for a given office might regard one of the alleged violations as a real violation that Congress should rectify, but the other as constitutionally permissible government behavior. If the candidates had conflicting views as to which alleged violation was really a problem, voters might be able to express their dissatisfaction with one of the alleged violations only by ostensibly expressing approval for the other. Again, the upshot is that election campaigns do not present a genuine opportunity for voters to resolve legal issues.

Moreover, even if a voter's attempt to remedy constitutional violations through the electoral process were somehow successful, the legal situation would not be much different. The unfocused nature of elections points to another problem that must plague even successful efforts to right constitutional violations through the ballot box: the electoral process is *inscrutable*. Let us imagine that a would-be plaintiff, finding her lawsuit blocked by the political question doctrine,

---

[69] Donald Doernberg makes this point in his comments on *United States v. Richardson*. See Donald L. Doernberg, *"We the People": John Locke, Collective Constitutional Rights, and Standing to Challenge Government Action*, 73 Cal. L. Rev. 52, 99 (1985) ("[T]he political process . . . is particularly unresponsive to single-issue candidacies, especially at the national level. The more diverse the electorate and the more complicated the issue facing it, the less any single issue is likely to be dispositive in the electoral process.").

attempts to make the alleged unconstitutionality of government action an issue in a subsequent election; more than that, let us imagine that, against all odds, she is successful! Her issue captures electoral attention, and the incumbent she attacks, who had brought about the allegedly unconstitutional action, is defeated at the polls. Now what?

The problem is that one can never really know *why* the incumbent was defeated. Even after the bum is duly thrown out, one is left to read electoral tealeaves and watch pundits opine on the "meaning" of the election. Perhaps the electorate voted the losing candidate out of office because of its anger at his allegedly unconstitutional actions, but, on the other hand, perhaps not. Perhaps the election was really about economic conditions, or national defense, or the challenger's personal charm, or a scandal afflicting the incumbent's political party, or any of a hundred other possibilities.

This hypothetical illustrates another critical difference between the electoral and the judicial process. A fundamental attribute of judicial decisions is that they come with a statement of reasons.[70] One knows not only *who* wins, but *why*; the process not only yields a result, but articulates a norm.[71] By contrast, even in the event that someone successfully used the electoral process to air a constitutional grievance, we could never really know it. The electoral process yields only a result. It does not tell us what caused that result, and usually there are so many contributing factors that it would be impossible to say that the election had decided a constitutional question. The electoral process does not articulate norms.

Closely related to this point is the further problem that the electoral process *does not operate within a system of precedent*. This problem follows, in part, from the last one: because elections are inscrutable and have no ascertainable meaning, they cannot set binding precedents for subsequent elections. Even if voters wanted to adhere to decisions on constitutional issues made via elections, and somehow agreed to do so, there would be no ascertainable decisions for voters to follow.

Moreover, of course, voters have no such agreement. Each election presents a new set of candidates and issues. Even assuming that, somehow, voters managed to turn some members of Congress out of office for their perceived constitutional misbehavior, nothing guarantees a similar result the next time the issue arises. Political actors may, of course, be chastened by experience—no president, for example, has repeated President Franklin Roosevelt's ill-fated attempt to pack the Supreme Court by adding additional justices—but, with regard to constitutional provisions that are not susceptible to judicial enforcement, the political branches

---

[70] In articulating the factors that constitute elements of a fair hearing, Judge Friendly remarked that he would put the requirement of a statement of reasons for the result "close to the top rather than near the bottom of the scale." Henry J. Friendly, *Some Kind of Hearing*, 123 U. Pa. L. Rev. 1267, 1292 (1975).

[71] Cf. Richard H. Fallon, Jr., *Some Confusions about Due Process, Judicial Review, and Constitutional Remedies*, 93 Colum. L. Rev. 309, 371 (1993) ("Due process doctrine assumes that there is less of a systemic interest in ensuring correct fact-finding than in achieving judicial articulation and enforcement of generally applicable constitutional norms.").

could repeat behavior even if, in the past, it had stirred up voter anger. A new electorate would have to decide what to do.

For this reason, elections are not capable of finally resolving constitutional questions and providing long-term redress for constitutional grievances in a fashion comparable to the judicial process. Of course, one might point out that, because courts may overrule past decisions, the judicial process never absolutely resolves constitutional questions either. Still, the role of precedent is obviously quite different in the two processes. A president or a member of Congress contemplating action of a kind that the courts have held to be unconstitutional will have a quite strong expectation that the action will be unsuccessful. With regard to actions raising nonjusticiable constitutional questions that in the past led to electoral defeat (even assuming one could accurately identify the causes of past electoral defeats), a politician may sense that the temper of the electorate has changed and that comparable action might not be electorally punished.

Finally, the electoral process is of course *majoritarian*: the electorate will pick the candidate that a majority of voters like best.[72] This is a virtue from the standpoint of democracy, but with regard to attempts to use the process to redress constitutional grievances, it poses a problem: the majority might like a candidate best precisely because of the candidate's willingness to ignore constitutional constraints on majoritarianism. A likely reason for politicians to violate constitutional norms in the first place is that they sense some political advantage in doing so.[73] Thus, while a charge of constitutional violation might have some "debate value" that could be used in the electoral process,[74] that debate value could be overwhelmed by the political popularity of the constitutional violation.

Moreover, whether or not a particular constitutional violation is in fact politically popular, the whole purpose of putting constraints into the Constitution was to put certain matters beyond majoritarian political control.[75] The judicial process provides a forum to which plaintiffs can come with a claim of right that is independent of majority support. To require plaintiffs to resort to the political process is to require them to win current majoritarian support for a point that, if valid, should be conclusive whether it has such support or not.

---

[72] Actually, there are numerous impediments to the implementation of majoritarianism in the electoral process, such as the electoral college system in presidential elections, the disproportionate ability of wealthy voters to persuade their fellow citizens, and the possibility of a victory, in a three-way congressional or presidential race, of a candidate who would be the last choice for a majority of voters. But the point here is that the electoral process is predominantly majoritarian, unlike the judicial process.

[73] See Bickel, *supra* n. 49, at 25 ("when the pressure for immediate results is strong enough and emotions ride high enough, men will ordinarily prefer to act on expediency rather than take the long view").

[74] See Mulhern, *supra* n. 3, at 153 n. 202.

[75] *Marbury v. Madison,* 5 U.S. 137, 176 (1803); Doernberg, *supra* n. 69, at 99–100; Dana S. Treister, *Standing to Sue the Government: Are Separation of Powers Principles Really Being Served,* 67 S. Cal. L. Rev. 689, 715 (1994).

This point, incidentally, demonstrates once again the vital importance of maintaining a clear distinction between real political question doctrine cases and bogus political question doctrine cases. The argument that plaintiffs should seek their remedy at the ballot box is, in fact, perfectly appropriate for the latter. Where government action is not subject to legal constraint (the hallmark of a bogus political question case), pure political struggle among competing forces legitimately determines the government's choice of action. The Constitution provides no answer to innumerable vital questions about the structure of our society, such as whether taxes should be high or low, whether the government should help farmers or let them battle market forces unaided, or whether the president should sign or veto any given bill. A plaintiff who goes to court over such a question is quite properly told to turn to the political process instead of the judicial one. The court is simply saying that the question presented is one that our legal system entrusts to unconstrained majoritarian decision. Thus, for example, the Tenth Circuit's comment that the farmer plaintiffs in *Schroder v. Bush* should seek relief "at the polling place, not the courts"[76] was exactly correct.

The appropriateness of such an argument in bogus political doctrine cases may, however, have the unfortunate consequence of causing courts to use the same argument in *real* political question doctrine cases, which present entirely different circumstances. The essence of a real political question case is that the plaintiff is seeking to enforce an actual legal constraint on government action. A court telling the plaintiff that his remedy lies "at the ballot box" is saying that plaintiff must attempt to use the electoral process to enforce a legal constraint on that very process. The result is that plaintiffs are entitled to enforce constitutional constraints on political actions only if they can "convince a sufficient number of their fellow electors that elected representatives are delinquent,"[77] but the representatives may have taken the actions precisely because they were likely to win votes despite their violation of constitutional norms. Usually, we think of constitutional constraints as existing for the very purpose of reining in the political process in cases where short-term political expediency might cause government officials to take actions that deviate from our constitutional values.[78]

The use of the "political question" label for these two very different situations is therefore doubly unfortunate. It does more than simply lead to the application of an unnecessary layer of doctrine in those bogus political question cases that could be dismissed for failure to state a claim. It creates an inappropriate line of thinking that may spill over into the real political question cases. Courts accustomed to telling plaintiffs—rightly—that they should be organizing electorally rather than litigating bogus question cases may erroneously apply this same point in cases concerning legal constraints designed to protect plaintiffs from the results of the electoral process.

---

[76] 263 F.3d at 1171 (quoting district court's opinion).

[77] *Richardson*, 418 U.S. at 179.

[78] Bickel, *supra* n. 49, at 23–28.

In any event, for all of the reasons stated above, the suggestion that voters might use the electoral process to remedy nonjusticiable constitutional grievances is inappropriate. The suggestion will often be entirely impractical, the electoral process provides no focused mechanism for raising legal questions, it leads to an inscrutable result, and, even if it is successful, it may need to be fought afresh every election cycle. Possibly worst of all, the majoritarian election process provides a poor mechanism for the enforcement of restraints on majoritarianism.

B. The Political Process As a Substitute for Judicial Remedies

Perhaps, one might argue, the suggestions that voters may use the electoral process to remedy nonjusticiable constitutional grievances should not be taken quite so literally. Although courts have expressly referred to the remedy of "the ballot box" and the possibility of turning politicians out of office because of unconstitutional (but not judicially remediable) misbehavior, perhaps what courts really meant was that voters could attempt to obtain redress using the political process more generally, not specifically the electoral process.[79] Voters could simply agitate for change through legislation. Politicians might want to keep special-interest voters happy in the legislative process without testing their ultimate electoral strength.

Moreover, one might argue that the legislative process avoids some of the problems associated with the electoral process that were discussed above. In particular, the legislative process can be more focused and less inscrutable than the electoral process. Particular issues, such as whether the CIA's budget should be published, can be brought to a clean, up-or-down vote. They need not always be entangled with other issues, as is inevitable in elections, and a particular legislative vote may provide a clear indication of the political judgment as to the constitutionality of the measure involved.

However, while the legislative process is different from the electoral process, it shares most of the problems noted above for the electoral process and adds at least one additional, very important problem not found in the judicial or electoral process. The electoral process, for all of its difficulties, is mandatory; elections are held at required intervals. The judicial process, too, has the vital characteristic that plaintiffs can invoke it as of right. As Chief Justice Marshall remarked in *Cohens v. Virginia*, "[t]he judiciary cannot, as the legislature may, avoid a measure because it approaches the confines of the Constitution. We cannot pass it by, because it is doubtful."[80] The judiciary is obliged to give relief to a plaintiff who is entitled to it.[81]

---

[79] See, e.g., *Richardson*, 418 U.S. at 179 (referring to the plaintiff's right to assert his views "in the political forum *or* at the polls") (emphasis added).

[80] *Cohens v. Virginia*, 19 U.S. 264, 404 (1821).

[81] Of course, one aspect of the political question doctrine is that, at least according to some, it affords courts discretion to decline to grant a remedy when they regard doing so as

There is, however, no guaranteed way to invoke the legislative process. Citizens can always ask for legislation, but there is no way to compel Congress to bring any matter to a vote. A court faced with a claim (in a properly posed case) that a statute is unconstitutional has a duty to rule on the claim—perhaps rejecting it, of course, but not ignoring it altogether. A legislature faced with a claim that it should change an existing statute because it is unconstitutional may choose to ignore the issue indefinitely.[82] Those making the claim would then be thrown back on the electoral process, with all of its attendant difficulties.[83]

Moreover, the legislative process also, like the electoral process, lacks a system of precedent: what one Congress does, the next may undo. In addition, the legislative process, although capable of stating reasons for its actions, is not required to do so; Congress may pass a law with or without adopting official findings and purposes, and the legislature's rejection of a law certainly does not necessarily imply a judgment as to its constitutional validity. Similarly, the legislative

---

inexpedient. E.g., Bickel, *supra* n. 49, at 187, 197. Moreover, as Henkin observed, courts may consider the demands of equity in deciding whether to grant certain forms of relief. But the point here is that the judiciary does not have, as the legislature does, a general discretion to do nothing in response to petitions for redress.

[82] Cf. Kramer, *supra* n. 50, at 27 (noting that American colonists first challenged the Stamp Act by petitioning Parliament, but Parliament ignored the petitions and failed even to consider them).

[83] A similar difficulty would attend the possibility of seeking relief in the executive branch, by simply calling the executive's attention to the allegedly unconstitutional practice and asking that it stop. Executive officials, one might argue, would be bound by their constitutional oaths to consider and act on the claim of unconstitutionality (possibly rejecting the claim on its merits, but not ignoring it). In practice, however, the executive does not have a tradition, comparable to the judiciary's, of regarding itself as having a mandatory duty to respond to such claims. The Department of Justice's Office of Legal Counsel (OLC) does address focused legal issues, provides reasons for its decisions, and operates within a system of precedent. See H. Jefferson Powell, *The President's Authority over Foreign Affairs: An Executive Branch Perspective*, 67 Geo. Wash. L. Rev. 527, 535–37 (1999); John O. McGinnis, *Models of the Opinion Function of the Attorney General: A Normative, Descriptive, and Historical Prolegomenon*, 15 Cardozo L. Rev. 375, 426 (1993); but cf. Harold Hongju Koh, *Protecting the Office of Legal Counsel from Itself*, 15 Cardozo L. Rev. 513, 517–23 (1993) (lamenting OLC's failure to publish all of its opinions and to respect precedent sufficiently). A private citizen, however, has no mandatory way to invoke the OLC opinion process. One may call a cabinet officer's attention to allegedly unconstitutional action by his or her department, and the officer may choose to respond, including choosing to seek OLC's advice, but the officer may also decline to act. Indeed, even when its opinion is sought by a government agency, OLC may decide that controversial opinion requests should "be allowed to languish." (McGinnis, *supra*, at 427). Also, if the agency involved is acting pursuant to a statutory command, the officer will almost certainly decline to consider the statute's constitutionality, because "[a]djudication of the constitutionality of congressional enactments has generally been thought beyond the jurisdiction of administrative agencies." *Johnson v. Robison*, 415 U.S. 361, 368 (1974) [quoting *Oestereich v. Selective Service Bd.*, 393 U.S. 233, 242 (1968) (Harlan, J., concurring in result)].

process *may* provide a clean up-or-down vote on a particular issue, but frequently it entangles many issues together in a single bill, thus denying clear opportunities for resolution of particularized questions of constitutionality. And the legislative process, like the electoral process, is majoritarian in nature and can hardly be expected to serve as a good enforcement mechanism for those constitutional provisions that are intended to restrain majoritarianism. ***

One might argue—in fact, Justice Scalia has argued—that justiciability doctrines serve to distinguish those constitutional provisions that restrain majoritarianism by giving individuals rights against the majority from those constitutional provisions that grant rights to the people as a whole, to be exercised by a majority of the people. Justice Scalia (when a D.C. Circuit judge) argued that the doctrine of standing, with its rule against the litigation of generalized grievances, "is an essential means of restricting the courts to their assigned role of protecting minority rather than majority interests"[84] Where the majority, expressing its will through the political process, chooses to allow government behavior that involves no harm to individual interests, courts should, Justice Scalia claims, ignore any legal constraints that may be violated; indeed, the majority's ability to choose to allow certain legal constraints to fall into desuetude is, he argues, one of the majoritarian process's useful features.[85]

Of course, there is no guarantee that political questions will involve the kind of widely shared injuries to which Justice Scalia's argument is appropriate.[86] But even where they do, the argument still suffers from the same problem that was pointed out above with regard to the electoral process. The Constitution places certain things beyond majoritarian control; to suggest that the majority may choose when to obey constitutional constraints and when to ignore them drains those constraints of their basic purpose. The best interpretation of the Statement and Account Clause may or may not require the government to publish the CIA's budget, but it is a little hard to fathom what purpose the clause serves if it means no more than "publish that part of the budget which the Congress, acting through the normal political process, decides ought to be published." No constitutional provision is needed to tell Congress that it may publish such part of the budget as it likes; that is the default starting point under Congress's ordinary powers. Justice Scalia's argument turns certain constitutional constraints (the ones that, according to him, protect majority interests rather than individual interests) into admonitions that not only are merely hortatory, but also are pointless, in that, in his view, they do no more than redundantly confirm the majority's ability to do what it likes.

---

[84] Antonin Scalia, *The Doctrine of Standing as an Essential Element of the Separation of Powers*, 17 Suffolk Univ. L. Rev. 881, 895 (1983).

[85] *Id.*, at 896–97.

[86] Judge Nixon's allegedly flawed removal, for example, was not a widely shared injury. (Justice Scalia, it should be noted, made the argument with regard to standing doctrine, not the political question doctrine; the argument is invoked here only in an effort to see if it could support the suggestion that the electoral process may serve as a substitute for the judicial process in political question cases.)

Moreover, the legislative process imposes numerous impediments to the ability of even a majority to work its will. The bicameral division of the legislature, the committee structure and the attendant power given to selected members of Congress, the possibility of filibusters in the Senate, the ever-present press of business, and other obstacles to the passage of legislation considerably weaken the strength of the inference that if a statute that violates a constitutional provision remains on the books, the people must approve of it. Justice Scalia suggests that widely shared injuries (generalized grievances of the *Richardson* type) should be left to the political process for resolution because "[t]here is surely no reason to believe that [such injuries] would not receive fair consideration in the normal political process,"[87] but the obstacles imposed by the political process may thwart the ability of even a majority to obtain something the Constitution was supposed to guarantee for it.

Thus, if by steering plaintiffs with nonjusticiable complaints to the electoral process, courts really meant the political process generally, including the legislative process, the result is not really better than if they meant the electoral process specifically. The general political process provides no mandatory way to raise issues; it does not operate within a system of precedent; its majoritarian nature suggests that, like the electoral process, it will not do a good job of enforcing constraints on majoritarianism; and the obstacles that the political process imposes mean that even a majority may not be able to navigate it successfully.

C. Implications for the political question doctrine

For these reasons, the argument that voters can use the electoral process to remedy constitutional violations should be banished from discussions of the political question doctrine. Even when used as a mere grace note to accompany more important arguments, it strikes a discordant tone. It represents an unfair appeal to our democratic instincts. Seeing the argument flash by in the brief form in which it is usually made, we are invited to think "ah, elections—voting—democracy—that must be good," and to ignore the profound practical and theoretical difficulties that would lie in the path of any attempt to put the point to actual use. The fundamental differences between the judicial and the electoral processes mean that the ability to resort to the electoral process is not an appropriate substitute for judicial relief for constitutional violations.

Of course, this does not prove that the political question doctrine is wrong. The main point of this essay has merely been to refute one argument used in support of that doctrine. It may still be that our Constitution does not permit judicial review of certain claims, even though it provides no adequate substitute for such review.

Still, thinking about what would actually happen if someone tried to use the electoral process to remedy a constitutional grievance perhaps provides an insight

---

[87] Scalia, *supra* n. 84, at 896.

into the more general arguments over the validity of the political question doctrine. Defenders of the political question doctrine often focus on characteristics of the judicial and political branches of government that impact the suitability of the different branches for resolution of constitutional questions. Scholars and courts observe that the political branches have an institutional advantage with regard to certain questions, such as those that require extensive fact-finding or choices between competing policies.[88] The judiciary, these defenders also note, has no monopoly on constitutional interpretation; the Constitution vests the president and members of Congress with interpretive authority that makes the political branches suitable to enforce constitutional norms.[89]

The characteristic of the judiciary most prominently mentioned in these discussions is its political insulation and independence—a characteristic that is said to make the judiciary the appropriate branch to enforce some constitutional constraints, but not others.[90] Examination of the differences between the judicial and the electoral processes, however, brings out other, critical characteristics of the judiciary that strongly impact its suitability for the enforcement of constitutional constraints. These other characteristics—the mandatory nature of the judicial process, its focus on precisely stated issues, its articulation of reasons for decisions, and its use of precedent—all contribute to the way in which judicial review serves to enforce the Constitution.

These other characteristics of judicial review are vital to a system in which constitutional constraints on political action are real constraints and not mere hortatory admonitions. The mandatory nature of the judicial process is obviously vital in that it creates a forum in which constitutional grievances can be aired and in which official decision makers must respond to them.[91] The focused nature of judicial review ensures that constitutional grievances are not lost because of the entanglement with other issues that would inevitably occur in the electoral, and might sometimes occur in the political, processes. The statement of reasons that accompanies judicial decisions ensures that the process articulates constitutional norms so that both the public and political actors can know what constraints the Constitution imposes on government behavior. The system of precedent ensures that once a constitutional norm is established, it will tend to remain established;

---

[88] E.g., Barkow, *supra* n. 4, at 240, 301–02, 329.

[89] Mulhern, *supra* n. 3, at 124–28.

[90] Barkow, *supra* n. 4, at 325–28.

[91] It is for this reason that defenders of the political question doctrine have a good point when they observe that other restrictions on justiciability, such as the standing requirement, may prevent certain constitutional questions from ever coming before the judiciary in a proper Article III case. E.g., Mulhern, *supra* n. 3, at 119–21. A full answer to this point would be too long for this short essay to contain, but the brief response is that there are problems with these other justiciability doctrines as well. See, e.g., Mark Tushnet, *The Sociology of Article III: A Response to Professor Brilmayer*, 93 Harv. L. Rev. 1698, 1706 (1980) (arguing for a "barebones" approach to standing doctrine); Henry Monaghan, *Constitutional Adjudication: The Who and the When*, 82 Yale L. J. 1363 (1973).

while the force of precedent is not absolute, it does mean that constitutional victories once won do not have to be re-fought every election cycle.

These characteristics of judicial review, and their absence from the electoral and political process, must be considered by defenders of the political question doctrine. Defenders need to explain why it is appropriate to entrust the enforcement of constitutional constraints on government behavior to a process that not only, because of its majoritarian nature, seems a poor one for enforcing constraints on majoritarianism, but that lacks certain characteristics that play an important role in enforcing any constraints on government behavior, even constraints that might have majoritarian support. The political question doctrine cuts constitutional constraints off from the process best designed to enforce constraints.

Conclusion

In justifying what he called the "deviant"[92] and "counter-majoritarian"[93] institution of judicial review, Bickel suggested that the courts' insulation from politics puts them in a good position to enforce enduring values when such values conflict with presently expedient measures adopted by political actors.[94] This feature of judicial review—the Constitution's placement of most important societal decisions in the hands of politically accountable actors, subject to review for constitutionality by judges insulated by life tenure—is indeed the chief brilliance of our constitutional system. But there is more to it than that. Judicial review works not only because of the political insulation of judges, but also because of the distinctive nature of the judicial process: because the judicial process is focused, because it is mandatory, because it articulates norms explicitly, and because it operates within a system of precedent. These special characteristics of judicial review, not found in the electoral or legislative processes, impose an additional burden of explanation on those who would defend the way the political question doctrine bars judicial review of constitutional issues. They also demonstrate why defenders of the political question doctrine should not suggest, even as a minor argument, that the electoral or legislative process provides an adequate substitute for judicial review.

---

[92] Bickel, *supra* n. 49, at 18.

[93] *Id.*, at 16.

[94] *Id.*, at 23–28.

About the Authors

David Gray Adler is professor of political science at Idaho State University. A prominent scholar on the subject of presidential war powers, he specializes in public law, the Supreme Court, presidency, and American political thought. Adler is the author, most recently, of the forthcoming, "The Presidency and the Law: The Clinton Legacy." He is completing a book-length manuscript on *United States v. Curtiss-Wright* (1936), and its impact on presidential power, constitutional law, and the conduct of American foreign policy and is researching and writing a book on presidential prerogative. A former president of the Pacific Northwest Political Science Association, he presently serves on the executive council of the Western Political Science Association and the board of directors of the Presidency Research Group, an arm of the American Political Science Association.

Pierre Avril, professor emeritus at the University of Paris II, worked with then *Président du Conseil* Pierre Mendès France from 1955 to 1962 and was a journalist until 1969. He became *professeur agrégé des facultés de droit* in 1972 and taught political science and constitutional law at the universities of Poitiers, Nanterre, and Paris II, as well as the Institut d'études politiques de Paris. He was a member of the *Conseil supérieur de la magistrature* (1998–2002) and served as the chair of the Committee on the Penal Status of the President of the Republic in France (2002). Among his books are *Essais sur les partis politiques*, *Le régime politique de la Ve République*, *Les conventions de la Constitution*, and, with Jean Gicquel, *Droit parlementaire* and *Le Conseil constitutionnel*. He is coeditor, with Jean Gicquel, of the Constitutional Chronicle of the French journal *Pouvoirs*, since 1977.

Rachel E. Barkow is associate professor at New York University School of Law. After graduating with honors from Northwestern University (B.A. 1993), Barkow attended Harvard Law School (J.D. 1996, magna cum laude), where she was an editor of the *Harvard Law Review* and won the Sears Prize. Barkow served as a law clerk to Judge Laurence H. Silberman of the U.S. Court of Appeals for the District of Columbia Circuit, and for Justice Antonin Scalia of the U.S. Supreme Court. Before joining the faculty at NYU, Barkow was an associate at Kellogg, Huber, Hansen, Todd & Evans in Washington, D.C. from 1998–2002. She took a leave from the firm in 2001 to serve as the John M. Olin Fellow in Law at Georgetown University Law Center. Her principal interests include administrative law, criminal law, and the separation of powers.

Bruce E. Cain, Robson Professor of Political Science, director of the Institute of Governmental Studies, UC Berkeley and the UC, Washington Center, came to Berkeley in 1989 from the California Institute of Technology. A graduate of

269

Bowdoin College and a Rhodes Scholar, he received his Ph.D. in political science from Harvard University. His writings include *The Reapportionment Puzzle; The Personal Vote*, with John Ferejohn and Morris Fiorina; and *Congressional Redistricting*, with David Butler. His co-edited books include *Developments in American Politics*, Volume I-IV, with Gillian Peele; *Constitutional Reform in California*, with Roger Noll; and *Voting at the Political Fault Line: California's Experiment with the Blanket Primary* with Elisabeth R. Gerber. Cain has served as a polling consultant for state and senate races; redistricting consultant to the Justice Department, Los Angeles County, San Diego Citizens Commission on Redistricting, City and County of San Francisco, and as Special Master in Arizona's 2002 Legislative Redistricting. He is a political commentator for numerous radio and television stations in Los Angeles and the Bay Area. He received the Zale Award for Outstanding Achievement in Policy Research and Public Service and is a member of the American Academy of Arts and Sciences.

Jesse Choper, Earl Warren Professor of Public Law, served as law clerk to Chief Justice Earl Warren of the U.S. Supreme Court, and taught at the Wharton School of the University of Pennsylvania and the University of Minnesota Law School. He has been a visiting professor at Harvard Law School and Fordham Law School. In 1965 he joined the Boalt Hall faculty and served as dean from 1982 to 1992. He has served on the executive committee of the Association of American Law Schools, and on the executive council of the American Academy of Arts and Sciences (of which he is vice president). He was a national president of the Order of the Coif and is a member of the American Law Institute. He received UC Berkeley's Distinguished Teaching Award and Boalt Hall's Faculty Lifetime Achievement Award. His major publications include the books, *Judicial Review and the National Political Process: A Functional Reconsideration of the Role of the Supreme Court*, which received the Order of the Coif Triennial Book Award in 1982, and *Securing Religious Liberty: Principles for Judicial Interpretation of the Religion Clauses*. Recent publications include the ninth edition of his *Constitutional Law* casebooks; the sixth edition of his *Corporations* casebook; the second edition of *The Supreme Court and Its Justices*.

Erwin Chemerinsky, Alston & Bird Professor of Law and professor of political science, joined the Duke faculty in 2004 after teaching at the University of Southern California Law School and DePaul College of Law He practiced law as a trial attorney, United States Department of Justice, and at Dobrovir, Oakes & Gebhardt in Washington, D.C. He received a B.S. from Northwestern University and a J.D. from Harvard. He is the author of *Federal Jurisdiction; Constitutional Law: Principles and Policies;* and *Interpreting the Constitution*. He writes a regular column on the Supreme Court for *California Lawyer, Los Angeles Daily Journal*, and *Trial Magazine*, is a frequent contributor to newspapers and magazines, and comments on legal issues for national and local media. He has been named one of the top twenty legal thinkers in America and one of the 100 most influential lawyers in California. He frequently argues cases before the United States Supreme Court and the United States Courts of Appeals. He was elected to Los Angeles Charter Reform Commission and served as its Chair.

Louis Fisher is Senior Specialist in Separation of Powers at the Congressional Research Service, the Library of Congress. He joined CRS in 1970 and served as research director of the House Iran-Contra Committee in 1987, writing major sections of the final report. His recent books include *American Constitutional Law, Military Tribunals and Presidential Power*, *Presidential War Power*, and *The Politics of Executive Privilege*. Fisher also co-edited, with Leonard Levy, a four-volume encyclopedia on the American presidency. Fisher has been invited to testify before congressional committees on such topics as war powers, executive privilege, legislative vetoes, the item veto, the balanced budget amendment, CIA whistleblowing, covert spending, the pocket veto, executive lobbying, and recess appointments. The views expressed in this article are personal, not institutional.

John W. Fox, a political anthropologist, researches political organization and ideational change in the U.S., the Arab Middle East and among the Maya of Guatemala. In the U.S., he has focused on the broad generational changes from Colonial times to the present, where the law is seen as one idea system articulated with and attendant to changes in society. Fox was most recently chair of international studies at the American University in Sharjah in the UAE. He has held positions at the University of Pennsylvania, Union College, and Baylor University. His books on changing political organization have been published by Cambridge University Press and the University of New Mexico Press; his most recent volume, *Globalization and the Gulf*, is published by Routledge Publishers. His articles on political process and changing idea systems have appeared in *Current Anthropology*, *American Anthropology*, and *American Antiquity* among others, and chapters have appeared in university press volumes by Oxford University Press and University of Arizona Press.

Richard L. Hasen is the William H. Hannon Distinguished Professor of Law at Loyola Law School in Los Angeles. Hasen clerked for the Honorable David R. Thompson of the United States Court of Appeals for the Ninth Circuit and then worked as a civil appellate lawyer at the Encino firm of Horvitz and Levy. Hasen taught at the Chicago-Kent College of Law, joined Loyola's faculty in 1997 as a visiting professor and became a member of the full-time faculty in 1998. A nationally recognized expert in election law and campaign finance regulation, Hasen is co-author of a leading casebook on election law, co-editor of the quarterly peer-reviewed publication, *Election Law Journal* and a member of the advisory board of the Campaign Legal Center. In 2002, Hasen was named one of the twenty top lawyers in California under age forty by the Los Angeles (and San Francisco) *Daily Journal*. Hasen writes the widely read "Election law blog."

His most recent book, *The Supreme Court and Election Law: Judging Equality from* Baker v. Carr *to* Bush v. Gore, was published by NYU Press in 2003.

Nancy Kassop is professor and chair of the Department of Political Science and International Relations at the State University of New York at New Paltz. She received her B.A. in political science from the University of Pennsylvania and her Ph.D. in politics from New York University. She writes on issues at the intersection of the presidency and law. Her most recent articles are "Not Going Public: George W. Bush and the Presidential Records Act" in Lori Cox Han and Diane J. Heith, eds., *In the Public Domain: Presidents and the Challenge of Public Leadership*; "When Law and Politics Collide: Presidents and the Use of the Twenty-Fifth Amendment" in *Presidential Studies Quarterly*; "The View from the President" in Mark C. Miller and Jeb Barnes, eds., *Making Policy, Making Law: An Interbranch Perspective*; "The White House Counsels Office," co-authored with MaryAnne Borrelli and Karen Hult in Martha J. Kumar and Terry Sullivan, eds., *The White House World: Transitions, Organization and Office Operations*; "The War Power and Its Limits" in *Presidential Studies Quarterly*; and "The Power to Make War" in Katy Harriger, ed., *Separation of Powers: Documents and Commentary*. She is president of the Presidency Research Group organized section of the American Political Science Association.

Nada Mourtada-Sabbah is chair of the Department of International Studies at the American University of Sharjah and visiting professor of public law at the Université Paris II. She received her Ph.D. in public law with distinction from the University of Paris II, and was recently appointed a faculty fellow in the Center for Congressional and Presidential Studies at American University (Washington, D.C.). She is also a research associate with the Thucydides Research Center at the University of Paris. Her books include *Le Privilège de l'Exécutif aux Etats-Unis*, *Les Tribunaux Militaires aux Etats-Unis*, and *Is War a Political Question*, with Louis Fisher. Her articles on the Supreme Court of the United States, the political question doctrine, military tribunals and the war powers have appeared in the *Revue du Droit Public et de la Science Politique en France et à l'Etranger*, the *Journal of Church and State*, the *Revue Internationale de Droit Comparé*, the *Annuaire Français de Relations Internationales*, *Public Integrity*, the *Harvard Middle Eastern and Islamic Review*, and *White House Studies* among others. Mourtada is member of the scientific board of the French journal *Politique Américaine* and the editorial board of the *Annuaire Français de Relations Internationales*. She has held visiting appointments at the University of California at Berkeley, the Congressional Research Service, the University of Michigan, and the Institut d'Etudes Politiques de Paris.

Nathaniel Persily is professor of law at the University of Pennsylvania Law School with a secondary appointment in political science. He is a nationally recognized expert on election law and a frequent practitioner and media commentator in the field. He has published dozens of articles and book chapters on election law, voting rights, political parties, redistricting, and campaign finance. He also has been appointed by courts on three occasions to draw states' redistricting plans. He received his B.A. and M.A. in political science from Yale, his J.D. from Stanford Law School, and his Ph.D. in political science from the University of California, at Berkeley.

Jonathan R. Siegel is professor of law at the George Washington University Law School. After graduating from Yale Law School, Siegel clerked for the Honorable Patricia M. Wald, Chief Judge of the U.S. Court of Appeals for the District of Columbia Circuit. Siegel then practiced for four years as a member of the Appellate Staff of the Civil Division of the United States Department of Justice. Siegel's teaching and scholarly interests include federal courts, administrative law, civil procedure, intellectual property, and statutory interpretation.

Mark Tushnet, Carmack Waterhouse Professor of Constitutional Law at the Georgetown University Law Center, received a J.D. and M.A. in history from Yale University in 1971. He clerked for Judge George Edwards and Justice Thurgood Marshall before beginning to teach at the University of Wisconsin Law School in 1973 and moved to the Georgetown University Law Center in 1981. He is the co-author of four casebooks, including the most widely used casebook on constitutional law, has written thirteen books, including a two-volume work on the life of Justice Thurgood Marshall, and has edited five others. He was president of the Association of American Law Schools in 2003. In 2002 he was elected a fellow of the American Academy of Arts and Sciences.